# CAMBRIDGE LIBRAR

*Books of enduring sch(*

## Physical Sciences

From ancient times, humans have tried to understand the workings of the world around them. The roots of modern physical science go back to the very earliest mechanical devices such as levers and rollers, the mixing of paints and dyes, and the importance of the heavenly bodies in early religious observance and navigation. The physical sciences as we know them today began to emerge as independent academic subjects during the early modern period, in the work of Newton and other 'natural philosophers', and numerous sub-disciplines developed during the centuries that followed. This part of the Cambridge Library Collection is devoted to landmark publications in this area which will be of interest to historians of science concerned with individual scientists, particular discoveries, and advances in scientific method, or with the establishment and development of scientific institutions around the world.

## Memoirs of the Life, Writings, and Discoveries of Sir Isaac Newton

Sir David Brewster (1781–1868) was a Scottish physicist, mathematician, astronomer, inventor, and writer of international reputation. His biography of Sir Isaac Newton, published in 1855 and reissued in 1860, was the result of over twenty years' research, undertaken while publishing hundreds of scientific papers of his own. Brewster made use of previously unknown correspondence by Newton, and his own scientific interests, particularly in optics, meant that he was able to understand and explain Newton's work. It covered the many facets of Newton's personality and work, remaining the best available study of Newton for over a century. Brewster reveals much about the science of his own time in his handling of earlier centuries, and as a cleric was obviously uncomfortable about the evidence of Newton's unorthodox religious views and alchemical studies. Volume 1 covers the period up to about 1700, and includes disputes with Leibniz over the development of calculus.

# Memoirs of the Life, Writings, and Discoveries of Sir Isaac Newton

VOLUME 1

DAVID BREWSTER

CAMBRIDGE
UNIVERSITY PRESS

CAMBRIDGE UNIVERSITY PRESS

Cambridge, New York, Melbourne, Madrid, Cape Town, Singapore,
São Paolo, Delhi, Dubai, Tokyo, Mexico City

Published in the United States of America by Cambridge University Press, New York

www.cambridge.org
Information on this title: www.cambridge.org/9781108025560

This edition first published 1855
This digitally printed version 2010

ISBN 978-1-108-02556-0 Paperback

Isaac Newton.

# MEMOIRS

OF

## THE LIFE, WRITINGS, AND DISCOVERIES

OF

# SIR ISAAC NEWTON.

BY SIR DAVID BREWSTER, K.H.

A.M., LL.D., D.C.L., F.R.S., AND M.R.I.A.,

One of the Eight Associates of the Imperial Institute of France—Officer of the Legion of Honour—
Chevalier of the Prussian Order of Merit of Frederick the Great—Honorary or Corresponding
Member of the Academies of St. Petersburg, Vienna, Berlin, Turin, Copenhagen,
Stockholm, Munich, Göttingen, Brussels, Haerlem, Erlangen, Canton de
Vaud, Modena, Florence, Venice, Washington, New York, Boston,
Quebec, Cape Town, etc. etc. ; and Principal and Vice-
Chancellor of the University of Edinburgh.

Second Edition.

VOL. I.

EDINBURGH:
EDMONSTON AND DOUGLAS.
MDCCCLX.

Ergo vivida vis animi pervicit, et extra
Processit longe flammantia mœnia mundi ;
Atque omne immensum peragravit mente animoque.

LUCRETIUS, Lib. i. l. 73.

TO HIS ROYAL HIGHNESS

# PRINCE ALBERT, K.G.

CHANCELLOR OF THE UNIVERSITY OF CAMBRIDGE.

SIR,

IN dedicating this Work to your Royal Highness, I seek for it the protection of a name indissolubly associated with the Sciences and the Arts. An account of the Life, Writings, and Discoveries of Sir Isaac Newton might have been appropriately inscribed to the Chancellor of the University of Cambridge, the birthplace of Newton's genius, and the scene of his intellectual achievements ; but that illustrious name is more honourably placed beside that of a Prince who has given such an impulse to the Arts and Sciences of England, and whose views, were they seconded by Statesmen willing to extend Education and advance Science, would raise our country to a higher rank than it now holds among the nations of Europe, in the arts of Peace and of War. It is from the trenches of Science alone that war can be successfully waged ; and it is in its patronage and liberal endowment that nations will find their best and cheapest defence.

That your Royal Highness may be enabled to realize those noble and patriotic views respecting the national encouragement of Science, and the consolidation of our Scientific Institutions, which you have so much at heart, and that you may long live to enjoy the reputation which you have so justly earned, is the ardent wish of,

SIR,

Your Royal Highness's

Humble and obedient Servant,

DAVID BREWSTER.

St. Leonard's College,
St. Andrews, *May* 12, 1855.

# PREFACE.

In consequence of the wide circulation of the Life of Sir Isaac Newton, which I drew up for the "Family Library" in 1831, I was induced to undertake a larger work, in order to give a more detailed account of his Life, Writings, and Discoveries. For this purpose I applied in 1837 to the Honourable Newton Fellowes, one of the trustees of the Earl of Portsmouth, for permission to inspect the Manuscripts and Correspondence of Sir Isaac, which, through his grandniece, Miss Conduitt, afterwards Lady Lymington, had come into the possession of that noble family. Mr. Fellowes kindly granted my request, and his amiable and accomplished son, Mr. Henry Arthur Fellowes, who, had he lived, would now have been Earl of Portsmouth, met me in June 1837, at Hurtsbourne Park, to assist me in examining and making extracts from the large mass of papers which Sir Isaac had left behind him.

In this examination our attention was particularly directed to such letters and papers as were calculated to throw light upon his early and academical life, and, with the assistance of Mr. Fellowes, who copied for me several important documents, I was enabled to collect many valuable materials unknown to preceding biographers.

After the death of Sir Isaac, his nephew, Mr. Conduitt, drew up a memorial, containing a sketch of his life, for the use of Fontenelle, the Secretary to the Academy of Sciences in Paris, whose duty it was to write his Eloge, as one of the eight Associates of the Academy. This memorial was published by Edmond Turnor, Esq., in his " Collections for the History of the Town and Soke of Grantham," and was supposed to contain all the information that Mr. Conduitt could collect from persons then alive, and from other sources, respecting Sir Isaac's life. This, however, was a mistake. After the publication of Fontenelle's Eloge, Mr. Conduitt resolved to draw up a Life of his illustrious relative, and, with this view, he wrote the following letter, requesting the assistance of Sir Isaac's personal friends :[1]—

" *6th February* 172⅘.

" SIR,—I have taken the liberty to trouble you with some short hints of that part of our honoured friend, Sir I. Newton's life, which I must beg the favour of you to undertake, there being nobody, without dispute, so well qualified to do it as yourself. I send you, at the same time, Fontenelle's Eloge, wherein you will find a very imperfect attempt of the same kind ; but I fear he had neither abilities nor inclination to do justice to that great man, who had eclipsed the glory of their hero, Descartes. As Sir I. Newton was a national man, I think every one ought to contribute to a work intended to do him justice, particularly those who had so great a share in his esteem as you had ; and as I pretend to nothing more than to compile it, I shall acquaint the public in the Preface, to whom they are indebted for each particular part of it.

---

[1] This letter is docqueted by Conduitt, " Letter sent by me concerning Sir I. N.'s Inventions."

" I am persuaded that the hints I have sent you are very imperfect, and that your own genius will suggest to you many others much more proper and significant, and I beg of you to put down everything that occurs to your thoughts, and you think fit to be inserted in such a work.

" I conjure you not to put off what I take the liberty to recommend to you. As on one hand the. complying with my request will be a mark of your gratitude to your old friend, and an eternal obligation on me, so your delaying it will be the most mortifying disappointment to,

" Sir,

" Your most humble Servant,

" JOHN CONDUITT."[1]

Although Mr. Conduitt had at this time resolved to compile a Life of Sir Isaac, and had obtained much information from Dr. Stukely, Mr. Wickins, and Dr. Humphrey Newton of Grantham, yet he seems to have so far relinquished his design, that in June 1729, nearly eighteen months after the date of his letter, he intimates to a friend[2] that " he has *some thoughts* of writing the Life of Sir Isaac Newton himself." That he made the attempt, appears from an indigested mass of manuscript which he has left behind him, and which does not lead

[1] I have not succeeded in ascertaining to whom this letter was addressed. It was probably a circular sent to more than one person. I have found a letter from John Craig, and a paper by De Moivre, which have the appearance of being answers to it, but the dates of both are earlier than that of Conduitt's letter. In a letter dated April 16, 1729, Conduitt made a similar application to Professor Machin.

[2] In a letter on the subject of a large " monumental picture to Newton's memory," for Conduitt himself. This letter is docqueted, " sent to Westgarth," who seems to have been then in Italy.

us to regret that he abandoned his design. The materials, however, which he obtained from Mrs. Conduitt, and from the friends of Newton then alive, are of great value ; and, in so far as Mr. H. A. Fellowes and I could make an abstract of these and other manuscripts during a week's visit at Hurtsbourne Park, I have availed myself of them in composing the first volume of this work, which was printed before the papers themselves came into my hands.

Before I began the second volume, which contains the history of the Fluxionary controversy, and the Life of Newton subsequent to the publication of the first edition of the *Principia*, I had the good fortune to obtain from the Earl of Portsmouth, through the kindness of Lord Brougham, the collection of manuscripts and correspondence which the late Mr. H. A. Fellowes had examined and arranged as peculiarly fitted to throw light on the Life and Discoveries of Sir Isaac. In these manuscripts I found much new information respecting the history of the *Principia*, which, though it might have been more appropriately placed in the first volume, I have introduced into those chapters of the second which relate to the period when the other editions of the *Principia* were published.

In the different controversies in which Newton's discoveries involved him, his moral character had never been the subject of suspicion. In Hooke, he found a jealous but an honest rival, who, though he claimed discoveries which substantially belonged to Newton, never cast a reproach upon his name ; and amid all the bitterness of the Fluxionary controversy, Leibnitz and Bernoulli, and their anonymous auxiliaries, never hesitated to acknowledge the purity of Newton's motives, and the scrupulous correctness of his conduct. It was reserved for two English astronomers, the one a contemporary and the other a disciple, to misrepresent and calumniate their illustrious countryman.

In 1835, the scientific world was startled by the publication of Baily's Life of Flamsteed, a huge volume, deeply affecting the character of Newton, and, strange to say, printed and circulated throughout the world, at the expense of the Board of Admiralty. The friends of the great philosopher were thus summoned to a painful controversy, which, had it been raised in his lifetime, would have been summarily extinguished ; but a century and a quarter had elapsed before the slumbering calumnies revived, and it was hardly to be expected that the means of defence would have enjoyed the same vitality. Under these circumstances Mr. Fellowes and I anxiously searched, but in vain, for the letters of Flamsteed to Newton, and other relative documents which were necessary for his defence. In this difficulty, some of the admirers of Newton, among whom I must mention my friend Mr. Robert Brown, the distinguished President of the Linnean Society, sent me some important facts ; but valuable as they were, they were not sufficient to refute the calumnies of the Astronomer-Royal. From this embarrassment, however, I have been relieved by the receipt of all Flamsteed's letters and other important- papers which Newton had carefully preserved, and which Mr. Fellowes had discovered and set aside for my use. With these documents I trust I have been able, though at a greater length than I could have wished, to defend the illustrious subject of this work against a system of calumny and misrepresentation unexampled in the history of science.

When I published my *Life of Newton* in 1831, I had not

seen his correspondence with Mr. Cotes and other mathematicians in the Library of Trinity College. Mr. Halliwell,
however, who had made copious extracts from 'these manuscripts, kindly put them into my hands ; but the subsequent
publication of the correspondence by Mr. Edleston, has enabled
me to make a more advantageous use of these valuable materials.

Dr. Monk, Bishop of Gloucester and Bristol, had "often
expressed in private a wish and request that some one of the
many accomplished Newtonians who are resident in that society
would favour the world by publishing the 'whole collection,"[1]
and I have no doubt that it was from this public expression of
it, in his able and interesting *Life of Dr. Bentley*, that the
Masters and Seniors of Trinity College resolved to publish the
correspondence.

This valuable work, edited by Mr. Edleston, Fellow of
Trinity, is a most important contribution to the History of
Mathematical and Physical Science. The admirable synopsis
which it contains of Newton's Life ;—the learned and able
annotations illustrative of his history ; and the explanatory
notes on the letters themselves, throw much light on the subjects to which they refer, and have been of essential service to
me in the composition of this work. But in addition to the
obligations which I owe to Mr. Edleston, in common with
every friend of science, I have to acknowledge others of a more
personal kind. During the printing of the second volume,
which he has had the kindness to peruse, I have received from
him much new and important information, and availed myself
of his judicious criticisms and useful suggestions.

To Professor De Morgan, to whom the public owes a brief

---

[1] *Life of Bentley*, p. 180.

but interesting biographical sketch of Newton, and who has carefully investigated various points in the Fluxionary controversy, I have been indebted for much information, and for his kind revision of the sketch I had given of the early history of the Infinitesimal Calculus. On a few questions in the life of Newton, and the history of his discoveries, my opinion differs somewhat from his ; but I have been able to confirm, from the documents in my possession, many of his views on important points which he was the first to investigate and to publish.

From my late amiable and distinguished friend Professor Rigaud of Oxford, too early cut off in his scientific career, I obtained valuable aid whenever I encountered difficulties or required information. His "Historical Essay on the Principia," which he generously offered to withhold from the public, till I had finished the present work, is a most important contribution to the history of Newton's discoveries, and I am glad to be able to complete the correspondence between Newton and Halley, which Mr. Rigaud was the first to publish in its genuine state.

The Rev. Jeffrey Ekins, Rector of Sampford, whose family, from their connexion with Newton, have been long in possession of several of his theological manuscripts and letters, has obligingly sent me copies of many of them, and has otherwise favoured me with much useful information.

To Lord Brougham, Sir John Lubbock, Mr. Cutts Barton, and other friends, I have to return my best thanks for the assistance they have given me.

In concluding this Preface, I can hardly avoid referring to Sir Isaac Newton's religious opinions. In the chapter which relates to them I have touched lightly, and unwillingly, on a subject so tender ; and in publishing the most interesting of the manuscripts in which these opinions are recorded, I have done little more than submit them to the judgment of the reader. Though adverse to my own, and I believe to the opinions of those to whom his memory is dearest, I did not feel myself justified, had I been so disposed, to conceal from the public that which they have long suspected, and must have sooner or later known. What the gifted mind of Newton believed to be truth, I dare not pronounce to be error. By the great Teacher alone can truth be taught, and it is only at His tribunal that a decision will be given on those questions, often of words, which have kept at variance the wisest and the best of men.

ST. LEONARD'S COLLEGE,
ST. ANDREWS, *May* 12, 1855.

# CONTENTS OF VOLUME I.

## CHAPTER I.

PAGE

Great Discoveries previous to the Birth of Sir Isaac Newton—Pre-eminence of his Reputation—The Interest attached to the Study of his Life and Writings—His Birth and Parentage—An only and Posthumous Child—Notice of his Descent—Inherits the small Property of Woolsthorpe—His Mother marries again—Is sent to a Day-school—His Education at Grantham School—His idle Habits there—His Love of Mechanical Pursuits—His Windmill, Water-clock, Self-moving Carriage, and Kites—His Attachment to Miss Storey—His Love of Drawing and Poetry—His Unfitness to be a Farmer—His Dials, Water-wheels, and Anemometer—Leaves Grantham School—His Commonplace Book and College Expenses,    1-16

## CHAPTER II.

Newton enters Trinity College, Cambridge—Origin of his Love of Mathematics—Studies Descartes' Geometry, and the Writings of Schooten and Wallis—Is driven from Cambridge by the Plague—Observes Lunar Halos in 1664—Takes his Degree of B.A. in 1665—Discovers Fluxions in the same Year—His first Speculations on Gravity—Purchases a Prism to study Colours—Revises Barrow's Optical Lectures, but does not correct his erroneous Opinions about Colours—Is elected a Minor Fellow of Trinity in 1667, and a Major Fellow in 1668—Takes his Degree of M.A.—His Note-Book, with his Expenses from 1666 to 1669—Makes a small Reflecting Telescope—His Letter of Advice to Francis Aston, when going upon his Travels—His Chemical Studies—His Taste for Alchemy—His Paper on Fluxions sent to Barrow and Collins in 1669,    .    .    .    .    17-32

## CHAPTER III.

Newton succeeds Barrow in the Lucasian Chair—Hyperbolic Lenses proposed by Descartes and Others—Opinions of Descartes and Isaac Vossius on Colours—Newton discovers the Composition of White Light, and the dif-

PAGE

ferent Refrangibility of the Rays that compose it—Having discovered the
Cause of the Imperfection of Refracting Telescopes, he attempts the Construction of Reflecting ones—Constructs a second Reflecting Telescope in
1668, which is examined by the Royal Society, and shown to the King—
Discussions respecting the Gregorian, Newtonian, and Cassegrainian Telescope—James Gregory the Inventor of the Reflecting Telescope—Attempts to construct one—Newton makes a Speculum of silvered glass—
Glass Specula by Short in 1730, and Airy in 1822—Hadley constructs two
fine Reflecting Telescopes—Telescopes by Bradley, Molyneux, and Hawksbee—Short's Reflecting Telescopes with Metallic Specula—Magnificent
Telescope of Sir William Herschel with a .four-feet Speculum—Munificence of George III.—Astronomical Discoveries of Sir Wm. Herschel—Telescopes of Sir J. Herschel and Mr. Ramage—Gigantic Telescope of the
Earl of Rosse with a six-feet Speculum—Progress of Telescopic Discovery
—Proposal to send a fine Telescope to a Southern Climate,      .     .     33-60

## CHAPTER IV.

Newton writes Notes on Kinkhuysen's Algebra—and on Harmonic and Infinite Series—Delivers Optical Lectures at Cambridge—Is elected a Fellow
of the Royal Society—Communicates to them his Discoveries on the different Refrangibility and Nature of Light—Popular account of them—
They involve him in various Controversies—His Dispute with Pardies—
With Linus—With Gascoigne and Lucas—The Influence of these Disputes
on his Mind—His Controversy with Dr. Hooke and Monsieur Huygens,
arising from their Attachment to the Undulatory Theory of Light—
Harassed with these Discussions he resolves to publish nothing more on
Optics—Intimates to Oldenburg his Resolution to withdraw from the Royal
Society from his Inability to make the Weekly Payments—The Council
agree to dispense with these Payments—He is allowed by a Royal Grant
to hold his Fellowship along with the Lucasian Chair without taking
Orders—Hardship of his Situation in being obliged to plead Poverty to
the Royal Society—Draws up a Scheme for extending the Royal Society,
by paying certain of its Members—The Scheme was found among his
Papers—Soundness of his Views relative to the Endowment of Science
by the Nation—Arguments in support of them,      .      .      .     61-95

## CHAPTER V.

Mistake of Newton in supposing the Length of the Spectra to be the same in all
Bodies—And in despairing of the Improvement of Refracting Telescopes
—In his Controversy with Lucas he was on the eve of discovering the dif-
ferent Dispersive Powers of Bodies—Mr. Chester More Hall makes this Dis-
covery, and constructs Achromatic Telescopes, but does not publish his
Discovery—Mr. Dollond rediscovers the Principle of the Achromatic Tele-

PAGE

scope, and takes out a Patent—Principle of the Achromatic Telescope
explained—Dr. Blair's Aplanatic Telescopes—Great Improvements on the
Achromatic Telescope by the Flint-Glass of Guinant, Fraunhofer, and
Bontemps—Mistake of Newton in forming his Spectrum from the Sun's
Disc—Dark Lines in the Spectrum—Newton's Analysis of the Spectrum
incorrect—New Analysis of the Spectrum by Absorption, &c., defended
against the Objections of Helmholtz, Bernard, and others—Change in the
Refrangibility of Light maintained by Professor Stokes—Objections to
his Theory, . . . . . . 96-111

## CHAPTER VI.

Newton on the Cause of the Moon's Libration—Is occupied with the subject
of Planting Cider Trees—Sends to Oldenburg his Discourse on Light and
Colours, containing his Hypothesis concerning Light—Views of Descartes
and Hooke, who adopt the Hypothesis of an Ether, the vibrations of
which produce Light—Rejected by Newton, who proposes a Modification
of it, but solely as an illustration of his Views, and not as a Truth—Light
is neither Ether, nor its vibrating Motion—Corpuscles from the Sun act
upon the Ether—Hooke claims Newton's Hypothesis as contained in his
Micrographia—Discussions on the subject—Hooke's Letter to Newton proposing a Private Discussion as more suitable—Newton's Reply to this
Letter, acknowledging the value of Hooke's Discoveries—Oldenburg the
cause of the Differences between Hooke and Newton—Newton's Letter to
Boyle on the subject of Ether—His conjecture on the Cause of Gravity—
Newton supposed to have abandoned the Emission Theory—Dr. Young's
supposition incorrect—Newton's mature judgment in favour of the Emission
Theory, . . . . . . . . 112-132

## CHAPTER VII.

Newton's Hypothesis of Refraction and Reflexion—Of Transparency and
Opacity—Hypothesis of Colours—The Spectrum supposed to be divided
like a Musical String—Incorrectness of this Speculation—Hooke's Observations on the Colours of Thin Plates explained by the vibrations produced
in the Ether by the Luminous Corpuscles—Hooke claims this Theory as
contained in his Micrographia—Newton's Researches on the Colours of
Thin Plates—Previous Observations of Boyle—Hooke's elaborate Experiments on these Colours—His Explanation of them—Dr. Young's Observations upon it—Newton acknowledges his obligations to Hooke—Newton's
Analysis of the Colours seen between two Object-Glasses—Corrections of
it by MM. Provostayes and Desains—Newton's Theory of Fits of easy Reflexion and Transmission—Singular Phenomenon in the Fracture of a
Quartz Crystal—Newton's Observations on the Colours of Thick Plates—
Recent Experiments on the same subject, . . . . 133-153

## CHAPTER VIII.

PAGE

Influence of Colour in the Material World—Newton's Theory of the Colours of Natural Bodies—Coloured Bodies reflect only Light of their own Colour, absorbing all the other parts of White Light—The Colours of Natural Bodies are those of Thin Plates—The transparent parts reflecting one Colour and transmitting another—Arrangement of the Colours exhibited in Natural Bodies into Seven Classes—Coloured Juices and Solutions, Oxidated Films, Metals, &c. &c.—Newton's Theory applicable only to one class of Colours—Objections to it stated—Mr. Jamin's Researches on the Colours of Metals—Cause of Colours must be in the Constitution of Bodies—Examples of the Effect of Heat upon Rubies and Nitrous Gas—Effect of Sudden Cooling—On Phosphorus—Effect of Mechanical Action on Iodide of Mercury—Indication of a New Theory—And of the Cause of the Absorption of Definite Rays—Illustration of these Views in a remarkable Tourmaline, 154-168

## CHAPTER IX.

Newton's Discoveries on the Inflexion of Light—Previous Researches of Hooke—Newton's Animadversions on them offensive to Hooke—Newton's Theory of Inflexion as described by Grimaldi, having made no experiments of his own—Discoveries of Grimaldi, which anticipate those of Hooke—Hooke suggests the Doctrine of Interference—Newton's Experiments on Inflexion—His Views upon the subject unsettled—Modern Researches—Dr. Young discovers the Law of Interference—Discoveries of Fresnel and Arago—Fraunhofer's Experiments—Diffraction by Grooved Surfaces—Diffraction by Transparent Lines—Phenomena of Negative Diffraction—Experiments and Discoveries of Lord Brougham—Explanation of Diffraction by the Undulatory Theory, . . . . . . 169-183

## CHAPTER X.

Miscellaneous Optical Researches of Newton—His Experiments on the Absolute Refractive Powers of Bodies—More Recent Experiments—His Conjecture respecting the Inflammability of the Diamond, confirmed by more Direct Experiments—His Erroneous Law of Double Refraction—His Observations on the Polarity of Doubly Refracted Images—Discoveries on Double Refraction in the present Century—His Experiments on the Eye of a Sheep—Results of them—His Three Letters on Briggs's New Theory of Vision—His Theory of the Semi-Decussation of the Optic Nerves—Partly anticipated by Rohault—Opinions of later writers on Vision, of Reid, Brown, Wollaston, Twining, and Alison, discussed—The true Laws of Sensation and Vision—Newton's Observations on the Impression of Strong Light upon the Retina—More recent Observations—His Reflecting Sextant—His Reflecting Microscope—His Reflecting Prism for Reflecting Telescopes—His Method of varying the Magnifying Power of Newtonian Telescopes—Newton's Treatise on Optics—His Lectiones Opticæ, . . 184-218

# CHAPTER XI.

PAGE

Astronomical Discoveries of Newton—Combined exertion necessary for the completion of Great Discoveries—Sketch of the History of Astronomy previous to the time of Newton—Discoveries of Nicolas Copernicus, born 1473, died 1553—He places the Sun in the Centre of the System—His Work on the Revolutions of the Heavenly Bodies, printed at the expense of Cardinal Schonberg, and dedicated to Pope Paul III.—Tycho Brahe, born 1546, died 1601—His Observatory of Uraniburg—Is visited by James VI.—Is persecuted by the Danish Minister—Retires to Germany —His Discoveries and Instruments—The Tychonic System—John Kepler, born 1571, died 1631—His Speculation on the Six Regular Solids— Discovers the Ellipticity of Mars' Orbit—His Laws of the Planetary Motions—His Ideas of Gravitation—His Religious Character—Galileo, born 1564, died 1642—The first to apply a Telescope to the Heavens—Discovers the Four Satellites and Belts of Jupiter—His Researches in Mechanics—Is summoned before the Inquisition for Heresy—Retracts his Opinions, but persists in teaching the Doctrine of the Earth's Motion—Is again summoned before the Inquisition—His Sentence to Imprisonment for Life—Becomes Blind—His Scientific Character—Labours of Bouillaud, and of Borelli—Suggestions of Dr Hooke on Gravity—His Circular Pendulum—His Experiments with it—His Views respecting the Cause of the Planetary Motions, . . . . . 219-251

# CHAPTER XII.

The first Idea of Gravity occurs to Newton in 1665—His first Speculations upon it—He abandons the Subject from having employed an erroneous measure of the Earth's Radius—He resumes the Subject in consequence of a discussion with Dr. Hooke, but lays it aside, being occupied with his Optical Experiments—By adopting Picard's Measure of the Earth, he discovers the Law of Gravity, and the Cause of the Planetary Motions— Dr. Halley goes to Cambridge, and urges him to publish his Treatise on Motion—The Germ of the Principia, which was composed in 1685 and 1686—Correspondence with Flamsteed—Manuscript of Principia sent to the Royal Society—Halley undertakes to publish it at his own expense— Dispute with Hooke, who claims the discovery of the Law of Gravity— The Principia published in 1687—The new edition of it by Cotes begun in 1709, and published in 1713—Character and Contents of the Work— General Account of the Discoveries it contains—They meet with opposition from the followers of Descartes—Their reception in foreign countries —Progress of the Newtonian Philosophy in England and Scotland, 252-299

# CHAPTER XIII.

PAGE

The Newtonian Philosophy stationary for half a century, owing to the imperfect state of Mechanics, Optics, and Analysis—Developed and extended by the French Mathematicians—Influence of the Academy of Sciences— Improvements in the Infinitesimal Calculus—Christian Mayer on the Arithmetic of Sines—D'Alembert's Calculus of Partial Differences—Lagrange's Calculus of Variations—The Problem of Three Bodies—Importance of the Lunar Theory—Lunar Tables of Clairaut, D'Alembert, and Euler —The Superior Tables of Tobias Mayer gain the Prize offered by the English Board of Longitude—Euler receives part of the English Reward, and also a Reward from the French Board—Laplace discovers the cause of the Moon's Acceleration, and completes the Lunar Theory—Lagrange's Solution of the Problem of Three Bodies as applied to the Planets—Inequalities of Jupiter and Saturn explained by Laplace—Stability of the Solar System the Proof of Design—Maclaurin, Laplace, and others, on the Figure of the Earth—Researches of Laplace on the Tides, and the Stable Equilibrium of the Ocean—Theoretical Discovery of Neptune by Adams and Leverrier —New Satellites of Saturn and Neptune—Extension of Saturn's Ring and its Partial Fluidity—Twenty-seven Asteroids discovered—Leverrier's theory of them—Comets with Elliptic Orbits within our System—Law of Gravity applied to Double Stars—Spiral Nebulæ—Motion of the Solar System in Space, . . . . . . . . . . 300-333

# CHAPTER XIV.

History of the Infinitesimal Calculus—Archimedes—Pappus—Napier—Edward Wright—Kepler's Treatise on Stereometry—Cavalieri's Geometria Indivisibilium—Roberval—Toricelli—Fermat—Wallis's Arithmetica Infinitorum—Hudde—Gregory—Slusius—Newton's Discovery of Fluxions in 1655—General Account of the Method, and of its Applications—His Analysis per Equationes, &c.—His Discoveries communicated to English and Foreign Mathematicians—The Method of Fluxions and Quadratures —Account of his other Mathematical Writings—He solves the Problems proposed by Bernoulli and Leibnitz—Leibnitz visits London, and corresponds with the English Mathematicians, and with Newton through Oldenburg—He discovers the Differential Calculus, and communicates it to Newton—Notice of Oldenburg—Celebrated Scholium respecting Fluxions in the Principia—Account of the changes upon it—Leibnitz's Manuscripts in Hanover, . . . . . . . . . . 334-363

# APPENDIX TO VOLUME I.

PAGE

No. I.—Letter from Mr. Newton to Francis Aston, Esq., a young Friend who
    was on the eve of setting out upon his Travels,   .   .   .   365

  II.—An Hypothesis explaining the Properties of Light discoursed of in my
    several Papers, .   .   .   .   .   .   .   .   368

  III.—Drawing and Measures of the Eye of a Sheep, .   .   .   388

  IV.—Letter from Newton to Dr. Wm. Briggs,   .   .   .   390

  V.—Second Letter of Newton to Dr. Briggs, .   . .   .   .   394

  VI.—Newton's Fifteenth Query,   .   .   .   .   .   395

  VII.—Description of the Optic Nerves and their Juncture in the Brain, by
    Sir Isaac Newton,   .   .   .   .   .   .   395

  VIII.—Correspondence between Halley and Newton, .   .   .   .   399

  IX.—Halley's Verses prefixed to the Principia,   .   .   .   417

  X.—Brief Notice of Professor Cotes,   .   .   .   . .   418

  XI.—Newton's Directions to Dr. Bentley for Studying the Principia, and
    John Craige's list of Authors to be read before Studying the Principia,   420

  XII.—Draught Copies of the Scholium to Lemma ii. Book ii.,   .   .   426

XIII.—Letters from Wallis to Newton, .   .   .   .   .   428

# LIST OF ENGRAVINGS AND WOODCUTS.

## VOL. I.

PORTRAIT OF SIR ISAAC NEWTON, . . . *Frontispiece.*

THE HOUSE AT WOOLSTHORPE, THE BIRTHPLACE OF NEWTON, . 4

SIR ISAAC NEWTON'S REFLECTING TELESCOPE, . . . 41

FRONT VIEW OF LORD ROSSE'S TELESCOPE, . . . 56

BACK VIEW OF DO. DO., . . . 57

## VOL. II.

ROUBILLIAC'S STATUE OF NEWTON IN TRINITY COLLEGE, *Frontispiece.*

THE ROOMS OF SIR ISAAC NEWTON IN TRINITY COLLEGE, . 46

THE HOUSE OF SIR ISAAC NEWTON IN MARTIN STREET, . 193

ENGRAVING FROM A CAST OF SIR ISAAC NEWTON'S FACE, TAKEN

    AFTER DEATH, . . . . . 338

ENGRAVING OF A BOX BELONGING TO SIR GEORGE HAMILTON

    SEYMOUR, G.C.B., WHICH WAS PRESENTED BY SIR ISAAC

    NEWTON TO THE EARL OF ABERCORN, . . . 342

# MEMOIRS

OF THE

## LIFE AND WRITINGS OF SIR ISAAC NEWTON.

## CHAPTER I.

Great discoveries previous to the birth of Sir Isaac Newton—Pre-eminence of his reputation—The interest attached to the study of his life and writings—His birth and parentage—An only and posthumous child—Notice of his descent—Inherits the small property of Woolsthorpe—His mother marries again—Is sent to a day-school—His education at Grantham School—His idle habits there—His love of mechanical pursuits—His windmill, water-clock, self-moving carriage, and kites—His attachment to Miss Storey—His love of drawing and poetry—His unfitness to be a farmer—His dials, water-wheels, and anemometer—Leaves Grantham School—His commonplace book and college expenses.

THE seventeenth century has always been regarded as the most interesting and eventful period in the history of positive knowledge. The discoveries and speculations of a preceding age had prepared the way for some grand generalization of the phenomena of the material world ; and sages of lofty intellect heralded the advent of that Master-mind by which it was to be accomplished. The establishment by Copernicus of the true Solar System, and of its independence of the sidereal universe, led to the investigation of those general laws with which Kepler laid the foundations of Physical Astronomy ; while, in combination with these, the observations of Tycho, the telescopic discoveries of Galileo, and the speculations of Hooke and Borelli, contributed in no slight degree to the establishment of the theory of universal gravitation, by which Sir Isaac Newton has im-

A

mortalized his name, and perpetuated the intellectual glory of his country.

A generalization of such vast extent, enabling us to determine the position and aspects of the planets during thousands of years that are past, and for thousands of years to come, could not but be regarded as an achievement of the highest order : and the name of Newton, therefore, has, by universal consent, been placed at the head of those great men who have been the benefactors and ornaments of their species. Imposing as are the attributes with which Time has invested the sages of antiquity—its poets and its philosophers ; and dazzling as are the glories of its heroes and its lawgivers, their reputation pales in the presence of his ; and the vanity of no presumptuous school, and the partiality of no rival nation, has ventured to question the ascendency of his genius. The philosopher, indeed, to whom posterity will probably assign the place next to Newton, has characterized his great work,—*The Principles of Natural Philosophy*, as pre-eminent above every other production of human genius,[1] and has thus divested of extravagance the encomium of contemporary friendship.

Nec fas est propius mortali attingere Divos.
                                   HALLEY.
So near the gods—man cannot nearer go.

But while the history of such discoveries must, to the intellectual world, be a subject of exciting interest, the biography of him who made them,—the details of his life, his studies and his opinions, cannot fail to arrest the attention and influence the judgment of every cultivated mind. Though the path of such a man may have lain in the secluded vale of humble life, unmarked by those dramatic incidents which throw a lustre even round perishable names, yet the inquiring spirit will linger over the history of a mind so richly endowed, will study its intellectual and moral phases, and will seek the shelter of its

[1] The Marquis La Place. See his *Exposition du Système du Monde*, Livre cinquième, chap. vi. p. 336.

authority on those solemn questions which Reason has abandoned to Faith and Hope.

If we look for instruction from the opinions of ordinary men, and watch their conduct as an exemplar for our own, how interesting must it be to follow the most exalted genius through the labyrinth of common life,—to mark the steps by which he attained his lofty pre-eminence,—to see how he performs the functions of the social and the domestic compact;—how he wields his powers of invention and discovery;—how he comports himself in the arena of intellectual strife; and in what sentiments, and with what aspirations, he leaves the world which he has adorned.

In each and all of these phases, the writings and the life of Sir Isaac Newton abound with the richest counsel. Here the philosopher will learn the art of patient observation by which alone he can acquire an immortal name; the moralist will trace the lineaments of a character exhibiting all the symmetry of which our imperfect nature is susceptible; and the Christian will contemplate with delight the High Priest of Science quitting the study of the material universe—the scene of his intellectual triumphs, to investigate with humility and reverence the mysteries of his faith.

ISAAC NEWTON was born in the Manor-house of Woolsthorpe, a hamlet in the parish of Colsterworth, in the county of Lincoln, close to the village of Colsterworth, and about six miles south of Grantham, between one and two o'clock in the morning of the 25th December, old style, 1642, in the same year in which Galileo died. His father, Isaac Newton, who was proprietor and farmer of the manor of Woolsthorpe, died in the thirty-seventh year of his age, a little more than a year after the death of his father Robert Newton, and only a few months after his marriage to Hannah Ayscough, daughter of James Ayscough of Market Overton, in Rutlandshire. Mrs. Newton had thus been left in a state of pregnancy, and appears to have

given a premature birth to her only and posthumous child.
The infant thus ushered into the world was of such a diminutive
size, that, as his mother afterwards expressed it to Newton
himself, he might have been put into a quart-mug, and so
feeble apparently was his constitution, that two women who
were sent to Lady Pakenham's at North Witham, to obtain for
him some tonic medicine, did not expect to find him alive
on their return.    Providence, however, disappointed their
fears, and that frail tenement which seemed scarcely able to
imprison its immortal mind, was destined to enjoy a vigorous
maturity, and to survive even the average term of human
existence.

Manor-house, Woolsthorpe ; the Birthplace of Sir Isaac Newton, showing the
Solar Dials which he made when a boy.

The small Manor of Woolsthorpe is said to have been more
than a hundred years in the possession of the family, who,

according to one account, were descended from Sir John Newton
of Westby, in Lincolnshire, and, according to another, from a
Scotch family in East Lothian.  The Manor-house is situated
in a pleasant little hollow on the west side of the valley of the
river Witham, which rises near it, and one spring of which is
in the Manor.  From the house there is an agreeable prospect
of the village of Colsterworth to the east, and, according to
Dr. Stukely, the air is so good, combining the sharpness of the
midland part of the kingdom with the more genial temperature
of the low parts of Lincolnshire, that the country round Woolsthorpe was called the Montpellier of England.  The Manor-
house consists of two storeys, and is built of stone.  Sir Isaac's
study before he went to college, and when he visited his
mother from the University, was in the upper flat.  The book-
shelves are described by Dr. Stukely as having been made by
Sir Isaac himself with pieces of deal-boxes, and as having
contained 200 or 300 books belonging to his father-in-law,
Dr. Smith, which Sir Isaac presented to Dr. Newton of
Grantham.

The Manor of Woolsthorpe, Sir Isaac's paternal estate, purchased by his grandfather in 1623, from Robert Underwood,
was worth only £30 per annum, but his mother possessed a
small estate at Sewstern, on the borders of Leicestershire, and
about three miles south-east of Woolsthorpe, which was worth
about £50 per annum ; and it is probable that the cultivation
of the little farm, on which she resided, added to the limited
rental upon which she had to support herself and educate
her son.

Under the guardianship of his uncle, James Ayscough, and
the tender care of his mother, young Newton remained at
Woolsthorpe acquiring gradually that strength of constitution
which was essential to the development of his intellectual
powers.  Before, however, he had reached his fourth year, he
was deprived of his mother's care, in consequence of her marriage, on the 27th January 1645, to the Rev. Barnabas Smith,

rector of North Witham ;[1] and her duties devolved upon her mother, the wife of James Ayscough, and a daughter of Mr. Blythe of Stroxton, who, for this purpose, took up her residence at Woolsthorpe. At the usual age Isaac was sent to two little day-schools at Skillington and Stoke, two hamlets about a mile to the north of Woolsthorpe, and about the same distance from each other, acquiring the education in reading, writing, and arithmetic, which such seminaries afforded.

When he reached the age of twelve he was sent to the public school at Grantham, then taught by Mr. Stokes, who had the character of being a good teacher, and was boarded at the house of Mr. Clark, an apothecary in the town, whose grandson, Mr. Clark, exercised the same profession there in 1727, the year of Newton's death. The house in which our young philosopher lodged, was next to the George Inn, "northward in the High Street, which was rebuilt about 1711." According to the confessions which Sir Isaac himself made to Mr. Conduit, he was extremely inattentive to his studies, and stood very low in the school. When he was the last in the lowermost form but one, the boy next above him, as they were going to school, gave him a kick on the stomach, which occasioned a great degree of pain. As soon as the scholars were dismissed, New-

---

[1] The issue of this marriage was a son and two daughters—Benjamin, Mary, and Hannah Smith, from whom were descended the four nephews and nieces who inherited Sir Isaac's personal estate.

The following account, from Conduit's MSS., of Mrs. Newton's marriage to Mr. Smith, was given to Mr. Conduit " by Mrs. Hutton, whose maiden name was Ayscough :—

" Mr. Smith, a neighbouring clergyman, who had a very good estate, had lived a bachelor till he was pretty old, and one of his parishioners advising him to marry, he said he did not know where to meet with a good wife. The man answered, The widow Newton is an extraordinary good woman. But, saith Mr. Smith, how do I know she will have me, and I don't care to ask and be denied; but if you will go and ask her, I will pay you for your day's work. He went accordingly. Her answer was, she would be advised by her brother Ayscough. Upon which Mr. Smith sent the same person to Mr. Ayscough on the same errand, who, upon consulting with his sister, treated with Mr. Smith, who gave her son Isaac a parcel of land, being one of the terms insisted upon by the widow if she married him." This parcel of land was given by Mrs. Smith, and was probably her property of Sewstern.—See the *Annual Register* 1776, Characters, p. 25.

ton challenged the boy to fight, and for this purpose they went into the churchyard. The schoolmaster's son came up to them during the fight, and, " clapping one on the back and winking to the other," encouraged them both to continue the encounter. Though Sir Isaac was not so robust as his antagonist, yet he had much more spirit and resolution, and therefore succeeded in the combat, beating his opponent till he declared he would fight no more. The schoolmaster's son, who seems to have been an amateur in the art, told Sir Isaac that he must treat the other as a coward by rubbing his nose against the wall. The victor accordingly took the advice, and dragging his victim by the ears, thrust his face against the wall of the church. The success which thus attended his first struggle for superiority induced him to repeat it in a better cause. Although vanquished in the churchyard, his antagonist still stood above him in the school, a victory more honourable than that which Newton had achieved ; and though the schoolmaster and his son would have given a different decision on the relative merits of the youthful combatants, yet Newton took the right view of his own position, and resolved to possess the moral as well as the physical supe- riority. He accordingly exerted himself in the preparation of his lessons, and, after many a severe struggle in which he and his adversary were alternately successful, he not only gained the individual victory, but rose to the highest place in the school.

It is very probable that Newton's idleness arose from the occupation of his mind with subjects in which he felt a deeper interest. He had not been long at school before he exhibited a taste for mechanical inventions. With the aid of little saws, hammers, hatchets, and tools of all sorts, he was constantly occupied during his play-hours in the construction of models of known machines, and amusing contrivances. The most import- ant pieces of mechanism which he thus constructed, were a wind-mill, a water-clock, and a carriage to be moved by the person who sat in it. When a wind-mill was in the course of

being erected near Grantham, on the way to Gunnerby, Sir
Isaac frequently watched the operations of the workmen, and
acquired such a thorough knowledge of its mechanism, that he
completed a working model of it, which Dr. Stukely says was
" as clean and curious a piece of workmanship as the original."
This model was frequently placed upon the top of the house in
which he lived at Grantham, and was put in motion by the
action of the wind upon its sails.   In calm weather, however,
another mechanical agent was required, and for this purpose a
mouse was put in requisition, which went by the name of the
miller.   It does not distinctly appear how the mouse was compelled to perform a function so foreign to its ordinary habits,
but it was supposed to act upon something like a tread-wheel
when attempting to reach some corn placed above it ; or, according to another supposition, it was placed within a wheel,
and by pulling a string tied to its tail, it went forward " by
way of resistance," as Dr. Stukely observes, and thus turned
the mill.

The water-clock constructed by Sir Isaac was a more useful piece of mechanism than his wind-mill.   It was made out
of a box which he begged from Mrs. Clark's brother, and,
according to Dr. Stukely, to whom it was described by those
who had seen it, " it resembled pretty much our common clocks
and clock-cases," but was less in size, being about four feet in
height, and of a proportional breadth.   There was a dial-plate
at top with figures of the hours.   The index was turned by a
piece of wood, which " either fell or rose by water dropping."
The clock stood in Sir Isaac's bedroom, and it was his daily
practice to supply it every morning with the proper quantity of
water.   It was frequently resorted to by the inmates of Mr.
Clark's house to ascertain the hour of the day, and it remained
there long after Sir Isaac went to Cambridge.   Dr. Stukely
informs us, that having had occasion to talk of clepsydræ, or
water-clocks, Newton remarked that their chief inconvenience
arose from the furring up of the small hole through which the

water passed, by the impurities which it contained,—a cause of inequality in its measure of time, the reverse of what takes place in clocks made with sand, which enlarges the hole through which it descends.

The mechanical carriage which Sir Isaac is said to have invented, was a four-wheeled vehicle, and was moved with a handle or winch wrought by the person who sat in it. We can find no distinct information respecting its construction or use, but it must have resembled a Merlin's chair, which is fitted only to move on the smooth surface of a floor, and not to overcome the inequalities of a common road.[1]

Although Sir Isaac was at this time a " sober, silent, and thinking lad," who never took part in the games and amusements of his school-fellows, but employed all his leisure hours in " knocking and hammering in his lodging-room," yet he was anxious to please them by " inventing diversions for them above the vulgar kind." In this way he often succeeded in alluring them from trifling amusements, and teaching them, as Dr. Stukely says, " to play philosophically ;" or, as Dr. Paris has better expressed it, in the title of his charming little work, to make " philosophy in sport science in earnest." With this view he introduced the flying of paper kites, and he is said to have investigated their best forms and proportions, as well as the number and position of the points to which the string

---

[1] It is a curious fact that Leibnitz, the rival of Newton, had laboured at similar inventions. In a letter written to Sir Isaac from Hanover, about a month after Leibnitz's death, on the 14th November 1716, the Abbé Conti informs him that Leibnitz had laboured all his life to invent machines, which had never succeeded, and that he was particularly desirous of constructing a wind-mill for mines, and a carriage to be moved without horses. Fontenelle, in his Eloge on Leibnitz, mentions these two inventions in different terms. He had bestowed, says he, much time and labour upon his wind-mill for draining the water from the deepest mines, but was thwarted in its execution by certain workmen who had opposite interests. In the matter of carriages, his object was merely to render them lighter and more commodious ; but a doctor, who believed that Leibnitz had prevented him from getting a pension from the King of Hanover, stated in some printed work, that he had contemplated the invention of a carriage which would perform the journey from Hanover to Amsterdam in twenty-four hours.—*Mém. Acad. Par.* 1718. Hist. p. 115.

should be attached. He constructed also lanterns of "crimpled paper," in which he placed a candle to light him to school in the dark winter mornings ; and in dark nights he tied them to the tails of his kites, in order to terrify the country people, who took them for comets.

Hitherto the attention of Sir Isaac had not been directed to any of the celestial phenomena, and when he did study the apparent daily motion of the sun, he was probably led to it by the imperfect measure of time which he obtained from his water-clocks. In the yard of the house where he lived, he was frequently observed to watch the motion of the sun. He drove wooden pegs into the walls and roofs of the buildings, as gnomons to mark by their shadows the hours and half-hours of the day. It does not appear that he knew how to adjust these lines to the latitude of Grantham ; but he is said to have succeeded, after some years' observation, in making them so exact, that anybody could tell what o'clock it was by *Isaac's Dial,* as it was called. It was probably at the same time that he carved two dials on the walls of his own house at Woolsthorpe ; but, though we have seen them there, we were not able to determine whether they were executed by a tentative process like those in Mr. Clark's yard, or were more accurately projected, from a knowledge of the doctrine of the sphere.[1]

But saws and hammers were not the only tools which our young philosopher employed. He was expert also with his pencil and his pen, drawing with the one and inditing verses with the other. It is not improbable that he received some in-

---

[1] One of these dials was taken down in 1844, along with the stone on which it was cut, by Mr. Turnor of Stoke Rochford, and presented by his uncle, the Rev. Charles Turnor, to the Museum of the Royal Society. The dial was traced on a large stone in the south wall, at the angle of the building, and about six feet from the ground. The name NEW-TON, with the exception of the first two letters, which have been obliterated, may be seen under the dial in rude and capital letters. The other dial is smaller than this, but not in good preservation. The gnomons of these dials have unfortunately disappeared. In the woodcut representing the manor-house of Woolsthorpe, the birthplace of Sir Isaac, are shown the places on the wall where the dials were traced.—See *Phil. Trans.* 1845, pp. 141, 142.

struction in drawing from his writing-master, called "Old Barley," who lived in the place occupied, in Dr. Stukely's time, by "the Millstone Alehouse in Castle Street." But whether he was instructed or self-taught, he seems to have made some progress in the art. His room was furnished with pictures drawn by himself, some of them being copied from prints, and some from life. The frames of these pictures were made by himself, and " coloured over in a workmanlike manner." Among these portraits Dr. Stukely enumerates " several of the King's heads, Dr. Donne, Mr. Stokes, his teacher at Grantham, and King Charles I." In addition to these portraits, there were well-designed drawings of " birds, beasts, men, ships, and mathematical diagrams, executed with charcoal on the wall, which remained till the house was pulled down in 1711."

Although Sir Isaac told Mr. Conduit that he " excelled particularly in making verses," yet it is strange that no authentic specimen of his poetry has been preserved. Beneath his portrait of Charles I. the follow verses were written :—

> A secret art my soul requires to try,
> If prayers can give me what the wars deny.
> Three crowns distinguished here, in order do
> Present their objects to my knowing view.
> Earth's crown thus at my feet I can disdain,
> Which heavy is, and at the best but vain.
> But now a crown of thorns I gladly greet,—
> Sharp is this crown, but not so sharp as sweet ;
> The crown of glory that I yonder see,
> Is full of bliss and of eternity.

Mrs. Vincent, who repeated these lines to Dr. Stukely from memory, fancied that they were written by Sir Isaac ; but even if he had thus early tasted of the Pierian spring, he must have lost his relish for its sparkling waters, as he often expressed in his later years a dislike for poetry ;—" not unlike Plato," as Conduit observes when mentioning this fact, " who, though he had addicted himself to poetry in his younger days, would not, in his serious years, allow even Homer a place in his commonwealth."

During the seven years which Sir Isaac spent at Grantham, there were some female inmates in Mr. Clark's house, in whose society he took much pleasure, and spent much of his leisure time. One of these, Miss Storey, sister to Dr. Storey, a physician at Buckminster, near Colsterworth, and the daughter of Mr. Clark's second wife, was two or three years younger than Newton, and seems to have added to great personal attractions more than the usual allotment of female talent. To the society of his school-fellows he preferred that of the young ladies at home, and he often made little tables, cupboards, and other utensils for Miss Storey and her playfellows, to set their dolls and their trinkets upon. Miss Storey, who after her second marriage bore the name of Mrs. Vincent, confessed to Dr. Stukely, when he visited her at Grantham in 1727, when she had reached the age of 82, that Newton had been in love with her, but that the smallness of her portion and the inadequacy of his own income, when the fellow of a college, prevented their marriage. Newton's esteem for her continued unabated during his life. He paid her a regular visit whenever he went to Woolsthorpe, and he liberally relieved her from little pecuniary embarrassments which seem to have occasionally beset her family.

At the death of the Rev. Mr. Smith in 1656, his widow, Sir Isaac's mother, left the rectory of North Witham, and, accompanied with her three children, Mary, Benjamin, and Hannah Smith, took up her residence at Woolsthorpe, which Mr. Smith had rebuilt. At this time Newton had reached his fifteenth year, and had acquired all the learning which a provincial school could supply. It does not appear that he had thought of following any particular profession, and it is probable that his mother intended to bring him up as a farmer and grazier,[1] and, like his ancestors, to take charge of her little property. He was therefore recalled from the school at Grantham, and

---

[1] Mrs. Hutton mentioned to Mr. Conduit that this was the profession to which Newton was to be brought up.

entered upon the new and not very welcome duties of tilling the ground and disposing of its produce. He was thus frequently sent to Grantham on Saturday, the market-day, in order to dispose of grain and other kinds of agricultural produce, and purchase articles of a domestic nature which the family required. On these occasions he was accompanied by an old and trustworthy man-servant, till he acquired sufficient experience to do business by himself. The inn which they frequented was the Saracen's Head in Westgate, but no sooner had they put up their horses than Isaac deserted his commercial duties, intrusted his marketings to the management of his rural Mentor, and went in search of knowledge to his former haunt in Mr. Clark's garret, where a parcel of old books afforded an interesting occupation of his time till the hour arrived when it was necessary to return. When the luxuries in the garret had lost their novelty, our young philosopher thought it a waste of time to go so far as Grantham and do nothing ; he deserted his duties, therefore, at an earlier stage, and entrenched himself under a hedge on the wayside between Woolsthorpe and Grantham, devouring some favourite author till his companion roused him on his return. With such tastes and habits it was not to be expected that the more urgent affairs of 'the farm would prosper under his management. When his mother ordered him into the fields to look after the sheep, or to watch the cattle when they were treading down the crops, he was equally negligent of the obligations which were imposed upon him. The sheep went astray, and the cattle enjoyed themselves among the growing corn, while he was perched under a tree with a book in his hands, or shaping wooden models with his knife, or luxuriating over the movements of an undershot water-wheel whirling the glittering spray from its float-boards, or arresting the passing traveller by its aqueous pulsations.

It was about this time, also, that he seems to have paid some attention to the subject of the resistance of fluids, to which his experiments with water-wheels would naturally lead him.   Mr. Conduit,[1] apparently on the authority of Mrs. Vincent, informs us that even when he was occupied with his paper kites, he was endeavouring to find out the proper form of a body which would experience the least resistance when moving in a fluid.   Sir Isaac himself told Mr. Conduit that one of the earliest scientific experiments which he made was in 1658, on the day of the great storm when Cromwell died, and when he himself had just entered his sixteenth year.   In order to determine the force of the gale, he jumped first in the direction in which the wind blew, and then in opposition to the wind ; and after measuring the length of the leap in both directions, and comparing it with the length to which he could jump in a perfectly calm day, he was enabled to compute the force of the storm.   Sir Isaac added, that when his companions seemed surprised at his saying that any particular wind was a foot stronger than any he had known before, he carried them to the place where he had made the experiment, and showed them the measure and marks of his several leaps.   This mode of jumping to a conclusion, or reaching it *per saltum*, was not the one which our philosopher afterward used.   Had he, like Coulomb, employed a shred of paper instead of his own person, and observed the time that it took to fly through a given distance, he would have obtained a better substitute for an anemometer.

Such were the occupations of Newton when his mother intrusted to him the management of her farm.   Experience soon convinced her that he was not destined to be a cultivator of the soil ; and as his love of study and dislike of every other occupation increased with his years, she resolved to give him all the advantages which education could bestow.   He was accordingly sent back to the school at Grantham, where he remained for nine months in active preparation for his academical studies.   His uncle, the Rev. W. Ayscough, who was rector of Burton Coggles, about three miles east of Woolsthorpe,

---

[1] MSS. of Conduit among the family papers.

having one day discovered Newton under a hedge, occupied in the solution of a mathematical problem, confirmed Mrs. Smith in the resolution which she had taken ; and as he had himself studied in Trinity College, it was arranged that Newton should follow his example, and proceed to Cambridge at the approaching term.

We have not been able to discover the exact year in which Newton was sent back to school, or the nature of the studies by which he was to be prepared for the University. It is stated by Conduit that he went to Cambridge in 1660 ; but the records of the University place it beyond a doubt that he was not admitted there till 1661, so that he had a year more than has been supposed to fit him for college. This period of preparation must have extended from 1658 to 1661, from the 16th to the 19th year of his age, and we accordingly find in one of his memorandum books, a small volume of about $3\frac{1}{2}$ inches square, and dated March 19, 1659,[1] that he was en-

---

[1] Mr. Conduit, in his MS. notes, mentions *two* of these memorandum books in the following manner :—" I find in a paper book of his to which he has put his name, and dated 1659,—Rules for drawing and making colours;" and in another of the same year, " *Prosodia* written out." The *first* of these books I did not find among the family papers ; but the *second* is the one referred to in the text. The following is its title :—

Quisquis in hunc librum
Teneros conjecit ocellos,
Nomen subscriptum perle-
gat ipse nomen.
Isaac Newton,
Martii 19, 1659.

On the second page is the title *Utilissimum Prosodiæ Supplementum*, which terminates on the 33d page with the date March 26, and is followed by an Appendix of three pages.

At the end of the book there is a list of his expenses, entitled *Impensa propria*, occupying fourteen pages.   On the 4th page the expenses are summed up thus:—

Totum,   .   .   .   .£3   5   6
Habui,   .   .   .   .   4   0   0
                        _____
Habeo,   .   .   .   .   0  14   6

On the 5th page there are fourteen loans of money extended thus:

Lent Agatha, .   . £0  11   1
Lent Gooch,   .   .   1   0   0

and he then adds at the bottom of the page, Lent out 13 shillings more than £4.

gaged in the study of prosody. This little volume contains various entries of his expenses during the first year that he was at college, but nothing, excepting the purchase of a dial, to indicate that he was engaged in physical or mathematical studies.

The day in which he quitted Grantham was one of much interest not only to himself but to his school-fellows and his venerable teacher. Mr. Conduit[1] has recorded it as a tradition in Grantham, that on that day the good old man, with the pride of a father, placed his favourite pupil in the most conspicuous part of the school, and having, with tears in his eyes, made a speech in praise of his character and talents, held him up to the scholars as a proper object of their love and imitation. We have not heard that the schoolmaster of Grantham lived long enough to feel a just pride in the transcendent reputation of his pupil; but many of the youth to whom his affectionate counsel was addressed, may have had frequent opportunities of glorying in having been the school-fellows of Sir Isaac Newton.

Among the entries are Chessmen and dial, . £0 1 4
Effigies amoris, . 0 1 0
Do. . . . . 0 0 10

and on the last page are entered seven loans, amounting to £3, 2s. 6d. There is likewise an entry of "Income from a glasse and other things to my chamber-fellow, £0 0 9." Another page is entitled

OTIOSE ET FRUSTRA EXPENSA.

| | |
|---|---|
| Supersedeas. | Sherbet and reaskes. |
| China ale. | Beere. |
| Cherries. | Cake. |
| Tart. | Bread. |
| Bottled beere. | Milk. |
| Marmelot. | Butter. |
| Custards. | Cheese. |

[1] MSS. of Conduit among the family papers.

# CHAPTER II.

Newton enters Trinity College, Cambridge—Origin of his Love of Mathematics—Studies Descartes' Geometry, and the Writings of Schooten and Wallis—Is driven from Cambridge by the Plague—Observes Lunar Halos in 1664—Takes his degree of B.A. in 1665—Discovers Fluxions in the same year—His First speculations on Gravity—Purchases a Prism to study Colours—Revises Barrow's Optical Lectures—But does not correct his erroneous Opinions about Colours—Is elected a Minor Fellow of Trinity in 1667—and a Major Fellow in 1668—Takes his degree of M.A.—His Note-book, with his expenses from 1666 to 1669—Makes a small Reflecting Telescope—His Letter of advice to Francis Aston, when going upon his Travels—His Chemical Studies —His Taste for Alchemy—His Paper on Fluxions sent to Barrow and Collins in 1669.

To a young mind thirsting for knowledge, and ambitious of the distinction which it brings, the transition from a provincial school to a university like that of Cambridge,—from intellectual solitude to the society of men imbued with all the literature and science of the age, must be an event of the deepest interest. To Newton it was a source of peculiar excitement. The history of science affords many examples where the young aspirant had been early initiated into her mysteries, and had even exercised his powers of invention and discovery before he was admitted within the walls of a college ; but he who was to give Philosophy her laws did not exhibit such early talent. No friendly counsel regulated his youthful studies, and no work of a scientific character guided him in his course. In yielding to the impulse of his mechanical genius, his mind obeyed the laws of its own natural expansion, and following in the line of least resistance, it was thus drawn aside from the precipitous path which it was fitted to climb, and the unbarred strongholds which it was destined to explore.

When Newton, therefore, entered Trinity College, he brought

with him a more slender portion of science than at his age falls
to the lot of ordinary scholars ; but this state of his acquirements was perhaps not unfavourable to the development of his
powers.  Unexhausted by premature growth, and invigorated
by healthful repose, his mind was the better fitted to make
those vigorous and rapid shoots which soon covered with foliage
and with fruit the genial soil to which it had been transferred.
Cambridge was consequently the real birthplace of Newton's
genius.  Her teachers fostered his earliest studies,—her institutions sustained his mightiest efforts,—and within her precincts
were all his discoveries made and perfected.  When he was
called to higher official functions, his disciples kept up the
pre-eminence of their master's philosophy, and their successors
have maintained this seat of learning in the fulness of its glory,
and rendered it the most distinguished among the universities
of Europe.

With letters of introduction from his uncle, the Rev. James
Ayscough, to his friends in Cambridge, Sir Isaac left Woolsthorpe in June 1661, and was admitted Subsizar at Trinity
College on the 5th of that month, and matriculated Sizar[1] on
the 8th of July.  Neither history nor tradition has handed
down to us any distinct account of the studies which Newton
pursued at Cambridge during the first three or four years of his
residence in that University.  In Conduit's Memoirs of Newton,

---

[1] "This class of students," says Mr. Edleston, " were required to perform various
menial services, which now seem to be considered degrading to a young man who is
endeavouring, by the force of his intellect, to raise himself to his proper position in
society.  The following extract from the *Conclusion Book* of Trinity College, while it
affords an example of one of their duties, will also serve to illustrate the rampant buoy-
ancy of the academic youth at the time of the Restoration."

"Jan. 1660-1.  Ordered also that no Bachelor, of what condition soever, nor any
Undergraduate, come into the upper butteries, save only a Sizar that is sent to see his
tutor's quantum, and then to stay no longer than is requisite for that purpose, under
penalty of 6d. for every time ; but if any shall leap over the hatch, or strike a butler or
his servant upon this account of being hindered to come into the butteries, he shall
undergo the censure of the Masters and Seniors."—Edleston's *Correspondence of Sir
Isaac Newton and Professor Cotes*, Lond. 1850, p. xli.

transmitted to Fontenelle,[1] we find very little information on this point, and even that little is by no means correct.   Before Newton left Woolsthorpe, his uncle had given him a copy of Sanderson's Logic, which he seems to have studied so thoroughly, that when he afterwards attended the lectures on that work, he found that he knew more of it than his tutor.   Finding him so far advanced, his tutor intimated to him that he was about to read Kepler's Optics to some Gentlemen Commoners, and that he might attend the Readings if he pleased.   Newton immediately studied the book at home, and when his tutor gave him notice that his Lectures upon it were to commence, he was was surprised to learn that it had been already mastered by his pupil.

About the same time probably he bought a book on Judicial Astrology at Stourbridge fair,[2] and in the course of perusing it he came to a figure of the Heavens, which he could not understand without a previous knowledge of trigonometry.   He therefore purchased an English Euclid, with an index of all the problems at the end of it, and having turned to two or three which he thought likely to remove his difficulties, he found the truths which they enunciated so self-evident that he expressed his astonishment that any person should have taken the trouble of writing a demonstration of them.   He therefore threw aside Euclid " as a trifling book," and set himself to the study of Descartes' Geometry,[3] where problems not so simple seem to have baffled his ingenuity.   Even after reading a few pages, he got beyond his depth, and laid aside the work ; and he is said to have resumed it again and again, alternately retreating and advancing till he was master of the whole,

---

[1] Collections for the History of the Town and Soke of Grantham, &c.  By EDMUND TURNOR, F.R.S., F.S.A.  Lond. 1806, pp. 159, 160.  Conduit's MSS. were written subsequently to the Memoirs above referred to.

[2] Demoivre says that the book on Astrology was bought at Stourbridge, the seat of the Cambridge fair, close to the town.

[3] Newton's copy of Descartes' Geometry I have seen among the family papers.  It is marked in many places with his own hand, *Error, Error, non est Geom.*

without having received any assistance.[1]  The neglect which he had shown of the elementary truths of geometry he afterwards regarded as a mistake in his mathematical studies ; and on a future occasion he expressed to Dr. Pemberton his regret that " he had applied himself to the works of Descartes, and other algebraic writers, before he had considered the Elements of Euclid with that attention which so excellent a writer deserved." [2]

The study of Descartes' Geometry seems to have inspired Newton with a love of the subject, and to have introduced him to the higher mathematics.    In a small commonplace book, bearing on the 7th page the date of Jan. 1663-4, there are several articles on angular sections, and the squaring of curves and " crooked lines that may be squared," several calculations about musical notes ;—geometrical propositions from Francis Vieta and Schooten ;—annotations out of Wallis's Arithmetic of Infinites, together with observations on Refraction,—on the grinding of " spherical optic glasses,"—on the errors of lenses, and the method of rectifying them, and on the extraction of all kinds of roots, particularly those " in affected powers." [3]

This commonplace book is particularly interesting from its containing the following important entry by Newton himself, after the lapse of thirty-five years, and when he had completed all his discoveries.

" *July* 4, 1699.—By consulting an account of my expenses at Cambridge,[4] in the years 1663 and 1664, I find that in the year 1664, a little before Christmas, I, being then Senior

---

[1] This statement is different from that of Conduit in his *Memoirs,* but I give it on his own authority, as founded on later inquiries.

[2] Pemberton's *View of Sir Isaac Newton's Philosophy.*  PREF.

[3] In this commonplace book we find the date November 1665, so that its contents were written in 1664 and 1665.

[4] In the commonplace book which contains the "annotations out of Schooten and Wallis," no expenses are entered, so that there must be another note-book which I have not found, in which the purchase of Schooten's Miscellanies and Descartes' Geometry is recorded.  It is not likely that the *second* note-book of 1659, mentioned by Conduit, contained expenses incurred in 1663 and 1664.

Sophister, bought Schooten's Miscellanies and Cartes' Geometry (having read this Geometry and Oughtred's *Clavis*[1] clean over half a year before), and borrowed Wallis's works, and by consequence made these annotations out of Schooten and Wallis, in winter between the years 1664 and 1665. At such time I found the method of Infinite Series ; and in summer 1665, being forced from Cambridge by the plague,[2] I computed the area of the Hyperbola at Boothby,[3] in Lincolnshire, to two and fifty figures by the same method.

Is. NEWTON."

In consequence of the devotion of his mind to these abstract studies, and his long-continued observations upon a comet in 1664,[4] which made him sit up late at night, Sir Isaac's health was impaired to such a degree, as Mr. Conduit informs us, that from this illness " he learnt to go to bed betimes." In the beginning of the same year, on the 19th February, Sir Isaac's attention was directed to the subject of circles round the moon, by two coronas of three and five-and-a-half degrees each, accompanied by the halo of $22°\ 35'$, of which he subsequently gave the theory in his Treatise on Optics.[5] In this year there were forty-four vacancies in the scholarships of Trinity College, and Newton was elected to one of them on the 28th of April. On this occasion he was examined in Euclid by Dr. Barrow, who

---

[1] Conduit remarks that in reading this work he did not entirely understand it, especially what "relates to Quadratic and Cubic Equations."—MSS. A translation of the Clavis was published and recommended by Halley in 1694.

[2] The plague commenced in Westminster about the end of 1664. It raged during the hotter months of 1665, and had so far abated before the end of the year, that the inhabitants returned to their homes in December. The date of Newton's quitting Cambridge, viz., 1665, as written under his own hand in his commonplace book, coincides with these facts, and is on this account probably the correct one ; but Pemberton makes the date 1666, which is adopted by Professor Rigaud, and seems to be given by Newton himself in the *Phil. Trans.* vol. vi. p. 3080. Rigaud's *Hist.  Essay on the first publication of Sir Isaac Newton's Principia*, p. 1, note.

[3] A village in Lincolnshire, near Sleaford, where Newton was probably on a visit.

[4] This comet passed its perihelion on the 4th December at midnight.

[5] Book II. Part IV. Obs. 13.

formed an indifferent opinion of his knowledge, and hence he was led not only to read Euclid with care, but to form a more favourable estimate of the ancient geometer when he came to the interesting propositions on the equality of parallelograms on the same base and between the same parallels.[1] In the month of January 1665, Newton took the degree of Bachelor of Arts, along with twenty-five other members of Trinity College, but we are not able to ascertain the academical rank which he held among the graduates, as the grace for that year does not contain the order of seniority of the Bachelors of Arts. The Proctors at this time were John Slader of Trinity, and Benjamin Pulleyn of Trinity, Newton's tutor, and the persons appointed in conjunction with them to examine the Questionists, were John Eachard of Catherine Hall, the satirical author of the *Grounds, &c., of the Contempt of the Clergy*, and Thomas Gipps of Trinity.[2]

In the same year Newton committed to writing his first discovery of Fluxions. This paper, written by his own hand, and dated May 20, 1665, represents in pricked letters the fluxions applied to their fluents, and in another leaf of the same waste book the method of fluxions is described without pricked letters, and bears the date of May 16, 1666. In the same book, with the date of November 13, 1665, there is another paper on Fluxions, with their application to the drawing of tangents, and " the finding the radius of curvity of any curve."[3] In the month of October 1666, Newton drew up another small tract, in which the method of Fluxions is again put down without pricked letters, and applied to Equations involving roots or surds.[4]

[1] Conduit's MSS.
[2] Edleston's *Correspondence*, &c. &c , App. xxi. xlv.
[3] Rigaud's *Hist. Essay, &c.*, App. No. II. p. 20. From the Macclesfield MSS. Raphson *Historia Fluxionum*, Cap. I. p. 1, Cap. xiii. p. 92, and English Edition, pp. 115, 116.
[4] These papers in the Macclesfield Collection are quoted by Newton himself in his Observations on Leibnitz's celebrated Letter to the Abbé Conti, dated 9th April 1716. See Raphson's *Hist. of Fluxions*, pp. 103 and 116.

It was doubtless in the same remarkable year 1666, or perhaps in the autumn of 1665, that Newton's mind was first directed to the subject of Gravity.  He appears to have left Cambridge some time before the 8th of August 1665, when the College was " dismissed " on account of the Plague, and it was therefore in the autumn of that year, and not in that of 1666, that the apple is said to have fallen from the tree at Woolsthorpe, and suggested to Newton the idea of gravity. When sitting alone in the garden, and speculating on the power of gravity, it occurred to him that as the same power by which the apple fell to the ground, was not sensibly diminished at the greatest distance from the centre of the earth to which we can reach, neither at the summits of the loftiest spires, nor on the tops of the highest mountains, it might extend to the moon and retain her in her orbit, in the same manner as it bends into a curve a stone or a cannon ball, when projected in a straight line from the surface of the earth.   If the moon was thus kept in her orbit by gravitation to the earth, or, in other words, its attraction, it was equally probable, he thought, that the planets were kept in their orbits by gravitating towards the sun.   Kepler had discovered the great law of the planetary motions, that the squares of their periodic times were as the cubes of their distances from the sun, and hence Newton drew the important conclusion that the force of gravity or attraction, by which the planets were retained in their orbits, varied inversely as the square of their distances from the sun.   Knowing the force of gravity at the earth's surface, he was, therefore, led to compare it with the force exhibited in the actual motion of the moon, in a circular orbit; but having assumed that the distance of the moon from the earth was equal to sixty of the earth's semidiameters, he found that the force by which the moon was drawn from its rectilineal path in a second of time was only 13·9 feet, whereas at the surface of the earth it was 16·1 in a second.   This great discrepancy between his theory and what he then considered to be the fact, induced him to

abandon the subject, and pursue other studies with which he
had been previously occupied.[1]

It does not appear from any of the documents which I have
seen, at what time Newton made his first optical discoveries.
On the authority of one of his memorandum books, containing
an account of his expenses, it is stated by Conduit that he
purchased a prism, in order to make some experiments on Descartes' Theory of Colours, and that he not only detected the
errors of the French philosopher, but established his own views
of the subject ; but this is contradicted by Newton himself,
who distinctly informs us that it was in the beginning of the
year 1666, that he procured a glass prism "to try therewith
the phenomena of colours."[2]   There is no evidence, however,
that he used it for this purpose, and there is every reason to
believe that he was not acquainted with the true composition
of light when Dr. Barrow completed his Optical Lectures,
published in 1669.[3]   In the preface of this work, Dr. Barrow
acknowledges his obligation to his colleague Mr. Isaac Newton,
as a man of a fine disposition and great genius, for having
revised the MSS., and corrected several oversights, and made
some additions of his own.[4]   Now, in the twelfth Lecture there

1 Neither Pemberton nor Whiston, who received from Newton himself the history of
his first ideas of Gravity, records the story of the falling apple. It was mentioned,
however, to Voltaire by Catherine Barton, Newton's niece, and to Mr. Green by Martin
Folkes, the President of the Royal Society. We saw the apple-tree in 1814, and brought
away a portion of one of its roots. The tree was so much decayed that it was taken
down in 1820, and the wood of it carefully preserved by Mr. Turnor of Stoke Rocheford.
See Voltaire's *Philosophie de Newton*, 3me part. Chap. III. Green's *Philosophy of Ex-
pansive and Contractive Forces*, p. 972, and Rigaud's *Hist. Essay*, p. 2.

2 *Phil. Trans.* vol. vi. p. 3075.

3 " Verum quod tenellæ matres factitant, a me depulsum partum amicorum haud
recusantium nutriciæ curæ commisi, prout ipsis visum esset, educandum aut exponen-
dum, quorum unus (ipsos enim honestum duco nominatim agnoscere) *D. Isaacus
Newtonus*, collega noster (peregregiæ vir indolis ac insignis peritiæ) exemplar revisit,
aliqua corrigenda monens, sed et de suo nonulla penu suggerens quæ nostris alicubi
cum laude inexa cernes." The other friend was John Collins, whom he calls the Mersennus of our nation. *Epist. ad Lectorem.* The imprimatur of this volume is dated
March 1668-9.

4 The addition by Newton is a singularly elegant and expeditious method at the end

are some observations on the nature and origin of colours, which are so erroneous and unphilosophical, that Newton could not have permitted his friend to publish them had he been then in the possession of their true theory. According to Barrow, who introduces the subject of colours as an unusual digression, *White* is that which discharges a copious light, scattered equally in every direction. *Black* is that which emits light not at all, or very sparingly. *Red* is that which emits light more condensed than usual, but interrupted by shady interstices. *Blue* is that which discharges a rarefied light, or one excited by a weaker force, as in bodies which consist of white and black particles arranged alternately, such, for example, as the *clear ether* in which there float fewer particles that reflect light, while the rest take away light, the *sea* in which the *white* salt is mixed with the *black* water, and the *blue shadows* seen at the same time by candle and day light, which are produced by the whiteness of the paper mixed with the faint light or blackness of the twilight. *Yellow* consists of much *white* and a little *red* interspersed, and *Purple* of much blue and some red. *Green* seems to have puzzled Dr. Barrow. He says that it is somehow allied to *Blue ;* but he adds, let wiser men find out the *difference,* I dare not conjecture. These opinions are so unsound, that they could not fail to have attracted the attention of Newton, who had certainly begun to study the subject of colours ; and if he had discovered at this time that *white* was a mixture of all the colours, and *black* a privation of them all, he could not have permitted the absurd speculations of his friend and master to pass uncorrected.[1]

While Newton was thus occupied with the subjects of Fluxions and Gravity, he " applied himself also to the grinding of optic glasses of other figures than spherical." Descartes, in

of Lect. xiv., of determining geometrically in every case the image formed by lenses, and describing the lens which projects the image on a given point.

[1] Barrow introduces the subject of colours by the following remarkable sentence : " *Quoniam colorum incidit mentio, quid si de illis (etsi præter morem et ordinem) paucula divinavero ?*"—*Lect.* xii. *ad finem.*

his *Dioptrics*, published in 1629, and more recently James
Gregory, in his *Optica Promota*, published in 1663, had shown
that parallel and diverging rays could only be reflected or
refracted to a point or focus by mirrors or lenses, whose surfaces were paraboloidal, ellipsoidal, or hyperboloidal, or of some
other form not spherical. Descartes had even invented and
described machines by which lenses of these shapes could be
ground and polished, and it was the universal opinion that the
perfection of refracting telescopes and microscopes depended on
the degree of accuracy with which lenses of these forms could
be executed.

While engaged in this work Newton made his first experiments with the prism, and he was soon induced to abandon
what he calls his "glass-works," in consequence of having
found "that the perfection of telescopes was limited not so
much for want of glasses truly figured according to the pre-
scriptions of optick authors (which all men have hitherto imagined), as because *light* itself is a heterogeneous mixture of
differently refrangible rays, so that were a glass so exactly
figured as to collect any one sort of rays into one point, it
could not collect those also into the same point, which having
the same incidence upon the same medium, are apt to suffer a
different refraction." He was therefore led to "take reflections into consideration," but in consequence of the interruption
produced by the Plague, "it was more than two years before
he proceeded."

After his return to Cambridge,[1] on the disappearance of the

[1] The only information which we have relative to the times of Newton's leaving and
returning to Cambridge, in consequence of the Plague, is contained in the following note
by Mr. Edleston:—

"The College was 'dismissed' June 22d, on the reappearance of the Plague. The
Fellows and Scholars were allowed their commons during their absence. Newton received on this account 3s. 4d. weekly, for 13 weeks, ending Michaelmas 1666.

    „  „  „   12  „      Dec. 21.
    „  „  „   5  .,     Ladyday 1667."

The College had been also dismissed the previous year, August 8th, on the breaking
out of the plague, but Newton must have left Cambridge before that, as his name does

Plague, he was, on the 1st of October 1667, elected Minor
Fellow, and an apartment called "The Spiritual Chamber,"
assigned to him by the Master,—a locality which Mr. Edleston
conjectures to be the ground room next the chapel in the north-
east corner of the great court. A few weeks after this he went
to Lincolnshire, and returned on the 12th February 1667-8.
On the 16th March 1668, he took his degree of M.A., and
was the twenty-third on the list of 148 signed by the Senior
Proctor.[1]

About this time, and during the period extending from 1666
to 1669, when he succeeded to the Lucasian chair, his studies
were of a very miscellaneous kind, and were doubtless interrupted not only by the appearance and reappearance of the
plague, but by the preparations necessary for taking his degree.
In his common note-book,[1] which I found among the family
papers, and which, along with a number of problems in
geometry and the conic sections, contains an account of his
expenses from 1665 to 1669, there are many entries which
throw some light upon his social character as well as upon his
studies. During his absence from College in 1665 and 1666,
we find him purchasing Philosophical Intelligences, the History
of the Royal Society, Gunter's Book and Sector from Dr. Fox,
together with magnets, compasses, glass-bubbles, drills, mandrels,
gravers, hones, and hammers. In 1667, he purchased Bacon's

not appear in the list of those who received *extra commons* for 6½ weeks on the occasion.
"Aug 7, 1665.—A month's commons (beginning Aug. 8th) allowed to all Fellows and
Scholars which now go into the country upon occasion of the pestilence."—(*Conclusion
Book.*)

" On the continuance of the scourge, we find him with others receiving the allowance
for commons for 12 weeks, in the quarter ending Dec. 21, 1665, and for 13 weeks ending
Ladyday 1666."—Edleston's *Correspondence, &c.* p. xlii. note 8.

[1] Thomas Burnet, author of the *Theoria Telluris Sacra*, and a future friend and correspondent of Sir Isaac.

[2] This note-book, of which three-fourths is white paper, begins at one end with three
pages of short-hand, which is followed by his expenses. At the other end of the book
there is a *Novi Cubi . . . . Tabella*, and a number of problems in geometry and the
conic sections.

Miscellany, three prisms, and four ounces of putty.[1]  He
records his jovial expenses, not only on the occasion of his
taking his two degrees, but " at the tavern several other times."
He acknowledges his having " lost at cards twice ; " but this
is compensated by his liberality to his " cousin Ayscough," on
whom, and " on other acquaintance," he " spends" considerable
sums,—by his generosity to his sister, for whom he buys
oranges,—and his kindness to D. Wickins, to whom he lends
considerable sums of money.  It appears, too, from this note-
book, that Newton went to London on Wednesday the 5th
August 1668, and returned to Cambridge on Monday the
28th September, after an absence of nearly two months ; but
the object of his journey is nowhere mentioned.  It is not improbable that he went there to purchase lenses, and apparatus
and materials for chemical experiments,—a new branch of
science which seems at this time to have occupied his attention,
and which he continued to prosecute with much zeal during
the most active period of his life.  In April 1669, he records
the purchase of lenses in London, and there follows a long list
of chemical substances, headed by mercury, together with a
furnace, and an air-furnace.[2]

[1] Flowers of Putty, an oxide of zinc used in polishing lenses and metallic specula.

[2] As this list of expenses is very interesting, and as the book which contains them has
obviously been preserved by Newton himself as evidence of the priority of some of his
researches, the following abstract of it is presented to the reader :—

1665.

| | | |
|---|---|---|
| Received, May 23d, whereof I gave my tutor 5s., | | £5 0 0 |
| Remaining in my hands since last quarter, | | 3 8 4 |
| In all, | | £8 8 4 |

This account of expenses extends only to six and a half pages, and records many loans.
The following are among the entries :—

| | | |
|---|---|---|
| Drills, gravers, a hone, a hammer, and a mandrel, | | £0 5 0 |
| A magnet, | | 0 16 0 |
| Compasses, | | 0 3 6 |
| Glass bubbles, | | 0 4 0 |
| My Bachelor's account, | | 0 17 6 |

Towards the end of 1668, Newton carried into effect, on a small scale, his resolution to "take reflections into consideration." Thinking it "best to proceed by degrees," he first "made a small perspective to try whether his conjecture would hold good or not."[1] The telescope was six inches long. The

| | | | |
|---|---|---|---|
| At the tavern several other times, | £1 | 0 | 0 |
| Spent on my cousin Ayscough, | 0 | 12 | 6 |
| On other acquaintance, | 0 | 10 | 0 |
| Cloth, 2 yards, and buckles for a vest, | 2 | 0 | 0 |
| Philosophical Intelligences, | 0 | 9 | 6 |
| The Hist. of the Royal Society, | 0 | 7 | 0 |
| Gunter's Book and Sector to Dr. Fox, | 0 | 5 | 0 |
| Lost at cards twice, | 0 | 15 | 0 |
| At the tavern twice, | 0 | 3 | 6 |
| I went into the country, Dec. 4, 1667. | | | |
| I returned to Cambridge, Feb. 12, 1667. | | | |
| Received of my mother, | 30 | 0 | 0 |
| My journey, | 0 | 7 | 6 |
| For my degree to the College, | 5 | 10 | 0 |
| To the proctor, | 2 | 0 | 0 |
| To three prisms, | 3 | 0 | 0 |
| Four ounces of putty, | 0 | 1 | 4 |
| Lent to D. Wickins, | 1 | 7 | 6 |
| Bacon's Miscellanies, | 0 | 1 | 6 |
| Expenses caused by my degree, | 0 | 15 | 0 |
| A Bible binding, | 0 | 3 | 0 |
| For oranges for my sister, | 0 | 4 | 2 |
| Spent on my journey to London, and 4s. or 5s. more which my mother gave me in the country, | 5 | 10 | 0 |
| I went to London, Wednesday, August 5th, and returned to Cambridge on Monday, September 28, 1668. | | | |
| Lent D. Wickins, | 0 | 11 | 0 |

APRIL 1669.

| | | | |
|---|---|---|---|
| For glasses in Cambridge. | | | |
| For glasses in London. | | | |
| For aquafortis, sublimate, oyle pink, fine silver, antimony, vinegar, spirit of wine, white lead, salt of tartar, ☿ | 2 | 0 | 0 |
| A furnace, | 0 | 8 | 0 |
| Air furnace, | 0 | 7 | 0 |
| Theatrum chemicum, | 1 | 8 | 0 |
| Lent Wardwell 3s., and his wife 2s., | 0 | 5 | 0 |

[1] See Letter to Oldenburgh, Feb. 1671-2, in Newtoni *Opera*, by Horsley, tom. iv. p. 295 ; and Letter to a Friend, Feb, 23, 1668-9, in Gregory's *Catoptrics*, edit. 3d, p. 259 ; or in the *Macclesfield Collections*, vol. ii. p. 289.

aperture of the large speculum was something more than an
inch, and, as the eye-glass was a plano-convex lens, with a focal
length of one-sixth or one-seventh of an inch, " it magnified
about forty times in diameter," which he believed was more
than any six-feet refracting telescope could do with distinctness.
Owing to the badness of the materials which he used, and the
want of a good polish, it did not represent objects so distinctly
as a six-feet refractor, yet Sir Isaac was of opinion that it
would discover as much as any three or four feet refractor,
especially if the objects are luminous.   He saw with it Jupiter
distinctly round, with his four satellites, and also the horns or
" moonlike phase of Venus," though this last phenomenon
required a nice adjustment of the instrument.   He therefore
considered this small telescope as " an epitome" of what may
be done by reflections ; and he did not doubt that, in time, a
six-feet reflector might be made which would perform as much
as any sixty or hundred feet refractor.   In consequence of
interruptions, Sir Isaac did not proceed any farther in the
construction of reflectors till the autumn of 1671.

It was during this period of his history, on the 18th of May
1669, that Sir Isaac wrote the celebrated letter of advice to
his young friend, Mr. Aston, who, at the age of twenty-seven,
was about to make a tour on the Continent.   This " letter" is
a very interesting production.[1]   It does not evince much acquaintance with the ways of the world, but it shows some
knowledge of the human heart, and throws a strong light on
the character and opinions of its author.   In his chemical
studies, which, as we have just seen, he had recently commenced, his mind was impressed with some belief in the doctrines of alchemy, and he certainly pursued his experiments to
a late period of his life, with the hope of effecting some
valuable transmutations.   Among the subjects, therefore, to
which he requests Mr. Aston to pay attention, there are several
which indicate this tendency of his mind.   He desires him to

[1] See APPENDIX, No. I.

observe the products of nature, especially in mines, with the circumstances of mining, and of extracting metals or minerals out of their ores, and refining them ; and, what he considered as far more important than this, he wishes him to observe if there were any transmutations out of one species into another, as, for example, out of iron into copper, out of one salt into another, or into an insipid body, &c.    Such transmutations, he adds, are above all others worth his noting, being *the most luciferous, and many times lucriferous experiments, too, in philosophy !*    Among the particular observations to which he calls the attention of his friend, is that of a certain vitriol, which changes iron into copper, and which is said to be kept a secret for the lucrative purpose of effecting that transmutation. He is to inquire also whether in Hungary, or in the mountains of Bohemia, there are rivers whose waters are impregnated with gold, dissolved by some corrosive fluids like aqua regis ; and whether the practice of laying mercury in the rivers till it be tinged with gold, and then separating the gold by straining the mercury through leather, be still a secret or openly practised.    There was at this time in Holland a notorious alchemist of the name of Bory, who, as Sir Isaac says, was some years since imprisoned by the Pope, in order to extort from him secrets of great worth, both " as to medicine and profit," and who made his escape into Holland, where they granted him a guard.    " I think," adds Sir Isaac, " he usually goes clothed in green : pray inquire what you can of him, and whether his ingenuity be any profit to the Dutch ! "    We have not been able to discover the results of Mr. Aston's inquiries, but whatever they were they did not damp the ardour of Newton in his chemical researches, nor extinguish the hope which he seems to have cherished, of making " philosophy lucriferous," by transmuting the baser metals into gold.

But however fascinating these studies were to our young philosopher, he did not permit them to interfere with his nobler pursuits.    At the very time when writing to Mr. Aston, we

find him occupied with his fluxionary calculus, and transmitting
to Dr. Barrow his celebrated paper *On Analysis by Equations
with an infinite number of terms*, with permission to communicate it to their mutual friend, Mr. Collins. In announcing this
communication on the 20th June 1669, and promising to
send it by the next opportunity, Dr. Barrow keeps the name of
its author a secret, and merely tells Mr. Collins that he is a
friend staying at Cambridge, who has a powerful genius for such
matters. In his next letter of the 31st July, accompanying
the paper, he expresses the hope that it will not a little delight
him : and, in a third letter to Collins of the 20th August, he
mentions how much he is pleased with the favourable opinion
which his correspondent has of it, and adds, that " the name
of the author is Newton, a Fellow of our College, and a young
man, who is only in his second year since he took the degree of
Master of Arts, and who, with an unparalleled genius, has
made very great progress in this branch of mathematics."

# CHAPTER III.

Newton succeeds Barrow in the Lucasian Chair—Hyperbolic Lenses proposed by Descartes and Others—Opinions of Descartes and Isaac Vossius on Colours—Newton discovers the Composition of White Light, and the different Refrangibility of the Rays that compose it—Having discovered the cause of the imperfection of Refracting Telescopes, he attempts the construction of Reflecting ones—Constructs a second Reflecting Telescope in 1668, which is examined by the Royal Society, and shown to the King—Discussions respecting the Gregorian, Newtonian, and Cassegrainian Telescope—James Gregory the Inventor of the Reflecting Telescope—Attempts to construct one—Newton makes a Speculum of silvered glass—Glass Specula by Short in 1730, and Airy in 1822—Hadley constructs two fine Reflecting Telescopes—Telescopes by Bradley, Molyneux, and Hawksbee—Short's Reflecting Telescopes with Metallic Specula—Magnificent Telescope of Sir William Herschel with a four-feet Speculum—Munificence of George III.—Astronomical Discoveries of Sir Wm. Herschel —Telescopes of Sir J. Herschel and Mr. Ramage—Gigantic Telescope of the Earl of Rosse with a six-feet Speculum—Progress of Telescopic Discovery—Proposal to send a fine Telescope to a Southern Climate.

In 1669, when Dr. Barrow had resolved to devote himself to the studies and duties of his profession, he resigned the Lucasian Professorship of Mathematics in favour of Newton. His appointment took place on the 29th October, and we may now consider him as having entered on that brilliant career of discovery, the history of which will form the subject of some of the following chapters. It had been long known to every writer on optics, and to every practical optician, that lenses with spherical surfaces, such as those now in common use, did not give distinct images of objects. This indistinctness was believed to arise solely from their spherical figure, in consequence of which the rays which passed through the marginal or outer parts of the lens were refracted to a focus nearer the lens than those which passed through its central parts. The distance between these foci was called the *spherical aberration* of the lens, and various methods were suggested for diminishing or removing this source of imperfection.  Descartes[1] had shown that hyperbolic lenses refracted the rays of light to a single focus, and we accordingly find the early volumes of the Philosophical Transactions filled with schemes for grinding and polishing lenses of this form.  Newton had made the same attempt, but finding that a change of form produced a very little change in the indistinctness of the image, he thought that the defect of lenses, and the consequent imperfection of telescopes, might arise from some other cause than the imperfect convergency of the incident rays to a single point.  This happy conjecture was speedily confirmed by the brilliant discovery of the different refrangibility of the rays of light,—a discovery which has had the most extensive applications to every branch of science, and (what is very rare in the history of inventions) one to which no other person has made the slightest claim.

No plausible conjecture, even, had been formed by the predecessors of Newton respecting the nature and origin of colours. Descartes believed them to be a modification of light depending on the direct or rotatory motion of its particles.  Grimaldi, Dechales, and others, regarded them as arising from different degrees of rarefaction and condensation of light.  Gregory defines colour to be the hue (*tinctura*) of igneous corpuscles emerging from radiant matter;[2] and we have already seen that the views of Barrow on this subject were equally absurd.  In recounting the opinions of preceding writers, Newton alleges that in all of them the colour is supposed not to be innate in light, but produced by the action of the bodies which reflect or refract it.  This, however, is not strictly true, as Isaac Vossius, in a dissertation which Newton probably never saw, distinctly maintains that all the colours exist in light itself, or, to use another of his expressions, that all light carries its colours along

[1] Dioptrice, cap. viii. ix. 1629.

[2] Optica Promota: *Definitiones*, 3.  Lond. 1663.

with it.[1] This, however, was a mere conjecture, which cannot be regarded as in any way anticipating the great discovery of Newton, " that the modification of light from which colours take their origin, is innate in light itself, and arises neither from reflection, nor refraction, nor from the qualities or any other conditions of bodies whatever, and that it cannot be destroyed or in any way changed by them."

After our author had purchased his glass prism at Stourbridge Fair, he made use of it in the following manner. Having made a hole H in his window-shutter SHT, and darkened the room, he admitted a ray of the sun's light RR, which after

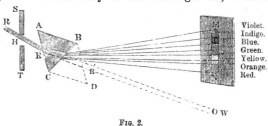

Violet.
Indigo.
Blue.
Green.
Yellow.
Orange.
Red.

Fig. 2.

refraction at the two surfaces AC, BC of the prism ABC, exhibited on the opposite wall MN what is called the *Solar* or *Prismatic Spectrum*. This spectrum was an elongated image of the sun

[1] Isaaci Vossii *De Lucis Natura et Proprietate*, Amstel. 1662. As the opinions of Vossius have not been referred to by any of our historians of science the following passages may be interesting.

" Primus itaque color, si tamen color dicendus sit, is est albus, pelluciditatem proxime hic accedit. Insunt itaque et lumini omnes colores, licet non semper visibiliter ; nempe ut flamma intensa alba et unicolor apparet, eadem si per nebula aut aliud densius corpus spectetur, varios induit colores. Pari quoque ratione, Lux, licet invisibilis aut alba ut sic dicam, si per prisma vitreum, aut aerem roridum transeat, similiter varios colores induit."—P. 6.

" Omnem tamen lucem secum colores deferre et eo colligi potest quod si per lentem vitream, aut etiam per foramen, lumen in obscurum admittatur cubiculum in muro aut linteo remotiore manifeste omnes videantur colores, cum tamen in punctis decussationis radiorum et locis minimum lenti vicinis, nullus color sed purum tantum compareat lumen."—P. 64.

" Quapropter non recte ii sentiunt qui colorem vocant Lumen modificatum."—P. 59.

about *five* times as long as it was broad, and consisted of *seven* different colours, *Red, Orange, Yellow, Green, Blue, Indigo,* and *Violet.* " It was at first," says Newton, " a very pleasing divertisement to view the vivid and intense colours produced thereby ;" but this pleasure was immediately succeeded by surprise at various phenomena which were inconsistent with the received laws of refraction. The " extravagant disproportion between the length of the spectrum and its breadth," excited him to a more than ordinary curiosity of examining from whence it might proceed. He could scarcely think that the various thickness of the glass, or the termination with shadow or darkness could have any influence on light to produce such an effect ; yet he thought it not amiss first to examine these circumstances, and he therefore tried what would happen by transmitting light through parts of the glass of different thickness, or through holes in the window of different sizes, or by setting the prism without (on the left hand of ST), so that the light might pass through it and be refracted before it was terminated by the hole ; but he found none of these circumstances material. The fashion of the colours was in all these cases the same.

Newton then suspected that by some unevenness of the glass, or other accidental irregularity, the colours might be thus dilated. In order to try this he took another prism BCD, and placed it in such a manner that the light passing through them both might be refracted contrariwise, and thus returned by BCD into the path RRW, from which the first prism ABC had diverted it, for by this means he thought that the regular effects of .the prism ABC would be destroyed by the second prism BCD, and the irregular ones more augmented by the multiplicity of refractions. The result was, that the light which by the first prism was diffused into an oblong form MN, was reduced by the second prism into a circular one W with as much regularity as when it did not pass through them, so that whatever was the cause of the length of the image MN, it did not arise from any irregularity in the prism.

Sir Isaac next proceeded to examine more critically the effect that might be produced by the difference in the angles of incidence, at which rays from different parts of the sun's disc fell upon the face AC of his prism, and for this purpose he measured the lines and angles belonging to the spectrum MN, and obtained the following results :

| | |
|---|---|
| Distance of MN from the hole H, | 22 feet. |
| Length of MN, . | 13¼ inches. |
| Breadth of MN, | 2⅜ ,, |
| Diameter of the hole H, | 0¼ ,, |
| Angle of WR with the middle of MN, . | 44° 56′. |
| Angle ABC of the prism, | 63° 12′. |
| Refractions at R and R′, | 54° 4′. |

" Now, subducting the diameter of the hole from the length and breadth of the image, there remains 13 inches in the length and 2¾ inches in the breadth comprehended by those rays which passed through the centre of the hole, and consequently the angle of the hole which that breadth subtended was about 31′, answerable to the sun's diameter ; but the angle which its length subtended was more than five such diameters, namely, 2° 49′."

With the refractive power of the prism, which he found to be 1·55, he found the refractions of two rays proceeding from opposite parts of the sun's disc, so as to differ 31 minutes in their obliquity, to be such as to comprehend an angle of 31 or 32 minutes.

Although Newton could not doubt the correctness of the law of the Sines on which these calculations were founded, yet " his curiosity caused him again to take his prism, and satisfy himself by direct experiment that even a motion of the prism about its axis of four or five degrees, did not sensibly change the position of the spectrum MN on the wall," so that " there still remained some other cause to be found out," from which the spectrum could subtend an angle of 2° 49′.

Having set aside all these explanations of the length of his spectrum, Newton hazarded the strange suspicion that the rays after passing through the prism "might move in curve lines, and according to their more or less curvity lead to different parts of the wall," and " it increased his suspicion," he adds, " when he remembered that he had often seen a tennis-ball struck with an oblique racket describe such a curve line.   In this case a circular and a progressive motion being communicated to it by that stroke, its parts on that side where the motions conspire, must press and beat the contiguous air more violently than on the other, and there excite a reluctancy and reaction of the air proportionally greater.   And for the same reason, if the rays of light should possibly be (composed of) globular bodies, and by their oblique passage out of one medium into another acquire a circulating motion, they ought to feel the greater resistance from the ambient ether on that side where the motions conspire, and thence be continually bowed to the other.   But notwithstanding this plausible ground of suspicion, when I came to examine it, I could observe no such curvity in them.   And besides (which was enough for my purpose) I observed that the difference betwixt the length of the image, and the diameter of the hole through which the light was transmitted, was proportional to their distance."

Having thus gradually removed these different hypotheses, or suspicions, as Newton calls them, he was led to the *experimentum crucis* for determining the true cause of the elongation of the spectrum MN.   He placed a board with a hole in it behind the face BC of the prism, and close to it, so that he could transmit through the hole any one of the colours in MN, and keep back the rest.   When the hole was near C, for example, no other rays but the *red* fell on the wall at N.   He then placed behind the *red* space at N another board with a hole in it, and behind this board he placed another prism, so as to receive the red light at N, which passed through the hole in the board.   He then turned round the first prism ABC, so as to make all the colours pass successively through the two holes, and he marked their places on the wall.   From the variation of these places he saw that the *red* rays at N were less refracted by the second prism than the *orange* rays, the *orange* less than the *yellow*, and so on, the *violet* being more refracted than all the rest.   Hence he arrived at the grand conclusion, *that light was not homogeneous, but consisted of rays of different refrangibility.*

We have given this full account of Newton's mode of investigation, in order to show the cautious manner in which he proceeded ; and were it not for the inconceivable stupidity of the men who called in question his results, we should have considered all his suspicions and precautions unnecessary, and adopted the opinion of Arago, that the *compound nature of white light* was clearly involved in the very phenomenon of the prismatic spectrum, and that the words in which Newton stated it as a conclusion, were " nothing else than a literal description or translation of that familiar experiment." [1]

Having established this important truth, Newton immediately perceived that the different refrangibility of the rays of

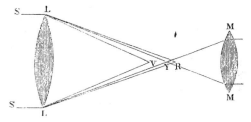

FIG. 3.

light was the real cause of the imperfection of refracting telescopes.   If LL is a convex lens receiving rays SL, SL, the *violet* rays in the *white* ray SL will be refracted in the line LV to V, the *yellow* rays to Y, and the *red* rays to R, forming a

[1] *Phil. Trans.* vol. vii. No. 80.   Feb. 19, 1672.

*violet* image of the *sun*, or any other object from which the white light proceeds at the point v, a *yellow* image at y, and a *red* one at R, images of intermediate colours being formed at intermediate points between v and R. If this image is received on a sheet of white paper at v, or y, or R, it will be exceedingly indistinct, and tinged with these different colours. Newton found that the space vR, which is called the *chromatic aberration*, or the *aberration of colour*, was in glass the fiftieth part of the diameter LL of the lens, so that in lenses about six inches in diameter, such as those used in the telescopes about 150 feet long, of Campani, Divini, and Huygens, the space vR would be about ·17 of an inch. Hence if LL be the object-glass of a telescope directed to any luminous body, and MM an eye-glass through which the eye sees magnified the image or picture of the body between v and R, it cannot see distinctly all the different images of the body formed there. If it is adjusted to see distinctly the *yellow* image at y as it is in the figure, it will not see distinctly either the *red* or the *violet* images, nor indeed any but the *yellow*, and that very imperfectly, as it is mixed up with hazy images of all the other colours, producing great confusion and indistinctness of vision.

As soon as Sir Isaac saw this result of his discovery, he left off his " glass-works," as he called his attempts to improve the refracting telescope, and, in the autumn of 1668, constructed the little reflecting telescope which we have already described. The success of this experiment, small as it was, inspired Newton with fresh zeal, and, though his mind was now occupied with his optical discoveries, with the elements of his method of fluxions, and with his speculations on gravity, yet, with all the ardour of youth, he set himself to the task of executing another reflecting telescope with his own hands. This telescope, of which we have given a drawing in the annexed figure, was a better one than the first ; and, we presume from its not being much superior either to the first, or to the one executed by his colleague, he allowed it to lie by him for several years. The

existence of these telescopes having become known to some of
the members of the Royal Society, Newton was requested to

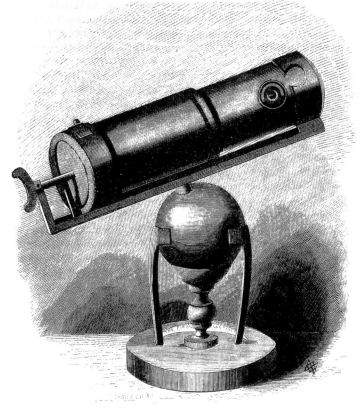

Fig. 4.

send his instrument to that learned body.    This telescope consisted of a concave metallic speculum, the radius of curvature of

which was $12\frac{2}{3}$ or 13 inches, so that "it collected the sun's rays at the distance of $6\frac{1}{3}$ inches." The rays reflected by the speculum were received upon a plain metallic speculum inclined 45° to the axis of the tube, so as to reflect them to the side of the tube in which there was an aperture to receive a small tube with a plano-convex eye-glass, whose radius was one-twelfth of an inch, by means of which the image formed by the speculum was magnified 38 times.

Newton did not hesitate to obey the request of the Royal Society, and it was accordingly sent, and we believe presented to that distinguished body near the end of 1671. It was also shown to the King, and a description of it published in the Philosophical Transactions.[1] The instrument itself is carefully preserved in the Library of the Royal Society, with the inscription,—

"THE FIRST REFLECTING TELESCOPE INVENTED BY SIR ISAAC NEWTON, AND MADE WITH HIS OWN HANDS."

Previous to March 16, 1672, a Fellow of Trinity College had made a similar telescope of nearly the same size, which Newton found to "magnify more, and also more distinctly," than a six-feet refractor, and which he considered better than his own. A description of Newton's instrument in Latin was drawn up and corrected by Newton, and when signed by Lord Brouncker, Wren, and Hooke, was sent to Huygens, who expressed his approbation of it, and suggested the propriety of giving the concave speculum a parabolic form. Various observations were made upon the instrument, particularly by Monsieur Auzout and Monsieur Denys ; and Monsieur Bercé claimed for M. Cassegrain the invention of a telescope which he considered "almost like Newton's," and "more ingenious."[2] Newton replied to this communication, and acknowledging that he had been ac-

---

[1] *Phil. Trans.* vol. vii. No. 81, p. 4004    March 25, 1672.

[2] See *Journal des Savans*, 1672, pp. 80 and 121 ; and *Phil. Trans.* No. 83, p 4056, May 20, 1672.

quainted with the telescope proposed by Gregory before he had
contrived his own, he points out the superiority of the Gregorian to the Cassegrainian form, and of his own to both.   This
letter led to a little amiable controversy between Gregory and
Newton on the merits of their reflecting telescopes, in which
neither of them gained the victory.[1]

Newton's occupations were at this period too numerous, and
his time too valuable to be spent in mechanical labour ; and he
therefore never resumed the construction of reflecting telescopes.
The Royal Society, however, employed a London optician of the
name of Cox to execute a Newtonian reflector, with a speculum
whose focal length was no less than *four feet*, but he failed in
polishing the speculum ; and though Sir Isaac himself contemplated the construction of another instrument, he seems to have
wholly abandoned the attempt, and to have bequeathed to another age the honour of making his telescope an instrument of
discovery.   The want of a good material for the specula seems
to have been the difficulty which perplexed the optician ; and
it would appear from the following observations of Newton
himself, that the specula for the instrument, ordered by the
Royal Society, were to be made of a new material.   " You will
gratify me much," says he in a letter to Oldenburg, " by ac-
quainting me with the particular dimensions, fashion, and success

---

[1] Gregory's *Catoptrics*, App. 261.  In this controversy, Newton never claimed any
credit for the invention of a new form of the reflecting telescope, and was certainly surprised at the notice it excited among persons that either were, or ought to have been,
acquainted with the previous invention of Gregory. In his letter to Mr. Collins, he speaks
in the kindest manner of Gregory.  " I doubt not that when Mr. Gregory wrote his *Optica
Promota*, he could have described more fashions than one of these telescopes, and perhaps have run through all the possible cases of them, if he had thought it worth his
pains.  Because Mr. Cassegrain propounded his supposed invention pompously, as if the
main business was the contrivance of these instruments, I thought fit to signify that that
was none of his contrivance, nor so advantageous as he imagined. And I have now sent
you these farther considerations on Mr. Gregory's answer, only to let you see that I chose
the most easy and practicable way to make the first trials. Others may try other ways,
nor do I think it material which way these instruments are perfected, so they be perfected.—Dec. 10, 1672."  See the *Macclesfield Collections*, vol. ii. pp. 346, 847, or Newtoni
*Opera* by Horsley, vol. iv. p. 288.

of the four-feet tube, which, I presume, Mr. Cox by this time hath finished. And to inform myself of the advantages of the steely matter which is made use of, you will much oblige me if you can procure me a fragment of it. I suppose it is made by melting steel with a little antimony, perhaps without separating the sulphureous from the metalline part of that mixture. And so though it may be very hard, and capable of a good polish, yet I suspect whether it be so strongly reflective as a mixture of other metals. I make this inquiry, because if I should attempt anything farther in the fabric of the telescope, I would first inform myself of the most advantageous materials. On which account, also, you would farther oblige me if you can inquire whether Mr. Cox, or any other artificer, will undertake to prepare the metals, glass, tube, and frame of a four-feet telescope, and at what rates he will do it, so that there may remain nothing for me to do but to polish the metals. A gross account of this will at present suffice, until I send you a particular design of the fabric of the instrument, if I resolve upon it." [1]

Such is a brief account of the first reflecting telescope that was successfully constructed and applied to the heavens ; but though we make this admission in its favour, we must also acknowledge that it was a small and ill-made instrument, incapable of showing the beautiful celestial phenomena which had been long seen by the refracting telescopes of Hevelius and Huygens. No discovery was made by any of the three instruments to which we have referred, and more than fifty years elapsed before telescopes of the Newtonian form became useful in astronomy. A similar fate befell the reflecting telescope of James Gregory, who was the undoubted inventor of that noble instrument, and whose merits were thrown into the shade by the display which accompanied the invention of his friend. In his *Optica Promota*, published in 1663, Gregory describes a reflecting telescope, with the view of making telescopes shorter and more manageable. When compared with other telescopes,

---

[1] July 13, 1672, in the *Macclesfield Collections*, vol. ii. p. 333.

he gives it the character of a *golden one*, as " it has no incon-
veniences, and may have all the properties of the other telescopes, whether dioptric or catoptric." He then goes on to
describe " a telescope of this most perfect kind." It consists
of a parabolic concave speculum, with a hole in its centre,
having near its focus a small elliptic concave speculum. The
image formed by the large parabolic speculum is received by
the small elliptical one, and reflected through the aperture in
the former upon a lens which magnifies it. In the reflecting
telescope proposed by Cassegrain, the image formed by the
larger speculum is received by a small *convex* speculum, the
effect of which is to shorten the telescope, and prevent the
crossing, or " decussation of the rays," as Newton calls it, in
the focus of the larger speculum.[1] Gregory never attempted
to construct this instrument with his own hands, but he employed Messrs. Reeves and Cox, celebrated glass-grinders, to
execute a concave speculum three feet in focal length, together
with a little concave and a little convex speculum ; but as Mr.
Reeves " could not polish the large concave on the tool, but
merely with cloth and putty,"[2] and as Gregory was on the eve

[1] Sir Isaac seems to have been the first person who suggested the idea that vision
might be rendered indistinct by the collision of the rays when they cross one another at
the focus of mirrors or lenses. In speaking of the use of more than one eye-glass in the
Gregorian telescope, he states, that " *by the iterated decussations of the rays, objects
will be rendered less distinct,* as is manifest in dioptric telescopes, where two or three
eye-glasses are applied to erect the object."—Letter to Collins, Dec. 10, 1672 ; *Macclesfield Collections,* vol. ii. p. 344. In the course of some experiments on this subject, I
found that the sections of the cone of rays are never so distinct and well-defined *after*
*the rays have crossed as before.*—(*Treatise on New Phil. Inst.* pp. 44 and 193.) And
Captain Kater, in comparing two equal telescopes, the one Gregorian and the other
Cassegrainian, found that the intensity of the light within the focus was nearly double of
what it was without the focus. In other experiments, he found the ratio as 1000 to
788.—*Phil. Trans.* pp. 13, 14. Mr. Tulley, however, in making similar experiments,
did not confirm the results obtained by Captain Kater. I have found, in confirmation
of these facts, that the negative diffractive fringes produced by rays which do not cross
one another before they enter the eye, are more distinct than the positive ones which do
cross.—*Treatise on Optics,* Edit. of 1853, p. 117.

[2] Dr. Hooke made several experiments with the speculum executed by Mr. Reeves, and
did not find it so bad as Gregory thought. See Newton's Letter to Collins above
referred to.

" of going abroad, he thought it not worth the pains to trouble himself any farther with it, so that the tube was never made. Yet," he adds, " I made some trials with a little concave and *convex* speculum, which were but rude, seeing I had but transient views of the object." [1]

‑Although Newton did receive through Oldenburg the information he requested from Mr. Cox,[2] yet he never availed himself of it in proceeding any farther with metallic reflectors. In consequence, however, of Gregory having suggested to him the use of glass specula silvered on the back for burning glasses, and shown how to make the foci of each surface coincident, Newton proposed, we believe in 1678, to substitute these specula instead of metallic ones in the reflecting telescope. In this manner he attempted to make a telescope four feet long, and with a magnifying power of 150; but though the glass was wrought by a London artist, and seemed well finished, yet, when it was quicksilvered on its convex side, it exhibited all over the glass innumerable inequalities, which rendered every object indistinct. He expresses, however, his conviction, that nothing but good workmanship is wanting to perfect such telescopes, and he recommends their consideration " to the curious in figuring glasses." This recommendation remained unnoticed for upwards of fifty years. At last Mr. James Short, a Scotch artist of consummate skill, executed, about the year 1730, no fewer than six reflecting telescopes, with glass specula, three of which were fifteen inches, and three nine inches in focal length; but some of them turned out useless from the veins in the glass. Maclaurin,[3] who, with one of nine inches, could read the Philosophical Transactions very easily at the distance of 130 feet, informs us that they were excellent instruments. Short, however, found that their light was fainter than he expected, and from this cause, combined with the difficulty of

[1] Letter from Gregory to Collins and Newton, Sept. 26, 1672.
[2] *Biog. Brit.*, Art. Newton, p. 3217.
[3] Smith's *Optics*, vol. ii. Remarks, p. 80.

finishing them, he afterwards limited himself to the use of metallic specula.[1]

The subject of glass specula was resumed in 1822 by Mr. Airy, one of the distinguished successors of Newton in the Lucasian chair.   Having demonstrated that the aberration both in figure and colour might be corrected in these instruments, he executed more than one ; but though the result of the experiment was such as to excite hopes of ultimate success, the construction of such an instrument is still a desideratum in practical science.

Notwithstanding these failures, we would not discourage the young artists of the present day from endeavouring to surmount the difficulties experienced by their predecessors.   Discs of glass can now be obtained entirely free of veins, and what is of great importance, instead of coating the convex surface with a plate of mercury and tin, which reflects even less light than speculum metal, we can now, by the electrotype, deposit pure silver on the glass, and give it a reflective power far surpassing that of any other metal.

Such is a brief history of the attempts which were made by Newton and Gregory to construct reflecting telescopes.   They were certainly far from being successful ; nor were their contemporaries more fortunate, though guided by the light of their experience.

After the lapse of fifty years, however, and several years before his death, Sir Isaac had the satisfaction of seeing a Newtonian telescope, six feet long, mounted upon a commodious stand, and capable of exhibiting some of the most interesting phenomena in the heavens.   A Gregorian telescope, of an inferior size, was executed with similar success, and from that time the art of making telescopes with metallic reflectors was gradually brought to perfection.   The history of these improve-

---

[1] Caleb Smith proposed to correct the colour produced by the two refractions, by a concave lens placed between the speculum and the small receiver, or by making the surface of a rectangular glass prism concave.—*Phil. Trans.* 1739, p. 326.

ments, and of the grand discoveries in astronomy to which they led, would of itself form an interesting volume. We shall endeavour, in a few pages, to present it to our readers.

The person to whom we owe the first step in the improvement of the reflecting telescope, was John Hadley, one of the inventors of the Reflecting Quadrant, which bears his name.[1] This gentleman, who was a Fellow of the Royal Society, and possessed of considerable scientific attainments, began his experiments in 1719, and, probably after many failures, completed a telescope toward the end of 1720. It was shown and presented to the Royal Society, in whose Journals for January 12, 1721, the following notice of it occurs :—" Mr. Hadley was pleased to show the Royal Society his reflecting telescope, made according to our President's (Sir Isaac Newton) directions in his Optics, but curiously executed by his own hand, the force of which was such as to enlarge an object near *two hundred times*, though the length thereof scarce exceeds *six* feet ; and having shown it he made a present thereof to the Society, who ordered their hearty thanks to be recorded for so valuable a gift." The instrument consisted of a metallic speculum, about six inches in diameter, and its focal length was five feet two inches and a half. Its plane speculum was made of the same metal, about the 15th of an inch thick, and it had six eye-pieces, three convex lenses 1-3d, 3-10ths, and 11-40ths of an inch, magnifying 190, 208, and 230 times, two concave lenses magnifying 200 and 220 times, and an erecting eye-piece of three convex lenses, magnifying about 125 times. It had also a small refracting telescope as a finder, which, we believe, was first suggested by Descartes, and the whole was mounted upon a stand, ingeniously and elegantly constructed.[2] The celebrated Dr. Bradley, and the Rev. Mr. Pound of Wanstead, compared it with the great Huygenian refractor 123 feet long, and they saw with the reflector, though less brightly, " whatever they had hitherto disco-

[1] See Prof. Rigaud's *Biographical Account of John Hadley, Esq.*, pp. 7-11.
[2] *Phil Trans.* vol. xxxii. No. 376, March and April, 1723, p. 303.

vered with the Huygenian, particularly the transits of Jupiter's satellites, and their shadows over the disc of Jupiter, the black list in Saturn's ring, and the edge of the shadow of Saturn cast on his ring. They also saw with it several times the five satellites of Saturn."[1]  Mr. Hadley himself and others likewise saw the preceding phenomena together with the belts of Saturn, and the first and second satellites of Jupiter, as bright spots on the body of the planet.[2]

After executing another Newtonian telescope of the same size, Mr. Hadley directed his attention to those of the Gregorian form, upon which he made great improvements.  In 1726 he communicated to Dr. Desaguliers an account of the instrument as perfected by himself, with tables showing the relative proportions of its different parts ; and in 1734 he made an additional communication to the same writer, in reference to the use of a double eye-glass, for " preventing the objects being coloured near the edges of the field."[3]  Not content with the labours of his own hands, Mr. Hadley, who was now Vice-President of the Royal Society, was desirous of enabling astronomers and opticians to manufacture these valuable instruments, the former for use in their observatories, and the latter for public sale. He accordingly inspired Dr. Bradley with the desire of constructing these instruments, and with his directions " he succeeded pretty well, and would probably have perfected one of them, had he not been obliged suddenly to remove from the place where he then dwelt, and been since diverted from it by other avocations." Soon afterwards, however, Dr. Bradley with Mr. Samuel Molyneux, renewed the attempt at Kew, by making an instrument about 26 inches long ; but notwithstanding Dr. Bradley's experience and Mr. Hadley's frequent instructions, a long time elapsed before they could " tolerably succeed." At last, however, they completed to their satisfaction a telescope of the Newtonian form of the above focal length. They afterwards

---

[1] *Phil. Trans.* July and August 1723, p. 382.
[2] Gregory's *Catoptrics*, pp. 250, 285.    [3] *Ibid.*, p. 385.

made a pretty good one of seven inches, and one of eight feet, the largest that had yet been made.[1] The first of these instruments was elegantly fitted up on a highly ornamented stand, and presented by Mr. Molyneux to his Majesty John v. of Portugal.[2]

Hitherto no optician but Mr. Hawksbee had ventured to construct these instruments for sale. He executed a good one of about $3\frac{1}{2}$ feet in focal length,[3] and other two of six and twelve feet, and he was the first person, as Molyneux informs us, " who had attempted it without the assistance of a fortune, which could well bear the disappointment."

Having acquired, by his own experience and Mr. Hadley's instructions, a sufficient knowledge of the art, Mr. Molyneux communicated the whole process[4] to Mr. Edward Scarlet, his Majesty's optician, and to Mr. Hearne, a mathematical instrument maker, and both these artists attained to such perfection in constructing them, that they manufactured them for public sale. In this way the Reflecting Telescope came into general use, and, principally in the Gregorian form, it has been an article of trade with every regular optician.

While the English opticians, with the aid of Molyneux and Hadley, were thus practising the new art of grinding and polishing specula, Mr. James Short of Edinburgh, without any such aid, was devoting to the subject all the energies of his youthful mind. In the year 1732, and in the 22d year of his age, he began his labours ; and to such perfection did he carry the art of grinding and polishing metallic specula, and of giving them the true parabolic figure, that with a telescope of 15 inches in focal length, he and Mr. Bayne, Professor of Law

1 The Hon. Samuel Molyneux and Hadley in Smith's *Optics*, vol. ii. p. 302, § 782.

2 *Ibid.*, p. 363, § 913.

3 This telescope, according to Dr. Smith, was so excellent that it was scarcely inferior to Hadley's of 5 feet 2½ inches in length. It bore a power of 226, as determined by Mr. Hawksbee, Mr. Folkes, and Dr. Jurin. See Smith's *Optics ;* Remarks, p. 79.

4 This process, drawn up partly by Molyneux and partly by Hadley, is printed in Dr. Smith's *Optics*, vol. ii. p. 301.

in the University of Edinburgh, read the Philosophical Transactions at the distance of 500 feet, and several times, particularly on the 24th of November and the 7th of December 1734,
they saw the five satellites of Saturn together, an achievement
beyond the reach of Hadley's six-feet telescope.  Mr. Short
had constructed several instruments, 9, 6, 4, and $2\frac{6}{10}$ inches
in focal length.  With those four inches long he saw the
satellites of Jupiter very well, and read in the Philosophical
Transactions at the distance of 125 feet.  With the six-inch
ones he read at the distance of 160 feet, and with the nine-
inch ones at the distance of 160 feet.  The celebrated Colin
Maclaurin compared one of the six-inch ones with one of the
best London ones of $9\frac{3}{10}$ inches, and found that it exceeded it
in brightness, distinctness, and magnifying power.  It surpassed
also another London one, $11\frac{1}{2}$ inches in focal length.[1]  After
Short had established himself in London in 1742, he received
£630 for a twelve-feet reflector from Lord Thomas Spencer.
In 1752 he executed one for the King of Spain for £1200 ;
and a short time before his death, which took place in 1768,
he finished the specula of the magnificent telescope which was
mounted equatorially for the Observatory of Edinburgh, by his
brother Thomas Short.  The King of Denmark offered twelve
hundred guineas for this instrument, through which we have
often seen the leading celestial phenomena, but not till the
large speculum had been greatly injured in consequence of
having been repolished by an inferior artist.[2]

Notwithstanding these great improvements on the Reflecting
Telescope, no discovery of importance had yet been achieved by
them.  The ordinary refractors of Huygens, and those of Campani in the hands of Cassini, though they laboured under all
the imperfections of coloured light, had made the latest dis-

[1] Maclaurin in Smith's *Optics*, vol. ii., Remarks, p. 81.
[2] This telescope was removed from the Observatory upon the establishment of the
Astronomical Institution, and is, we believe, now lying dismantled in some garret of
the city.

coveries in the heavens ; and nearly three quarters of a century had elapsed without any extension of our knowledge of the Solar and Sidereal Systems. This, however, was only one of those stationary intervals during which human genius holds its breath, in order to take a new and a loftier flight. The power of the Refracting Telescope, extended to the unmanageable length of above *two hundred* feet, had been strained to the very utmost, and the Reflectors, vigorous and promising in their infancy, were about to attain an efficiency and magnitude which the most sanguine astronomer had never ventured to anticipate. It was reserved for Sir William Herschel and the Earl of Rosse to accomplish this great work, and by the construction of telescopes of gigantic size to extend the boundaries of the Solar System—to lay open the hitherto unexplored recesses of the sidereal world, and to bring within the grasp of reason those nebular regions to which imagination had not ventured to soar.

Anxious to observe with his own eyes the wonders of the planetary system, and, fortunately for science, unable to purchase a telescope for himself, Sir William Herschel resolved, in 1774, to construct one with his own hands. With this instrument, which was a Newtonian reflector of five feet, he saw distinctly the ring of Saturn and the satellites of Jupiter. Dissatisfied with its performance, he afterwards executed *two hundred* specula of *seven* feet focal length, *one hundred and fifty* of *ten* feet, and above *eighty* of *twenty* feet ! In 1781 he began a thirty-feet aerial reflector, with a speculum three feet in diameter, but as it was cracked in the operation of annealing, and as another of the same size was lost in the fire from a failure in the furnace, his hopes were disappointed. In minds like his, however, disappointment is often a stimulus to higher achievements, and the double accident which befell his specula suggested, no doubt, the idea of making a still larger instrument, and of obtaining pecuniary aid for its accomplishment. He accordingly conveyed, through Sir Joseph Banks, to the King his intention to execute such a telescope, and his Majesty, with the munificent spirit of a great sovereign, instantly offered to defray the whole expense of its construction.   Encouraged by this noble act of liberality, Sir William Herschel began in 1785, and completed in 1789, his gigantic telescope, *forty feet* in focal length, with a speculum *forty-seven and a half inches* in diameter !   Its tube, about *forty feet* long and *five* wide, was made of iron, and the observer, suspended in a moveable seat at the mouth of it, examined, with what is called the *front view,* the celestial objects to which it was directed.    This noble instrument, now dismantled, stood in the lawn of Sir William Herschel's house, and some of our readers may remember, like ourselves, its extraordinary aspect when visiting the great astronomer himself, or resting in the Crown Hotel at Slough, or journeying on their way to Windsor.

It is due to the memory of George III., that the friends of science should cherish it with respect and gratitude.    By enabling Sir William Herschel to construct his colossal tube, and to spend the whole of his time in applying it to the heavens, he was entitled to share in the glory of his discoveries ; and we owe it to historical truth to say, that none of the sovereigns who either preceded or followed him have an equal claim on the homage of astronomers.    If, in his imperial rule, he sometimes transcended the limits of constitutional government, let us remember that he left the throne more secure and glorious than he found it.    If he ventured, on some occasions, to thwart the counsellors of his choice, we may find some apology for the exercise of a high prerogative in the factious character of the age, and in the acknowledged incapacity of his advisers ;—and if he lost a transatlantic empire by persisting to levy tribute from its people, he followed the advice of distinguished counsellors, and was but the instrument of a higher power in establishing a mighty nation veined with Saxon blood, and nerved with British spirit,—destined to give lessons of civilisation to the Eastern World—to afford a home to science unpatronized—to religion in persecution, and to patriotism in exile.

Stimulated by such patronage, the genius and perseverance which created instruments so transcendent in magnitude, were not likely to be baffled in their practical application.  In the examination of the starry heavens, the ultimate object of his labours, Sir William Herschel exhibited the same exalted qualifications ; and in a few years he rose from the level of humble life to the enjoyment of a name more glorious than that of the sages and warriors of antiquity, and as enduring as the objects with which it will be for ever associated.  Nor was it in the ardour of the spring of life that these triumphs were achieved.  He had reached the middle of his appointed course before his career of discovery began, and it was in the autumn and winter of his days that he reaped the full harvest of his glory.  The discovery of a new planet at the verge of the Solar System, was the first trophy of his skill, and new double and multiple stars, and new nebulæ and groups of celestial bodies, were added in hundreds to the system of the universe.  The spring tide of knowledge, which was thus let in upon the human mind, continued for a while to spread its waves over Europe, but when it sank to its ebb in England, there was no other bark left upon the strand but that of the Deucalion of science, whose home had been so long upon its waters.[1]

When Sir William Herschel's great telescope was taken down in 1822, a telescope of 20 feet in focal length, and with an aperture of $18\frac{1}{4}$ inches, was erected in its place by his son, Sir John Herschel.  This instrument, with three mirrors of the same size, was carried to the Cape of Good Hope, and it was with it that Sir John made those valuable observations which have added so greatly to our knowledge of Sidereal Astronomy.

About the same time, the late Mr. John Ramage, a merchant

[1] For an account of the Decline of Science in England, here alluded to, we refer the reader to Sir John Herschel's *Treatise on Sound*, to Mr. Airy's *Report on Astronomy*, in the Report of the British Association for 1833, and to Mr. Babbage's interesting volume, *On the Decline of Science.*  See also *Quarterly Review*, October 1830, and *North British Review*, vol. xiv. p. 235.

in Aberdeen, devoted much of his attention to the construction
of large Newtonian reflectors.    He ground and polished specula
of 13½, 15, and 21 inches in diameter.    One of these was
erected at the Royal Observatory of Greenwich, in 1820,[1] with
a focal length of 25 feet, and a speculum 15 inches in diameter ;
another of the same size at Sir John Ross's Observatory, near
Stranraer ;—and the large speculum of 21 inches is, we believe,
in the Observatory of Glasgow.[2]

The long interval of half a century seems to be the period
of hybernation during which the telescopic mind rests from its
labours, in order to acquire strength for some great achievement :  Fifty years elapsed between the dwarf telescope of Newton and the large instruments of Hadley :  Other fifty years
rolled on before Sir William Herschel constructed his magnificent telescope ; and fifty years more passed away before the
Earl of Rosse produced that colossal instrument which has
already achieved such brilliant discoveries.

This distinguished nobleman began his experiments so early
as 1828, and he ground and polished specula fifteen inches, two
feet, and three feet in diameter, before he commenced the Herculean attempt of executing a speculum *six feet* in diameter, and
with a focal length of *fifty* feet.    The speculum was cast on the
13th April 1842, ground in 1843, polished in 1844, and, in
February 1845, the telescope was ready to be tried.    The focal
length of the speculum is fifty-four feet.    It weighs four tons,
and, with its supports, it is seven times as heavy as the four-
feet speculum of Sir William Herschel.    The speculum is placed
in one of the sides of a cubical wooden box s, *Fig.* 6, about
eight feet wide ; and to the opposite end of this box is fastened
the tube, which is about fifty feet long, eight feet in diameter
in the middle, but tapering to seven at the extremities, and

---

[1] See *Transactions of the Astronomical Society,* vol. ii. p. 413.

[2] A fine reflecting telescope, with a speculum two feet in diameter, and a focal length
of twenty feet, has been recently constructed by Mr. Lassels, who has made with it several
important discoveries within the limits of our own system.

furnished with diaphragms $6\frac{1}{2}$ feet in aperture. The tube is made of deal staves an inch thick, hooped with strong iron clamp rings, and it carries at its upper end, and in the axis of the tube, the small oval speculum A, six inches in its lesser diameter.

The telescope, as shown in the annexed figure, is established between two lofty castellated piers sixty feet high, and is raised to different altitudes by a strong chain cable B attached to the top of the tube. This cable passes over a pulley T on the frame

Fig. 5.—Lord Rosse's Telescope from the South-East.

F down to a windlass shown at U in *Fig.* 6, on the ground, which is wrought by two assistants. To the frame F are attached, at X, X, chain guys fastened to the counterweights E, E. The telescope is balanced by these counterweights suspended by chains D, D, which are fixed to the sides of the tube, and pass over large iron pulleys C, C.

To the *eastern* pier is fixed a strong semicircle of cast-iron

v v, about eighty-five feet in diameter. The telescope is connected with this circle by a strong racked bar w, with friction-
rollers attached to the tube by wheel-work, so that by means of
a handle near the eye-piece, the observer can move the telescope
along the bar on either side of the meridian to the distance of
an hour for an equatorial star.

FIG. 6.—Lord Rosse's Telescope from the North-West.

On the *western* pier are erected the stairs and galleries for
the observers. The *first* gallery, shown at H, H below the tube,
*Fig.* 5, commands an altitude of 42°. It is a light but strong

framing of wood, which slides between two ladders I, I, fixed
to the southern face of the piers.   It is counterpoised by a
weight, and raised to the height required by a windlass K.
Upon its upper plane is a railway upon which the observing
gallery L can be moved about 24 feet east and west by means
of two wheels turned by a winch M near the observer.   Other
three galleries, N, O, P, command all altitudes above 42°, and
within 5° of the zenith.   They are each carried by two beams
Q, Q, which run between pairs of grooved wheels R, R, and these
beams, with their respective galleries, are drawn forward when
the wheels are turned by a very ingenious piece of mechanism.
These galleries hold twelve persons, and strangers are not a little
startled when they find themselves suspended, midway between
the piers, over a chasm 60 feet deep.[1]

   We have enjoyed the great privilege of seeing and using this
noble instrument, one of the most wonderful combinations of
art and science which the world has yet seen.   We have, in the
morning, walked again and again, and ever with new delight,
along its mystic tube, and, at midnight, with its distinguished
architect, pondered over the marvellous sights which it discloses,
—the satellites, and belts and rings of Saturn,—the old and new
ring, which is advancing with its crest of waters to the body of
the planet,—the rocks, and mountains, and valleys, and extinct
volcanoes of the moon,—the crescent of Venus, with its moun-
tainous outline,—the systems of double and triple stars,—the
nebulæ and starry clusters of every variety of shape,—and
those spiral nebular formations which baffle human compre-
hension, and constitute the greatest achievement in modern discovery.

   Such is a brief description of the gigantic telescope completed
by the Earl of Rosse.   In order to form a correct idea of its
effective magnitude, we must compare it with other instruments,
as in the following table, in which the specula are supposed to
be square in place of round :—

———————————

[1] A box containing a second speculum is shown at Y.

| Names of Makers. | Diameter of Speculum. | | | Area of Surface. |
|---|---|---|---|---|
| Newton, | . . . | 1 inch, | . . . | 1 square inch. |
| —— | . . . | 2·37 ,, | . . . | 5·6 ,, |
| Hadley. | . . . | 4·5 ,, | . . . | 20 ,, |
| —— | . . . | 5 ,, | . . . | 25 ,, |
| Hawksbee, | . . | 9 ,, | . . . | 81 ,, |
| Ramage, | . . . | 21 ,, | . . . | 441 ,, |
| Lassels, | . . . | 2 feet, | . . . | 576 ,, |
| Lord Rosse, | . . | 2 ,, | . . . | 576 ,, |
| —— | . . . | 3 ,, | . . . | 1296 ,, |
| Herschel, | . . | 4 ,, | . . . | 2304 ,, |
| Lord Rosse, | . . | 6 ,, | . . . | 5184 ,, |

Next in interest to the telescopes of Lord Rosse are those of M. Foucault, who deposits a film of pure silver upon the spherical surface of a disc of glass. After the silver surface has been polished by the hand, he modifies the figure by local retouches, and converts the sphere into an ellipsoid, and then into a paraboloid, so as to remove the spherical aberration. By this method he has produced a telescope with a speculum *thirteen* inches in diameter, and *eight* feet in focal length, which separates the two small stars which compose the *blue* star of γ Andromedæ, a result obtained by M. W. Struve with the great achromatic of Pulkova.

In looking back on what the telescope has accomplished since the time of Newton, and in reflecting on the vast depths of ether which have been sounded ;—on the number of planetary bodies which have been added to our system, and on the extensive fields of sidereal space which have been explored, can we hesitate to believe it to be the Divine plan that man shall yet discover the whole scheme of the visible universe, and that it is his individual duty, as well as his high prerogative, to expound its mysteries and to develop its laws ? Over the invisible world he has received no commission to reign, and into its secrets he has no authority to pry. It is over the material and the visible that he has to sway the intellectual sceptre,—it is among the structures of organic and inorganic being that his functions of combination and analysis are to be chiefly exercised. However great have been the achievements of the past, and however magnificent the instruments to which we owe them, the limits of telescopic vision have not been reached, and space has yet marvellous secrets to surrender. A reflector *ten feet* in diameter will be due to science before the close of the century, and a disc of flint-glass,[1] 29 *inches* in diameter, awaits the command of some liberal government, or some munificent individual, to be converted into an achromatic telescope of extraordinary power.

In cherishing these sanguine expectations, we have not forgotten that the state of our northern atmosphere must set some limit to the magnifying power of our telescopes. In a variable climate, indeed, the vapours and local changes of temperature, and consequent inequalities of refraction, offer various obstructions to astronomical research. But we must meet the difficulty in the only way in which it can be met. The astronomer cannot summon the zephyrs to give him a cloudless sky, nor command a thunderstorm to clear it. He must transport his telescope to the purer air of Egypt or India, or climb the flanks of the Himalaya or the Andes, to erect his watch-tower above the grosser regions of the atmosphere. In some of those brief yet lucid intervals, when distant objects present themselves in sharp outline and minute detail, discoveries of the highest value might be grasped by the lynx-eyed astronomer. The resolution of a nebula,—the bisection of a double star,—the detection of new asteroids ;—the details of a planet's ring,—the evanescent markings on its disc,—the physical changes on its surface, and perchance the display of some of the dark worlds of Bessel, might be the revelations of a moment, and would amply repay in national glory the transportation of a huge telescope to the shoulder or to the summit of a lofty mountain.[2]

---

1 This disc of flint-glass was executed by Messrs. Chance Brothers and Company, of the Smethwick Glass-works, and was rewarded with a council medal of the Great Exhibition.—See *Reports of the Juries*, p. 529.

2 This proposal, which was first made by the author in September 1844, is likely to be now carried into effect. A committee of the British Association, and of the Royal Society, have applied to Government for the necessary funds.

# CHAPTER IV.

Newton writes Notes on Kinkhuysen's Algebra—and on Harmonic and Infinite Series— Delivers Optical Lectures at Cambridge—Is elected a Fellow of the Royal Society— Communicates to them his Discoveries on the different Refrangibility and Nature of Light—Popular account of them—They involve him in various Controversies—His Dispute with Pardies—with Linus—with Gascoigne and Lucas—The Influence of these Disputes on his Mind—His Controversy with Dr. Hooke and Monsieur Huygens, arising from their Attachment to the Undulatory Theory of Light—Harassed with these Discussions he resolves to publish nothing more on Optics—Intimates to Oldenburg his Resolution to withdraw from the Royal Society from his inability to make the Weekly Payments—The Council agree to dispense with these Payments—He is allowed by a Royal Grant to hold his Fellowship along with the Lucasian Chair without taking Orders—Hardship of his situation in being obliged to plead Poverty to the Royal Society—Draws up a Scheme for extending the Royal Society, by paying certain of its Members—The Scheme was found among his Papers—Soundness of his Views relative to the Endowment of Science by the Nation—Arguments in support of them.

WHILE Newton was constructing his Reflecting Telescope, and discussing with Gregory and others the question of its superiority to instruments of the Gregorian and Cassegrainian form, his mind was directed to a variety of other subjects. Dr. Barrow had requested him, through Collins, to write some notes to be appended to a Latin translation from the Dutch, of Kinkhuysen's Algebra, a task which he readily undertook, and which occupied some considerable portion of his time during the years 1669 and 1670. He at first did not think the work " worth the pains of a formal comment," and returned the book with his notes, " intermixed with the author's discourse," requesting Collins not to mention his name, but merely to say that " it was enriched by another author." In thanking him for his valuable additions, Collins intimated that the part on surd numbers had been " too lightly handled," and requested New-

ton to point out in several books on surds which he sent to
him, such passages as might be added to Kinkhuysen, to supply
the defect. Newton kindly offered to make the necessary
additions, and having learned from his correspondent that his
" pains" in this matter " would be acceptable to some very
eminent grandees of the Royal Society, who must be made
acquainted therewith," he got back his MSS., and added only
two or three examples more, as·upon revising the papers he
" judged it (the part on surds) not so imperfect as he thought
it had been."[1]

His attention had also been directed by Collins to problems
on the summation of harmonic series, and in the determination
of the rate per cent. in annuity problems, when all the other
quantities were given. In sending the solution of the problems,
he gives Collins permission " to insert it in the Philosophical
Transactions, so it be without his name to it." " For I see
not," he adds, " what there is desirable in public esteem were
I able to acquire and maintain it. It would perhaps increase
my acquaintance, the thing which I chiefly study to decline."

In the month of July 1670, he had intended, during the
Duke of Buckingham's installation as Chancellor of the University of Cambridge, to pay a visit to his friends in London, and
to give Mr. Collins " a verbal acknowledgment of his undeserved favours ;" but he was prevented " by the sudden sur-
prisal of a fit of sickness, which not long after (God be thanked)
I again recovered of."

During the winter of this year, Newton had begun to " me-
thodize his Discourse of Infinite Series,[2] designing to illustrate
it with problems," but he was " suddenly diverted from it by
some business in the country," and was not able to resume the

---

[1] Letters to Collins from 1669 to September 27, 1670.—*Macclesfield Correspondence,*
vol. ii.
[2] This work was never finished. It was published by Horsley, under the title of
*Geometria Analytica,* from three different MSS.—See Newtoni *Opera,* tom. i. pp. 391-518.
A translation of it had been published by Colson in 1736.

subject till towards the end of the year, when he was prevented by other avocations from preparing it for the press.

Although our author had read a course of lectures on Optics, in the University of Cambridge, in the years 1669, 1670, and 1671, containing his principal discoveries regarding the different refrangibility of light, and towards the end of 1671 was preparing a series of twenty of them for the press, yet it is a singular fact that these discoveries should not have become public through the conversation or correspondence of his pupils. The members of the Royal Society even had acquired no knowledge of them till the beginning of February 1672, and it was chiefly on his Reflecting Telescope that his reputation in that body was founded.   So great indeed was the interest which it excited, that Dr. Seth Ward, Bishop of Salisbury, who had written some able works on Astronomy, and filled the Savilian Chair of Astronomy at Oxford, proposed Mr. Newton as a Fellow of the Royal Society on the 23d December 1671.   In a letter to its secretary, Mr. Oldenburg, of the 6th January, he expressed his satisfaction with this event in the following words :—" I am very sensible of the honour done me by the Bishop of Sarum in proposing me a candidate, and which I hope will be further conferred upon me by my election into the Society ; and if so, I shall endeavour to testify my gratitude by communicating what my poor and solitary endeavours can effect towards the promoting your philosophical designs."   He was accordingly elected on the 11th January, on which day the Society, with the view of securing his invention of the telescope from foreign piracy, agreed to transmit a drawing and account of it to Huygens at Paris.   The notice of his election, and the thanks of the Society for the communication of his telescope, were contained in the same letter, with an assurance that the Society " would take care that all right should be done him in the matter of this invention."   In replying to this letter, Newton very justly expressed his surprise to see " so much care taken about securing an invention of which I have hitherto

had so little value, and therefore since the Royal Society is
pleased to think it worth the patronizing, I must acknowledge
it deserves much more of them for that, than of me, who, had
not the communication of it been desired, might have let it
still remain in private, as it hath already done some years."

Thus encouraged by the Royal Society, Newton lost no time
in making other communications to them. In his very next
letter to their secretary, dated 18th January 1672, he announces his optical discoveries in the following manner :—" I
desire that in your next letter you would inform me for 'what
time the Society continue their weekly meetings ; because, if
they continue them for any time, I am purposing them to be
considered of and examined on account of a philosophical discovery, which induced me to the making of the said telescope,
and which I doubt not but will prove much more grateful than
the communication of that instrument, being in my judgment
the oddest if not the most considerable detection which hath
hitherto been made in the operations of nature."

This " oddest and most considerable detection" was the discovery of the different refrangibility of the rays of light, which
it was necessary to explain in a previous chapter, as having
been made before the construction of his telescope. It was
communicated in a letter to Oldenburg on the 6th of February
1672, and excited great interest when read on the 8th February
to " that illustrious company." The " solemn thanks of the
meeting were voted to its author for his very ingenious discourse ;" and it was immediately printed in the 80th Number
of their Transactions, namely, on the 19th February, both for
the purpose of having it well considered by philosophers, and
for " securing the considerable notices thereof to the author
against the arrogations of others." At the same time a committee, consisting of Dr. Seth Ward, Bishop of Salisbury, Mr.
Boyle, and Dr. Hooke, was appointed to peruse and consider it,
and to give in a report upon it to the Society.

The kindness of this distinguished body, and the anxiety

which they had already shown for Newton's reputation in the affair of his telescope, excited on his part a reciprocal feeling, and he accepted of their proposal to print his discourse in the following humble terms :—" 'Twas an esteem," he says, " of the Royal Society, for candid and able judges in philosophical matters, which encouraged me to present them with that discourse of light and colours, which since it has been so favourably accepted of, I do earnestly desire you to return them my cordial thanks. I before thought it a great favour to have been made a member of that honourable body ; but I am now more sensible of the advantage. For believe me, Sir, I do not only esteem it a duty to concur with them in the promotion of real knowledge, but a great privilege, that instead of exposing discourses to a prejudiced and censorious multitude (by which means many truths have been baffled and lost), I may with freedom apply myself to so judicious and impartial an assembly. As to the printing of that letter, I am satisfied in their judgment, or else I should have thought it too strait and narrow for public view. I designed it only to those that know how to improve upon hints of things, and therefore, to shun tediousness, omitted many such remarks and experiments as might be collected by considering the assigned laws of refraction, some of which I believe, with the generality of men, would yet be almost as taking as any of those I described. But yet since the Royal Society have thought it fit to appear publicly, I leave it to their pleasure ; and, perhaps, to supply the aforesaid defects, I may send you some more of the experiments, to record it (if it be so thought fit) in the ensuing Transactions."

Having in the preceding chapter given an account of the leading doctrine of the different refrangibility of the rays of light, and of the attempts to improve the reflecting telescope which that discovery suggested, we shall now endeavour to make the reader acquainted with the other discoveries respecting colours, which he at this time communicated to the Royal Society.

We have already seen that a beam of white light emitted from the sun, and refracted by a prism, is decomposed by its action into seven different colours, which compose what is called the *Prismatic Spectrum*, and which is nothing more than an elongated image of the sun, its length being *five* times its breadth, and the coloured spaces having the proportions shown in the annexed figure.

When this spectrum is distinctly formed by a good prism, so so that the different colours are clearly separated, Newton found that any particular colour, such as *red*, was not susceptible of any change either by refraction through prisms, or reflection from mirrors, or from natural bodies, nor by any other cause that he could observe, notwithstanding his utmost endeavours to change it. It might become fainter or brighter, but its colour never changed. Its refrangibility, too, was equally unchangeable, and hence he drew the conclusion that the same degree of refrangibility always belonged to the same colour, and the same colour to the same degree of refrangibility.

Red.

Orange.

Yellow.

Green.

Blue.

Indigo.

Violet.

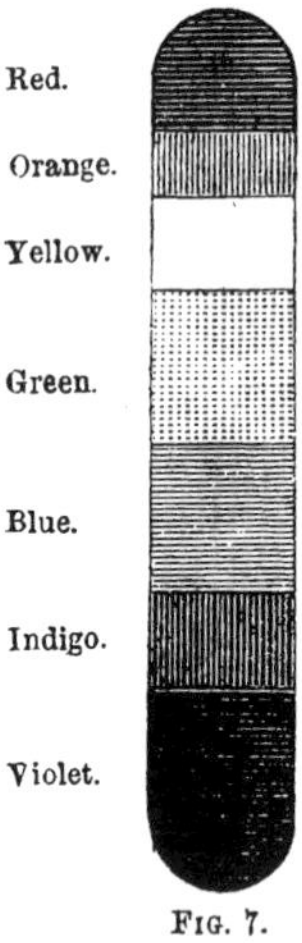

FIG. 7.

But while the colours in the spectrum are original and simple, such as *red, orange, yellow, green, blue, indigo,* and *violet,* other colours may be compounded of these, "for a mixture of *yellow* and *blue* makes *green,* and *red* and *yellow* makes *orange,* and *orange* and *yellowish green* makes *yellow.*" These compound colours, however, may be separated by the prism into their simple colours, and hence we are enabled by the prism to decompose all such colours, and however similar they may be to the primitive ones, their difference may always be discovered by the different refrangibility of their elements.

But, as Newton remarks, "the most surprising and wonderful composition is that of *whiteness.* No one sort of rays is alone capable of exhibiting it. It is ever compounded, and for its composition all the primary colours in their due proportion are required." In order to prove this doctrine, which is called the *Recomposition* of white light, he employed three different methods. When the beam of white light RR, *Fig.* 8, was separated into its component colours, as in the spectrum MN, he received the refracted pencil R' on a second prism BCD, held

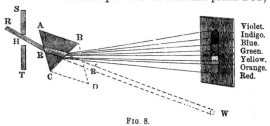

FIG. 8.

either close to the first, or a little behind it, and by the opposite refraction of this prism they were all refracted back into a beam of perfectly white light BW, which projected a white circular spot on the wall at W, exactly similar in form and in colour to the spot formed there by the beam RR, before the prism intercepted it.

Another mode of recomposing white light, which Newton tells us he " often beheld with admiration," is to cause the spectrum to fall upon a large lens at some distance from the prism, and then to converge all the colours into a spot, and mix them again as they were in the light before its incidence on the prism. The light thus reproduced is " entirely and perfectly white," and does not " at all sensibly differ from the direct light of the sun, unless when the glasses used were not sufficiently clear." Hence our author concludes, " that whiteness is the usual colour of light ; for light is a confused aggregate of rays endued with all sorts of colours, as they are promiscuously darted from the various parts of luminous bodies." When there is a due proportion of the ingredients, that is, of all the simple colours, *whiteness* is generated, but if any one colour predominate, the light will incline to that colour, as in the yellow flame of a candle, the blue flame of brimstone, and the various colours of the fixed stars.

From a consideration of these facts, our author regards it as very evident how colours are produced by the prism. Since such of the rays constituting white light as differ in colour, differ proportionally in refrangibility, they must in virtue of their unequal refraction be severed and dispersed into an oblong form, as in *Fig.* 7, in regular succession from the least refracted *red* to the most refracted *violet.* " And for the same reason it is," says Newton, " that objects, when looked upon through a prism, appear coloured. For the difform rays, by their unequal refraction, are made to diverge towards several parts of the retina, and there express the images of things coloured, as in the former case they did the sun's image upon a wall."

Having established these principles, Newton applies them to the explanation of several interesting phenomena. He shows that the colours of the primary and secondary rainbow are prismatic spectra, produced by the refraction of the drops of water. He explains the odd phenomena of *lignum nephriticum, leaf gold, fragments of coloured glass,* and other bodies, which appear in one position of one colour, and of another in another, in consequence of their disposition to reflect one sort of light and transmit another. He assigns the reason of Hooke's beautiful experiment, with two wedge-like transparent vessels, the one filled with *red,* the other with a *blue* liquor. Although they are each very transparent, yet when the two are put together they are opaque ; for since the one transmits only *red,* and the other only *blue,* no rays whatever can pass through both of them. And without giving more instances, he concludes with this general one, " That the colours of all natural bodies have no other origin than this ; that they are variously qualified to reflect one sort of light in greater plenty than another. For if we illuminate these bodies with uncompounded light of different colours, they always appear of the colour of the light cast upon them, the colour being most vivid in the light of their own day-light colour.   *Minium*, for example, though *red*, appears indif-ferently of any colour, though most luminous in *red ;* and *bise*, though blue, appears indifferently of any colour cast upon it, though most luminous in *blue*.   Hence, since *minium* reflects most copiously the red rays, it must appear *red* when illumi-nated with daylight, that is, with all sorts of rays promiscuously blended, and for the same reason *bise* appears *blue*.

No sooner were these important discoveries given to the world, than they were criticised and assailed with a degree of virulence and ignorance which have not often been combined in scientific controversy.   The Royal Society unfortunately con-tained few individuals of pre-eminent talent capable of appre-ciating the value of his discoveries, and of entering the lists against his envious and ignorant assailants.   While they held his labours in the highest esteem, they regarded his discoveries as fair subjects of discussion, and their secretary regularly com-municated to him, and even published in their Transactions, almost all the papers which were written in opposition to his views.

The first communication on this subject was the suggestion of four experiments with the prism, which seems to have been made by some friend at Cambridge, as Newton communicated them to the editor of the Philosophical Transactions, with his own observations.[1]   This letter was followed by a communica-tion from a Jesuit, Ignatius Pardies, Professor of Mathematics in the Parisian College of Clermont, containing animadversions upon the new Theory of Colours.   Although Newton in his original discourse had demonstrated the reverse, yet the French professor pretended that the elongation of the sun's image arose from the unequal incidence of the different rays on the first face of the prism ; that the mixture of differently coloured

[1] The communication is dated 13th April 1672, and is published in the *Transactions*, No. 82, p. 4059, April 22, 1672.

powders was not white, but dun and grey ; and that opacity was not produced when the two coloured liquors were mixed in the same vessel. Newton answered these shallow objections in the most satisfactory manner ;[1] but this disciple of Descartes, unwilling to be vanquished, took up a new position, and maintained that the elongation of the sun's image by the prism, might be explained by the diffraction of light on the hypothesis of Grimaldi, or by the diffusion of undulations on the hypothesis of Hooke.[2] Newton replied to these silly speculations on the 11th of June ; but he contented himself with reiterating his original experiments, and confirming them by more popular arguments.[3] Pardies replied on the 9th July, in terms highly complimentary to Newton.[4] He expressed himself satisfied with Newton's explanations, acknowledged that his only difficulty had been wholly removed, and that he cherished the warmest gratitude for the kindness with which his annotations had been examined and answered.

About this time Newton seems to have been peculiarly sensitive about the reception of his Doctrine of Colours. On the 8th of July, a month after he had written his second Reply to Pardies, he published in the Philosophical Transactions, with his name, " A Series of Queries, propounded by Mr. Isaac Newton, to be determined by experiment, positively and directly concluding his new Theory of Light and Colours, and here recommended to the industry of the lovers of Experimental Philosophy, as they were generously imparted to the Publisher in a letter of the said Mr. Newton."[5] This paper consists of eight queries, which are merely the different propositions he had established put into that form as if they were still matters of doubt, and it concludes with expressing the wish of the author, " that all objections be suspended taken from *Hypotheses*, or any other heads than these two ; of showing the insufficiency

[1] *Phil. Trans.* No. 84, p. 4091, June 17, 1672.
[2] *Phil. Trans.* No. 85, p. 5012, July 15, 1672.   [3] *Ibid.* p. 5014.   [4] *Ibid.* p. 5018.
[5] *Phil. Trans.* No 84, p. 4080, June 17, 1672. This paper is part of a letter to Oldenburg, dated July 6, 1672, from Stoake Park, Northamptonshire.

of experiments to determine these *Queries*, or prove any other parts of my theory by assigning the flaws and defects in my conclusions drawn from them ; or of producing other experiments which directly contradict me, if any such may seem to occur." In order to "invite and gratify foreigners" to consider and put to trial these Queries, the publisher "delivers Mr. Newton's letter in the language also of the learned."

This challenge to foreigners on the part of Oldenburg, summoned into the field a new combatant, in the person of Francis Linus, a physician in Liege, who, on the 6th October 1674, addressed a letter to a friend in London, entitled, "Animadversions on Newton's Theory of Light and Colours."[1] He asserts that he has often observed the same difference between the length and breadth of the spectrum ; but that he never found it so when the sky was clear and free of clouds near the sun. The difference only appeared when the sun either shone through a white cloud, or enlightened some such clouds near him. The elongation of the spectrum was therefore not affected by the true sunbeams, "and consequently the theory of light grounded on the experiment cannot subsist." In support of these gratuitous assertions, Linus appeals to frequently repeated experiments on the refractions and reflections of light which he had exhibited nearly thirty years ago, "together with divers other experiments on light, to that worthy promoter of experimental philosophy, Sir Kenelm Digby, who coming into these parts to take the Spa waters, resorted oftentimes to my darkened chamber, and took notes upon them ;" and he adds, that if Newton had used the same industry as he did, "he would never have taken so impossible a task in hand," as "to endeavour to explicate the aforesaid difference between the length and breadth of this coloured *spectrum*, by the received laws of refraction." When this letter was shown to Newton he refused to answer it ; but Linus was referred to his answer to Pardies, and assured that the experiments on which he animad-

[1] *Phil. Trans.* No. 110, p. 217.

verted were made in clear days when there was no bright cloud in the heavens. The Dutch philosopher, however, was not satisfied with this reply. He confesses in a second letter to his friend, that "*if the assertions be admitted*, they do indeed directly cut off what he had said of Mr. Newton's being deceived by a bright cloud;" but he endeavours to prove that Newton did not make the experiment in a clear day, because Newton describes the ends of the spectrum as semicircular, "and these semicircular ends are never seen in a clear day!" The rest of the letter abounds with the most erroneous statements, indicating the grossest ignorance, and calculated to irritate even the patient mind of Newton.

Oldenburg again attempted to prevail upon Newton to answer these observations, but he once more declined, on the ground that the dispute referred merely to simple matters of fact, which could only be decided before competent witnesses. The entreaties of Oldenburg, however, prevailed, and "lest Mr. Linus should make the more stir," this great man condescended to write a grave reply to reasonings utterly contemptible, and to assertions wholly unfounded. In this answer, dated November 13, 1675, and which Linus, who died on the 15th November, probably never saw, Newton gives the most minute and simple instructions for producing the prismatic spectrum. He mentions the size of the hole, "about the bigness of a pease," the position of the prism close to the hole, the mode of turning the prism round till the spectrum is placed in its stationary position, when the rays are equally refracted on both sides of the prism, and the nature and order of the colours. He tells him also that the experiment will not succeed well if the day is not clear, and he begs that "when Mr. Line has tried this he will proceed to try the *experimentum crucis*, which," he adds, "may be done, though not so perfectly, even without darkening a room, or the expense of any more time than half a quarter of an hour." [1]

1 *Phil. Trans.* No. 121, p. 503.

After the death of Linus, his pupil, Mr. Gascoigne, entered the field, and declared that Linus had shown to various persons in Liege his-experiment, proving the spectrum to be circular, and that Mr. Newton could not be more confident on his side than they were on the other, being fully "persuaded, that unless the diversity of placing the prism, or the bigness of the hole, or some other such circumstance, be the cause of the difference between them, Mr. Newton's experiment will hardly stand."[1] Pleased with "the handsome genius" of Mr. Gascoigne's letter, Newton replied again,[2] exerting himself to discover the reason why the elongated spectrum was not as visible to others as it was to himself. With this view, he describes the three different kinds of images that may be seen upon the wall when a prism refracting the sun's rays is turned round its axis. The first of these is the regular elongated coloured spectrum ; the second a round white image formed by reflection from one of the faces of the prism ; and the third, an image formed by two refractions and one reflection, which, with a good equi-angular prism, would be a round white image of the aperture, but more or less elongated and coloured, if the two refracting angles were more or less inequal. From this it becomes very probable that Linus never saw the real prismatic spectrum.[3]

As Mr. Gascoigne had not the means of making the experiment thus pointed out, he requested Mr. Anthony Lucas of Liege to make it for him. This ingenious individual, who succeeded Linus in the mathematical chair at Liege, confirmed the leading results of Newton, in so far as the prismatic spec-

[1] Phil. Trans. No. 121, p. 503.　　　　　　　[2] Ibid. No. 123, p. 556.

[3] A short time before the commencement of this controversy, Linus communicated to the Royal Society a paper entitled Optical Assertions concerning the Rainbow, which appeared in their Transactions, No. 117, p. 386. How such a paper could have been published by so learned a body seems very incomprehensible. Linus was celebrated as a dial-maker. Mr. Charles Ellis mentions one of his dials at Liege, in which the hours were distinguished by touch, and says that they were "the originals of those formerly in our Privy Gardens."—Phil. Trans. No. 283, 1703, vol. xv. p. 1418.

trum was concerned ; but he refused to acknowledge the truth
of his theory, and made a number of experiments with coloured
silks and coloured fluids, which he considered to be subversive
of it. His experiments on the length of the spectrum, however, possess a peculiar interest. With a prism having an
angle, of 60°, and a refractive power of 1·500, he formed the
spectrum at the distance of eighteen feet from the window.
The hole in the shutter was sometimes one-fifth and sometimes
one-tenth of an inch, the distance of the prism from the hole
about two inches, and the darkness of the room equal to that
of the darkest night when the hole was shut. Under these
circumstances, he never could find the spectrum longer than
*thrice the diameter* of its breadth, or, at most, *three and a half
times* that diameter when the refractions on both sides of the
prism were equal ; whereas Newton found it to be *five times*
that diameter, with a prism whose refracting angle was 63° 12'.

In taking into consideration this new difficulty, Newton
acknowledges that a difference of 3° 12' in the refracting angle
of the prism is too little to reconcile the two results, and he
conjectures that Mr. Lucas may have set down the round number of 60° as the angle of his prism, in the same manner as
he set down its refractive power, or the ratio of the sines, as
two to three, or 1·500. " Then," he adds, " if it be two or
three degrees less than 60°, if not still less, all this would take
away the greatest part of the difference between us." In order,
however, to determine the point experimentally, he measured
the length of the spectrum with prisms of different angles, and
obtained the following results :—In the first column of the
following table, he gives the six angles of two prisms which he
used, and " which were measured as exactly as he could *by
applying them to the angle of a sector.*" In the second he
gives in inches the length of the image made by each of these
angles, its breadth being *two* inches, its distance from the prism
*eighteen feet* and *four* inches, and the breadth of the hole in
the window-shutter one-fourth of an inch. We have added a

third column, showing the ratio of the length to the breadth of the spectrum.

| | Angles of the Prism. | Length of Image. | Ratio of its Length to its Breadth. |
|---|---|---|---|
| The first Prism, | 56° 10′ | $7\frac{3}{4}$ inches. | $3\frac{7}{8}$ to 1. |
| | 60 24 | $9\frac{1}{2}$ ,, | $4\frac{3}{4}$ to 1. |
| | 63 26 | $10\frac{1}{3}$ ,, | $5\frac{1}{6}$ to 1. |
| The second Prism, | 54° 0′ | $7\frac{1}{3}$ ,, | $3\frac{2}{3}$ to 1. |
| | 62 12 | $10\frac{1}{3}$ ,, | $5\frac{1}{16}$ to 1. |
| | 63 48 | $10\frac{3}{4}$ ,, | $5\frac{3}{8}$ to 1. |

On a clearer day, with the second prism, he found the lengths of the spectrum to be as follows, about one-fourth of an inch greater than before :—

| | | | |
|---|---|---|---|
| The second Prism, | 54° 0′ | $7\frac{2}{3}$ inches. | $3\frac{5}{6}$ to 1. |
| | 62 12 | $10\frac{1}{2}$ ,, | $5\frac{1}{4}$ to 1. |
| | 63 48 | 11 ,, | $5\frac{1}{2}$ to 1. |

In noticing the other experiments of Lucas with differently coloured silks, which he placed in a line, and viewing both through a prism and when placed at the bottom of a square vessel of water, Newton found that "unconcerned persons" always saw them in a line as if they had all suffered the same refraction. He does not, however, point out their insufficiency to prove an equality of refraction, but thanks Mr. Lucas for taking so much pains in examining them, "and so much the more, as he was the first that had sent him an experimental examination of them." He even goes so far as to say that, in a little Treatise on the subject, written before his first communication to the Royal Society, he had actually written down the principal of the experiments which Mr. Lucas had now sent him.

We have been thus minute in describing the experiments of Lucas and Newton on the length of the spectrum, because they have a close connexion with the determination of the different dispersive powers of bodies, which was one of the greatest discoveries of the following century, and led to the invention of the achromatic telescope. There are only two ways in which we can account for the shortness of the spectrum observed by Lucas. His eyes may have been to some extent insensible to violet and blue light, and therefore the spectrum would appear to him much shorter than it really was. If we cut off from Newton's spectrum one and a half inches, to reduce it to Lucas's, we cut off the whole of the indigo and violet spaces ; and, unless from an imperfection of vision, Lucas could not have failed to see these colours in an apartment so very dark as his. If he had no such imperfection, it becomes highly probable that his prism was made of glass of a low dispersive power. Newton's prisms may have been of flint-glass, and Lucas's of crown-glass ; and it is a remarkable circumstance, that in all these controversies the nature of the glass is never once mentioned. Had Newton been less confident than he was, that all other prisms must give a spectrum of the same length as his, in relation to its refracting angle and index of refraction, the invention of the achromatic telescope would have been the necessary result. The objections of Lucas drove Newton to make experiments which he never contemplated, namely, to measure accurately the lengths of spectra formed with prisms of different angles and different refractive powers ; and had the Dutch Professor maintained his opinions with more obstinacy and perseverance, he would have conferred a distinguished favour upon science, and rewarded Newton for all the vexation which had arisen from the minute discussion of his optical discoveries.

Thus terminated the disputes with Pardies, Linus, Gascoigne, and Lucas, and we think it can scarcely be doubted that Newton found it a more difficult task to detect the origin of his adversaries' blunders, and to expose their fallacy, than to establish the great truths which they had attempted to overturn.

Harassing as such a controversy was to a philosopher like Newton, yet it did not touch those deep-seated feelings which characterize the noble and generous mind. It was with ignorance and incapacity only that he had to strive. No personal invective ruffled his equanimity ;—no vulgar jealousy roused his indignation ;—no charge of plagiarism called in question his veracity or his honour.   These aggravations of scientific controversy, however, he was destined to endure, and in the disputes which he was called to maintain against Hooke, Huygens, and Leibnitz, the agreeable consciousness of grappling with minds of kindred power was painfully embittered by the personal feelings which were thrown into the contest.

Dr. Robert Hooke, born in 1635, was about seven years older than Newton, and was one of the ninety-eight original or unelected Fellows of the Royal Society.   He possessed great versatility of talent ; yet though his genius was of the most original cast, and his acquirements extensive, he had not devoted himself with fixed purpose to any particular branch of knowledge.   His numerous and ingenious inventions, of which we cannot speak too highly, gave to his studies a practical character, unfitting him for that continuous labour which physical researches so imperiously demand.   The subjects of light and colours, however, seem to have deeply occupied his thoughts before Newton descended into the same arena, and there can be no doubt that he had made considerable progress in their study.   With a mind less divergent in its pursuits, and more fixed in its purpose, he might have unveiled the mystery in which both these subjects were enveloped, and pre-occupied the intellectual throne which was destined for his rival ; but the infirm state of his health, the peevishness of temper to which it gave rise, the number of unfinished inventions from which he looked both for fortune and fame, and above all, his inordinate love of reputation, distracted and broke down the energies of his powerful intellect.   In the more matured inquiries of his rivals he recognised, and often truly, his own incompleted speculations ; and when he saw others reaping the harvest for which he had prepared the ground, and of which he had sown the seed, it was not easy to conceal the mortification which their success inspired.   In the arbitraments of science, it has always been a difficult task to adjust the rival claims of competitors, when the one was allowed to have completed what the other was acknowledged to have begun. He who commences an inquiry, and publishes its results, often goes much farther than he has announced to the world, and pushing his speculations into the very heart of the subject, frequently submits them to the ear of friendship. From the pedestal of his published labours his rival begins his researches, and brings them to a successful issue, while he has in reality done nothing more than complete the unfinished labours, and demonstrate the imperfect speculations of his rival or his predecessor. To the world and to himself he is no doubt in the position of the principal discoverer, but there is still some apology for his rival, when he brings forward his unpublished labours, and some excuse for the exercise of personal feeling, when he measures the speed of his rival by his own proximity to the goal.

The conduct of Dr. Hooke would have been viewed with some such feeling, had not his arrogance on other occasions checked the natural current of our sympathy. When Newton presented his Reflecting Telescope to the Royal Society, Dr. Hooke not only criticised the instrument with undue severity, but announced, what was never realized, that he possessed an infallible method of perfecting all kinds of optical instruments, so that "whatever almost hath been in notion and imagination, or desired in optics, may be performed with great facility and truth."

Descartes had long ago maintained that an ethereal medium pervaded all transparent bodies ;—that light consists in the action of this medium ;—that the ether is less implicated in the parts of solid bodies ;—that it moves more freely in them, and transmits light more readily through them, so as to accelerate the rays in a certain proportion ;—that refraction arises from this acceleration, and has the sines of incidence and refraction proportional ;—that light is at first uniform ;—that its colours are some disturbance or new modification of its rays by refraction or reflexion ;—that the colours of a prism are made by means of the quiescent medium accelerating some motion of the rays on one side where *red* appears, and retarding it on the other side where *blue* appears, and that there are but these two original colours, or colour-making modifications of light, which, by their various degrees or dilutings, as Hooke calls them, produce all intermediate ones.

These views were adopted by Dr. Hooke, who "changed Descartes' pressing or progressive motion of the medium to a vibrating one ;—the rotation of the globuli to the obliquation of pulses, and the accelerating their rotation on the one hand, and retarding it on the other, by the quiescent medium to produce colours, to the like action of the medium on the two ends of his pulses for the same end."[1]

Such were Hooke's opinions of the nature of light when Newton published his Theory of Colours, and it was through this theoretical medium that he viewed Newton's discoveries, when he sent his observations upon them to the Royal Society, on the 15th February 1672. Dr. Hooke was thanked "for the pains he had taken in bringing in such ingenious reflections ;" but it was not "thought fit to print the two papers together, lest Mr. Newton should look upon it as a disrespect in printing so sudden a refutation of a discourse of his which had met with so much applause at the Society but a few days before."

It is not easy to follow the train of thought which runs through the observations of Dr. Hooke. While he praises "the niceness and curiosity" of Newton's experiments, and expresses an entire agreement with him as to the truth of those which he brought forward, founded on hundreds of trials made by himself, yet he "cannot see in his hypothesis of solving the phenomena of colours thereby, any undeniable argument to convince

[1] This view of Descartes' theory and of Hooke's opinions, is given by Newton in his letter to Oldenburg, dated 21st December 1675. General Dict. vol. vii. p. 783, or *Macclesfield Correspondence*, vol. ii. p. 378.

him of its certainty." He considers them as proving his own hypothesis, which he endeavours, without much success, to explain and establish. This, indeed, seems to be the principal object of his paper, but even if he had succeeded, the truth of his theory would not have invalidated in the slightest degree the doctrines of Newton. " I most readily agree," says he, " with them (Newton's experiments) in every part thereof, and esteem it (his hypothesis) very subtle and ingenious, but I cannot think it to be the only hypothesis, nor so certain as mathematical demonstration." In remonstrating with Newton " on his wholly laying aside the thought of improving telescopes and microscopes by refractions," he is more successful ; but though this assertion, that the difficulties of removing the effects of colour are not insuperable, has received ample confirmation, yet the result was not obtained by any of the contrivances which he pretended to possess.

Newton lost no time in replying to Hooke's communication, and he expressed to Oldenburg the gratification which he felt, " that so acute an objector as Hooke had said nothing that could enervate any part of his theory." On the 11th July 1672, he transmitted to Oldenburg an elaborate answer to Hooke,[1] expressing his conviction that both of them " had a sincere endeavour after knowledge, without valuing uncertain speculations for their subtleties, or despising certainties for their plainness." After admitting that he had deduced the " corporeity of light" from his theory of colours, he asserts that the properties of light were in some measure capable of being explained, not only by that theory, but by many other mechanical hypotheses, and that " he had therefore declined them all, and spoken of light in general terms, considering it abstractedly as *something or other* propagated every way in straight lines from luminous bodies, without determining what that thing is." Conscious of the ingenuity and mental power of his opponent, Newton left him no loop-hole for escape, but replied to every

1 Newtoni *Opera*, tom. iv. pp. 322-342.

objection with a precision and force of argument which Hooke found to be unanswerable.    In this remarkable discussion Newton pointed out the true character of experimental philosophy, and the duties of those who cultivate it when rival theories demand their attention.    He has shown that the properties of light may be investigated, and its physical laws determined without any other principle than that it is "something propagated every way in straight lines," and that discoveries are not to be valued from their coincidence with the theoretical views of him who made them, or their repugnance to those of his opponents.    The discovery of an important fact, or a new law, may confirm one theory and shake another, but he is not a friend to truth who would over-estimate it in the one case, or depreciate it in the other.    The true philosopher who forgets his own reputation amid the triumphs of advancing science, and who confides in a theory as a branch of eternal truth, will be the last to spurn from him even experimental results, that may put his own views to the torture.    It is the self-seeking sciolist alone who pilfers a laurel at the expense of truth, or the intellectual coward who dreads the ordeal, and questions the decision of experiment and observation.    Should the eye of youthful genius rest upon these pages, we would counsel him to ponder over the reply to Hooke, and to remember, in the ardour of his pursuit, that Science has a court of appeal in which posterity is the arbiter.

It would have been well for the progress of science and the tranquillity of its friends, if experiment and observation had been, more than they have, our guides in philosophical inquiry. Even in the present day the disciples of Hooke, who " split pulses " with more success than he did, and whose theory of light has attained a lofty pre-eminence, have not scrupled to imitate their master in measuring optical truths by the undulatory standard, and in questioning and depreciating labours, that it cannot explain, or that run counter to its deductions.    There is fortunately, however, a small remnant in the Temple of

Science, who, while they give to theory its due honours and its proper place, are desirous, as experimental philosophers, to follow in the steps of their great Master.

After silencing the most powerful of his adversaries, Newton was unexpectedly summoned to defend himself against a new enemy. The celebrated Christian Huygens, an eminent mathematician and natural philosopher, who, like Hooke, had maintained the undulatory theory of light, transmitted to Oldenburg on the 14th January 1673, a letter from Paris, containing some considerations on Newton's Theory of Light ; but though his knowledge of optics was of the most extensive kind, his objections were as groundless, and his speculations as erroneous as those of his less enlightened countrymen. Attached to the undulatory hypothesis, he seems, like Dr. Hooke, to have viewed the theory of Newton as calculated to overturn it, and he therefore objects to its two leading doctrines, namely, the composition of white light by the union of all the colours, and the generality of the doctrine of their different refrangibilities. The objection which he urges against the theory of *whiteness* is, that it may be produced equally well by *yellow* and *blue*, and " he does not see why Mr. Newton doth not content himself with these two colours, as it will be much more easy to find a *hypothesis* by motion that will explicate these two differences, than for so many diversities as there are of other colours ; and till he hath found this hypothesis, he has not taught us what it is wherein consists the nature and difference of colours, but only this accident (which certainly is very considerable) of their different refrangibility." He then proposes that the experiment should be tried of stopping all the colours but *yellow* and *blue* and *green*, and then mixing them on paper to see if they make the paper white, " as well as when they all give light." Nay, he adds the following extraordinary opinion, as if it were a new and happy thought. " I even doubt," says he, " whether the *lightest place of the yellow colour may not all alone produce that effect*, and I mean to try it at the first conveniency ; for

this thought never came into my mind but just now.     Meantime you may see that if these experiments do succeed it can no
more be said that all the colours are necessary to compound
white ; and that 'tis very probable that all the rest are nothing
but degrees of *yellow* and *blue* more or less changed."

On the subject of the difference of refrangibility, he is equally
wrong, though with more reason for his error.     He remarks,
that the picture formed in a dark room by an object-glass of
twelve feet, is too distinct and too well defined to be " produced by rays that would stray the fiftieth part of the aperture ;
so that (as I believe I have told you heretofore) the difference
of the refrangibility doth not, it may be, always follow the
same proportion in the great and small inclinations of the rays
upon the surface of the glass." [1]

To these extraordinary objections, Newton replied on the 3d
April 1673,[2] and also in another paper which immediately follows the observations of Huygens, the first of these answers
having been, as we are informed by the editor, mislaid, otherwise it should have also immediately followed the letter of
Huygens.     In these answers, Newton shows that the *yellows*
and *blues* which could produce *white*, are not simple but compound ; and he explains more minutely how the existence of an
aberration equal to the fiftieth of the aperture, is compatible
with the distinctness of a picture formed by a twelve-feet object-glass.     Huygens, still dissatisfied with the explanations so
patiently given to him, informs Oldenburg that he has still
" matter to answer them, but seeing that Newton maintains his
opinion with so much concern, he list not to dispute."     Newton
was not pleased with this criticism upon his explanations, and
says in his letter to Oldenburg,—" As for Mr. Huygens' expression, I confess it was a little ungrateful to me to meet
with objections which had been answered before, without

[1] *Phil. Trans.* vol. viii. No. 96, p. 6086, July 1693.
[2] *Phil. Trans.* No. 97, p. 6108.

having the least reason given me why those answers were insufficient."[1]

But though Huygens appears in this controversy as a rash
and unreasonable objector to the Newtonian doctrine of colours,
it was afterwards the destiny of Newton to play a similar part
against the Dutch philosopher. When Huygens published his
beautiful law of double refraction, founded on the finest experimental analysis of the phenomena, though presented as a result
of the undulatory theory, Newton not only rejected it, but substituted for it another law entirely incompatible with the experiments of Huygens, which Newton himself had praised, but
with those of all succeeding philosophers.[2]

Although Hooke and Huygens were now driven from the
field, and the views of Newton established upon an impregnable

[1] Letter to Oldenburg, without a date, but probably in April 1673.

[2] It is curious to observe how little accurate knowledge of the great optical discoveries of the age was possessed by Leibnitz. In a letter addressed to Huygens, dated
8th September 1679, he says,—" I hear from Mr. de Mariotte that you are about to give
us your Dioptrics, so long wished for. I have a great desire to know beforehand if you
are satisfied with the ratio of refraction proposed by Descartes. I confess that I am
neither wholly satisfied with it, nor with the explanation of Mr. Fermat, given in the
third volume (Lett. 51) of Descartes' Letters."—Ch. Hugenii *Exercit. Math.*, tom. i. pp.
7, 8 : lett. iv. Hag. Com. 1833. Huygens made no reply to this question, though he answered Leibnitz's letter on the 22d November. In reply to this letter, Leibnitz repeats
the same question, confessing that he was neither satisfied with the ratio of Descartes,
nor that of Fermat deduced from an opposite supposition. To this question he adds,—
" I wish to know also if you believe that the irregularity of refraction,—for example,
that which Mr. Newton has remarked,—ought to hurt telescopes considerably ?"—*Ibid.*
lett. vi. p. 17. An answer to this question was given by Huygens in a subsequent letter,
for we find Leibnitz, in a letter dated 26th June 1680, expressing his satisfaction that
Huygens had formed the same opinion of the "pretended demonstration of the laws of
refraction given by Descartes."—*Ibid.* lett. viii. p. 20. No reply is made to the question
about Newton's doctrine of the cause of the imperfection of refracting telescopes ; but
*ten* years afterwards, when Leibnitz had received from Huygens a copy of his *Traité de
la Lumière*, we find the following curious passage in his letter to Leibnitz, dated 24th
August 1690 :—" I have said nothing respecting colours in my *Traité de la Lumière*,
finding this subject very difficult, and particularly from the great number of different
ways in which colours are produced. Mr. Newton promised something on the subject,
and communicated to me some very fine experiments which he had collected. It seems
that you have also thought on the subject, and apparently to some purpose."—*Ibid.*
lett. xi. pp. 27, 28.

basis, yet these prolonged and exciting controversies ruffled his temper, and disturbed his tranquillity.  Even the satisfaction of humbling all his antagonists he did not regard as a compensation for the time he had wasted, and the intellectual labour which he had thrown away.  " I intend," says he to Oldenburg, " to be no farther solicitous about matters of philosophy ; and therefore I hope you will not take it ill if you never find me doing anything more in that kind ; or rather that you will favour me in my determination, by preventing, so far as you can conveniently, any objections or other philosophical letters that may concern me."  In a subsequent letter in 1675, he says,—" I had some thoughts of writing a farther discourse about colours, to be read at one of your assemblies, but find it yet against the grain to put pen to paper any more on that subject ;" and in a letter to Leibnitz, of the 9th December 1675, he observes,—" I was so persecuted with discussions arising out of my theory of light, that I blamed my own imprudence for parting with so substantial a blessing as my quiet to run after a shadow."  Nor was this a temporary resolution arising from some disagreeable expressions of a personal nature, which often embitter controversy even in its most temperate form.  Nearly a year after his complaint to Leibnitz, he uses the following remarkable expressions in a communication to Oldenburg :—" I see I have made myself a slave to philosophy ; but if I get free of Mr. Linus's business, I will resolutely bid adieu to it eternally, excepting what I do for my private satisfaction, or leave to come out after me ; for I see a man must either resolve to put out nothing new, or to become a slave to defend it." [1]

In this state of mind, perplexed, as we shall presently see, with some pecuniary difficulties, and feeling, as he expressed it to Collins in 1674, " that mathematical speculations were at least dry, if not somewhat barren," there is reason to believe

[1] This letter is dated November 18, 1676, and was written after receiving an account of the experiments of Lucas.—*Macclesfield Correspondence*, vol. ii. p. 405.

that Newton, "who, in the usual course of things, would vacate his Fellowship in a few months, had seriously thought of directing his mind to the study of law." In an obituary notice of the Rev. Robert Uvedale, Rector of Langton, in Lincolnshire,[1] it is stated that his grandfather, Mr. Uvedale, when one of the Divinity Fellows of Trinity College, Cambridge, had become candidate for the Law Fellowship in that College when made vacant, on the 14th February 1673, by the death of Dr. Crane ;—that Mr. Newton was his competitor ;—that Dr. Barrow, as Master of Trinity, decided it in favour of Mr. Uvedale ; and that the ground of his decision was, that though Mr. Uvedale and Mr. Newton were at that time equal in literary attainments, yet he must give the Fellowship to Mr. Uvedale as the senior. Mr. Edleston[2] is disposed to consider this story as mythical, and he thinks that the real facts of the case were, that Uvedale was appointed to a Law Fellowship, and that Newton would have been glad to have had one. This opinion he rests on the ground that the tenure of the Law Fellowship could scarcely be considered compatible with the duties of the Lucasian chair, and "he believes that it would argue much misconception of the characters of the two great men concerned, to suppose them capable of being parties to a lax interpretation of the statute which they had sworn to obey." We can hardly admit the force of this argument in opposition to the precise statements, even if traditional, of the Uvedale family. The necessities of Newton, and the ardent friendship of Barrow, might have induced the one to adopt a lax interpretation of the Lucasian statutes, and the other to accept the Fellowship, had it been in his power, without any great loss of character ; and we are the more inclined to adopt this opinion, when we know that in modern times the same statutes have been imperfectly observed.

While Newton was harassed with these discussions, and

---

[1] *Gentleman's Magazine*, 1799, Supplement, pp. 1186 and 999.

[2] *Correspondence, &c.*, pp. xlviii. xlix. *note*, 38.

chagrined, it may be, with the loss of the Law Fellowship, he came to the resolution of resigning his place in the Royal Society.  On the 8th of March 1673, he writes in the follow-ing terms to Oldenburg :—" SIR,—I desire that you will procure that I may be put out from being any longer a member of the Royal Society ; for though I honour that body, yet, since I see I shall neither profit them, nor (by reason of this distance) can partake of the advantage of their assemblies, I desire to with-draw." Oldenburg expressed his surprise[1] "at his resigning for no other cause than his distance, which he knew as well at the time of his election ;" and he probably then intimated to him, that he would apply to the Society to excuse him his weekly payments.  That such an intimation was made, appears from Newton's letter to Oldenburg, dated June 23, 1673, in which he says,—" For your proffer about my quarterly pay-ments, I thank you, but I would not have you trouble yourself to get them excused, if you have not done it already." Nothing farther seems to have been said on the subject till the 28th January 1675, when Mr. Oldenburg mentioned " to the Society, that Mr. Newton was now in such circumstances that he desired to be excused from the weekly payments."[2]  Upon which " it was agreed to by the council that he should be dispensed with, as several others were." It does not appear, from any docu-ments we have seen, what the change of circumstances was to which Oldenburg alludes, but Mr. Edleston thinks it probable that it refers to the expected vacating of his Fellowship, from his being appointed to the Lucasian chair, which, in the usual course of things, would expire in the following autumn.  This anticipated event, however, did not take place, for, on the 27th April 1675, he obtained a patent from the Crown, permitting the Lucasian Professor to hold a Fellowship, without being obliged to go into orders.

---

[1] This appears from a memorandum on the back of Newton's letter to him.
[2] The admission-money to the Royal Society was £2, and the payments one shilling a week.

This permission seems to have been obtained on the application of Newton ; and Mr. Edleston is of opinion, that the draught of it in Newton's own hand, among the Lucasian papers, was composed by himself, and that his visit to London in February may have been connected with this application to the Crown.  When the grant was submitted to the King, the following memorandum, found also in Newton's handwriting, was recorded at Whitehall on the 2d March 1674 :—" His Majesty, being willing to give all just encouragement to learned men who are and shall be elected into the said Professorship, is graciously pleased to refer this draught of a patent unto Mr. Atturney-Generall to consider the same, and to report his opinion what his Majesty may lawfully do in favour of the said Professors, as to the indulgence and dispensation proposed and desired."  The original draught, which has been published by Mr. Edleston, was adopted, excepting in two unimportant particulars, and there is a copy of it in the archives of Trinity College, with the heading, —*Indulgentia Regia Professori Mathematico concessa, dignissimo viro Magistro Isaaco Newtono, hujus Collegii Socio, istud munus tunc temporis obeunte.*

It is obvious, we think, from these proceedings, that the change in Newton's circumstances must have been of a distressing nature, otherwise he would hardly have permitted Oldenburg to apply to the Royal Society for a remission of his weekly payments.  At no period of his life had he any regard for money, and, as he was always punctual and accurate in his pecuniary concerns, it is very probable, that when the income of his Fellowship [1] and the Lucasian chair were united, he may have resumed his payments to the Royal Society.[2]  If he did

---

[1] In reference to an application from Francis Aston for a dispensation similar to that received by Newton, Dr. Barrow, then Master of Trinity, in declining to grant it, says, —" Indeed a Fellowship with us is now so poor, that I cannot think it worth holding by an ingenuous person upon terms liable to so much scruple."—Edleston's *Correspondence*, p 1.

[2] In a volume of MSS. in the British Museum relating to the Royal Society, there is, as Mr. Weld informs us, a sheet containing the names of Fellows who will *probably pay,*

not do this, it could not have been from poverty, as we find him in 1676 subscribing forty pounds to the new Library of Trinity College.

But however this may be, it cannot fail to be remarked, especially by foreigners, as a singular example of the illiberality of England to her scientific institutions, that a Society, founded by the sovereign, and bearing the name of Royal, should have been established without any provision for the support of its members, for carrying on scientific inquiries, or for the publication of its Transactions. Nor is it less remarkable, that an Institution so useful to the country, so bright with immortal names, and so fitted to promote the intellectual glory of the nation, should have been continued under royal patronage for nearly two hundred years without any attempt being made to extend its usefulness, by placing it in the same advantageous position as the Academy of Sciences in Paris, and other similar institutions in the metropolitan cities of Europe.

If Newton did not feel it a hardship to pay a weekly pittance into the treasury of the Royal Society, he must have felt it a degradation to plead poverty for its remission. His colleagues in the Society, and men of science in a succeeding age, on whom the wealth of this world is never abundantly bestowed, must have often smarted under the injustice of paying for the publication of discoveries which it cost them much time, and frequently much money, to complete. Of all the taxes upon knowledge this is the most oppressive, and not the less oppressive that it is exacted from the feelings and patriotism of its victims.

There is reason to believe that Newton took this view of his own position, and of the inefficiency of any scientific body constituted upon the voluntary principle ; and it is not improbable,

*and give yearly one entertainment to the Society.* Opposite the names of Dr. Grew, Hooke, and Newton, are the words, "No pay, but will contribute experiments." The date of this list, if it has any, is not mentioned. See Baily's *Life of Flamsteed*, p. 90, *note*, and Weld's *Hist. of the Royal Society,* vol. i. p. 250, *note*.

that he committed to writing his opinions on this subject at the
time when he had resolved to withdraw from the Society.   In
support of this opinion, we have great pleasure in submitting
to the reader a very remarkable document in Newton's handwriting, which we found among the family papers at Hurtsbourne Park, entitled " A Scheme for Establishing the Royal
Society." We give it without abridgment or change, as the
opinions of so competent a judge on the subjects which ought
to occupy the attention of a national institute, and on the best
method of making it efficient in promoting the advancement of
profound science and of useful knowledge, cannot fail to be
appreciated by every class of readers.[1]

## " SCHEME FOR ESTABLISHING THE ROYAL SOCIETY.

" Natural Philosophy consists in discovering the frame and
operations of Nature, and reducing them, as far as may be, to
general Rules or Laws,—establishing these rules by observations and experiments, and thence deducing the causes and
effects of things ; and for this end it may be convenient, that
*one* or *two* (and at length perhaps *three* or *four*) Fellows of the
Royal Society, well skilled in any one of the following branches
of Philosophy, and as many in each of the rest, be obliged by
pensions and forfeitures (as soon as it can be compassed), to
attend the meetings of the Royal Society. — The Branches
are—

" 1. Arithmetic, Algebra, Geometry, and Mechanics, with
relation to the figures, surfaces, magnitudes, forces, motions,
resistances, weights, densities, centres of gravity, and other
mathematical affections of solids and fluids ;—the composition
of forces and motions ;—the shocks and reflexions of solids ;—
the centrifugal forces of revolving bodies ;—the motion of pen-

[1] We found six copies of this scheme, one of which is more complete than the others.
The first paragraph of the copy given in the text is wanting in the less perfect copies, but
in other respects they are nearly the same.   There is no date upon any of the copies.

dulums, projected and falling bodies ;—the mensuration of time and distance ;—the efficacy of the five powers, the running of rivers ;—the propagation of light and sound, and the harmony and discord of tunes and colours.

" 2. Philosophy relating to the Heavens, the Atmosphere, and the surface of the Earth, viz., Optics,—Astronomy,— Geography,—Navigation, and Meteorology ; and what relates to the magnitudes, distances, motions, and centrifugal forces of the heavenly bodies ; and to the weight, height, form, and motions of the Atmosphere, and of the things therein, and to instruments for observing the same ; and to the figure and motions of the Earth and Sea.

" 3. Philosophy relating to animals, viz., their species,—qualities,—passions,—anatomy, diseases, &c., and the knowledge of the frame and use of their Stomachs,—entrails, blood-vessels, heart, lungs, liver, spleen, glands, juices, and organs of sensation, motion, and generation.

" 4. Philosophy relating to vegetables, and particularly the knowledge of their species, parts, leaves, flowers, seeds, fruits, juices, virtues, and properties, and the manner of their generation, nutrition, and vegetation.

" 5. Mineralogy[1] and Chemistry, and the knowledge of the nature of Earths, Stones, Corals, Spars, Metals, semi-metals, Marchasites, Arseniates, Bitumens, Sulphurs, Salts, Vitriols, Rain-Water, Springs, Oils, Tinctures, Spirits, Vapours, Fumes, Air, Fire, Flames and their parts, Tastes, Smells, Colours, Gravity, Density, Fixity, Dissolutions, Fermentations, Coalitions, Separations, Congelations, Liquefactions, Volatility, Distillation, Sublimation, Precipitation, Corrosiveness, Electricity, Magnetism, and other qualities ;—and the causes of subterraneous Caves, Rocks, Shells, Waters, Petrifactions, Exhalations, Damps, Heats, Fires, and Earthquakes, and the rising or falling of Mountains and Islands.

" To any one or more of these Fellows, such Books, Letters,

[1] Written by mistake *Meteorology ;* but in one of the other copies it is *Mineralogy.*

and things as deserve it, may be referred by the Royal Society at their meetings from time to time ; and as often as any such Fellowship becomes void, it may be filled up by the Royal Society with a person who hath already invented something new, or made some considerable improvement in that branch of philosophy, or is eminent for skill therein, if such a person can be found. For the reward will be an encouragement to Inventors ; and it will be an advantage to the Royal Society to have such men at their meetings, and tend to make their meetings numerous and useful, and their body famous and lasting."

It is very evident, from this interesting document, that Newton was desirous of converting the Royal Society into an institution like that of the Academy of Sciences in Paris ; but we have not been able to learn that he ever communicated this plan either to the Society itself, or to any of its members. During the last twenty years, and long before we could have known the views of so competent a judge, we have cherished the same desire, and embraced every opportunity of pressing it upon the notice of the public.[1] Several years ago we communicated Sir Isaac Newton's scheme to Sir Robert Peel, and it was so far carried into effect by the establishment of the *Museum of Practical Geology*, which is neither more nor less than an enlargement of the *Mineralogical, Geological, and Chemical* sections of an Academy of Sciences, or a National Institute. The services of all the members of this important body are of course at the entire disposal of the State, though its members are frequently employed in other duties than those which strictly belong to their office. If mineralogy, geology, and chemistry, therefore, have obtained a national establishment for their improvement and extension,—astronomy, me-

---

[1] See especially the *Quarterly Review*, October 1830, vol. xliii. pp. 305-342 ; *Edinburgh Review*, January 1835, vol. lx. p. 363 ; *Edinburgh Journal of Science, passim ; North British Review*, vol. iv. pp. 410-412 ; vol. vi. p. 506 ; vol. xiv. pp. 281-288 ; from the last of which articles some of the paragraphs in the text are transferred.

chanics, natural history, medicine, and literature, and the arts, are entitled to the same protection. If any real objections exist to such an establishment, they can be founded only upon two causes ;—on the unwillingness of existing voluntary societies to be merged in a general institution, and on the apprehension that the expense would be a burden to the state. Men will always be found who oppose every change, however salutary, and who regard the reform of existing institutions as dangerous innovations. In political and educational questions, the rights and interests of individuals often obstruct the march of civilisation, but in matters of science and literature, such rights have neither been conferred nor claimed. Were the Royal, the Astronomical, the Geological, the Linnæan, the Zoological, and the Geographical Societies, together with the Society of Civil Engineers, and the Museum of Practical Geology, all united into an Academy of Sciences, and divided into distinct sections as in France, the really working members would occupy a more distinguished position, while the nobility and gentry would preserve all their rights and privileges as honorary members.[1] The Royal Society of Literature, and the Antiquarian Society, would readily coalesce into the Academy of Belles Lettres, and the existing Royal Academy would form the Academy of the Fine Arts, divided, as in France, into the three sections of Painting, Sculpture, and Engraving. In the magnificent grove acquired by Prince Albert and the Royal Commissioners at Kensington Gore, a Palace of Arts would be reared for the Institute, and there would be one library, one museum, and one record of their weekly proceedings. Each member of the now insulated societies would listen to the memoirs and discussions of the assembled Academy, and science and literature would thus receive a new impulse from the number and variety of their worshippers.

The second difficulty to which we have referred, namely, the expense of endowment, scarcely merits our consideration. A

[1] Corresponding to the *Académiciens Libres* of the Academy of Sciences in Paris.

very large sum is annually expended by the State in support of the existing societies, and a considerable number of those who would be members of the General Institute, already enjoy the liberality of Government. But, independently of these considerations, the organization of a National Institute would be a measure of real and direct economy. The inquiries connected with the arts, whether useful or ornamental, which are required by the Government, have hitherto been carried on by Committees of Parliament ; and had we a return of all the sums annually spent in scientific inquiries, and for scientific purposes, the amount would be found to exceed greatly that of the annual expense, however liberal, of a National Institution. Every question connected with ship-building, with our steam navy, our light-houses, our harbours, our railways, our mines, our fisheries, our sanitary establishments, our agriculture, our statistics, our fine and useful arts, would be investigated and reported upon by a Committee of Academicians ; and while the money of the State would thus be saved, the national resources would be augmented, and all the material interests of the country, under the combined energies of her Art and her Science, would advance with a firm and accelerated step.

But there are grounds higher than utilitarian, on which we would plead the national endowment of science and literature. In ancient times, when knowledge had a limited range, and was but slightly connected with the wants of life, the sage stood even on a higher level than the hero and the lawgiver, and History has preserved his name in her imperishable record, when theirs have disappeared from its page. Archimedes lives in the memory of thousands who have forgotten the tyrants of Syracuse, and the Roman consul who subdued it. The halo which encircled Galileo under the tortures of the Inquisition, extinguishes in its blaze even the names of his tormentors ; and Newton's glory will throw a lustre over the name of England, when time has paled the light reflected from her warriors. The renown of military achievements appeals but to the country which they benefit and adorn : It lives but in the obelisk of granite : It illuminates but the vernacular page.  Subjugated nations turn from the proud monument that degrades them, and the vanquished warrior spurns the record of his humiliation or his shame.  Even the patriot traveller makes a deduction from military glory, when he surveys the red track of desolation and of war, and the tears which the widow and the orphan shed corrode the inscription that is written in blood.  How different are our associations with the tablet of marble, or the monument of bronze, which emblazon the deeds of the sage and the philanthropist !  Their paler lustre irradiates a wider sphere, and excites a warmer sympathy.  No trophies of war are hung in the temple which they adorn, and no assailing foe desecrates its shrine.  In the anthem from its choir the cry of human suffering never mingles, and in the procession of the intellectual victor, ignorance and crime are alone bound to his car.  The achievements of genius, on the contrary, could the wings of light convey them, would be prized in the other worlds of our system,—in the other systems of the universe. They are the bequests which man offers to his race,—a gift to universal humanity—at first to civilisation—at last to barbarism.

Views like these must have influenced the mind of Newton, when, in an elaborate document which he left in duplicate behind him, he recommended the systematic endowment of Science.  Were the British Parliament to try this question at its bar, and summon as witnesses the wisest of their race, what name, or what constellation of names, could countervail against the High Priest of Science, when he proposes to rebuild its Temple upon a broader basis, and give its arches a wider span, and its domes a loftier elevation !

## CHAPTER V.

Mistake of Newton in supposing the Length of the Spectra to be the same in all Bodies—
And in despairing of the Improvement of Refracting Telescopes—In his Controversy
with Lucas he was on the eve of discovering the different Dispersive Powers of Bodies
—Mr. Chester More Hall makes this Discovery, and constructs Achromatic Telescopes,
but does not publish his Discovery — Mr. Dollond re-discovers the Principle of the
Achromatic Telescope, and takes out a Patent—Principle of the Achromatic Telescope explained—Dr. Blair's Aplanatic Telescope—Great Improvement on the Achromatic Telescope by the Flint-Glass of Guinant, Fraunhofer, and Bontemps—Mistake
of Newton in forming his Spectrum from the Sun's Disc—Dark Lines in the Spectrum
—Newton's Analysis of the Spectrum incorrect—New Analysis of the Spectrum by
Absorption, &c., defended against the Objections of Helmholtz, Bernard, and others
—Change in the Refrangibility of Light maintained by Professor Stokes—Objections
to his Theory.

THE two great doctrines of the different refrangibility of the
rays of light, and of the composition of white light, by mixing
all the rays of the spectrum, having been established by Newton
on an impregnable basis, we come now to describe some of the
other results which he obtained regarding the prismatic spectrum and its colours, to point out the errors which he committed, to show the influence which they had on the progress
of optics, and to give an account of the remarkable discoveries
which have been made in this branch of science during the last
and the present century.

There are few facts in the history of optics more singular
than that Newton should have believed that all bodies when
shaped into prisms produced prismatic spectra of equal length,
or separated, or dispersed the red and violet rays to equal distances, when the mean refraction, or the refraction of the
middle ray of the spectrum, was the same.    This opinion,
which he deduced from no direct experiments, and into which

no theoretical views could have led him, seems to have been impressed on his mind with all the force of an axiom.   In one of his experiments he had occasion to counteract the refraction of a prism of glass by a prism of water ; and had he completed the experiment, and studied the result of it when the mean refraction of the two prisms was the same, he could not have failed to observe that the prism of water did not correct the colour of the prism of glass, and would have thus been led to one of the most important truths in optics,—that different bodies have different dispersive powers, or produce prismatic spectra of different lengths, when their mean refraction is the same.    It is curious to observe, as happened in this experiment, what trifling circumstances often arrest the philosopher when on the very verge of a discovery.    Newton had mixed with the water which he used in his prism a little *sugar of lead*, in order to increase the refractive power of the water ; but the sugar of lead having a higher dispersive power than water, made the dispersive power of the water prism equal to that of the prism of glass ; so that if Newton had completed the experiment, the use of the sugar of lead would have prevented him from making an important discovery, which was almost in his possession.    Had he, on the contrary, increased the angle of his water prism till it produced the same deviation of the mean ray of the spectrum, he would have found that the one prism did not correct the colour of the other, and that the glass had a greater dispersive power than the water, and gave a longer spectrum.

Nor is it less extraordinary that the same discovery escaped from his grasp during his controversy with Lucas.    When the Dutch philosopher and his numerous friends who saw his experiments, pronounced his spectrum to be only $3\frac{1}{2}$ times its breadth, Newton found it to be at least five times its breadth ; and it is strange that neither party ever thought that this might arise from using different kinds of glass, and never made the least inquiry regarding the material of which their prism was made.   It is highly probable that Lucas's prism had a very low dispersive power, which would account for the great difference between his spectra and those of Newton, but whether this was the case or not, Newton, under the blind conviction that all spectra must, *cæteris paribus*, be of equal length, pronounced " the improvement of telescopes by refractions to be desperate," [1] and thus checked for a long time the progress of this branch of science.

About two years after the death of Sir Isaac, an individual unknown to fame, broke the spell in which the subject of the spectrum had so long been bound.   In the year 1729, Mr. Chester More Hall, of More Hall in Essex, while studying the mechanism of the human eye, was led to suppose that telescopes might be improved by forming their object-glass with two lenses of different refractive powers.   He published no memoir on the subject, and has not even left behind him any record of the steps by which he arrived at such a conclusion. It is probable that he may have adopted David Gregory's idea of combining lenses of different density, and as crown and flint-glass differed most in this respect, that in combining them he discovered the great difference in their dispersive powers, and was thus led to the invention of the achromatic telescope.   Mr. Hall employed working opticians to grind his lenses, and furnished them with the proper radii of their surfaces for correcting the colour arising from the difference of refrangibility in the rays, and the aberration occasioned by the spherical

[1] Optics, Prop. vii. Book ii. p. 91.   In his reply to Hooke, who justly "reprehended him for laying aside the thoughts of improving optics by refractions," he seems to modify his opinion by saying that he tried what might be done " by two or more glasses or crystals, with water or some other fluid between them." " But what the results by theory or by trials have been, he might possibly find a more proper occasion to declare." This was written in 1672, and we can therefore say with certainty that he failed in this attempt, as it was in 1684 that he pronounced the case to be desperate.   It is a curious circumstance that David Gregory, in his Lectures delivered in Edinburgh in 1684, suggests that, in imitation of the human eye, the object-glasses of telescopes might be composed of media of different density.   In Brown's translation of Gregory, the sense of the passage is not brought out.   See Gregory's *Catoptrics*, Prop xxiv. Schol. pp. 110, 111.

figure of the lenses. Mr. Bass, a well-known working optician, was one of his assistants, and it was probably through him that the knowledge of Mr. Hall's invention has been preserved. About the year 1733 he had completed several achromatic object-glasses, which bore an aperture of more than $2\frac{1}{2}$ inches, though their focal length did not exceed twenty inches. One of these telescopes, which in 1798 was in the possession of the Rev. Mr. Smith of Charlotte Street, Rathbone Place, was examined by several gentlemen of scientific eminence, and found to be a genuine achromatic telescope.

Many years after the death of Mr. More Hall, Mr. John Dollond and others had turned their attention to the improvement of telescopes. Euler, believing the eye to be achromatic, had attempted, but in vain, to discover a combination of media, by which the object-glasses of telescopes could give colourless images. Klingenstierna had endeavoured to show that refraction without colour might be produced according to the laws of refraction laid down by Newton himself ; but none of these philosophers made a single step towards the great discovery which was made by Mr. Dollond, when the previous labours of Hall were unpublished. In 1758, he communicated to the Royal Society an account of his experiments on the different refrangibility of light. In this valuable paper, he proved that glass had a greater dispersive power than water, and attempted to make achromatic object-glasses by enclosing water between two lenses of glass. In this attempt he found the spherical aberration difficult to correct, and he was therefore led to try crown and flint glass, which he found to have such different dispersive powers, that he was at once able to make achromatic object-glasses. In order to secure his right to this invention, Dollond took out a patent ; but in consequence of its having been discovered that the same invention had been made before, some of the London opticians tried the question at law, and produced in court the telescope of Mr. Hall. It was in vain to deny the prior claims of Mr. Hall ;

but as it was certain that Dollond was unacquainted with his labours, and as no achromatic telescope had ever been exposed to sale, Lord Mansfield justly decided the case in favour of Dollond.[1]

It is not easy to explain to the general reader the principle of the Achromatic Telescope ; but we think it may be apprehended from an inspection of the annexed diagram.    In crown glass the index of refraction is 1·526 for red rays, and 1·547 for violet rays.    If L L then be a convex lens of crown glass, it will refract the violet rays more than the red, the former in the direction L R, and the latter in the direction L V, so that R will be the focus of red, and V that of the violet rays.    If we now place behind it a concave lens C C of the same kind of glass and the same curvature, it will by its opposite and equal refractions unite again the rays L R, L V, in the direction L $l$, so as to form a white ray ; but in this case the compound lens acts like a piece of plane glass, or rather like a watch glass which

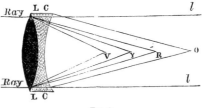

FIG. 9.

has no focus.    But if we make the concave lens C C of flint glass with less curvature than L L, then since it has a greater refractive and dispersive power than the lens L L of crown glass, it will, notwithstanding its inferior curvature, unite the rays L R, L V, and leave such a balance of refraction in favour of the lens L L, that the rays will be united, and a colourless image

[1] See Tilloch's *Philosophical Magazine*, Nov. 1789, vol. ii. p. 177.

formed at o, so that the double object-glass L L C C will be an
achromatic one.

If the prismatic spectrum formed by crown and flint glass
had been exactly the same, that is, if the coloured spaces in
each were of the same length, telescopes constructed upon the
preceding principle, would have been perfect, in so far as colour
is concerned ; but this is not the case, and consequently in the
very best achromatic telescopes, there is left what has been
called a *secondary spectrum*, consisting of *green* and *purple*
colours, which appear on the border of the images of all luminous objects.

This *secondary* or *residual* spectrum, arising from what has
been called the *irrationality* of the coloured spaces in the two
equal spectra of crown and flint glass, may be corrected by an
ingenious contrivance discovered by Dr. Blair.   He found that
muriatic acid produced a prismatic spectrum, in which the
coloured spaces were nearly the same as in crown glass, and
that he could increase its low refractive and dispersive power,
by mixing it with metallic solutions, so as to fit it for being
used like flint glass for correcting the colour of the crown glass
without balancing its refraction.   This increase in its refractive
and dispersive powers, did not alter the proportion of the
coloured spaces in its spectrum, so that it was capable of giving
a perfectly colourless image, when placed as a concave lens
between two convex ones of crown glass.   The metallic solution
used by Dr. Blair was *muriate of antimony*, and in the lens
which he constructed, the rays of different colours were bent
from their rectilineal course with the same equality and regularity as in reflexion.   To this telescope he gave the name of
*Aplanatic.*   According to the testimony of Professor Robison,
those he examined surpassed greatly the best ordinary achromatic telescopes ; but they have been found difficult to construct, and in so far as we know, there is not in existence a
single aplanatic telescope.

The Achromatic Telescope, on the contrary, even with the

imperfection of its secondary spectrum, has undergone great improvements, and promises to rival Reflectors in excellence and power. By the labours of Guinand, Fraunhofer, and M. Bontemps, discs of flint glass of 12, 15, 24, and even 29 inches in diameter, have been made, and we hope soon to see the largest of them converted into a magnificent telescope. The disc of 24 inches has been converted into a telescope by the Rev. Mr. Craig of Leamington.[1]

But while Newton overlooked the remarkable property of the prismatic spectrum, on which the improvement of Refracting Telescopes depends, he committed other considerable mistakes in his examination of the spectrum. It does not seem to have occurred to him that the *Solar Spectrum* was not the spectrum from which the properties of the sun's rays ought to be deduced, and that the relations of the coloured spaces must depend on the angular magnitude of the luminous body, or of the aperture from which the spectrum is obtained. Misled by an apparent analogy between the length of the coloured spaces and the divisions of a musical chord,[2] which he ascertained " by an assistant whose eyes were more critical than his own," he adopted that division as representing the proportion of the coloured spaces in every dispersed beam of light. Had he studied the prismatic spectrum in Mercury and Jupiter by the same instruments, he would have obtained quite different results. In Mercury, where the sun's apparent magnitude is very large, he would have seen a spectrum without any green, and having *red, orange,* and *yellow* at one end, *white* in the middle, and *blue* and *violet* at the other end. In Jupiter, on the contrary, he would have obtained a spectrum in which the coloured spaces were much more condensed, and the pure colours more separated. The Solar spectrum described by Newton, has an intermediate character between these two extremes, and had he examined it under the same circumstances

1 See my *Treatise on Optics,* new edit. p. 506.
2 *Optics,* Part ii. Prop. iii. p. 110.

in winter and in summer, he would have found the analysis of the beams more perfect in summer, on account of the sun's diameter being less.   We are entitled, therefore, to assert, that neither the number nor the extent, nor the limits of the coloured spaces, as given by Newton, are those which belong to the true prismatic spectrum.

Had Newton received upon his prism a beam of light transmitted through a very narrow aperture, he would have anticipated Wollaston and Fraunhofer in their fine discovery of the lines in the prismatic spectrum.   In 1802, Dr. Wollaston, by transmitting the light of the sky through an aperture the twentieth of an inch wide, discovered *six* fixed dark lines in the spectrum, one in the red, one in the orange, one in the blue, and one in the violet spaces.   Without knowing of Wollaston's observations, the late celebrated M. Fraunhofer of Munich, dis-covered in sun light, nearly 600 lines, the largest of which subtended an angle of from 5″ to 10″.   We have found this angle to increase enormously by atmospherical absorption, as the sun passes from the meridian to the horizon, and in a long series of observations we have observed upwards of *two thousand* lines in the prismatic spectrum formed from the sun's rays.

From his analysis of the Solar spectrum, by examining with the prism its separate colours, Newton concluded, *that to the same degree of refrangibility ever belonged the same colour, and to the same colour ever belonged the same refrangibility*, and hence he inferred that *red, orange, yellow, green, blue, indigo, and violet*, were primary and simple colours.   This proposition is true in so far as the analysis of the spectrum by the prism is concerned ; but we have found another species of analysis, by which the colours of the spectrum may be decomposed. Though we cannot separate the *green* rays in the spectrum into *yellow* and *blue* by the refraction of prisms, yet if we possessed any solid or fluid which had a specific attraction for *blue* rays, that is, which absorbed them during the passage of the *green* light through the medium, and allowed the *yellow* rays to pass, we should then analyse the *green* into its component elements as effectually as if we separated them by the prism.  We have in this way subjected the colours in the spectrum to the analysis of a great variety of solid and fluid bodies of different colours, and we have found that in every part of the spectrum, the colours are more or less changed or decomposed by absorption.

The simplest way of observing these changes is to receive the spectrum in the eye by looking through the prism at a narrow line of light from the sky.  If we now interpose between the eye and the prism a plate of purplish blue glass, about the twentieth of an inch thick, we shall see the prismatic spectrum with its bright colours completely metamorphosed. The *red* part of the spectrum is divided into *two red* spaces, separated by a dark interval.  Next to the inner red space comes a space of bright yellow, separated from the red by a visible interval.  After the yellow comes the *green*, with an obscure space between them, then follow the *blue* and the *violet*, the last of which has suffered little or no diminution.  Now, in this experiment, the *blue* glass has absorbed the *red* rays which, when mixed with the *yellow*, on one side constituted *orange*, and the *blue* rays which, when mixed with the *yellow* on the other side, constituted *green*, so that the insulation of the yellow rays thus effected, and the disappearance of the *orange* and of the greater part of the *green* light, places it beyond a doubt that the *orange* and *green* colours in this spectrum are component colours, the former consisting of *red* and *yellow*, and the latter of *yellow* and *blue* rays *of the very same refrangibility*.  If we compare the *two red* spaces seen through the *blue* glass, with the red spaces seen without the *blue* glass, it will appear that the *red* has experienced such an alteration in its tint by the action of the blue glass, as would be effected by the absorption of a small portion of yellow light ; and hence we conclude that the red of this spectrum contains a slight tinge of yellow, and that the yellow space extends over more than one half of the spectrum, including the *red, orange, yellow, green,* and *blue* spaces.

By varying the absorptive media, I have found that *red* light exists in the *yellow* space, and we have ocular evidence, that in the *violet* space *red* light is combined with the *blue* rays. From these and other facts, which it would be out of place here to enumerate, I have been led to the conclusion that *the prismatic spectrum consists of three different spectra,* viz., *red, yellow,* and *blue, all having the same length, all superposed, and each having its maximum intensity at the point where it predominates in the combined spectrum.* Hence it follows :—

1. That *red, yellow,* and *blue,* rays of the same refrangibility exist at every point of the spectrum of intensities, represented by the ordinates of the curve of intensity in each separate spectrum.

2. That the colour of the spectrum at any one point will be that of the predominant ray modified by the smaller quantities of the other two rays ; and,

3. That if we could absorb the two predominant rays at any one point of the spectrum, in such quantities as when mixed with the remaining or unabsorbed ray, would make white light, we should be able to insulate *white light indecomposable by the prism.*

This view of the structure of the spectrum will be understood from the annexed diagrams, where *Figs.* 10, 11, and 12, represent the three separate spectra, which are shown in their combined state in *Fig.* 13. In all these figures, the point M is the *red* or *least* refrangible extremity of the spectrum, and N the *violet* or *most* refrangible extremity. The maximum intensity of each spectrum is opposite R, Y, and B, the intensity diminishing to nothing at the extremities M and N. When these three spectra are superposed, they will exhibit the colours shown in *Fig.* 13, in which we have inserted the three curves which represent the intensities in each spectrum.

Fig 10.

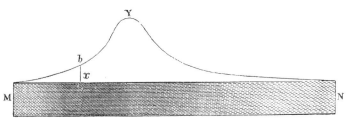

Fig. 11.

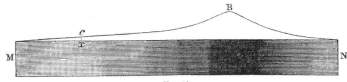

Fig. 12.

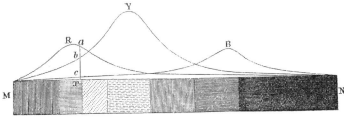

Fig. 13.

In order to explain how the *seven* colours, observed by Newton, are produced by the three primitive colours, we shall take the case of the *orange,* as shown in *Fig.* 13, where the *three* ordinates $ax$, $bx$, $cx$, will indicate the relative intensities of the *three* colours, combined at any point $x$ of the spectrum. Thus let

$$\text{The ordinate for red light be } ax = 30$$
$$\text{,,} \quad \text{yellow} \quad bx = 16$$
$$\text{,,} \quad \text{blue} \quad cx = 2$$
$$\text{Then } ax + bx + cx = 48 \text{ rays.}$$

Hence the point $x$ will be illuminated with forty-eight rays, namely, thirty of red, sixteen of yellow, and two of blue light. Now, as there must be certain quantities of red and yellow light, which, when combined with two blue rays, will form *white,* let us suppose that white light, whose intensity is ten, will be formed by three red, five yellow, and two blue rays, then it follows that the point $x$ will be illuminated with

| | | |
|---|---|---|
| Red rays, . . . . . | $30 - 3$ | or 27 rays. |
| Yellow rays, . . . . | $16 - 5$ | or 11 ,, |
| White light $+ .3$ red $+ 5$ yellow $+ 2$ blue, | | or 10 ,, |
| Orange $=$ red $+$ yellow $+$ white, | | $= 48$ rays. |

That is, the point $x$ will have the colour of *orange* rendered brighter by a mixture of *white* light. The *blue* rays consequently which exist at $x$ will not communicate any *blue* tinge to the prevailing *orange.*

In submitting to the scientific world this new analysis of light, by absorption, we were fully aware of the difficulties which we had to encounter, and we anticipated the opposition which would be made to it. " Even in physical science," we said,[1] " it is an arduous task to unsettle long-established and deeply-rooted opinions ; and the task becomes Herculean when these opinions are intrenched in national feeling, and associated with immortal names. There are cases, indeed, where the

---

[1] *Edinburgh Transactions,* 1831, vol. xii. p. 124.

simple exhibition of new truths is sufficient to dispel errors the most deeply cherished, and the most venerable from their antiquity ; but it is otherwise with doctrines which depend on a chain of reasoning where every step in the inductive process is not rigorously demonstrative ; and of this we require no other proof than is to be found in the history of Newton's optical discoveries, and particularly in the opposition they experienced from such distinguished men as Dr. Hooke and Mr. Huygens."

The preceding analysis of the spectrum embraces three propositions, which, to a certain extent, are independent of each other.

1. That the colours of the coloured spaces may be changed by absorbing media, acting by reflexions and transmissions.

2. That in pure spectra, *white light* can be insulated.

3. That the Newtonian spectrum of *seven* colours consists of *three* equal primary spectra, *red*, *yellow*, and *blue* superposed, having their maximum intensity of illumination at different points, and shading to nothing at their extremities.

The *first* of these propositions may be true, even though we could not insulate white light at any point of the spectrum ; and both the first and second may be true, without our being able to demonstrate that the three spectra have the same length, and diminish in intensity from their maxima to their extremities.

The general proposition that the colours of the spectrum are changed by absorption, has been questioned by three classes of critics,—by Mr. Airy,[1] M. Melloni,[2] and Mr. Draper,[3] who have never repeated our experiments, but made some very imperfect ones of their own ;—by Dr. Whewell,[4] and the' Abbé Moigno,[5] who have made no experiments at all ;—and by M.

[1] *Phil. Mag.* vol. xxx. p. 73.
[2] *Bibl. Univers.* Août 1847.
[3] *Silliman's Journal,* vol. iv. p. 388. 1847.
[4] *Hist. of Inductive Sciences,* vol. ii. p. 361 ; and *Edinburgh Review,* vol. lxvi. p. 136 ; and vol. lxxiv. p. 288.
[5] *Répertoire d'Optique,* tom. ii. p. 459.

Helmholtz[1] in Prussia, and M. Bernard[2] in France.   We have replied to the three first of these writers, and shall now make a few observations on the results obtained by MM. Helmholtz and Bernard.

M. Helmholtz has candidly stated, in contradiction of Mr. Airy, that " the changes of colour" which we have described, as produced by absorption, " are for the most part sufficiently striking to be observed without difficulty ;" and he adds, that " a careful repetition of at least the most important of my experiments, carried out in exact accordance with my method, and with every precaution hitherto deemed necessary, has indeed taught me that the facts which he affirms to have observed, are described with perfect accuracy."

*The change of colour, thus admitted as a physical fact,* M. Helmholtz ascribes to two causes :—

1. To the possible admixture of rays scattered from the prism, and the other transparent bodies used in the experiment ; and

2. To the mixture of complementary colours produced by the action of the other colours of the spectrum on the retina.

The first of these, as M. Helmholtz almost admits, is wholly uninfluential, and the second, if it does disturb the colorific impressions on retinæ tender and sensitive, had no such effect on ours.

If the subjective perception of colour, when we view the spectrum, or make experiments in which more than one colour reaches the eye, is capable of masking the colours under examination, then all that has been written on colours, thus seen, must be erroneous, and all the gay tints of art or of nature are but false hues under the metamorphosis of a subjective perception.   We must not now pronounce a *rose* to be *red*, and its leaves *green*, till we have stared at them through a chink, or torn them from their foot-stalk !   The phenomena of ab-

---

[1] Poggendorff's *Annalen.*  1852, No. 8.
[2] *Ann. de Chim. et de Phys.* tom. xxxv. p. 385, &c.

sorption which we have described *we have seen*, just as Newton saw his seven colours in the spectrum, and Hooke his composite tints in the soap-bubble ; and now that our eyes have nearly finished their work, we are not disposed to mistrust, without reason, such good and faithful servants.[1]

The observations of M. Bernard, who has repeated only a few of our experiments, differ very little from those of M. Helmholtz. He maintains that the conversion of the *blue* space into *violet* arises from the light being diminished. If the colours of the spectrum thus change, as he maintains, by their becoming fainter, we would desire to ask at what degree of illumination are we to see the spectrum in its *true colours ?* *Colour* cannot depend upon refrangibility, if the *blue space* is converted into *violet* either by diminution of light or absorption ; and therefore the doctrine of M. Bernard is as fatal to Newton's as to ours. If M. Bernard's experiment be correct, it only proves that the *blue rays, when enfeebled, lose their power over the retina sooner than the red.*

The Newtonian doctrine, " that the degree of refrangibility proper to any particular sort of rays is not mutable by refraction, nor reflection, nor by any other cause,"[2] has been recently questioned by Professor Stokes, one of the distinguished successors of Newton in the Lucasian chair. Mr. Stokes[3] found that the chemical rays in the violet space, between the lines G and H of the spectrum, produce, in a solution of sulphate of quinine, *light of a sky-blue* colour, which he assumes to have the refrangibility of that portion of the spectrum. By refracting

---

[1] The changes of colour in the spectrum at different seasons of the year, and the different hours of the day, and when formed from different portions of the illuminated sky, as well as from the direct light of the sun, are very remarkable. We have mentioned one or two of them in the *Edinburgh Review*, vol. lxxiv. p. 284. Jan. 1842. One of these observations is as follows :—" October 23, 1832. 11th, The *yellow* comes distinctly up to F, and a little beyond it ; *i.e.*, the *blue* has been all absorbed in the *green* space of Fraunhofer's spectrum from E to F." In another observation on the 5th February 1833, the *green* space was wholly *yellow*.

[2] Letter to Oldenburg, Feb. 6, 1672, in *Phil. Trans.* No. 80, p. 3081, § 3.

[3] *Phil. Trans.* 1852.

this light through a prism, he converts the *sky-blue rays* into a spectrum of all colours, and all refrangibilities.   Hence he concludes, that the *sky-blue light* having the fixed refrangibility due to its locality between G and H, is changed by refraction into all the other colours, with their respective refrangibilities. If this conclusion be admitted, our doctrine of the severance of colour and refrangibility is placed beyond a doubt.   We have in the first experiment *sky-blue* light with the refrangibility of *violet* light between G and H ; and, in the second experiment, we have the same *blue* light changed by refraction into *all the colours* of the spectrum.

We cannot, however, avail ourselves of this last fact, for, after a careful consideration of Mr. Stoke's important results,[1] we cannot but regard the *sky-blue* light as a *phosphorescence*, produced in the quinine solution by the chemical rays, which, like all other phosphorescences, is decomposable by the prism.

[1] See my *Treatise on Optics*, new edition, pp. 182, 183.

# CHAPTER VI.

Newton on the cause of the Moon's Libration—Is occupied with the subject of planting Cider Trees—Sends to Oldenburg his Discourse on Light and Colours, containing his Hypothesis concerning Light—Views of Descartes and Hooke, who adopt the Hypothesis of an Ether, the Vibrations of which produce Light—Rejected by Newton, who proposes a Modification of it, but solely as an Illustration of his Views, and not as a Truth—Light is neither Ether, nor its Vibrating Motion—Corpuscles from the Sun act upon the Ether—Hooke claims Newton's Hypothesis as contained in his Micrographia—Discussions on the Subject—Hooke's Letter to Newton proposing a Private Discussion as more suitable—Newton's Reply to this Letter, acknowledging the Value of Hooke's Discoveries—Oldenburg the Cause of the Differences between Hooke and Newton—Newton's Letter to Boyle on the Subject of Ether—His Conjecture on the Cause of Gravity—Newton supposed to have abandoned the Emission Theory—Dr. Young's Supposition incorrect—Newton's mature Judgment in favour of the Emission Theory.

In the years 1675 and 1676, when Newton was engaged in his fruitless controversy with the Dutch professors, his mind was directed to a great variety of subjects. Collins[1] informs his correspondent, James Gregory, that he had not written to Newton or even seen him for these *eleven* or *twelve* months ; that he did not wish to trouble him, as he was "intent upon chemical studies and practices," and that Newton and Barrow had "begun to think mathematical speculations at least dry, if not somewhat barren." His attention was at this time occupied with the subject of the moon's libration. In a letter to Oldenburg in 1673, in reference to Huygen's work on Central Forces, he mentions that "he had sometimes thought that the moon's libration might depend upon her *conatus* from the sun and earth compared together, till he apprehended a better cause." This better cause he communicated in 1675 to Nicholas

---

[1] October 19, 1675. *Macclesfield Correspondence*, vol. ii. p. 280.

Mercator, who published it in the following year in his Astronomical Institutions.[1] Galileo had discovered and explained the diurnal libration, arising from the spectator not viewing the moon from the centre of the earth, but it was reserved for Newton to explain the libration in longitude, which Hevelius, its discoverer, had ascribed to the displacement of the centre of the moon's orbit from the centre of motion. He showed that it was occasioned by the inequalities of the moon's motion in an elliptic orbit round the earth, combined with the uniformity of her motion round her axis. In the same letter to Mercator he showed that the libration in latitude arose from her axis of rotation being inclined 88° 17′ to the ecliptic.

About this time we find Newton occupied with a subject very different from his usual pursuits—taking an interest, like a country gentleman, in the planting of fruit trees for the manufacture of cider. It does not appear how his attention was directed to this subject. A reference is made to it in a letter to Oldenburg, in November 1676 ; but we have been fortunate enough to find among his papers a previous letter to the same gentleman, in September, which we need make no apology for inserting here.

" September 2, 1676.

" Sir,—I have now made what inquiry I can into the state we are in for planting, and find there are some gentlemen that of late have begun to plant, and seem to incline more and more to it, but I cannot hear of any professed nurseryman we have. Our gardeners find more profit in cherry trees, and so stock their ground almost wholly with them. The chief of them plant some fruit trees, but it is to find the gentry with plants : to whom I am apt to think your proposition will prove a very reasonable one, considering the new humour of planting that begins to grow among them. But in order to

---

[1] " Harum . . . librationum causas Hypothesi elegantissima explicavit nobis vir cl. Isaac Newton, cujus humanitati hoc et aliis nominibus plurimum debere me lubens profiteor."—Mercator's *Institutiones Astronomicæ,* p. 286.

promote the design, I am desired to inquire what sort of trees
your friend can furnish us with, at what rates, which way they
can most conveniently be conveyed to so great a distance, and
what may be the charges of carriage. Also, whether they are
to be sent in cions or grafts ; the first being more convenient
for carriage, and so rather to be wished, unless those trees be
found best which are grafted on their native soil. I perceive
the gardener I mentioned (Mr. Blackley by name) would gladly
embrace the proposal, and provide himself with more ground
than he has, for a nursery, to stock his neighbours, if he found
he can have good sorts of trees, and the carriage make them
not too dear.

" But, upon discoursing with people, I find we lye under one
great difficulty ; which is an opinion generally taken up here,
that Red Streaks (the famous fruit for cyder in other parts)
will not succeed in this country. The tree thrives well here,
and bears as much fruit, and as good to look as in other countries ; but the cyder made of it they find harsh and churlish,
and so this fruit begins here to be generally neglected, and
other fruit, and which they find does pretty well, but the cyder
will not keep above a year, whereas that made of Red Streaks
in other parts will keep three years or more. The ill success
of Red Streaks here, I perceive, is generally imputed to the
soil ; but since the tree thrives, and bears as well here as in
other parts, I am apt to think it is in the manner of making the
cyder. For upon inquiry of the gardiners, I cannot find that
they mixed any other fruit with the Red Streaks, which I
have been told they do in the cyder countries, and am apt to
believe it necessary ; the juice of the finer fruit, on the one
hand, sweetening and ripening the harsh juice of the Red
Streaks, as that juice, on the other hand, by its slow ripening,
makes the cyder keep long. Sir, if this prejudice we have
against Red Streaks could be removed, it would much promote
the design of planting, and double the benefit of it to us by
bettering the cyder ; and therefore I make bold to desire you

to inform me, if you know of any practical description of
making cyder, printed in any author ; and if not, to desire you,
if it lye in your way at any time, to inquire, about the manner
of making and ordering of it.   For which end give me leave
to make these queries :—What sort of fruit are best to be
used, and in what proportion they are to be mixed, and what
degree of ripeness they ought to have ?  Whether it be material
to press them as soon as gathered, or to pare them ?  Whether
there be any circumstances to be observed in pressing them ?
or what is the best way to do it ?   If you can direct us to, or
procure for us a short narrative of the way of making and
ordering cyder in the cyder countries, which takes in a resolution of these, or the most material of these queries, you will
oblige your humble servant,

                               "Is. Newton."


   "Sᴿ. If my last letter be not yet sent to Mr. Lucas, I desire you would, for preventing any suspicion of insincerity, insert this parenthesis (as is well known here) between the words
[and written a tractate on that subject], and [wherein I had set
down] in the latter part of my letter."[1]


   In November 1676, Newton addresses another letter to
Oldenburg in the following terms :—
   " I am desired to write to you about procuring a recommendation of us to Mr. Austin, the Oxonian planter.  We hope
your correspondent will be pleased to do us that favour as to
recommend us to him, that we may be furnished with the best
sort of cider fruit-trees.  We desire only about 30 or 40 graffs
for the first essay, and if these prove for our purposes, they will
be desired in greater numbers.  We desire graffs rather than
sprags, that we may the sooner see what they will prove.  They

---

[1] Newton's letter had been forwarded to Mr. Lucas, and therefore the sentence does
not appear in it.—See *Phil. Trans.* No. 128, p. 703.

are not for Mr. Blackley, but some other persons about Cambridge."[1]

The friend mentioned in one of these letters, and the correspondent in the other, was the Rev. Dr. John Beal, Rector of Yeovil, in Somersetshire, who, in imitation of his father and great-grandfather, had distinguished himself by his zeal in the plantation of orchards for the making of cider.[2]

But though thus occasionally occupied with other subjects, he was at this time diligent in the prosecution of his optical researches. On the 13th November 1675, he intimated to Oldenburg, "that he had some thoughts of writing a further discourse about colours, to be read at one of your assemblies, but find it yet against the grain to put pen to paper any more on that subject. But, however, I have one discourse by me on that subject, written when I sent my first letter to you about colours, and of which I then gave you notice. This you may command when you think it may be convenient, if the custom of reading weekly discourses still continues." Mr. Oldenburg having been desired by the Society to thank him for this offer, and to desire him to send this discourse as soon as he pleased, Newton again writes to him on the 30th November, "that he intended to have sent the papers this week, but that upon reviewing them it came into his mind to write another little scribble to accompany them." This little scribble was his "Hypothesis," to which we shall presently refer.

The discourse above referred to was produced in manuscript on the 9th December 1675, with the title of—"A Theory of Light and Colours, containing partly an Hypothesis to explain the properties of light discoursed of by him in his former papers, partly the principal phenomena of the various colours exhibited by thin plates or bubbles, esteemed to be of a more difficult consideration, yet to depend also on the said properties of

[1] Edleston's *Correspondence*, App. No. XVI. p. 260.
[2] He wrote a work entitled, *Herefordshire Orchards a Pattern for England*, 1656. See Birch's *Hist. of the Royal Society*, vol. iv. p. 235.

light." This paper was introduced by the following letter to Oldenburg, which possesses considerable interest.

"Sir,—I have sent you the papers I mentioned, by John Stiles. Upon reviewing them I find some things so obscure as might have deserved a further explication by schemes ; and some other things I guess will not be new to you, though almost all was new to me when I wrote them. But as they are, I hope you will accept of them, though not worth the ample thanks you sent. I remember in some discourse with Mr. Hooke, I happened to say that I thought light was re-flected, not by the parts of glass, water, air, or other sensible bodies, but by the same confine or superficies of the ethereal medium which refracts it, the rays finding some difficulty to get through it in passing out of the denser into the rarer medium, and a greater difficulty in passing out of the rarer into the denser ; and so being either refracted or reflected by that superficies, as the circumstances they happened to be in at their incidence make them able or unable to get through it. And for confirmation of this, I said further, that I thought the reflexion of light, at its tending out of glass into air, would not be diminished or weakened by drawing away the air in an air-pump, as it ought to be if they were the parts of air that re-flected ; and added, that I had not tried this experiment, but thought he was not unacquainted with notions of this kind. To which he replied, that the notion was new, and he would the first opportunity try the experiment I propounded. But upon reviewing the papers I sent you, I found it there set down for trial ; which makes me recollect that about the time I was writing these papers, I had occasionally observed in an air-pump here at Christ's College, that I could not perceive the re-flexion of the inside of the glass diminished in drawing out the air. This I thought fit to mention, lest my former forgetfulness, through my having long laid aside my thoughts on these things, should make me seem to have set down for certain what I never tried.

" Sir,—I had formerly purposed never to write any hypothesis of light and colours, fearing it might be a means to
engage me in vain disputes ; but I hope a declared resolution
to answer nothing that looks like a controversy, unless possibly
at my own time upon some by-occasion, may defend me from
that fear.  And therefore, considering that such an hypothesis
would much illustrate the papers I promised to send you, and
having a little time this last week to spare, I have not scrupled
to describe one, so far as I could on a sudden recollect my
thoughts about it ; not concerning myself, whether it should
be thought probable or improbable, so it do but render the
paper I send you, and others sent formerly, more intelligible.
You may see by the scratching and interlining it was done in
haste ; and I have not had time to get it transcribed, which
makes me say I reserve a liberty of adding to it, and desire
that you would return these and the other papers when you
have done with them.  I doubt there is too much to be read
at one time, but you will soon see how to order that.  At the
end of the hypothesis you will see a paragraph, to be inserted
as is there directed.  I should have added another or two, but
I had not time, and such as it is I hope you will accept it.—
SIR, I am your obedient servant,        " Is. NEWTON."

The Hypothesis,[1] to which this letter is introductory, possesses many points of historical interest.  Descartes was the
first philosopher who maintained the existence of an ether, a
medium more subtle than air, filling the interstices of air, and
occupying the pores of glass and all transparent bodies.  He
considered the ether to be composed of a continued series of
molecular globules, along which a motion was propagated constituting light and colour.[2]  Dr. Hooke, who adopted the

---

[1] See APPENDIX, No. II.

[2] Dr. Whewell states that Descartes regarded light as " consisting of small particles
emitted by the luminous body," but Mr. Vernon Harcourt (Letter to Lord Brougham,
p. 32) has shown the incorrectness of this opinion.  See Œuvres de Descartes, tom. vii.
pp. 193, 240.

general view of Descartes, maintained that " the parts of bodies
when briskly agitated excite vibrations in the ether which are
propagated every way from these bodies in straight lines, and
cause a sensation of light by beating and dashing against the
bottom of the eye ; something after the manner that vibrations
in the air cause a sensation of sound by beating against the
organs of hearing."[1]    In his reply to Hooke, on the 11th of
July 1673, Newton distinctly states that this, which he calls
the fundamental supposition in Hooke's hypothesis, " *seems
itself impossible ;* namely, that the waves or vibrations of any
fluid can, like the rays of light, be propagated in straight lines,
without a continual and very extravagant spreading and bending every way into the quiescent medium where they are
terminated by it. *I am mistaken if there be not both experiment and demonstration to the contrary.*"

In thus summarily rejecting Hooke's hypothesis, Newton
suggests a modification of it, or a form in which it will be better
fitted to account for the phenomena, or to use his own expression,—" The most free and natural application of this
hypothesis I take to be this—that the agitated parts of bodies,
according to their several figures, sizes, and motions, do excite
vibrations in the ether of various depths or sizes, which being
promiscuously propagated through that medium to our eyes,
effect in us a sensation of light of a white colour ; but if by
any means those of unequal sizes be separated from one
another, the largest beget a sensation of a red colour, the least
or shortest of a deep violet, and the intermediate ones of intermediate colours."[2]    Now this modification of Hooke's hypothesis has been very erroneously regarded as an expression of
Sir Isaac's own views, whereas he merely gives it as a better
form of a hypothesis, the fundamental position of which he
pronounces impossible, and contrary both to experiment and
demonstration.    In judging of Sir Isaac's Hypothesis of 1675,

[1] Newtoni *Opera*, tom. iv. pp. 325, 326.
[2] *Phil. Trans.* 1672, No. 88, p. 5088.

it is necessary to keep this in view, as it appears to be quite clear that this hypothesis is not what he believes, but what he found it necessary to draw up for the information of many of his friends. " Having observed," he says, " the heads of some great virtuosos to run much upon hypotheses, as if my discourses wanted a hypothesis to explain them by, and found that some, when I could not make them take my meaning, when I spoke of the nature of light and colours abstractedly, have readily apprehended it when I *illustrated* my discourse with an hypothesis ; *for this reason* I have here thought fit to send you a description of the circumstances of this hypothesis, as much tending to the *illustration* of the papers I herewith send you."

In order to prevent any misapprehension of his meaning, he goes on to say, " that he shall not assume either this or any other hypothesis ;" yet while he is describing this hypothesis " he shall *sometimes, to avoid circumlocution, and to represent it more conveniently, speak of it as if he assumed it, and propounded it to be believed.*"

With this caution, he supposes an ethereal medium rarer than air, subtler, and more elastic, not one uniform matter, but " compounded of various ethereal spirits or vapours, with the phlegmatic body of ether. The whole frame of nature may be nothing but various contextures condensed by precipitation, and after condensation, wrought into various forms, at first by the immediate hand of the Creator, and ever since by the power of nature ; which, by virtue of the command, increase and multiply, became a complete imitator of the copies set her by the protoplast." " Thus," he adds, " perhaps may all things be originated from ether." Newton then proceeds to describe an electrical experiment, which afterwards excited much interest in the Society. He laid upon a table a round piece of glass about two inches broad, set 'in a brass ring, so as to keep the glass about the sixth of an inch from the table, the air being enclosed on all sides by the ring. Having placed some small pieces of paper within the ring, and rubbed the glass briskly with some rough substance, the pieces of thin paper began to be attracted and fly about even after the friction had ceased. From this result he conceived that some subtle matter lying condensed in the glass was rarefied by friction as water is rarefied into vapour by heat, and by " moving and circulating variously, actuates the pieces of paper till it returns into the glass and be re-condensed there." He next supposes that this ether may be imbibed by the earth, and also copiously by the sun, in order to preserve his shining, and keep the planets from receding farther from him ; that is, to increase his " gravitating attraction, which may be caused by the continual condensation of some very subtle gummy or unctuous substance diffused through the ether." And as if he were amusing himself with the extravagance of his speculations, he adds, " And *they that will may also* suppose that this spirit affords, or carries with it thither, the solary fuel, and material principle of light, and that the vast ethereal spaces between us and the stars are for a sufficient repository for this food of the sun and planets !" If we laugh at Kepler's firm belief that the earth and other planets are enormous living animals taking their daily and nightly alternations of sleeping and waking, we may be allowed to smile when Newton condescends to feed them with the nectar and ambrosia of the ethereal domains. In the same extravagance of speculation he supposes that the soul may have an immediate power over the whole ether in any part of the body, producing, by processes which he invents, the swelling and shrinking of the muscles, and the animal motions which result from it.

In passing from " the effects and uses of ether" to the " consideration of light," he supposes that light " is neither ether, nor its vibrating motion, but something of a different kind propagated from lucid bodies," such as " multitudes of small and swift corpuscles of various sizes springing from shining bodies, at great distances, one after another, but yet

without any sensible interval of time." That it is different
from the vibrations of the ether, he infers from the existence
of shadows, and the colours of thin plates. His next supposition is, " that light and ether mutually act upon one another,
ether in refracting light, and light in warming ether ;" and,
after some farther observations on this mutual action, he goes
on to explain the manner in which refraction and reflexion are
produced upon this hypothesis, and the cause of transparency,
opacity, and colour. His discourse concludes with an application of the hypothesis to the colours of thin plates, to the inflexion of light, and to the colours of natural bodies,—subjects
to which we shall presently direct the reader's attention.

After the reading of the first part of this discourse on the
9th December, Mr. Hooke said, " that the main of it was contained in his *Micrographia*, which Mr. Newton had only carried
farther in some particulars." When this remark was communicated to Newton, he seems to have been greatly offended,
and, on the 21st December, he wrote a letter to Oldenburg,
pointing out the difference between his hypothesis and that of
Dr. Hooke. Although " he is not much concerned at the
liberty of Mr. Hooke's insinuation," yet he wishes to " avoid the
savour of having done anything unjustifiable or unhandsome "
to him. He therefore separates the part of the hypothesis that
belongs to Descartes and others, and leaves to Hooke the merit
of having changed Descartes' progressive motion of the ether
into a vibrating one,—" the rotation of the globuli to the
obliquation of pulses, and the accelerating their rotation on the
one hand, and retarding it on the other, by the quiescent
medium to produce colours, to the like action of the medium
on the two ends of his pulse for the same end." He gives
Hooke the credit also of explaining the phenomena of thin
plates, and also the colours of natural bodies, fluid and solid.[1]
In the other two paragraphs of the letter, he details more

[1] Newtoni *Opera*, tom. iv. pp. 378-381; or Birch, vol. iii. p. 278.

specifically the difference between his explanations and those of his rival.[1]

These controversial discussions seem to have annoyed Hooke as much as they did Newton, and, instead of publicly replying to the two last communications of Newton, he addressed a letter to him, which, with Newton's answer, we had the good fortune to discover among the family papers. These letters are highly interesting ; and we are persuaded that those who have had occasion to animadvert on the conduct of Hooke, will peruse this letter with much satisfaction.

Robert Hooke—" These to my much esteemed friend, Mr. Isaack Newton, at his chambers in Trinity College in Cambridge.

" S$^R$,—The hearing a letter of yours read last week in the meeting of the Royal Society, made me suspect that you might have been some way or other misinformed concerning me ; and this suspicion was the more prevalent with me, when I called to mind the experience I have formerly had of the like sinister practices. I have therefore taken the freedom, which I hope I may be allowed in philosophical matters to acquaint you of myself. First, that I doe noe ways approve of contention, or feuding or proving in print, and shall be very unwillingly drawn to such kind of warre. Next, that I have a mind very desirous of, and very ready to embrace any truth that shall be discovered, though it may much thwart or contradict any opinions or notions I have formerly embraced as such. Thirdly, that I do justly value your excellent disquisitions, and am extremely well pleased to see those notions promoted and improved which I long since began, but had not time to compleat.

---

[1] In a paper entitled "Observations," which accompanied this letter, but which was not printed, Newton says that Hooke, in his *Micrographia*, had " delivered many very excellent things concerning the colours of thin plates, and other natural bodies, which he had not scrupled to make use of as far as they were for his purpose."

That I judge you have gone farther in that affair much than I did, and that as I judge you cannot meet with any subject more worthy your contemplation, so I believe the subject cannot meet with a fitter and more able person to inquire into it than yourself, who are every way accomplished to compleat, rectify, and reform what were the sentiments of my younger studies, which I designed to have done somewhat at myself, if my other more troublesome employments would have permitted, though I am sufficiently sensible it would have been with abilities much inferior to yours. Your design and mine are, I suppose, both at the same thing, which is the discovery of truth, and I suppose we can both endure to hear objections, so as they come not in a manner of open hostility, and have minds equally inclined to yield to the plainest deductions of reason from experiment. If, therefore, you will please to correspond about such matters by private letters, I shall very gladly embrace it ; and when I shall have the happiness to peruse your excellent discourse (which I can as yet understand nothing more of by hearing it cursorily read), I shall, if it be not ungrateful to you, send you freely my objections, if I have any, or my concurrences, if I am convinced, which is the more likely. This way of contending, I believe, to be the more philosophical of the two, for though I confess the collision of two hard-to-yield contenders may produce light, [yet] if they be put together by the ears by other's hands and incentives, it will [produce rath]er ill concomitant heat, which serves for no other use but . . . . kindle—cole. S$^r$, I hope you will pardon this plainness of, your very affectionate humble serv$^t$,

" 1675-6.                ROBERT HOOKE."

To this letter Newton sent the following reply :—

" CAMBRIDGE, *February* 5, 1675-6.

" DR. SIR,—At the reading of your letter I was exceedingly pleased and satisfied with your generous freedom, and think

you have done what becomes a true philosophical spirit. There
is nothing which I desire to avoyde in matters of philosophy
more than contention, nor any kind of contention more than
one in print ; and, therefore, I most gladly embrace your proposal of a private correspondence. What's done before many
witnesses is seldom without some further concerns than that
for truth ; but what passes between friends in private, usually
deserves the name of consultation rather than contention ; and
so I hope it will prove between you and me. Your animadversions will therefore be welcome to me ; for though I was
formerly tyred of this subject by the frequent interruptions it
caused to me, and have not yet, nor I believe ever shall recover so much love for it as to delight in spending time about
it ; yet to have at once in short the strongest objections that
may be made, I would really desire, and know no man better
able to furnish me with them than yourself. In this you will
oblige me, and if there be any thing else in my papers in which
you apprehend I have assumed too . . . . . . If you please to
reserve your sentiments of it for a private letter, I hope you
[will find that I] am not so much in love with philosophical
productions but that I can make them yield. . . . . . . But,
in the mean time, you defer too much to my ability in searching into this subject. What Descartes did was a good step.
You have added much several ways, and especially in considering the colours of thin plates. *If I have seen farther, it is
by standing on the shoulders of giants.* But I make no question you have divers very considerable experiments beside those
you have published, and some, it's very probable, the same
with some of those in my late papers. Two at least there are,
which I know you have often observed,—the dilatation of the
coloured rings by the obliquation of the eye, and the apparition
of a black spot at the contact of two convex glasses, and at the
top of a water-bubble ; and it's probable there may be more,
besides others which I have not made, so that I have reason to
defer as much or more in this respect to you, as you would to

me.[1]  But not to insist on this, your letter gives me occasion
to inquire regarding an observation you was propounding to
me to make here of the transit of a star near the zenith.  I
came out of London some days sooner than I told you of, it
falling out so that I was to meet a friend then at Newmarket,
and so missed of your intended directions ; yet I called at your
lodgings a day [or] two before I came away, but missed of you.
If, therefore, you continue . . . . . . to have it observed, you
may, by sending your directions, command . . . . . . your
humble servant,                              " Is. NEWTON."

These beautiful letters, emulous of good feeling and lofty
principle, throw some light on the character and position of
two of the greatest of our English philosophers, and we cannot
read their mutual confessions and desires without an anxious
hope that two such men may never again be placed in a state
of intellectual collision.  In alluding to the sinister practices
of some intermeddling friend, and to the evil consequences of
two hard-to-yield contenders being put together by the ears
by other's hands and incentives, Hooke evidently refers to his
colleague, Mr. Oldenburg.  It was not unlikely that the secretary to the Royal Society, and its Curator and Professor of
Mechanics, might have occasional grounds of difference without
any imputation upon their social or moral character ; but this
official jealousy, whatever was its amount, was increased in a
high degree during the disputes between Hooke and Hevelius
on the subject of plain and telescopic sights, and between Hooke
and Huygens respecting the invention of pendulum clocks.
These disputes were running high about the time when Newton's discourse on colours was before the Royal Society, and
in both of them Oldenburg took a keen and active part against
Hooke.  It was, therefore, no improbable supposition, that in
communicating to Newton what Hooke had said at the Society,

[1] In his *Optics*, published many years after this, in 1704, Newton does not give Hooke
the credit of having made these observations.

Oldenburg had given it too high a colouring, or even artfully misrepresented it. In a subsequent dispute, in 1686, about the law of gravity, when Newton made some severe animadversions on Hooke's claim, Dr. Halley informs him in reply, that " he feared Mr. Hooke's *manner* of claiming the discovery had been *represented in worse colours than it ought.*" With his usual good feeling, Newton thus expressed his regret : " Now that I understand he was *in some respects misrepresented to me, I wish I had spared the postscript in my last.*"

When Hooke, in the case more immediately before us, stated " that the main of Newton's discourse was contained in his *Micrographia,* which he had only carried further in some particulars," he did not do justice to the valuable communication of his rival ; but, on the other hand, we have it on the evidence of Newton himself, that he did not, in his discourse, give Hooke the same credit for his discoveries which he afterwards did in the letter that he addressed to him. It has been too much the practice of the admirers of Newton to assail the memory of Hooke with ungenerous animadversions, and unmanly abuse. M. Biot has even ventured to describe him as " a bad man," as if he added to the intellectual fame of Newton by the moral depreciation of his rival. We cannot give our sanction to so harsh a judgment. Under a due sense of the imperfections of our common nature, and influenced by the charity which thinketh no evil, we may find in the physical constitution and social position of Hooke, and to a certain extent in the injustice of his enemies, some apology for that jealousy and quickness of temper which may have been more deeply regretted by himself than it was felt by others.

After the publication of his " Hypothesis, explaining the Properties of Light," Newton seems to have been conversing with Robert Boyle on its application to chemistry, and on the 28th February 1679, he addressed a letter to him on the subject, in fulfilment of a long deferred promise. The views which he here presents to his friend, he characterizes as in digested and unsatisfactory to himself, and he adds, that "as it is only an explication of qualities that is desired," he "sets down his apprehensions in the form of suppositions." He supposes a subtle and elastic ether to pervade all gross bodies, and to stand rarer in their pores than in free space, being so much the rarer as their pores are less. The ether within solid and fluid bodies diminishes in density towards their surface, while the ether without all such bodies diminishes in density towards their surface. According to this theory there is a certain space within solid and fluid bodies, and a certain space without them, which Newton calls " the space of the ether's graduated rarity." On these suppositions he tries to explain the inflexion of light in passing through this space, the colours of minute particles, and of natural bodies, the repulsion and attraction of bodies coming into contact, the action of menstrums upon bodies, the phenomena of effervescence and ebullition, and the transmutation of gross substances into aërial ones. He conceives the confused mass of vapours, air, and exhalations, which we call the atmosphere, to be nothing else but the particles of all sorts of bodies of which the earth consists, separated from one another, and kept at a distance by the said principle, and he concludes this remarkable speculation with a conjecture about the cause of gravity.

"I shall set down," he says, "one conjecture more, which came into my mind even as I was writing this letter ; it is about the cause of gravity. For this end I will suppose ether to consist of parts differing from one another in *subtlety* by indefinite degrees ; that in the pores of bodies there is less of the grosser ether in proportion to the finer, than in open spaces ; and consequently, that in the great body of the earth there is much less of the grosser ether in proportion to the purer, than in the regions of the air ; and that yet the grosser either in the air affects the upper regions of the earth, and the finer ether in the earth the lower regions of the air, in such a manner, that from the top of the air to the surface of the earth, and again from the surface of the earth to the centre thereof, the ether is insensibly finer and finer.  Imagine now any body suspended in the air or lying on the earth ; and the ether being by the hypothesis grosser in the pores which are in the upper parts of the body, than in those which are in its lowest parts, and that grosser ether being less apt to be lodged in these pores than the finer ether below, it will endeavour to get out and give way to the purer ether below, which cannot be without the bodies descending to make room above for it to go out into."[1]

The Hypothesis of Newton, and his other speculations regarding ether, have led some writers to suppose that he had abandoned the corpuscular or emission theory, in which light is supposed to be produced by material particles projected from luminous bodies, and that he had adopted views not very different from those of the supporters of the undulatory theory. This opinion has been entertained chiefly on the authority of Dr. Thomas Young, in his theory of light and colours.[2]  In introducing this theory, he remarks, that "a more extensive examination of Newton's writings has shown me, that he was in reality the first that suggested such a theory as I shall endeavour to maintain ; and that his own opinion varies less from this theory than is now almost universally supposed."[3]   "I shall collect," he adds, "from Newton's various writings, such passages as seem to be most favourable to its admission (Dr. Young's theory), and although I shall quote some papers which may be thought to have been *partly retracted* at the publication of the ' Optics,' yet I shall borrow nothing from them that can be supposed to militate against his *maturer judgment*."  In another place he states in language still more explicit, "that *Newton considered the operation of an ethereal medium as absolutely necessary to the production of the most remarkable effects of light*."

[1] Letter to Boyle, Newtoni *Opera*, tom. iv. pp. 385-395.
[2] *Phil. Trans.* 1801 ; or, Lectures on Natural Philosophy, vol. ii. p. 614.
[3] *Ibid.* vol. i. p. 477.

VOL. I.                                        I

In direct contradiction to these statements, we have already
found Newton distinctly maintaining "that light is neither
ether nor its vibrating motion, but something of a different
kind propagated from lucid bodies," such as "multitudes of
small and swift corpuscles of various sizes springing from shining bodies;" and when in order to please his friends and illustrate his views, he invents a speculation "not propounded to be
believed," he cannot be regarded as maintaining views at all
approximating to the undulatory theory. We cannot understand how Dr. Young could overlook the language of caution
in which he everywhere guards himself against its being supposed that he believes even in the existence of an ether,—
language, too, so precise, that the honest meaning of its author
cannot be misinterpreted.

The matured judgment of Newton, of which Dr. Young
speaks, and against which his quotations directly militate, is
given in the following explicit passage, published in 1717, in
the second edition of his *Optics*, revised by himself.[1]

"Are not all hypotheses erroneous in which light is supposed
to consist in pression or motion propagated through a fluid
medium? For in all these hypotheses the phenomena of light
have been hitherto explained by supposing that they arise
from new modifications of the rays, which is *an erroneous
supposition.*

"If light consisted only in pression propagated without
actual motion, it would not be able to agitate and heat the
bodies which refract and reflect it. If it consisted in motion
propagated to all distances in an instant, it would require an
infinite force every moment in every shining particle to generate
that motion. And if it consisted in pression or motion propagated either in an instant or in time, it would bend into the
shadow. For pression or motion cannot be propagated in a
fluid in right lines, beyond an obstacle which stops part of the

motion, but will bend and spread every way into the quiescent medium which lies beyond the obstacle. . . .

" And it is as difficult to explain by such hypotheses how rays can be alternately in fits of easy reflexion and easy transmission ; unless perhaps one might suppose that there are in all space two ethereal vibrating mediums, and that the vibrations of one of them constitute light, and the vibrations of the other are swifter, and as often as they overtake the vibrations of the first, put them into those fits.  But how two *ethers* can be different through all space, one of which acts upon the other, and by consequence is reacted upon, without retarding, shattering, dispersing, and compounding one another's motions, is inconceivable.  And against filling the heavens with fluid mediums, unless they be exceeding rare, a great objection arises from the regular and very lasting motions of the planets and comets in all manner of courses through the heavens.  For thence it is manifest that the heavens are void of all sensible resistance, and by consequence of all sensible matter."

That this passage contains the mature and the latest judgment of Newton on the subject of light cannot be doubted.  All the quotations from Newton referred to by Dr. Young bear the date of 1672 and 1675, and the letter to Boyle the date of 1679 ; but the preceding passage was published in 1704, 1717, and 1721, in the lifetime of Newton, when it was in his power to alter or retract it.  But in addition to this argument, we have the evidence of Leibnitz in a letter to Huygens, dated 26th April 1694, that Newton at that time was more convinced than ever of the truth of the emission theory.  " I have learned," says Leibnitz, "from Mr. Fatio,[1] by one of his friends, that Mr. Newton and he have been more than ever led to believe that light consists of bodies which come actually to us from the sun, and that it is in this way that they explain the different refrangibility of light and colours, as if there were primitive bodies

---

[1] Fatio D'huillier, the particular friend of Newton.

which always kept their colours, and which come materially
from the sun to us.    The thing is not impossible, but it appears
to me difficult to understand how by means of these little arrows
which, according to them, the sun darts, we can explain the
laws of refraction." [1]

[1] Huygenii *Exercitationes Mathematicæ, &c.*, Fascic. i. p. 173.

# CHAPTER VII.

Newton's Hypothesis of Refraction and Reflexion—Of Transparency and Opacity—
Hypothesis of Colours—The Spectrum supposed to be divided like a Musical String—
Incorrectness of this Speculation—Hooke's Observations on the Colours of thin Plates
explained by the Vibrations produced in the Ether by the luminous Corpuscle—
Hooke claims this Theory as contained in his Micrographia—Newton's Researches on
the Colours of Thin Plates—Previous Observations of Boyle—Hooke's elaborate Experiments on these Colours—His Explanation of them—Dr. Young's Observations upon
them—Newton acknowledges his Obligations to Hooke—Newton's Analysis of the
Colours seen between two Object-Glasses—Corrections of it by MM. Provostayes and
Desains—Newton's Theory of Fits of easy Reflexion and Transmission—Singular Phenomenon in the Fracture of a Quartz Crystal—Newton's Observations on the Colours
of Thick Plates—Recent Experiments on the same Subject.

IN the preceding chapter we have given an account of the
first part of Newton's discourse on light and colours, read on
the 9th December 1675, and explaining his hypothesis concerning " ether and ethereal substances, and their effects and uses."
In the second part of the portion read at the same meeting he
proceeds to " the consideration of light " as connected with the
supposed ether, that is to the cause of refraction, reflexion,
transparency, and opacity.

Regarding the ether as more dense in free space than in solid
bodies, and as diminishing in density towards their surface both
from without and from within, Newton supposes the incurvation or bending of a ray of light, incident on such a surface, in
one direction to produce refraction, and in another to produce
reflexion, to be effected within " the space of ether's graduated
rarity," or " physical superficies." In the case of refraction,
from air to glass, the ray passes from denser into rarer ether,

and is incurvated from the perpendicular in its passage through the physical superficies ; whereas in reflexion from a dense medium, such as glass into air, it is incurvated upwards or towards the glass, and the incurvation may be such that the ray does not emerge but suffer total reflexion.

In order to account by the agency of ether for the simultaneous refraction and reflexion of light incident upon the same surface of glass or water, Newton supposes " that ether in the confine of two mediums is less pliant and yielding than in other places, and so much the less pliant (or, ' more rigidly tenacious') by how much the mediums differ in density." When light therefore, that is small corpuscles, falls upon " this rigid resisting ethereal superficies, it puts it into a vibrating motion, so that *the ether therein is continually expanded and compressed by turns.*" When a ray of light is incident upon it " while it is much compressed, it is too dense and stiff to let the ray pass through, and so *reflects* it ; but the rays that are incident upon it at other times, when it is either expanded by the interval of two vibrations, or not too much compressed or condensed, go through and are *refracted.*"

When the ether. is of the same rarity in every pore, or when the ether is evenly spread by its continual vibrations into all the pores when they do not exceed a certain size, the light will pass freely through the body, or the body will be *transparent.* But when the pores exceed a certain size, the density of the ether will be greater than that which surrounds it, and the light being refracted or reflected at its superficies, the body will be *opaque.*

On the 16th December the second portion of Newton's discourse was read, in which he applies his hypothesis to the explanation of *colours.* For this purpose he supposes the particles of light to have different degrees of " bigness, strength, or power," *red* having the *largest,* and *violet* the *least* degree of any of these qualities. When light, therefore, is incident on the " refracting superficies," the smallest particles, namely, the violet, will be most incurvated or refracted, and the red the least ; and when these fall upon the refracting superficies of the retina, they will there excite " the sensation of various colours according to their bigness and mixture, the *biggest* with the *strongest* colours *reds* and *yellows*, the *least* with the *weakest blues* and *violets*, the *middle* with *green*, and a *confusion of all* with *white ;* much after the manner that in the sense of hearing, nature makes use of aërial vibrations of several bignesses to generate sounds of divers tones." Pursuing this idea, " the analogy of nature," he conjectures, " that colour may possibly be distinguished into its principal degrees, *red, orange, yellow, green, blue, indigo,* and *deep violet,* on the same ground that sound within an eighth is graduated into tones." In order to test this speculation by experiment, he forms a distinct spectrum, and, " because his own eyes are not very critical in distinguishing colour," he employs a friend to whom he has not communicated his thoughts, to measure the lengths of the different coloured spaces. The differences between the measures thus obtained, he says, " were but little, especially towards the red end, and taking means between these differences, the length of the image (reckoned not by the distance of the verges of the semicircular ends, but by the distance of the centres of those semicircles, or length of the strait sides as it ought to be) was divided *in about* the same proportion *that a string is between the end and the middle to sound the tones in the eighth.*"

Ingenious as this speculation is, it is contradicted by all the recent discoveries respecting the prismatic spectrum, of which we have given an account in a preceding chapter. It is not even true in the spectrum which Newton himself observed. There are not *seven* colours in any spectrum, and even if we divide it into such a number of parts, the divisions have no resemblance to those of a musical string.

From the explanation of colours produced by refraction, Newton proceeds to explain those produced by reflexion, namely, the colours of thin plates described by Hooke in his Micrographia.

In order to do this, he supposes that the ethereal vibrations excited by a ray move faster than the ray itself, and so " overtake and outrun it, one after another." When light, therefore, is incident upon a thin transparent plate, the waves, excited by its passage through the first surface, overtaking it one after another, till it arrive at the second surface, will cause it to be there reflected or refracted according as the condensed or the expanded part of the wave overtakes it there. If the plate be so thin that the condensed part of the first wave overtakes the ray at the second surface, it must be reflected there ; if *double* that thickness, so that the following rarified part of the wave, that is, the space between that and the next wave, overtake it, there it must be transmitted ; if *triple* the thickness, so that the condensed part of the *second* wave overtake it, there it must be reflected, and so where the plate is *five, seven,* or *nine* times that thickness, it must be *reflected* by reason of the *third, fourth,* or *fifth* wave overtaking it at the second surface ; but when it is *four, six,* or *eight* times that thickness, so that the ray may be overtaken there, by the dilated interval of those waves, it shall be *transmitted,* and so on ; the second surface being made able or unable to reflect according as it is condensed or expanded by the waves.

In this way he explains the coloured rings produced by pressing a convex lens against a plain glass ; and he concludes this portion of his discourse, namely, his " Hypothesis," by applying it to certain phenomena of Inflexion or Diffraction, as observed by Grimaldi.

It was after the reading of this portion of his discourse that Hooke said, " that the main of it was contained in his Micrographia, which Mr. Newton had only carried farther in some particulars,"—a remark which led to the correspondence with Oldenburg and Hooke, which we have given in the preceding chapter.

In the remainder of his discourse, Newton gives an account of his beautiful experiments on the colours of thin plates ; but before we enter upon their consideration, we must notice the previous observations of Boyle and Hooke, in order that we may apportion to Hooke and to Newton the discoveries which they actually made.  In the details into which this will lead us, we shall see two great minds striving for victory,—calling forth all their powers to surmount the difficulties which beset them in their path,—deviating from the rigorous process of research which both of them recognised, and perhaps forgetting, in the ardour of their pursuit, some of those courtesies which are now deemed essential in intellectual warfare.

In his book on Colours,[1] Mr. Boyle informs us, that divers, if not all essential oils, as also spirit of wine, when shaken, " have a good store of bubbles, which appear adorned with various and lively colours.'' He mentions also, that bubbles of soap and turpentine exhibit the same colours, which " vary according to the incidence of the sight and the position of the eye ;'' and he had seen a glass-blower blow bubbles of glass, which burst, and displayed " the varying colours of the rainbow, which were exceedingly vivid.''

In the year 1664, Hooke published, in his *Micrographia*,[2] a very interesting *chapter of the colours observable in Muscovy glass* (mica), *and other thin bodies*, in which he has described many new phenomena.

1. In several parts of plates of mica, he found white specks or flaws diversely coloured with all the colours of the rainbow, the colours being ranged in rings, encompassing, and having the same form as the speck.  The colours from the middle of the spot were *blue, purple, scarlet, yellow*, and *green*, the same series of colours recurring *nine* or *ten* times.

[1] Experiments and Observations touching Colours.  Exp xix. p. 243  London, 1064.
[2] " *Micrographia, or some Physiological Descriptions of Minute Bodies made by magnifying-glasses, with Observations and Inquiries thereupon.''  In many of the copies the date is 1667, but the title-page which bears this date was a trick of the printer, to indicate a second edition, which was never printed.  The imprimatur of the President of the Royal Society is Nov. 23, 1664.  See Ward's *Life of Hooke*, in the Lives of the Gresham Professors, p. 190.

2. By pressing together two pieces of plate-glass with his
forefingers and thumbs, he produced the same series of colours
as in mica, the colours changing with the thin plate of air
between the glasses. The same phenomena were produced by
placing different fluids between the plates, the colours being
more strong and vivid in proportion as the refractive power of
the fluids differed from that of the glass-plates.

3. If the plate of air or fluid is *thickest* in the middle like a
*convex* lens, or *thinnest* as in a *concave* lens, the colours will
also be produced, the order of colours in the *first* case being *red,
yellow, green, blue,* &c. ; and, in the *second,* quite *contrary.*

4. As the colours cease when the plates have a certain thickness, so they cease also when the plate has a certain thinness,
the colours ending in a white and colourless ring.

5. When we cleave a plate of mica with a needle, we shall
come to one of such a thickness as to exhibit a uniform colour,
every different degree of thinness below this giving a different
colour.

6. When *two* or *three* or more of these coloured plates are
laid one upon another, they exhibit such compound colours " as
one would scarce imagine would be the result of such ingredients." A faint *yellow,* for example, and a *blue,* may produce
a very deep *purple.*

7. The same coloured laminæ may be obtained by blowing
glass very thin ; and also from bubbles of pitch, rosin, colophony,
turpentine, solutions of gums, or any glutinous liquor, such as
wort, wine, spirit of wine, oil of turpentine, glare of snails, soap-
water, &c.

8. The same colours are produced upon polished steel by
gradually tempering or softening it with a sufficient degree of
heat. They are also produced on brass, copper, silver, gold, tin,
but most conspicuously upon lead ; and the colours that cover
the surface of the metal are nothing else than a very thin vitrified
part of the heated metal.

9. The same colours are exhibited in animal bodies, as in

pearls, mother-of-pearl shells, oyster shells, and almost all other kinds of stony shells. They are seen also in muscles and tendons.

10. If we take any glutinous substance, and run it exceedingly thin upon the surface of a smooth glass, or a polished metalline body, the same colours are produced; " and in general wheresoever you meet with a transparent body thin enough, that is terminated by reflecting bodies of differing refractions from it, there will be a production of these pleasing and lovely colours."

Such is a brief account of Hooke's elaborate inquiry into the colours of thin plates. We shall now consider the theory which he invented to explain them. He considers light as produced by "a very short vibrating motion propagated every way through a homogeneous medium by direct or straight lines extended every way like rays from the centre of a sphere, and with equal velocity, so that the pulse or vibration of the luminous body will generate a sphere which will continually increase, and grow bigger, just after the same manner (though indefinitely swifter) as the waves on the surface of the water do swell into bigger circles about a point of it where, by the sinking of a stone, the motion was begun ;—whence it necessarily follows, that all the parts of these spheres, undulated through a homogeneous medium, cut the rays at right angles." Our author then proceeds to explain how refraction and reflexion take place at the confines of media, in which the " fluid undulating substance " (or ether) has different densities.

In applying this theory to the explanation of the colours of thin plates, he considers it " most evident that the reflexion from the under or farther side of the body, is the principal cause of the production of these colours." Supposing a ray " to fall obliquely on the thin plate, part thereof is reflected back by the first superfices," but, as the body is transparent, another part of the ray is refracted by the first surface, reflected by the second, and refracted again by the first surface, so that after two refractions and one reflexion, there is propagated a kind of fainter ray, whose pulse, by reason of the time spent in passing and repassing between the two surfaces, comes behind the former reflected pulse, so that hereby (the surfaces being so near together that the eye cannot discriminate them from one) this confused or duplicated pulse, whose strongest part precedes, and whose weakest follows, does produce on the retina the sensation of a yellow.    If the two reflecting surfaces be yet farther removed asunder, then will the weaker pulse be so far behind, that it may be coincident with the second, third, fourth, fifth, &c., as the plate grows thicker ; " so that if there be a thin transparent body that, from the greatest thinness requisite to produce colours, does, in the manner of a wedge, by degrees grow to the greatest thickness that a plate can be of to exhibit a colour by the reflexion of light from such a body, there shall be generated such a consecution of colours, whose order, from the thin end towards the thick, shall be *yellow, red, purple, blue, green*, and these so often repeated, as the weaker pulse does lose pace with its primary or first pulse, and is coincident with a second, third, fourth, &c., pulse behind the first.    And this, as it is coincident, or follows from the first hypothesis I took of colours, so upon experiment have I found it in multitudes of instances that seem to prove it."

Dr. Thomas Young has quoted nearly the whole of these passages as such an approximation to the true explanation of the colours of thin plates, that if he had not satisfied himself respecting the phenomena of this class of colours, these passages would have led him earlier to a similar opinion.    The doctrine of interference is distinctly stated in them, and had Hooke adopted Newton's views of the different refrangibility of light, and applied them to his own theory of the coincidence of pulses, he would have left his rival behind in this branch of discovery.

Relying on the correctness of his views respecting the colours produced by *reflexion*, Hooke very ingeniously applied the same principle to the colours produced by *refraction :* and his objection to Newton's doctrine always was, that it was contrary to his theory. It is very obvious that hypotheses, however much they were abjured by the experimental philosophers of that day, were not only invented but admired ; and Newton was thus driven to propose a hypothesis to satisfy his friends, he himself declaring that he neither believed it, nor wished them to believe it.

When this hypothesis was read, Hooke, as we have already seen, stated " that the main of it was contained in his *Micrographia*, which Mr. Newton had only carried farther in some particulars." The reader will, we think, be able to judge, from our abstract of Hooke's theory and observations, of the truth of this remark. We think it substantially true, and do not hesitate to say, that Newton has not done justice to Hooke. Excepting once, in reference to the inflexion of light, Hooke's name is never mentioned. The results of his experiments are made use of, and his theory partly adopted and altered, without any acknowledgment of the one, or notice of the other. In his vindication, read on the 21st December 1675, Newton admits that he made use of some of Hooke's observations ; that he adopted the idea of a vibrating ether ; and he thanks him for his explanation of opacity, and for his notice of the colours of plated bodies. In his interesting letter to Hooke, which we have given in the preceding chapter, he goes much farther, acknowledging that Hooke had added much several ways to Descartes' theory, especially in considering the colours of thin plates, and giving him the credit of two important discoveries (which we do not find in the *Micrographia*), namely, the dilatation of the coloured rings by the obliquation of the eye, and the apparition of a black spot at the contact of two convex glasses, and at the top of a water bubble. In thus justifying the criticism of Hooke, and throwing some blame on Newton, we revert with pleasure to the noble amends which he made in his private letter, when there was no " intermeddling friend" to pervert the native generosity of his character.

We have hitherto considered only that part of Newton's discourse which contained his hypothesis, and its application to refraction, reflexion, transparency, and opacity. The remaining portions of it were read at the Royal Society on the 20th January, the 3d and the 10th February 1675-6, and contain all the optical discoveries of Newton.

The portion which was read on the 20th January, contains fifteen observations. In the first three of these he describes the arcs and circles of colours, which are exhibited by pressing together the imperfectly flat surfaces of two prisms. The place where they touched was absolutely transparent, appearing like a black spot " when looked upon," and " when looked through" it seemed like a hole in the thin plate of air between the prisms. The arcs and rings were generally of many colours, and about eight or nine in number. By turning the prisms about their common axis, the rings became black and white, and were sometimes about *thirty* in number. In order to see them distinctly, and without any other colour, it was necessary to hold the eye at a considerable distance from them, and also to view them through a slit or oblong hole narrower than the pupil of the eye.

In order to observe the order of the colours more correctly, and obtain measures of the rings at different thicknesses of the plate of air between the glasses, Newton took two object-glasses, the one a plano-convex for a *fourteen* feet telescope, and the other a large double convex for one of *fifty* feet, and having laid upon this the other with its plane side downwards, he pressed them slowly together, and observed the following orders of colours, next to the pellucid or dark central spot.

> Order 1st,—Dark spot, violet, blue, white, yellow, and red.
> Order 2d,—Violet, blue, green, yellow, and red.
> Order 3d,—Purple, blue, green, yellow, and red.
> Order 4th,—Green and red.

The succeeding orders became more and more imperfect, " till after three or four more revolutions they ended in perfect whiteness." [1]

When his eye was placed perpendicularly over the glasses, he found the diameter of the first six rings, at the most luminous " part of their orbits," to be, when squared in arithmetical progression of the odd numbers, 1, 3, 5, 7, 9, 11, and the diameter of the dark rings between the more luminous ones, when squared, to be in arithmetical progression of the even numbers, 2, 4, 6, 8, 10, 12. When the rings were viewed obliquely, they became bigger, as Hooke had observed, continually swelling as the eye was removed farther from their axis.

" By measuring the diameter of the same ring at several obliquities of the eye, partly by other means, as also by making use of the two prisms for very great obliquities," Newton found its diameter, and consequently the thickness of the air at its perimeter, to be " proportional to the secant of an angle whose sine is a certain mean proportional between the sines of incidence and refraction. And that mean proportional is the first of 106 arithmetical mean proportionals between the sines of incidence and refraction counted from the lesser sine, that is, from the sine of refraction when the refraction is made out of air into water, otherwise from the sine of incidence." [2]  That is, the angle to whose secant the thickness of the air is proportional, is one whose sine is to the sine of the real angle of incidence in the constant ratio of

$$\frac{106 + \frac{1}{m}}{107}$$

$m$ being the index of refraction of the glass.

In repeating the experiment with the light of a monochromatic lamp, and measuring the angles with great care, and at

<hr/>

[1] The reader will observe that the orders here given, and their colours, differ somewhat from those published nearly thirty years afterwards in his " Optics."

[2] *Optics*, Book ii. Part i. Obs. 7, 18.

incidences so great as 85° 21', MM. Provostayes and Desains obtained the following results. At an incidence of 85° 21 the diameter of the *seventh* black ring in millionths of a millimetre, was

| | | |
|---|---|---|
| By observation, · . . . | 47·53 |
| By Newton's Formula, . . | 40·11 |

According to the doctrine of interference, the thickness of the plate of air should be proportional to the secant of the angle of incidence, which, in the present case, would give 47·55 for the diameter of the seventh ring, a coincidence with the experiment so remarkable, as to leave no doubt of the truth of the theory.[1]

The difference between Newton's experiment and the result of theory, is so great as to call forth the remark from Sir John Herschel,[2] that " it might be drawn into an argument against the theory, were we sure that the law of refraction at extreme incidences, and with very thin laminæ, does not vary sensibly from that of the proportional sines." The important results obtained by MM. Provostayes and Desains will teach us rather to doubt the accuracy of an unconfirmed experiment, and carefully to repeat it, than to explain it by calling in question a well established law.

By various modes of observation, Newton found the following relations between the diameter of the rings and the thickness of the plate of air :—

Diameter of the ring, } 10, $10\frac{1}{13}$, $10\frac{1}{4}$, $10\frac{3}{4}$, $11\frac{2}{3}$, $12\frac{1}{2}$, 14, $15\frac{1}{4}$, $16\frac{3}{4}$, $19\frac{1}{4}$. $22\frac{5}{7}$, 29, **35.**

Thickness of the plate of air, } 10, $10\frac{2}{13}$, $10\frac{3}{4}$, $11\frac{1}{2}$, 13, $15\frac{1}{2}$, 20, $23\frac{1}{3}$, $28\frac{1}{2}$, 37, $52\frac{1}{4}$, 84, $122\frac{1}{2}$.

Our author next proceeded to examine the effects of homogeneous coloured light, and was thus led to more important results. In place of *eight* or *nine* rings which he saw in the open air, he now saw more than *twenty*. In *red* light the rings

1  *Comptes Rendus*, &c. &c., tom. xxv. p. 498.  1850
2  *Treatise on Light*, Art. 670.

were much *larger* than in *blue* and *violet*. The thickness of
the plate of air at which any red ring was produced, was to
that at which the same *violet* ring was produced, as *nine* to
*fourteen.* The rings were not of various colours, as before,
when white light was used, but of the prismatic colour which
was employed, and each ring was separated from the other by
a dark ring or space. Upon placing a white paper behind the
rings, Newton observed rings painted upon it of the same
colour with those which were reflected, and of the same size
as their intermediate dark space. Hence he concluded that
the light which fell on the dark spaces was transmitted through
the glasses without any change of colour, and that *the aërial
interval of the glasses according to its various thickness is disposed in some places to reflect, and in others to transmit, the
light of any colour, and in the same place to reflect one colour
where it transmits another.*

From the examination of the colours of thin plates of air,
Newton proceeded to that of the colours of thin plates of water,
as exhibited in the soap-bubble. Having covered the soap-
bubble with a glass shade, he saw its colours emerge in a
regular order, like so many concentric rings encompassing the
top of it. As the bubble grew thinner by the continual sub-
sidence of the water, the rings dilated slowly and overspread
the whole of it, descending to the bottom, where they vanished
successively. When the colours had all emerged from the top,
there arose in the centre of the rings a small round black spot,
like that in the centre of the rings formerly described, dilating
it to more than half an inch in breadth till the bubble burst.

Upon examining the rings between the object-glasses, Newton found that when they were only *eight* or *nine* in number,
more than *forty* could be seen by viewing them through a
prism ; and even when the plate of air seemed all over uniformly white, multitudes of rings were disclosed by the prism.
The same result was obtained with thin plates of water, mica,
and glass.

By means of these interesting observations, Newton proceeds to show how the system of coloured rings exhibited by white light, are produced by the superposition of the rings belonging to each separate colour in the spectrum, and he constructs a diagram, explaining a method of finding the colours of which the rings are composed at any distance from their centre. He then concludes this part of his discourse with a table showing, in millionths of an inch, the different thicknesses of plates of air, water, and glass, when they exhibit the different colours in the seven rings or orders of colours. The thicknesses, for example, of *air*, *water*, and *glass*, at which no light is reflected, or at which the black of the first ring is produced, are 2, $1\frac{1}{2}$, $1\frac{1}{4}$ millionths of an inch respectively, and the thicknesses at the margin of the seventh ring are 84, 63, and $54\frac{1}{2}$ millionths of an inch. This Table, which is known by the name of *Newton's Scale of Colours*, is of great value in all optical researches, and is constantly referred to by modern writers on Optics.

This celebrated discourse is concluded by nine propositions, showing how the phenomena of thin transparent plates stand related to the colours of all natural bodies, and how the size of the component parts of such bodies may be conjectured by their colours,—a subject which will be discussed in another chapter.

Such is a brief account of Newton's discoveries respecting the colours of thin plates, and of the hypothesis of ethereal vibrations, by which he proposed to explain them. The experiments from which they were deduced were all made previous to 1675 ; and it does not appear that, during the remaining fifty-two years of his life, he made any other communications on optical subjects to the Royal Society. In the preface to his Treatise on Optics, dated 1704, he tells us that "*part* of the ensuing discourse about light was written at the desire of some gentlemen of the Royal Society in the year 1675, and then sent to their secretary and read at their meetings ; and *the rest* was added about *twelve years after*, to complete the Theory, except the third book and the last proposition of the second, which were since put together out of scattered papers." These additions to the discourse, which were made in 1687, are no doubt his ampler discussion of the theory of the colours of natural bodies, and his theory of *fits of easy re1exion and easy transmission*, by which he explains the colours of thin plates ; and what was since put together out of scattered papers, was the first part of the third book on the *in1exion of light*, and the fourth part of the second book on the *colours of thick plates.* An explanation, therefore, of the theory of fits, will form an appropriate conclusion of our account of Newton's discoveries respecting the colours of thin plates.

In the propositions of his Optics, where he explains this theory, Newton does not attempt to assign any cause by which these fits are produced.   He does not inquire whether the kind of action or disposition in which they originate " consist in a circulating or vibrating motion of the ray or of the medium, or something else ;" but he says, that those who require a hypothesis, " which, whether it be true or false, he does not consider, may for the present adopt the one previously explained, in which the rays of light, by impinging on any refracting or reflecting surface, excite vibrations in the refracting or reflecting medium or substance," and that the ray is refracted or reflected according as it is in that part of the vibration which conspires with or impedes its motion.[1]   A popular idea may be formed of these fits of reflexion and transmission, by supposing that each particle of light, after its emission from a luminous body, revolves round an axis perpendicular to the direction of its motion, and presenting alternately to a refracting surface, which it approaches, an attractive and a repulsive pole, in virtue of which it will be refracted if the attractive pole is

---

[1] It is curious that Newton here makes no mention of an ethereal medium as that in which the vibrations are executed, as he does in his Hypothesis, formerly described. See p. 118.

nearest the refracting surface, and reflected if the repulsive pole is nearest that surface.

In order to explain this more clearly, let s be a ray of light which falls upon a trans-
parent surface MN, and is *transmitted* by that surface. It is obvious that it must have been nearer its fit of transmission than its fit of reflexion when it met the surface MN at T; but whether it was exactly in its fit of transmission, or a little way from it, the theory supposes that it is put by the action of the surface into the same state as if it had begun its fit of transmission at T. Let us now suppose that its fit of reflexion takes place at R, and that these fits

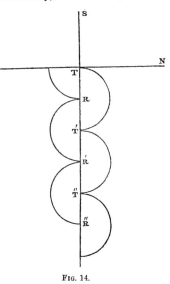

FIG. 14.

recur at T′, R′, T″, R″, &c., so that if there was a second trans-
parent surface at T′ or T″, the ray would be transmitted; and if there was a second transparent surface at R′, R″, it would be reflected. The spaces TT′, T′T″, are called the intervals of the fits of transmission, and the spaces RR′, R′R″, the intervals of the fits of reflexion. Now, as the spaces TT′ RR′ are equal for light of the same colour, it is obvious that the ray R will be transmitted, if the thickness of the body is TT′, TT″, &c., that is TT′, 2 TT′, 3 TT′, or any multiple whatever of TT′, the interval of a fit of easy transmission; and as TT′ is equal to RR′, the ray R will be reflected when the thickness of the body

is $\frac{1}{2}$ TT$'$, $1\frac{1}{2}$ TT$'$, $2\frac{1}{2}$ TT$'$, $3\frac{1}{2}$ TT$'$, &c.   If the body MN, therefore, were a plate with parallel surfaces, and if the eye were
placed above it so as to receive the rays reflected perpendicularly, it would in every case see the first surface MN by the
portion of light uniformly reflected from that surface ; but if
the thickness of the body were TT$'$, 2 TT$'$, 3 TT$'$, 4 TT$'$, or
1000 TT$'$, the eye would receive no rays from the second surface, because they would be all transmitted ; and, in like
manner, if the thickness were $\frac{1}{2}$ TT$'$, $1\frac{1}{2}$ TT$'$, $2\frac{1}{2}$ TT$'$, or
$1000\frac{1}{2}$ TT$'$, the eye would receive all the light reflected from
the second surface, because it would be all reflected.   When
this reflected light meets the first surface MN, on its way back
from the second surface, it will be all transmitted, because it is
then in its fit of transmission.   At intermediate thicknesses,
such as $\frac{3}{4}$ TT$'$, a portion only of the light will be reflected from
the second surface, increasing as the thickness increased from
TT$'$ to $1\frac{1}{2}$ TT$'$, and diminishing again as the thickness increased
from $1\frac{1}{2}$ TT$'$ to 2 TT$'$.

Let us now suppose that the plate whose surface is MN has

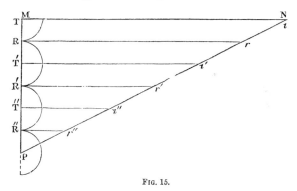

FIG. 15.

its thickness varying like a wedge MNP, *Fig.* 15, and that the
eye is placed above it to receive the light which it reflects.

The interval of the fits being TT′, RR′, as before, it is evident that, near the point N, the light that falls upon the second surface $t$P, will be transmitted, because it is in a fit of transmission, but at the thickness TR the light will be reflected from the second surface at $r$, because it is then in a fit of reflexion, and again transmitted in returning through the first surface MN. In like manner, the light will be transmitted at $t′$ and $t″$, and reflected at $r′$ and $r″$, so that the observer will see a series of dark and luminous bands, the middle of the dark ones being at $t$, $t′$, $t″$, and of the luminous ones at $r$, $r′$, $r″$.

Let us now suppose that the figure is adapted to *red* light ; then since the length of a fit is *greatest* in *red*, *least* in *violet*, and of an intermediate size in *yellow* light, it is obvious that in *yellow* light there will be a set of dark and luminous bands less than those in the figure, and in violet light another set less than in the yellow. When, therefore, the light incident on the plate is white, all these bands will be superimposed, and form the coloured bands already described. When the thin plate is wedge-shaped, the bands will be parallel. When it has the form of a concave lens, like air or vacuity between two object-glasses, the bands will be circular, with the lowest tints in the centre. When it has the form of a convex lens, like the plates of air in mica, the bands will also be circular, with the lowest tints at the margin ; and when the thin plate has different thicknesses like a film of blown glass, the bands will have no regular shape, the same thickness giving always the same colour.

The preceding doctrine of fits has always been regarded as an ingenious explanation of the colours of thin plates. It is not given by its author as a theory or a hypothesis, but simply as an expression of the facts which he has observed ; and yet it has to a certain extent the character of a hypothesis, in so far as it assumes that the second surface of the plate does not in every part of it reflect light like the first, whereas in the theory of interference, certain portions thus reflected are destroyed before they reach the eye of the observer.

With the exception of the interesting observations of MM. Provostayes and Desains already referred to, no discovery of any great importance has been made on the subject of thin plates since the time of Newton. We have had occasion to observe a number of curious phenomena in the thin plates of decomposed glass when acting upon light in a state of combination. The colours which they reflect and transmit are not deducible from any theory of light, and have an intimate connexion with the absorption of light by coloured media.[1]

Among natural phenomena illustrative of the colours of thin plates, we have found none more remarkable than one exhibited by the fracture of a large crystal of quartz of a smoky colour, and about two and a quarter inches in diameter. The surface of fracture, in place of being a face of cleavage, or irregularly conchoidal, as we have sometimes seen it, was filamentous like a surface of velvet, and consisted of short fibres so small as to be incapable of reflecting light. Their size could not have been greater than the third of the millionth part of an inch, or one-fourth of the thinnest part of the soap-bubble when it exhibits the black spot where it bursts.[2]

Although Newton did not communicate his observations on the colours of *thick plates* to the Royal Society in his discourse on light and colours, but " put them together out of scattered papers" some time before the publication of his Optics,[3] yet this is the proper place for bringing them under the notice of the reader.

The colours of thick plates arise from a quantity of light scattered in all directions from the little inequalities or imperfections which exist in the surface of a glass mirror either silvered or unsilvered. In order to observe them, a sunbeam is

---

[1] " On the Connexion between the Phenomena of the Absorption of Light and the Colours of Thin Plates."—*Phil. Trans.* 1837, p. 245.

[2] *Edinburgh Journal of Science,* vol. i. p. 108.   June 1824.

[3] These observations, thirteen in number, entitled, " *Observations concerning the Reflections and Colours of thick transparent polished Plates,* form the fourth part of the Second Book of Optics.

admitted through a small hole about a third of an inch in diameter into a dark room.   This beam is received perpendicularly
on a concavo-convex glass mirror, a quarter of an inch thick,
and having each surface ground to a sphere six feet in radius.
When the sunbeam passes through a small hole in the middle
of a sheet of white paper placed in the centre of the mirror's
concavity, the whole is surrounded with four or five coloured
rings.   The rings resembled those seen by transmission through
two object-glasses, but were larger and fainter in their colours.
When mirrors of different thicknesses were used, the diameters
of the rings were reciprocally as the square roots of the thicknesses ; and in homogeneous light they were largest in the
red, and smallest in the violet rays, like those formed by thin
plates.

These and other phenomena described by Newton, he explains by taking into consideration the fits of easy reflexion
and transmission of the faint scattered light already mentioned.
On the undulatory theory they are explained by the interference
of the portions of light scattered at the first surface by the rays
in passing and repassing through it.

The Duke de Chaulnes[1] observed similar rings when the
surface of the mirror was covered with fine gauze, or with a
thin film of milk dried upon it, and Sir William Herschel[2]
noticed analogous colours when hair-powder was scattered in
the air before a metallic mirror, on which a beam of light was
incident.

When we look through two plates of parallel glass of exactly
the same thickness, at a circular disc of light 1° or 2° in diameter, no coloured bands will be seen when the light is incident
perpendicularly, and when the plates are parallel.   But if we
incline them slightly to one another, we shall see, beside the
direct image of the luminous body which is crossed with no
fringes, a series of lateral images formed by successive reflexions
between the surfaces of the plates, which are crossed with

[1] *Mém. Acad. Par.* 1705.                    [2] *Phil. Trans.* 1807.

fifteen or sixteen highly coloured bands parallel to the common section of the surfaces of the plates. The breadth of these bands is inversely as the inclination of the plates, and at a given inclination their magnitudes are inversely as the thickness of the plates employed.

These brilliant bands, which we have described minutely in a separate memoir,[1] are explicable by the doctrine of fits of easy reflexion and transmission. They have been explained also on the undulatory hypothesis by Dr. Thomas Young,[2] and in greater detail by Sir John Herschel.[3]

Another species of coloured fringes, produced by the reflexion of a pencil of light between the lenses of a double or a triple achromatic object-glass, is equally explicable by Newton's theory of fits, and by the doctrine of interference. Owing to the curvature of the surfaces which produce them, the forms of the isochromatic lines, or the lines of equal tint, are various and beautiful.[4]

[1] *Edinburgh Transactions*, 1815, vol. vii. p. 435.
[2] Art. CHROMATICS in *Encyclopædia Britannica*.
[3] *Treatise on Light*, § 688-695.
[4] *Edinburgh Transactions*, 1832, vol. xii.

# CHAPTER VIII.

Influence of Colour in the Material World—Newton's Theory of the Colours of Natural Bodies—Coloured Bodies reflect only Light of their own Colour, absorbing all the other parts of White Light—The Colours of Natural Bodies are those of Thin Plates —The Transparent Parts reflecting one Colour and transmitting another—Arrangement of the Colours exhibited in Natural Bodies into Seven Classes—Coloured Juices and Solutions, Oxidated Films, Metals, &c. &c.—Newton's Theory applicable only to one Class of Colours—Objections to it stated—M. Jamin's Researches on the Colours of Metals—The Cause of Colours must be in the Constitution of Bodies—Examples of the effect of Heat upon Rubies and Nitrous Gas—Effect of Sudden Cooling—On Phosphorus—Effect of Mechanical Action on Iodide of Mercury—Indication of a New Theory—And of the Cause of the Absorption of Definite Rays—Illustration of these views in a remarkable Tourmaline.

HAD the objects of nature been rendered visible only by white light, and exercised upon it the same action in refracting and reflecting it to the human eye, all the combinations in the material world, and all the various forms of life, would have displayed no other tint than that which they exhibit in a pencil sketch, a China-ink drawing, or a photographic picture. The magnificent foliage of the vegetable world might have filled the eye with its picturesque and lovely forms, and given protection to its fruit and its flowers, but we should not have rejoiced in the verdure of its youth, nor mourned over the yellow of its age. The sober mantle of twilight would have replaced the golden vesture of the rising and the setting sun. The stars would have twinkled colourless in a grey sky, and the rainbow would have dwindled into a narrow arch of dusky light. The diamond, the ruby, and the sapphire might have displayed to science the nice geometry of their forms, and yielded to the arts their adamantine virtues ; but they would have ceased to sparkle in the chaplet of beauty, or adorn the diadem of princes. The human face divine might have expressed all the qualities of the mind, and beamed with all the affections of the heart ; but the purple light of love would not have risen on the cheek of beauty, nor the hectic flush have heralded its decay. Life would have breathed and perished in its pale marble ; and nature would have sprung and decayed in its russet brown. The material world, however, has been otherwise framed, and those exquisite models of organic and inorganic life, into which the great sculptor has chiselled the furniture of his terrestrial temple, have been enhanced by that ethereal beauty which the play of light and colour can alone impart.

Many attempts were made previous to the time of Newton, to explain the colours of natural bodies ; but they all necessarily failed, while philosophers were ignorant of the true nature of colours themselves. In his earliest communications to the Royal Society, Newton had clearly indicated his views respecting the colours of natural bodies ; and after showing " that they appear of divers colours, according as they are disposed to reflect most copiously the rays endued by these colours," he proceeds, in the last part of his " Discourse," read to the Royal Society on the 10th February 1675-6, to consider " the constitution of bodies on which their colours depend." This curious subject continued to occupy the attention of Newton, and he enters upon it more fully in two different parts of his *Optics*, where " by the discovered properties of light he explains the permanent colours of natural bodies,"[1] and points out the " analogy between such colours, and the colours of thin transparent plates."[2]

After showing that all bodies, whatever were their colours, exhibited these colours best in white light, or in light which contained their peculiar colour, he proves by experiment, that when coloured bodies are illuminated with homogeneous *red*

[1] *Optics*, Book i. Part ii. Prop. 10.      [2] *Optics*, Book ii. Part iii.

light, they appear *red*, with homogeneous *blue* light, *blue*, and so on, " their colours being most brisk and vivid under the influence of their own daylight colours." The leaf of a plant, for example, appeared *green* in the white light of day, because it had the property of reflecting *green* light in greater abundance than any other. When the leaf was placed in homogeneous *red* light, it no longer appeared *green*, because there were no green rays in the red ; but it reflected red light in a small degree, because there were some red rays in the compound green, which it had the property of reflecting. If the leaf had originally reflected a pure homogeneous green, unmixed with red, and reflected no white light (as all leaves do) from its outer surface, it would have appeared quite black, in pure homogeneous red light, as this light does not contain a single ray which the leaf is capable of reflecting. Hence it follows that the colours of natural bodies are owing to the property which they possess of stopping or absorbing certain rays of white light, while they reflect or transmit to the eye the rest of the rays of which white light is composed. The *green* leaf, for example, stops or absorbs the red, blue, and violet rays of the white light which falls upon it, and reflects and transmits only those which compose its peculiar green.

To this extent the views of Newton are demonstrable, and have been universally adopted ; but when he attempts to determine the manner in which the colour of any body is insulated from the other colours which fall upon it, and in which these other colours are stopped or lost, or, in other words, the physical constitution of natural bodies by which these processes are effected, he enters the region of hypothesis and fails in bringing conviction to the mind. His theory, however, is grand and imposing, but standing as it does, and as we shall presently show, on a perishable basis, it must soon be swept away in the progress of optical discovery.

The following are the principles on which this theory is founded.

1. Bodies that have the highest refractive powers, reflect the greatest quantity of light from their surfaces, and at the confines of equally refracting media there is no reflexion.

2. The least parts of almost all natural bodies are in some measure transparent.

3. Between the parts of opaque and coloured bodies, are many spaces or pores, either empty or filled with media of other densities.

4. The parts of bodies and their interstices or pores must not be less than of some definite bigness, to render them coloured.

5. The transparent parts of bodies, according to their several sizes, reflect rays of one colour, and transmit those of another, on the same grounds that thin plates do reflect or transmit these rays.

6. The parts of bodies on which their colours depend, are denser than the medium which pervades their interstices.

7. The bigness of the component parts of natural bodies may be conjectured by their colours.

In illustration of the *fifth*, or leading proposition of the theory, Newton remarks, " that if a thinned or plated body, which being of an even thickness, appears all over of one uniform colour, should be slit into threads or broken into fragments of the same thickness with the plate, he sees no reason why every thread or fragment should not keep its colour, and by consequence why a heap of those threads or fragments should not constitute a mass or powder of the same colour which the plate exhibited before it was broken. And the parts of all natural bodies being like so many fragments of a plate, must on the same grounds exhibit the same colours."

In order to prove this, Newton proceeds to describe various kinds of colours, to which he considers the theory specially applicable ; but before we follow him in this investigation, we must endeavour to classify all the varieties of colours which are exhibited in the natural world.

Colours may be arranged into *seven* classes, in each of which the colour has a different origin.

1. Transparent coloured fluids, such as the juices obtained from the coloured parts of plants, and coloured solutions, whether natural or artificial. Transparent coloured solids, such as coloured minerals, glasses, powders, and vegetable tissues.

2. Oxidated films on metals—colours of precious and hydrophanous opal—of Labrador felspar—of the feathers of birds—of the wings, &c., of insects—of the scales of fishes—of the tapetum of animals—of the *internal* films of mother-of-pearl and various shells—and of decomposed glass.

3. Superficial colours of mother-of-pearl, striated and grooved surfaces, which can be communicated by pressure to other surfaces.

4. Opalescences, or colours dispersed from the particles of different solid and fluid and gaseous bodies, some of which are coloured, and others colourless. These colours appear in ice, in water, in the atmosphere—in fluorspar and several glasses—in solutions of sulphate of quinine, &c., and in the juices of plants and several oils.

5. At the surfaces of media of different dispersive powers, and in which the index of refraction is the same in each medium for certain rays, but different for all the rest.

6. The colours produced by heat, and during combustion.

7. The colours of metals.

The colours referred to in the *first* of these classes are represented by red and yellow wines—by the coloured fluids shown in the windows of the apothecary—by the green leaves of plants—by the ruby, the cairngorm, the topaz, and the sapphire—and by the powders of cinnabar, red lead, ultramarine, sulphur, &c.

In all these bodies Newton supposes that the colour peculiar to each, namely, that which passes through its substance, is the *tint* reflected from the minute particles of which it is composed, the opposite or complementary tint, which is transmitted by the particles being lost within the body by a multitude of internal

reflexions.  In the *ruby*, for example, the particles are supposed
to have such a size as to appear *red* by reflexion, and the *green*
light which' would be seen by transmission through a single
particle, is supposed to be lost by repeated reflexions within the
body composed of such particles.  If we now examine the *ruby*,
or any other coloured solid or fluid, we shall find that neither
*red* nor *green* light is reflected from any of its external surfaces,
or any of its internal parts.  The *red* light which characterizes
the body is seen *only* by transmission through its substance.
If we now analyze the *red* light by the prism, we shall find that
it has not the composition of any of the red rings in Newton's
scale of colours.

In the case of the *ruby*, which we have purposely selected,
we are able to apply another test, and one which Newton himself authorizes, when he remarks that changes of colour may be
produced by the swelling or shrinking of the tinging corpuscles.
In subjecting the *balas ruby* to a high degree of heat, which
must have had the effect of swelling the tinging corpuscles, I
found that it became *green*, which, as the cooling advanced,
gradually faded into *brown*, the ruby resuming its original
brilliant *red* when it had returned to its former temperature.
Berzelius observed an analogous fact in the *spinelle* of Ceylon
and Aker, which became *brown* by heat, then *black*, and *opaque*
as the heat increased.  Upon returning to its former temperature, it passed through a fine *chrome green* before it recovered
its *red* colour.  Hence it is obvious that these colours and
changes of transparency, which have no relation to those of
thin plates, could not have arisen from the gradual swelling and
subsequent shrinking of tinging corpuscles.

A still more striking proof of the want of analogy between
the colours of natural bodies and those of thin plates, may be
obtained from the prismatic analysis of certain colours in which
Newton himself believed that analogy to exist.  A *green* of the
*third* order of colours is, as he observes, " constituted principally of original *green*, but not without a mixture of some *blue*

and *yellow*," and contains not a single ray of *orange, red, indigo*, or *violet*.   He considers the *green* of all vegetables, to be a green of the *third* order, not only because this green is the purest and most intense in colour, but because when vegetables wither, some of them turn to a *greenish yellow*, and others to a more perfect *yellow* or *orange*, or perhaps to *red*, passing first through all these intermediate colours.   " Now," he adds, " the *green* is *without doubt* one of the same orders with those colours into which it changeth, because the changes are gradual, and those colours, though usually not very full, yet are often too full and lively to be of the *fourth* order."   These changes from *green* to *red*, he considers as " effected by the exhaling of the moisture which may leave the tinging corpuscles more dense, and something augmented by the accretion of the oily and earthy part of that moisture."

In order to put these opinions to the test of direct experiment, we examined the brilliant *green juice* extracted by alcohol from the leaves of twenty different plants, and also the same juice when taken from the leaves in their yellow, orange, and red state, and found that their composition had not the least resemblance to that of the colours of any order whatever, and least of all to those of the *greens* of the third order.   The spectrum obtained from a sunbeam passing through these juices is one of singular beauty, divided by dark spaces into several coloured bands of unequal breadths, and possessing all the colours which ought not to exist in the green of the third order.   When the green fluid thus analyzed has stood for three or four days it loses its bright green colour, and becomes of an *olive green*, which grows more and more of a *brownish yellow*, till it becomes almost *colourless*, a series of changes which have no relation whatever to the effects that might be expected to arise from an increase or decrease in the density or size of the tinging corpuscles.

In some plants the green leaf decays in a different manner from that described by Newton.   In place of becoming *yellow*, the green leaves of the privet become of a deep *black violet*, when they wither ; a colour which has no resemblance whatever to any of the colours of thin plates.   The fluid obtained from these violet leaves was of a *deep red colour*,—much deeper than that of the *darkest port wine*.   It divided the red space of the spectrum into two red bands, absorbed the violet and blue spaces generally, and obliterated the middle of the green space.   Its action was so different from that of the green juice, that the two tints had no resemblance to those of adjacent colours of the same order.[1]

The pale *blue* of the sky is regarded by Newton as a blue of the first order, produced by the minute particles of " vapours which have not arrived at that grossness which is requisite to reflect other colours ;" and while he considers the *whiteness* of froth, paper, linen, &c., as that which arises " from a mixture of the colours of several orders," that is, from the action of particles of a much greater size than those of vapours which produce the blue of the first order.   Now, it is obvious that *froth*, when seen under a clear blue sky, must have the colour of the sky itself, as it is nothing more than an accumulation of images of the sky reflected from the innumerable aqueous vesicles which compose it.   The colour of froth, wherever it is placed, must be the average tint of all the differently coloured rays which fall upon it and are reflected to the eye.

The colours referred to in the *second* class are undoubtedly analogous to those of thin plates.   Newton has himself mentioned the colours of the feathers of some birds as those of thin plates, and the fine colours of the diamond and other beetles obviously have the same origin.   The splendid colours of the tapetum, or membrane behind the retina of animals, afford an interesting example of this class of colours.   Even when the membrane has been taken out, it exhibits the most beautiful colours by reflexion, but it becomes absolutely black

[1] A full account of these experiments, with coloured drawings of the spectra, will be found in the *Edinburgh Transactions*, 1833, vol. xii. pp. 538-545.

when dry.   The colours, however, may be revived by moisture, and, after remaining in the dry state for upwards of twenty years, we have succeeded in restoring the colours by steeping the membrane in warm water.   The black passes into a bright *blue*, the *blue* into *green*, and the *green* into *greenish yellow*.

In placing the internal colours of mother-of-pearl under this class, we must carefully distinguish them from the external colours communicable to wax.   By reducing the mother-of-pearl to exceedingly thin plates, we are able to exhibit the action of the colorific films which they enclose, and which, like those of thin plates, give one colour by reflexion, and its complementary colour by transmission.[1]

The splendid colours exhibited by decomposed glass, both in the light which it reflects and transmits, belong also to colours of the second class ; and though they are clearly those of thin plates, yet they exhibit peculiarities when produced by a great number of films, which place them in a certain interesting relation with the colours of the first class.[2]

The colours of Labrador felspar, and of precious and hydrophanous opal, which we have shown to be produced by thin plates and minute pores and tubes, belong also to the second class of colours.[3]

The superficial colours which we have placed in the *third* class, have obviously no relation whatever to the colours of thin plates.   They are spectra produced by interference, and, had he been acquainted with them, they would have been regarded by Newton himself as inexplicable by his theory.[4]

The very remarkable colours produced by internal dispersion, and which have recently excited so much interest from the discoveries of Professor Stokes, form a *fourth* class, which has

[1] See *Phil. Trans.* 1814, p. 397 ; and 1836, pp. 55, 56.
[2] See Layard's *Discoveries in the Ruins of Nineveh*, 1853, pp. 674-676 ; and *Phil. Trans.* 1837, p. 249.
[3] See *Edinburgh Transactions*, 1829, vol. xi. p. 322 ; and *Reports of the British Association*, 1844, p. 9.
[4] See *Phil. Trans.* 1814, p. 397 ; and 1829, p. 301.

not been identified with those of thin plates. The light thus dispersed must be reflected, in cases of ordinary opalescence, from the faces of minute pores in solids, or from particles of different densities disseminated through solids or suspended in fluids. The beautiful colours exhibited by fluor spar, by solutions of the sulphate of quinine, and various other solids and fluids, are emanations of a phosphoric nature, generated by certain rays in the solar spectrum, and have therefore no analogy with the colours of thin plates. These emanations have all colours,—*red* in the alcoholic juices of leaves, *violet, blue, pink*, and *whitish* in fluor spar, *sky-blue* in sulphate of quinine, bright *green* in alcoholic solutions of the *colchicum autumnale*, and in various glasses and oils, and *violet* in an alcoholic solution of guiacum.[1]

In the *fifth* class we have placed a new species of colours which we discovered many years ago, and which we believe have never been studied, or even alluded to by any other person. In the year 1814, when investigating the law of polarization for light reflected at the separating surface of different media, we had occasion to enclose oil of cassia between two flint-glass prisms, and were surprised to observe that the colour of the reflected light was *blue*. The cause of this we had some difficulty in discovering. The refractive power of oil of cassia exceeds greatly that of flint-glass for the mean rays of the spectrum, while the action of the two bodies on the less refrangible rays is nearly the same. Hence the *red* rays must be in a great measure *transmitted*, while there will be reflected a small portion of the *orange*, a greater portion of the *yellow*, and a much greater proportion of the *blue* and *violet*, so that the colour of the pencil, formed by reflexion, must necessarily be *blue*, mixed with some of the less refrangible rays.

By employing different kinds of glass, and different oils, we

[1] See *Edinburgh Transactions*, 1833, vol. xii. p. 542; and 1846, vol. xvi. p. 111; *Reports of the British Association*, 1838, pp. 10-12; *Phil. Trans.* 1845, p. 143; and 1852, p. 463.

obtained various analogous results, in which rays of different
colours were extinguished from the reflected pencil according to
the part of the spectrum where an equilibrium had been established between the refractive powers of the media in contact.
When the refractive indices were equal in the *blue* rays, the
colour of the reflected pencil was *yellow.*  As the indices of
refraction are the same for all obliquities of incidence,[1] the tint
of the reflected pencil, though it must vary in intensity, can
never vary in colour; and as that colour is abstracted from the
white incident light, its complementary tint must appear, however faintly, in the transmitted pencil.   Hence it follows as a
general result, that as all reflecting surfaces are the separating
surfaces of two media, the pencils which they reflect and transmit must necessarily have a different tint from the incident
pencil, excepting in the extreme case, and one not known to
exist, where the two bodies in contact have the same refractive
power, or the same differences of refractive power for every ray
of the spectrum.

Hitherto we have supposed the *irrationality* of the coloured
spaces to be *simple,* but it may be *compound,* and there may
be *two, three,* or more points in the spectrum of two adjacent
media where the indices of refraction are the same, or have
equal differences, while in other points they are not the same,
or have their differences unequal.   In these cases the reflected
and transmitted tints will be compound ; but as such colours
have not been observed, it would be out of place to make any
farther reference to such a supposition.   It may be sufficient to
remark, that even if we never discover spectra of such a character, they may exist in the refractions at the separating surfaces of the tinging corpuscles of Newton, and the media which
fill their interstices.

In the *sixth* class of colours may be ranked those produced

---

[1] In his Memoir on Diffraction, Fresnel has thrown out the idea that, at great incidences, and with very thin laminæ, the law of refraction may not follow the proportionality of the sines.

by heat in metals and other substances, the colours of different
bodies in combustion, and those exhibited in the deflagration of
metals.   There is no reason to believe that any of these colours
have the slightest analogy with those of thin plates, and their
nature and origin remain to be investigated.

The colours of metals, which form the *seventh* class in our
enumeration, have been referred by Newton to those of thin
plates, but without any plausible reason.   The polarization of
light by metallic bodies required to be investigated before the
problem of their colour could be solved, and we owe its solution
to the recent and beautiful researches of M. Jamin.   As it would
be foreign to the character of the present work to give an
account of the process by which M. Jamin obtained his results,
we must content ourselves with presenting them in the following
Table :—

COLOURS AFTER ONE REFLEXION.

| | | | | | D. | | C. |
|---|---|---|---|---|---|---|---|
| Copper, | . . . | Orange, very red, | . . | 69° | 56' | 0·113 |
| Brass, | . . . . | Yellow, | . . . . | 103 | 13 | 0·112 |
| Bell metal, | . . . | Orange, yellow, . | . . | 83 | 10 | 0·065 |
| Speculum metal, | . . | Orange, very red, | . . | 67 | 25 | 0·027 |
| Zinc, | . . . . | Blue, . . . . | . . | 180 | 57 | 0 021 |
| Silver, | . . . . | Orange, yellow, . | . . | 89 | 00 | 0·013 |
| Steel, | . . . . | White, | . . . . | — | — | —— |

COLOURS AFTER TEN REFLEXIONS.

| | | | | | D. | | C. |
|---|---|---|---|---|---|---|---|
| Copper, | . . . | Red, middle, | . . . | 42° | 29' | 0·812 |
| Brass, | . . . | Orange, very red, | . . | 62 | 50 | 0·349 |
| Bell metal, | . . . | Red, . . . . | . . | 40 | 40 | 0·767 |
| Speculum metal, | . . | Red, orange, | . . . | 53 | 59 | 0·292 |
| Zinc, | . . . . | Blue, indigo, | . . . | 267 | 58 | 0.188 |
| Silver, | . . . . | Orange, yellow, . | . . | 84 | 32 | 0·124 |
| Steel, | . . . . | White, | . . . . | — | — | —— |

The numbers in the column marked D are the distances of
the tint of the metal from the red end of the spectrum, whose
whole length is 360° ; and those under the letter C are the
intensities of the tints, that of the incident *white* light being
1·000.

After a careful study of these different classes of colours, philosophers will have no hesitation in concluding that Newton's theory of the colours of natural bodies has only a limited application, and that instead of any general theory such as he contemplated, we must look for a separate explanation of the different classes of phenomena.  The *first* class of our enumeration, which comprehends the largest number of coloured bodies, is the one which presents the greatest difficulty to philosophers; and to it the Newtonian hypothesis is certainly inapplicable. Within the solids, fluids, and gases of this class, certain rays of the intromitted pencil are absorbed or lost, while others are transmitted, or, what is the same thing, the coloured body has different degrees of transparency for different rays, being opaque for different portions of the spectrum at different thicknesses ; whereas, in colourless bodies, the rays are absorbed in equal proportions, so that the transmitted beam emerges colourless. The colour of a body, therefore, is not produced by particles having the same colour as itself, but it is the colour which arises from the mixture of all the transmitted rays, and these rays proceed from every part of the spectrum, though in different proportions.  Hence we must look for the cause of the colour in the constitution of the body itself, that is, in the manner in which its atoms are combined, and not in the size or nature of the atoms themselves.

In support and in illustration of this opinion, we may mention a few remarkable examples, in which the colour is changed by a change in the condition of its particles.  The most remarkable of these is *nitrous gas*.  This body is almost transparent in small thicknesses, and at low temperatures.  By heating it, its colour becomes in succession *straw yellow, orange, red,* and even absolutely *black.*[1]  When *phosphorus,* which in its ordinary state is of a *pale yellow* colour, is melted and thrown into cold water, it becomes *black,* and recovers its original colour when again melted.  It is therefore obvious, that in both these cases the blackness could not be produced by any diminution in the size

[1] See *Edinburgh Transactions,* vol. xii. p. 523.

of the particles. A similar change of colour is produced by simple mechanical pressure on the crystals of *iodide of mercury*, which change their colour by simply pricking them with a sharp point.

The various phenomena of colour in crystallized bodies, and the influence of the continued action of light upon coloured substances, indicate the existence of different causes of colour ; and the influence of structure, as one of these causes, is finely shown in the relation of the colours of dichroitic crystals to their axes of double refraction or crystallization.

The great diversity in the constitution of coloured bodies is peculiarly shown in the diversity of their action on the different rays of the spectrum ; and it is therefore probable that the cause of their difference of colour may be found in the diversity of action exercised upon light by their particles or elementary atoms. In describing the colours of the *fifth* class, we have already mentioned an experiment with flint glass and oil of cassia, and its indication of a new theory of the colours of natural bodies of the first class. In Fraunhofer's spectrum, the principal black lines which it contains are represented by the letters A, B, C, D, E, F, G, H, I ;—AI being nearly the whole of its length. If $a$, $b$, $c$, $d$, $e$, $f$, $g$, $h$, $i$, represent the same lines in a spectrum of equal length formed by any fluid or solid different from that which produces the spectrum A I, then though $ai$ be equal to A I, it frequently happens, and we venture to say, always happens, that $ab$ is not equal to A B, nor $cf$ to C F, while $ac$ may be equal to A C, and $dh$ to D H. The equal spectra may coincide in particular points, that is, individual lines in the one, indicating particular colours, may coincide with individual lines marking the same colours in the other spectrum, and yet other lines may not coincide, indicating different colours. When a ray of white light, therefore, is incident on the separating surface of the two media which give these two spectra, a very large portion, or rather the whole of the colours, indicated by the coincident lines, will be transmitted, while a very small portion of the colours indicated by the non-coincident lines will be reflected, the greatest quantity of the colours being reflected where the non-coincidence is greatest, and the greatest quantity being transmitted at the points of coincidence. Where there are many separating surfaces, and many elements in the body, the spectrum obtained by the prismatic analysis of the transmitted light will be cut up by obscure portions exactly as it is found to be in all coloured media.

When the constitution of any coloured body is altered by heat or pressure, the refractive and dispersive powers of its elements are changed, and the resulting colour altered, according to the ratio in which the refracting forces are changed in the elementary molecules. Changes of this kind are finely exhibited in the growth of certain coloured crystals. In the *tourmaline*, for example, we have sometimes a *red* nucleus which absorbs one of the doubly refracted pencils, namely, the *green* one, and transmits only the *red*. When this nucleus was completed, some change had taken place in the circumstances under which the crystallization was proceeding, and the molecules, though still combining as tourmaline, combine in such a manner as to produce no colour—no difference in the tint of the pencils—and no absorption of one of them. At a subsequent stage, the structure which produces the red colour again appears and disappears, forming in succession coloured and colourless laminæ round the original nucleus !

Another example of great interest is afforded by certain specimens of *fluor spar*, in which the colours of the *fourth* class are produced.[1] The structure which produces a white phosphorescence, is succeeded by one which produces a coloured phosphorescence, and this again by a structure which produces no phosphorescence at all. The changes of structure to which these different effects are owing, arise, in all probability, from a change in the arrangement of the atoms in the molecular groups of which the body is composed.

1 See *Edinburgh Transactions,* vol. xvi. p. 112.

# CHAPTER IX.

Newton's Discoveries on the Inflexion of Light—Previous Researches of Hooke—Newton's Animadversions on them offensive to Hooke—Newton's Theory of Inflexion as described by Grimaldi, having made no experiments of his own—Discoveries of Grimaldi, which anticipate those of Hooke—Hooke suggests the Doctrine of Interference—Newton's Experiments on Inflexion—His Views upon the Subject unsettled —Modern Researches—Dr. Young discovers the Law of Interference—Discoveries of Fresnel and Arago—Fraunhofer's Experiments—Diffraction by Grooved Surfaces— Diffraction by Transparent Lines—Phenomena of Negative Diffraction—Experiments and Discoveries of Lord Brougham—Explanation of Diffraction by the Undulatory Theory.

AMONG the optical discoveries of Newton, those which he made on the *inflexion* of light hold a high place. They were first published in his Treatise on Optics in 1704, but we have not been able to ascertain at what period they were made. In the preface to this work, Sir Isaac informs us, that the third book, which contains his experiments on inflexion, " was put together out of scattered papers ; " and he adds, at the end of his observations, that " he designed to repeat most of them with more care and exactness, and to make some new ones for determining the manner how the rays of light are bent in their passage by bodies for making the fringes of colours with the dark lines between them. But we were then interrupted, and cannot now think of taking these things into consideration."

The earliest notice of the inflexion of light by English philosophers was taken by Dr. Hooke in a discourse read to the Royal Society on the 27th November 1672, "containing diverse optical trials made by himself, which seemed to discover some new properties of light, and to exhibit several phenomena in his opinion not ascribable to reflection or refraction, or any other till then known properties of light." The Society desired him to pursue these experiments, and to register some account of them, in order "to preserve his discoveries from being usurped."

After an interval of more than two years, he communicated to the Society a second discourse "on the nature and properties of light, in which were contained several new properties of light, not observed that he knew of by optical writers." These properties were,—

" 1. That there is an *inflexion of light* differing both from refraction and reflexion, and seeming to depend upon the unequal density of the constituent parts of the ray, whereby the light is dispersed from the place of condensation, and rarefied, or gradually diverged into a quadrant.

" 2. That this *deflexion* is made towards the superficies of the opaque body perpendicularly.

" 3. That in this deflexion of the rays, those parts of diverged radiation that are deflected by the greatest angle from the strait or direct radiations are faintest ; those that are deflected by the least are the strongest.

" 4. That rays cutting each other in one common foramen, do not make the angles *ad verticem* equal.

" 5. That colours may be made without refraction.

" 6. That the true bigness of the sun's diameter cannot be taken with common sights.

" 7. That the same rays of light falling upon the same point of the object will turn into all sorts of colours, only by the various inclination of the object.

" 8. That colours begin to appear when two pulses of light are blended so very well and near together, that the sense takes them for one."[1]

These observations of Hooke on the Inflexion of Light, were

---

[1] See Birch's *Hist. Royal Society,* vol. iii. pp. 63, 194, and Hooke's *Posthumous Works.* pp. 186-190.

referred to, not very courteously, by Sir Isaac Newton, at the close of the celebrated Discourse on Colours, of which we have already given an account. After treating of the colours of natural bodies, he says, "that there is another strange phenomenon of colours which may deserve to be taken notice of. Mr. Hooke," he adds, "you may remember, was speaking of an odd straying of light, caused in its passage near the edge of a razor, knife, or other opaque body, in a dark room ; the rays which pass very near the edge being thereby made to stray at all angles into the shadow of the knife. To this Sir William Petty, then President, returned a very pertinent query,— Whether that straying was in curve lines? and that made me (having heard Mr. Hooke, some days before, compare it to the straying of sound into the quiescent medium) say, that I took it to be only a new kind of refraction, caused perhaps by the external ether's beginning to grow rarer a little before it came at the opaque body, than it was in free spaces, the denser ether without the body, and the rarer within it, being terminated not in a mathematical superficies, but passing into one another through all intermediate degrees of density ; whence the rays that pass so near the body, as to come within that compass where the outward ether begins to grow rarer, must be refracted by the uneven denseness thereof, and bended inwards towards the rarer medium of the body. To this Mr. Hooke was then pleased to answer, that though it should be but a new kind of refraction, yet it was a new one. What to make of this unexpected reply I knew not,—having no other thoughts but that a new kind of refraction might be as noble an invention as any thing else about light ; but it made me afterwards, I know not upon what occasion, happen to say, among some who were present to what passed before, that I thought I had seen the experiment before in some Italian author. And the author is Honoratus Faber, in his dialogue De Lumine, who had it from Grimaldi, whom I mention because I am to describe something further out of him."

This passage, which must have been very offensive to Hooke, may be fairly adduced as affording an additional apology for his statement that Newton had, in his Discourse, only carried farther, in some particulars, what was contained in his *Micrographia*. We have no doubt that Hooke discovered the *inflexion of light*, without knowing anything of the previous experiments of Grimaldi. Hooke was right in calling his discovery a new property of light, and Newton was wrong in calling it "*only* a new kind of refraction,"—thus stripping it of much of its value, and placing it in the same category with his own discoveries. Hooke felt the bitterness of the remark, and with more temper than might have been expected, replied, "that though it should be *but a new kind of refraction*, yet it *was a new one;*" thus taking to himself the credit of making a new discovery even when reduced in importance by another designation. Newton confesses that he knew not what to make of this unexpected reply. The reply was a proper one, and might have been expected; but though Newton felt its full significance, he had not the readiness to make the explanation which it required, and which he subsequently gave. He had no thoughts, he afterwards said, of undervaluing the discovery of a property of light by calling it "a new kind of refraction;" yet he did not give this explanation till he had ascertained that the new property had been previously discovered by Grimaldi; and though he now gave its true value to the new discovery, he but embittered the admission when he announced to the Society, that the discovery belonged to an Italian philosopher. On a former occasion, Newton had unnecessarily claimed for Descartes some of Hooke's theoretical opinions; and when a similar claim was made for Grimaldi, Hooke could not but feel the unkindness of his rival. Nearly two centuries have elapsed since these controversies raged; and it is not without its moral in intellectual strife, nor yet without its consolation to the humbler cultivators of science, that while Newton's Theory of the Inflexion of Light is maintained by nobody, the Theory of Hooke, imperfect as it is, is adopted by the greater number of modern philosophers.

It is obvious from these details, that Newton had at this time made no important experiments on the Inflexion of Light. " He propounded his theory with diffidence," as he had " not made sufficient observation about it." It is equally obvious that he had not seen the work of Grimaldi,[1] which he quoted from Honoratus Faber, although a copy of the work had been three years in the possession of the Royal Society, or at least of their secretary, Mr. Oldenburg, who published an analysis of it in the Philosophical Transactions for January 22, 1671-72. The analysis, indeed, is a very imperfect one, in so far as it refers to the *diffraction* of light, and could scarcely have led Hooke to his discovery, even if he had perused it with atten- tion. " The author," says the reviewer, " explains how many ways light is propagated or diffused, viz., not only *directly*, and by *refraction* and *reflexion*, but also by *diffraction ;* which last, according to him, is done when the parts of light, separated by a manifold dissection, do in the same medium proceed in dif- ferent ways,"—a definition of diffraction which Newton could scarcely have comprehended, and which, if he had, he would not have accepted.

That Newton had not seen Grimaldi's work in 1675, is avowed by himself ; and there is every reason to believe that he had not even seen it in 1704, when he published his Optics. If he had seen it, and was aware of the discoveries which it contains, he has not only done great injustice to the Italian philosopher, but neglected the opportunity which it afforded him of anticipating the discoveries of his successors. In the third book of his Optics, he gives to Grimaldi the credit merely of having observed that the shadows of all bodies, placed in light let into a dark room through a small hole, were larger than they ought to be, and that these shadows had three

[1] *Physico-Mathesis de Lumine, Coloribus, et Iride, aliisque annexis.* Bononiæ, 1665. 4to.

parallel fringes of coloured light adjacent to them, whereas the Italian philosopher had penetrated more deeply into the subject, and obtained, as we shall now see, very important results.

Having admitted a ray of light through a small hole into a dark room, Grimaldi observed that it was diffused in the form of a cone, and that all bodies placed in this light had their shadows larger than they should have been had the light passed by their edges in straight lines. Upon a closer examination of these shadows, he discovered that they were surrounded by *three* coloured fringes, growing narrower as they receded from the shadow. When the sun's light was strong, he perceived similar coloured fringes *within* the shadow of narrow bodies like a needle. These fringes were sometimes only *two* in number, and sometimes *four*, their number increasing and their size diminishing with the thickness of the body, and also, in the same shadow, when it was received on a sheet of paper at a greater distance from the body. From these new and valuable facts Grimaldi concluded that light is bent from its rectilineal direction in passing by the edges of bodies. By admitting the sun's rays through two small holes, so near each other that the two cones of light which they produced did not penetrate each other till they had reached to a considerable distance from the two holes, Grimaldi discovered the remarkable fact, that in consequence of the mutual interference of the two cones of light, the spot which was illuminated by both the pencils of light was more obscure than when it was illuminated by either of them singly, or, what is the same thing, "that a body actually illuminated may become more obscure by *adding* a light to that which it already receives." Grimaldi discovered also the beautiful phenomenon of the crested, or curved fringes exhibited within the shadow of the rectangular termination of bodies.

Although Hooke was anticipated by Grimaldi in the greater number of his observations, yet he is clearly entitled to share with the Italian philosopher in the discovery of the doctrine of the interference of light, though it was left to Dr. Thomas Young to complete the discovery.

Such was the state of the subject of Inflexion when Newton directed to it his powers of acute and accurate observation. His attention, however, was turned only to the enlargement of the shadow of inflecting bodies, and to the three fringes adjacent to it. He was therefore led to take exact measures of the shadow of a human hair, and of the breadth of the fringes at different distances behind it, and to repeat these observations with light of different colours. In this way he was led to two new and remarkable results.

1. That these breadths were not proportional to the distances at which they were measured ; and,

2. That the fringes made in homogeneous *red* light were *red*, and the largest ; that those made in *violet* light were *violet*, and the smallest ; and that those made in *green* light were *green*, and of an intermediate size, the rays which formed the red fringe passing by the hair at a greater distance than those which formed the violet.

When Newton made the preceding observations, he intended to repeat most of them with more care, and to make " some new ones, to determine the manner how the rays of light are bent in their passage by bodies ;" but having been then interrupted, he could not think of resuming the inquiry.

It is very difficult to ascertain his real views on the subject of *inflexion*. In his Discourse, read in 1675, he ascribes it to the variable density of the ether within and without the inflecting body, thus regarding it as a new species of refraction ; and in his letter to Robert Boyle in 1679, he takes the same view of the subject, and considers the several colours of the fringes as produced " by that refraction." Pursuing the same idea, he asserts in the Scholium to the 96th Prop. of the first book of the Principia, that the rays of light, in passing near bodies, are bent round them as if by attraction ; that the rays which pass nearest them are most bent, as if they were most attracted ;

that those which pass at a greater distance are less bent ; and that those which pass at still greater distances, are bent in an opposite direction.

In this remarkable passage, Newton introduces, for the first time, the idea of a force bending the rays ; or of an *inflecting* force bending the rays inwards, accompanied with a *deflecting* force bending them outwards. This opinion, however, he subsequently abandoned ; for in the third book of his *Optics*, he refers all the phenomena to a force which " bends the rays *not towards*, but *from* the shadow ;" and he distinctly asserts, " that light *is never known to follow crooked passages, nor to bend into the shadow.*"

These erroneous opinions, now wholly exploded, arose from Newton's having never observed the *internal fringes*, or those seen within the shadow. Grimaldi had described them minutely in his work, and, as they have been seen by every philosopher, it is not easy to explain how they should have escaped the notice of two such careful observers as Hooke and Newton. Without this cardinal fact our author stumbled in his path, and was misled into the erroneous propositions that bodies act upon light at a distance ;—that this action bends in rays with a force diminishing with the distance ;—and that rays which differ in refrangibility differ also in flexibility. Nor was he nearer the truth, when he conjectured in his third query that the rays of light, in passing by the edges of bodies, may be bent several times backwards and forwards with a motion like that of an eel, and that the three fringes of coloured light may arise from three such bendings.

A subject which had thus baffled the sagacity of Newton, was not likely to unfold its mysteries to ordinary observers. The experiments of Grimaldi and Newton were repeated by various philosophers in various lands. Observations better made, and measures more accurately taken, were continually accumulating. A Pelion of inferences was heaped upon an Ossa of facts, but no Baconian conjurer could elicit from them the vital spark. The cardinal facts were still wanting, and a century passed away before a single experiment dissipated the inflexion theories of a graduated ether, of refracting atmospheres, and molecular actions. This humble experiment, which neither merits nor claims any particular notice, was, we believe, first made by ourselves in 1798, and afterwards, extended in 1812 and 1813. We found that ice, cork, metals, and diamond, the lightest and the heaviest bodies, the least refractive and the most refractive substances, produced exactly the same fringes ; and that no change in the phenomena of inflexion was produced when a fibre of an opaque body was placed in fluids of precisely the same or of greater refractive power. Hence it followed that the light which passed by the edges of bodies was not inflected by any refracting agent, or by any action whatever of the bodies themselves.

It is to Dr. Thomas Young, however, that we owe the master fact which enabled philosophers to unveil the mysteries of diffraction, and to account for a great variety of hitherto unexplained phenomena. In studying the internal fringes, and the crested ones discovered by Grimaldi, he found that, by intercepting the rays which passed by one side of the diffracting body, the internal and the crested fringes completely disappeared ; and hence he concluded that the fringes were produced by the joint action, or by the interference, of the two portions of light which passed on each side of the diffracting body.

Having thus discovered the cause of the internal fringes, Dr. Young directed his attention to the external ones. He considered them as produced by the interference of the direct rays, or " those which have pursued their course without interruption," with those which are *reflected from* the margin of the diffracting body ; and as the fringes are on this supposition formed by light " *turned away* from the substance near which it passes," he has characterized the phenomenon as one of *de-flected light*.

M. Fresnel, to whose fine researches we owe the best experiments on diffraction, and the most perfect theory of it, followed Dr. Young in ascribing the external fringes to the influence of light reflected from the edge of the diffracting body,—an opinion which we never could reconcile with the palpable fact, that the fringes had always the same character, whatever was the reflecting power, or the shape of the edge of the body. Fresnel, influenced no doubt by the same consideration, suggested a different origin for the rays which interfere with the direct ones, namely, that the rays which pass at a sensible distance from the diffracting body deviate from their primitive direction towards the shadow, and thus interfere with the direct rays that pass near the body. In comparing these two hypotheses, and assuming with Dr. Young that half an undulation was lost by the reflected rays, he found that the real place of the fringe, on the hypothesis of a reflection, would be $\frac{17}{100}$ths of a millimètre different from what it really was.

In conducting his experiments on diffraction, Fresnel adopted a new and accurate method of observing and measuring the fringes. In place of using a small hole, he employed a convex lens of short focal length, which collected the solar rays into a focus, from which they again diverged, as if they had proceeded from a small aperture.[1] When bodies were placed in this divergent light, he examined the fringes adjacent to their shadows by means of an eye-glass furnished with a micro-. meter, instead of receiving them upon a white surface ; and he was thus able to measure their breadths even to the one hundred or two hundredth part of a millimètre. In this way he traced the external fringes to their origin, and with a lens of short focus he perceived the *third* fringe at a distance of less than the one-hundredth part of a millimètre from the edge of the inflecting body.

By measuring the angular inflection of homogeneous *red* light, when the radiant point was placed at different distances

---

[1] A concave lens is preferable to a convex one, for reasons which will presently be seen ; and we recommend that it should be achromatic.

in front of the diffracting body, and also when the radiant point remained fixed at different distances of the fringes behind the inflecting body, he was led to two important discoveries—

1. That the angular inflexion diminishes with the distance of the inflecting body from the radiant point ; and,

2. That when the radiant point remains fixed, the successive positions of the same fringe are not in a straight line, but form a curve whose concavity is turned towards the diffracting body,[1] the curves being hyperbolas, having for their common foci the radiant point and the edge of the diffracting body.[2]

The discovery of Dr. Young, that an opaque screen, on one side of the inflecting body, extinguished the interior fringes, was extended by M. Arago, who found that the same effect is produced by a transparent screen of sufficient thickness, and that thin screens merely displace the fringes, and transfer them from the side where they were formed. When such a screen is placed on each side of the diffracting body, the effect is equal to the difference of the transferences which each screen would have produced separately. As the amount of this trans- ference may be computed theoretically from the thickness and refractive power of the screen, MM. Arago and Fresnel em- ployed this method for measuring, with great exactness, the refractive power of gases.

The late M. Fraunhofer of Munich made a series of experi- ments on the diffraction of light on a large scale, and obtained many interesting results. The experiments were made with a telescope, which enabled him to obtain accurate measures of the fringes or rings produced by apertures of various forms ; and he has published beautiful drawings of the spectra, and groups of spectra produced by a great number of diffracted rays,—by small apertures variously arranged, and by wire-gratings either acting singly, or crossed at right angles.

[1] This result had been previously obtained by Sir Isaac Newton.

[2] The hyperbolic form of the fringes had been previously discovered by Dr. Young.— *Lect.*, vol. i. p. 287.

We have had occasion to study some of the same phenomena, when produced by lines cut upon polished steel with a diamond. The grooved surfaces which we employed were executed for us by the late Sir John Barton, and contained groups of lines varying from 500 to 10,000 in an inch. When divergent light was reflected from these surfaces, the central image formed by ordinary reflexion from the original surface of the steel-plate was, in general, *white*, as observed in every case by Fraunhofer and others, and the other spectra had their usual character. But when the bright spaces in the plate, or those between the grooves had a certain relation to the width of the groove, or the part of the steel that was excavated by the diamond point, a series of new and remarkable phenomena were produced. The light reflected from the original surface of the steel forming the central image was no longer *white*, but coloured, the colour varying with the angle of incidence at which the steel-plate received the divergent beam. In some of the groups of lines, the colour varied slightly from 0° to 90° of incidence. In others, it passed through the first order of colours; and in others, where the original steel surface was nearly removed, it passed through three or more orders of tints. The light which is obliterated from the central image, at any angle of incidence, or the complementary colour of the tint at that angle, is obliterated also from all the coloured spectra at less angles of incidence, the angle diminishing with the distance of the spectrum from the central one, and being less in each spectrum for the less refrangible rays.

If we cover the surface of the grooved steel with a fluid so as to reduce the refractive power of its surface, we develop more orders of colours on the *white* or central image, and consequently on all the spectra, higher tints being produced at a given incidence. But what is very remarkable, when the central image is perfectly white, and when the spectra are complete without any obliteration of their tints, the application of fluids to the grooved surface develops colours on the central or white image, and a corresponding obliteration of tints in the coloured spectra.[1]

In the experiments hitherto made on diffraction, the lines employed have been opaque, such as wires, hairs, or fibres of glass, which act upon light as if they were opaque. A series of beautiful phenomena are produced when we employ transparent lines drawn upon glass with solutions of gums of different kinds, and different degrees of strength. A section of these transparent lines varies with the nature and density of the solution, though it is generally thicker at its edges. The consequence of this is, that the light which passes through the transparent line not only interferes with that which passes on each side of it, but also with part of the light which has its direction changed by the refraction of its curvilineal edges. Hence it follows, that a series of new interferences takes place, and we accordingly have a splendid display of coloured fringes infinitely surpassing in variety and brilliancy of colour the ordinary phenomena of diffraction.[2]

In all the experiments on inflexion and diffraction made by Newton and Fresnel, the fringes were viewed either on paper, or in the focus of a lens when the rays had actually interfered and produced the coloured fringes. The fringes thus seen may be called *positive*, because they are formed in space and out of the eye, on the retina of which they are afterwards delineated ; but there is another form of these fringes, which I have examined, and which may be called *negative*, because they are not brought to a positive focus in space, or do not interfere till they reach the retina. In order to see these fringes, place the lens behind the diffracting body, so as to see the *positive* fringes, and then move it forward till these fringes disappear. The diffracting edge will now be in the anterior focus of the lens.

---

[1] See the *Phil. Trans.* 1829, pp. 301-317.

[2] These effects are so beautiful, that we have recommended the use of a diffracting apparatus for suggesting patterns for ribands.—See *Reports of British Association*, 1838, vol. vii. p. 12 ; *Treatise on Optics*, Edit. 1853, p. 117.

If we advance the lens towards the diffracting body, the *negative* fringes will appear, and will increase in size till the lens touches the body, when they will have the same magnitude as the *positive* fringes have when the lens is placed behind the body, at the distance of twice its focal length.

If we wish to see the fringes larger, we must use a lens with a longer focus ; and when it is placed in contact with the diffracting body, the fringes will in every case be the same as the positive ones seen by the same lens placed behind the body twice its focal length.    If the diffracting body is included in a fluid lens, or even placed in *front of the lens*, the negative fringes will be seen.,  In producing the negative fringes, the interfering rays are those which virtually radiate from the anterior focus of the lens, and which being refracted into parallel directions, enter the eye, and interfere on the retina ; and in consequence of their not interfering till they enter the eye, they are much more distinct than the positive fringes.[1]

The most recent experiments on the inflexion of light have been made by Lord Brougham, who had investigated the subject so early as 1796, and given an account of his experiments in two interesting papers printed in the Philosophical Transactions.[2]    These investigations were published before Dr. Young discovered the key to this class of phenomena, and before Fresnel had explained them on the principles of the undulatory theory. In his early papers, Lord Brougham considered the phenomena as produced by inflecting and deflecting forces emanating from the diffracting body, and acting, as Newton supposed, upon the passing rays ; but in his recent researches he has used these terms merely for the purpose of making the narrative shorter and more distinct, and has avoided all arguments and suggestions relating to the two rival theories.

The recent investigations of Lord Brougham were carried on under the clear sky of Provence, and with an excellent set of

[1] See *Reports of British Association*, vol. vii. p. 12.   1838.
[2] *Phil. Trans.* 1796, p. 227 ; and 1797, p. 352.

instruments constructed by M. Soleil of Paris. It would be impossible, without diagrams, to make them intelligible to the general reader, but some idea may be formed of the originality and importance of his discoveries from the two following propositions, which relate to a new property of the inflected and deflected rays :—

1. " The rays of light, when inflected by bodies near which they pass, are thrown into a condition or state which disposes them to be on one of their sides more easily deflected than before their first flexion, and disposes them on the other side to be less easily deflected ; and when deflected by bodies, they are thrown into a condition or state which disposes them on one side to be more easily inflected, and on the other side to be less easily inflected than they were before the first flexion.

2. " The rays disposed on one side by the first flexion are polarized[1] on that side by the second flexion ; and the rays polarized on the other side by the first flexion, are depolarized and disposed on that side by the second flexion."[2]    In continuing his researches, Lord Brougham was led to conclude that the rays of light differ in deflexibility and inflexibility, the least refrangible being the most flexible ; the law of different flexibility having this peculiarity, that the fringes or images by flexion are not rectilineal but curvilineal from the extreme violet to the extreme red.

Whatever opinion we may form of the undulatory theory in its physical aspect, the explanation which it affords of a vast variety of optical phenomena, entitles it to the highest consideration.   With the exception of Lord Brougham's discoveries, and the peculiar colours on the central image formed by grooved surfaces, to which we have already referred, the undulatory theory gives a satisfactory explanation of the leading phenomena of diffraction, while the Newtonian or atomical hypothesis has not even ventured to suggest a probable explanation.

---

[1] Lord Brougham uses the term polarization " merely because the effect of the first edge resembles polarization, and without giving any opinion as to its identity."

[2] *Phil. Trans.* 1850 ,pp. 235-260.

# CHAPTER X.

Miscellaneous Optical Researches of Newton—His Experiments on the Absolute Refractive Powers of Bodies—More recent Experiments—His Conjecture respecting the Inflammability of the Diamond confirmed by more direct Experiments—His Erroneous Law of Double Refraction—His Observations on the Polarity of Double Refracted Pencils—Discoveries on Double Refraction in the present Century—His Experiments on the eye of a Sheep—Results of them—His three Letters on Briggs's New Theory of Vision—His Theory of the Semi-Decussation of the Optic Nerves—Partly anticipated by Rohault—Opinions of later writers on Vision, of Reid, Brown, Wollaston, Twining, and Alison, discussed—The true laws of Sensation and Vision—Newton's Observations on the Impression of Strong Light upon the Retina—More recent Observations —His Reflecting Sextant—His Reflecting Microscope—His Reflecting Prism for Reflecting Telescopes—His Method of Varying the Magnifying Power of Newtonian Telescopes—Newton's Treatise on Optics—His Lectiones Opticæ.

ALTHOUGH the discoveries described in the preceding chapters are those on which Newton's reputation in optics chiefly rests, yet it is necessary to notice some of his less elaborate researches, which, though of inferior importance in the science of light, have either exercised an influence over the progress of discovery, or have been associated with the history of other branches of knowledge.

In the second book of his Optics,[1] Newton proves, with much fulness of detail, that " the cause of reflexion is not the impinging of light on the solid or impervious parts of bodies, as is commonly believed ;" and that " bodies reflect and refract light by one and the same power variously exercised in various circumstances." He then proceeds to show, that " if light be swifter in bodies than in vacuo, in the proportion of the sines which measure the refraction of the bodies, the forces of the bodies to reflect and refract light are very nearly proportional to the

[1] Part iii. Prop. viii. ix. &c.

densities of the same bodies, *excepting that unctuous and sulphureous bodies refract more than others of the same density.*" This remarkable exception led our author to point out the connexion between the refractive powers and the chemical composition of bodies. Having obtained measures of the refractive powers and densities, or specific gravities of twenty-two substances varying in density between *air* and *diamond*, and having computed their refracting forces, and compared them with their densities, he calculated their *refractive powers in respect of their density.* From this comparison he found that *topaz, selenite, rock-crystal, Iceland spar, common glass, glass of antimony,* and *air,* have their refractive powers almost in the same proportion as their densities, " excepting that the refraction of that strange substance, *Iceland spar,* is a little bigger than the rest."—" Again," he adds, " the refraction of *camphor, olive oil, lintseed oil, spirit of turpentine,* and *amber,* which are fat sulphureous unctuous bodies, and *diamond,* which probably is an unctuous substance coagulated, have their refractive powers in proportion to one another as their densities, without any considerable variation. But the refractive powers of these unctuous substances are two or three times greater in respect of their densities than the refractive powers of the former substances are in respect of theirs. *Water* has a refractive power in a middle degree between these two sorts of substances . . . . *salts of vitriol* between those of earthy substances and water, and spirit of wine between *water* and *oily* substances." The following are a few of the numbers in Newton's Table :—

| | Refractive Power. | | | Refractive Power. |
|---|---|---|---|---|
| Pseudo topaz,[1] . | . | 3,979 | Rain water, . . | 7,845 |
| Air, . . . . | . | 5,208 | Spirit of wine, . . | 10,121 |
| Rock crystal, . | . | 5,450 | Oil of olives, . . | 12,607 |
| Iceland crystal, | . | 6,536 | Amber, . . . | 13,654 |
| Rock salt, . | . | 6,477 | Diamond, . . | 14,556 |

To the results in this table we have added the following, computed chiefly from observations of our own, and interesting

---

[1] Probably *Sulphate of Barytes.*

as being, with the exception of three in *italics*, below the lowest
and above the highest in Newton's Table :—

| | Refractive Power. | | Refractive Power. |
|---|---|---|---|
| Tabasheer, | 976 | Realgar artificial, | 16,666 |
| Cryolite, . | 2,742 | Ambergris, | 17,000 |
| Fluor spar, | 3,426 | Sulphur, . | 22,000 |
| Sulphate of Barytes, | 3,829 | Phosphorus, | 28,857 |
| *Greenockite*, | 12,861 | Hydrogen, | 29,964 |
| *Octohedrite*, | 13,816 | Hydrogen, | 31,862 |
| *Diamond*, | 13,964 | | |

The enormous refractive powers possessed by the last six
bodies in the preceding table, when taken in connexion with
those given by Newton, exhibit in a striking degree the connexion between a high degree of inflammability and a great
refracting force. The conjecture of Newton that the diamond
" is an unctuous substance coagulated," has been generally regarded as a proof of singular sagacity, and as an anticipation
of the results of chemical analysis ; but it is certainly not
entitled to such praise. Its *solitary* position among the oils
and inflammable bodies led to the conjecture ; but had he
known the refractive index and specific gravities of *greenockite*
and *octohedrite*, he would have drawn the same conclusion respecting them, and been mistaken. The real inference respecting the composition of the diamond, which Newton's Table
authorizes, is not that it should consist of carbon, but of
sulphur. "So then," says he, "by the foregoing table, all
bodies seem to have their refractive powers proportional to
their densities (or very nearly), excepting so far as they partake
more or less of sulphureous oily particles, and thereby have
their refractive power made greater or less. Whence it seems
rational to attribute the refractive power of all bodies chiefly,
if not wholly, to the sulphureous particles with which they
abound. For it is probable that all bodies abound more or less
with sulphurs. And as light congregated by a burning glass
acts most upon sulphureous bodies, to turn them into fire and

flame ; so since all action is mutual, *sulphurs ought to act most upon light.*"[1]

That diamond is *a soft substance coagulated*, has been rendered probable by experiments of a more direct nature. We have shown by the examination of a great number of diamonds in polarized light, that the little cavities which many of them contain, have been pressed outward by an elastic force emanating from some gas or fluid with which they had been filled. Several such cavities we found in the Koh-i-noor diamond, and in the two smaller ones which accompanied it ; and in a specimen in the British Museum, we found a yellow crystal of diamond that had crystallized upon the cleavage surface of another which was colourless, having been expelled from an adjacent cavity, in which it had existed in a fluid state.[2]

Among the more interesting optical researches of Newton, we rank his observations on the double refraction and polarization of light. On the 12th of June 1689, when Huygens was in England, during the presidency of Sir Robert Southwell, he attended a meeting of the Royal Society, at which Newton was present. Huygens informed the Society that he was about to publish a treatise concerning the cause of gravity, and another about refraction, giving, among other things, the reasons of the doubly refracting Iceland crystal. " Mr. Newton, considering a piece of the Iceland crystal, did observe that of the two species wherewith things do appear through that body, the one suffered no refraction when the visual ray came parallel to the oblique sides of the parallelopiped ; the other, as is usual in all other transparent bodies, suffered more when the beam came perpendicular to the planes through which the object appeared."[3] It is remarkable that this observation of Newton, which had been made long before by Bartholinus, as

---

[1] *Optics*, Book ii. Part iii. Prop. x.

[2] See *Transactions of the Geological Society*, 2d Series, vol. iii. p. 455 ; and *North British Review*, vol. xviii. p. 227.

[3] *Journal Book* of the Royal Society.

Huygens knew at the time, and as the Royal Society ought to have known,[1] should not have been claimed for that author.

In the admirable Treatise on Light, to which Huygens referred at the Royal Society, and which was published in 1690, he has shown that the observation of Bartholinus, adopted by Newton, is erroneous,[2] and has explained the law of *unusual refraction*, as exhibited in one of the two pencils formed by the double refraction of *Iceland* or *calcareous spar*. This law he deduced from the principles of the undulatory theory, and he confirmed it by direct experiment. Viewing it probably as a theoretical result, Newton seems to have regarded it as incorrect, and though he has given Huygens the credit of describing the phenomena more exactly than Bartholinus, who first discovered and described the remarkable property of this spar, yet without assigning any reason, or even referring to the law of Huygens, he substitutes another in its place. The observations of Newton were first published in his *Optics* in 1704,[3] fourteen years after the appearance of Huygens's work. The law of unusual refraction, adopted by Newton, is not given as the result of theory. It is stated as an undoubted truth, and no experiments whatever are referred to as having been made either by himself or others. "One of these refractions," he says, "is performed by the usual rule of optics, the sine of incidence out of air into this crystal being to the sine of refraction as five to three. The other refraction, which may be called the *unusual*[4] refraction, *is performed by the following rule.*" This rule was first shown to be erroneous by the Abbe Hauy,[5] and it has been rejected by all succeeding philosophers.[6]

In his observations on the successive disappearance and re-

---

[1] It was published in the *Phil. Trans.* 1671, p. 2039.

[2] *Traité de la Lumière*, chap. v. p. 57 ; and Maseres' *Scriptores Opticæ*, p. 234.

[3] Query 25th and 26th at the end of the work.

[4] The term *unusual*, and the ratio of the sines, viz., 5 to 3, were given by Bartholinus in the abstract of his Paper in the *Phil. Trans.* No. 67, Jan. 1670-1, pp. 20, 39.

[5] *Traité de Mineralogie*, tom. i. p. 159, Note.

[6] Hauy's *Elements of Nat. Phil.* by Gregory, vol. ii. p. 337.

appearance of two of the four images which are formed when
a luminous object is viewed through two rhombs of Iceland
spar, one of which is made to revolve upon the other, Newton
has been more successful, though he has omitted to give to
Huygens the credit of having discovered these curious phenomena. He considers "every ray of light as having four sides
or quarters, two of which are originally endued with the property on which the unusual refraction depends, and the other
two opposite sides not endued with that property;" and he
adds, that "it remains to be inquired whether there are not
more properties of light by which the sides of the rays differ,
and are distinguished from one another."

In animadverting on Huygens's theory of two vibrating media
within the Iceland crystal, he asserts that the unusual refraction depends "not on new modifications, but on the original
and unchangeable dispositions of the rays," which, he says,
"had Huygens known, he would have found it difficult to explain how these dispositions, which he supposed to be impressed
on the rays by the first crystal, could be in them before their
incidence on that crystal ; and in general, how all rays emitted
by shining bodies can have these dispositions in them from the
beginning. To me, at least," he adds, "this seems inexplicable, if light be nothing else than pression or motion propagated
through ether."

After Newton wrote these imperfect observations, more than
a century elapsed before the double refraction and polarization
of light in Iceland spar and other bodies were reduced to regular
laws. In 1810, Malus announced to the Academy of Sciences,
the remarkable discovery that a ray of light reflected at a particular angle was polarized like one of the pencils formed by
Iceland spar, that is, exhibited the same properties in its four
sides or quarters which are exhibited in one of the pencils of
Iceland spar ; and the result of this fine discovery has been the
establishment of a new branch of Physical Optics, which possesses the highest interest, not only from the beauty of its laws

and the splendour of its phenomena, but from the new power with which it arms the philosopher in detecting organic or inorganic structures, which defy the scrutiny of the eye and the microscope.

Although Sir Isaac Newton has not published any of his opinions or experiments on Vision, or on the structure and functions of the eye, yet we fortunately possess some fragments of his researches, which are both valuable and interesting. Among these is a manuscript in his own handwriting, which we found among the family papers, containing some accurate observations and experiments on the form and dimensions of the eye of a sheep, and accompanied with an outline drawing, on a large scale, of a section of the eye.[1]  The following are the most interesting results contained in this manuscript.

In the first part of it, which is written in Latin, he makes the outer surface of the cornea part of a prolate spheroid, the major axis coinciding with the optical axis, or that of the eye, and having to the transverse axis the ratio of 1350 to 972.

He places the focus for parallel rays of the first surface of the cornea at a point behind the eye, and as far beyond the sclerotic coat as one-seventh of the diameter of the eye-ball, which he makes an oblate spheroid, having its vertical axis 1025, and its horizontal one 975, the anterior portion of the spheroid coinciding nearly with the front of the iris.

He represents the crystalline lens as having a great degree of convexity, differing not much from a sphere, and he remarks that the anterior superficies of the crystalline is more full than the posterior surface, which is certainly not the case, and is not so represented in the diagram.

The second part of the manuscript, which contains minute measurements of every part of the eye, is written in English, and concludes with an expression of regret, that " he was prevented by an accident from taking the distance of the crystalline humour from the horny tunic (the sclerotic coat), which I

would gladly have done to have had the conformity of all the
parts one to another, in one and the same eye." The elliptical
form of the cornea was detected not many years ago by M.
Chossat of Geneva, who, of course, could not know that he had
been anticipated by Newton.

We have not been able to ascertain at what time these observations were made, but it appears from the correspondence of
Newton with Dr. W. Briggs, published by Mr. Edleston,[1] that
in 1682 his attention was called to the subject of binocular
vision, in consequence of Dr. Briggs having communicated to
the Royal Society on the 15th March, a paper entitled, " A
New Theory of Vision."[2]   Briggs, who was a contemporary of
Newton's at Cambridge, and a Fellow of Corpus Christi College, seems to have sent him a copy of his paper, and to have
solicited his opinion of it.   The theory which he proposes
evinces neither sagacity nor genius.   Setting out on the erroneous principle which has so long disfigured the physiology of
the senses, and which has not yet been exploded, that sensation
is performed only in the brain, he seeks for an explanation of
single vision with two eyes, and of other visual phenomena in
" the rise of the optic nerve, the position of its fibres, and the
manner of their insertion into the eye."   He describes the
optic nerves as arising " from two gibbous protuberances,"[3] in
such a manner that those fibres that are in the *zenith* or apex
of the thalami have the greatest tension, while those in the
*nadir*, or opposite part, have the least tension by reason of a
less flexure.   Every fibre that passes into the upper part of the
right eye from the upper part of one thalamus, has a corresponding one passing from the upper part of the other thalamus into
the upper part of the left eye, and the same thing takes place
with the lower fibres.   The fibres which thus correspond in site

[1] *Correspondence*, &c. pp. 264-273.   From the Originals in the British Museum, Add.
MSS. 4237, fol. 32 and 34.
[2] Hooke's *Collections*, March 1682, No. 6, p. 167.
[3] The *Thalami Nervorum Opticorum*.

correspond also in tension, " so that when any impression from an object without moves *both fibres*, it causes not a *double sensation* any more than *unisons* in two *viols* struck together cause a *double sound.*" This theory may be called the *theory of corresponding fibres*, and is doubtless the parent of one more modern though equally inadmissible—the *theory of corresponding points.*

In his first letter to Briggs, Newton tells him that he has " perused his very ingenious theory of vision, in which (to be free with you as a friend should be) there seems to be some things more solid and satisfactory, others more disputable, but yet plausibly suggested, and well deserving the consideration of the ingenious. The more satisfactory I take to be your asserting that we see with both eyes at once,—your speculation about the *musculas obliquus inferior*,[1]—your assigning every fibre in the optic nerve of one eye to have its correspondent in that of the other, both which make all things appear to both eyes, in one and the same place, and your solving hereby the duplicity of the object in distorted eyes, and confuting the childish opinion about the splitting the optic cone. The more disputable seems your notion about every pair of fellow fibres being unisons to one another, discords to the rest, and this consonance making the object seen with two eyes appear but one, for the same reason that unison sounds seem but one sound." Newton here terminates his letter to " his honoured friend, Dr. Briggs," with the observation that he had intended to state his objections " against this notion," but that he thought it better " to reserve it for discourse at their next meeting."

Briggs, probably anxious for an earlier discussion than one living at Cambridge could concede, seems to have requested him to make his objections in writing. Newton accordingly addressed to his honoured friend a long letter of nearly seven printed pages,[2] a letter of very great interest, and utterly sub-

---

[1] Briggs considers this muscle necessary to prevent squinting, by "keeping the eye *even and in sight.*"—Hooke's *Coll.*, March 1682, p. 170.

[2] Dated Trin. Coll. Cambridge, September 12, 1682. APPENDIX, No. IV.

versive of the theory of his correspondent. In the commencement and conclusion of this letter, which is of a slightly
personal nature, we see finely displayed the modesty and peculiar character of its author.  " Though I am of all men," he
begins, " grown the most shy of setting pen to paper about
anything that may lead into disputes, yet your friendship overcomes me so far, that I shall set down my suspicions about
your theory, yet on this condition, that if I can write but plain
enough to make you understand me, I may leave all to your
use without pressing it further on.  For I design not to
confute or convince you, but only to present and submit my
thoughts to your consideration and judgment."

After showing that the *bending* of the nerves in the thalami
is no proof of a difference of tension, he states, that when the
ear hears two sounds in unison, it does not hear them as one
sound, unless they come from nearly the same spot ; and for
the same reason a similar tension of the optic fibres will not
make the object appear one to two eyes.

He then proceeds to show that the singleness of the picture
arises from the coincidence of the two pictures, and therefore
that the cause of single vision must be sought for in the *cause
that produces the coincidence.*  " But you will say," he adds,
" how is this coincidence made ?  I answer, what if I know
not ?  Perhaps in the sensorium after some such way as the
Cartesians would have believed,[1] or by some other way.  Perhaps by the mixing of the marrow of the nerves in their juncture before they enter the brain, the fibres on the right side of
each eye going to the right side of the head, those on the left
side to the left." [2]

In support of his theory, Briggs maintained that " it was

---

[1] Descartes himself distinctly states that we see objects single with two eyes in exactly
the same way as we feel objects single with two hands, forgetting that we see them
double by the displacement of the coincident images, and *never* feel them double by the
two hands.  See Descartes' *Dioptrice*, cap. 6, *De Visione*, Art. X.  The experiment of
feeling a pea double between two fingers, is not hostile to this observation.

[2] This is precisely the theory of Rohault, see p. 200.

not to be imagined that the nerves decussate one another, or
are blended together," at the place where they approach each
other before they set off to the right and left eye ; and he
adduces the case of many fishes, where the nerves are joined
only by simple contact, " and in the *chameleon* not at all (as is
said)," admitting, at the same time, that in *whitings*, and perhaps some other fishes, they do decussate.

To this Sir Isaac replies : " If you say that in the chameleon
and fishes the nerves only touch one another without mixture,
and sometimes do not so much as touch ; 'tis true, but makes
altogether against you. Fishes look one way with one eye, the
other way with the other ; to the right hand with this, to the
left hand with that, twisting their eyes severally this way or
that as they please. And in those animals which do not look
the same way with both eyes, what wonder if the nerves do not
join ? To make them join would have been to no purpose ;
and nature does nothing in vain. But then, whilst in these
animals, where 'tis not necessary, they are not joined, in all
others which look the same way with both eyes, so far as I can
yet learn, they are joined. Consider, therefore, for what reason
they are joined in the one and not in the other. For God, in
the frame of animals, hath done nothing without reason."

The last objection of Sir Isaac to the new theory is unanswerable. Admitting that consonance unites objects seen
with the fibres of *two* eyes, " much more," says he, " will it
unite those seen with those (consonant fibres) of the *same* eye,
and yet we find it much otherwise."

" You have now seen," he says in conclusion, " the sum of
what I think of worth objecting, set down in a tumultuary
way, as I could get time from my Stourbridge Fair friends.
If I have anywhere expressed myself in a more peremptory way
than becomes the weakness of the argument,—pray, look on
that as done not in earnestness, but for the mode of discoursing.
Whether anything be so material as that it may prove any way
useful to you, I cannot tell ; but pray, accept of it as written

for that end. For having *laid philosophical speculations aside,* nothing but the gratification of a friend would easily invite me to so large a scribble about things of this nature." [1]

Notwithstanding the force of these objections, Dr. Briggs continued to press his theory on public notice, and in May 1683, he published in Hooke's Philosophical Collections additional explanations of it, and a reply to *seven* different objections that had been sent him " by Mr. Newton, our worthy Professor of Mathematics at Cambridge, and other friends." It would be out of place to make any observations on this defence of his theory. We hear no more of it for two years ; but it appears that Newton had requested Briggs to print a Latin version of it, and we accordingly find that it was published in London in 1685, with a curious letter of Newton's prefixed. This letter [2] must have been solicited by Briggs, in order to call the attention of philosophers to his book ; and we confess that we feel great difficulty in appreciating the motives that could have induced its author to express the opinions which it contains.

In this letter, [3] written in Latin, Sir Isaac speaks of Briggs's two treatises [4] as advancing at once two sciences of great name, Anatomy and Optics. He compliments him on having diligently inquired into the mysteries of an organ so skilfully constructed, and he expresses the great delight which he had formerly received from the skill and dexterity with which he had dissected it. He tells him that he had so elegantly developed the muscles of the eye-ball, and expounded the other parts, that we could not only understand, but see the uses and functions of each,

---

[1] This letter contains, as will be seen in the Appendix, No. IV., a paragraph respecting the opinions of a Mr. Sheldrake, who, as Mr. Edleston informs us, was a Fellow of Corpus Christi College, and seven years senior to Newton. Mr. Sheldrake states that vision is more distinct when the eye is directed to the object, than when the object is *above* or *below* the optic axes. I do not recollect that this curious fact has been stated by any previous writer on vision.

[2] See APPENDIX, No. V.

[3] Dated Cambridge, May 1685.

[4] The one the Theory of Vision, and the other his *Ophthalmographia.* Cantab. 1676, and Lond. 1687.

and that this showed that nothing inaccurate could be expected from his scalpel. He then speaks of his excellent anatomical tract, in which he shows the value of accurate observation by " a most ingenious theory." After describing Briggs's theory in a few lines, and mentioning the analogy between unisons in music and in optics, he says that nature is simple—that a great variety of effects may be produced by the same mode of opera- tion, and that this was probable in the causes of the cognate senses. But notwithstanding all this general praise, which is certainly not merited, Newton does not adopt the theory. For though he *may suspect that there is another analogy* between these senses, than that contained in the theory, he must willingly confess that that of Briggs is very ingeniously excogitated. He then remarks that he does not think the second dissertation useless in which he *dilutes* the objections made against the theory. " Go on, then," he adds, " illustrious sir, as you are doing, and advance these sciences by your very great inventions, and teach the world that those difficulties in investigating physical causes which usually yield with difficulty to vulgar attempts, may be so easily overcome by talent."

While Newton was writing this letter, there is reason to believe that he had himself conceived another theory of single vision with two eyes, proceeding on the supposition that Briggs was wrong in his Anatomy as well as in his Optics. This, we think, is indicated by the " other analogy " of the senses of sight and hearing which he then suspected, and to which he was no doubt led by his correspondence with Briggs. It is evident, that in September 1682, the date of his second letter, he had laid aside philosophical speculations, and that he un- willingly wrote his opinion " about things of that nature ;" and it is equally obvious, from his supposition about the mixing of the marrow of the nerves in their juncture before they enter the brain, that if the idea of the semi-decussation of the fibres had been then in his view, he had not at that time given it any serious consideration.

That he had studied this subject with peculiar care, is manifest from the 15th Query of his Optics,[1] where he has given a brief abstract of his theory of corresponding points, or of the semi-decussation of the optic nerves, but particularly from an elaborate paper on the subject which was never published in his lifetime, but was found in MS. among the papers of William Jones, Esq., known as the celebrated Macclesfield Collection of scientific correspondence. A copy of this paper was given to Joseph Harris, who inserted it in his *Treatise of Optics*,[2] but from the manner in which he has garbled it, we cannot discover whether or not he has published the whole of the manuscript.[3]

The theory of Newton, as published in his Optics, and as more fully developed in the MS. in question, will be understood from the annexed diagram given by himself. Let P, Q represent the two eyes, T V E G, Y X E H the optic nerves, crossing at what has been called the *sella turcica*, G H, and passing between I L or M K towards the brain. Newton observes, that if the nerve be cut crosswise anywhere between T G or Y H, the section will

---

[1] See APPENDIX, No. VI.                    [2] See APPENDIX, No. VII.

[3] Although it is evident, from a careful perusal of the 15th Query, that it contains the same doctrine of the *semi-decussation of the optic nerves* which is given in the MS., yet it has been misunderstood by Dr. Reid, who obviously had not seen the copy of it in Harris's *Optics*. " Sir Isaac Newton," says Dr. Reid (*Inquiry*, cap. vi. sect. 13), " who was too judicious a philosopher and too accurate an observer to have offered even a conjecture which did not tally with the facts which had fallen under his observation, proposes a query with respect to the cause of it (namely, the relation and sympathy between corresponding points of the two retinæ)."—*Optics*, Query 15. Dr. Reid seems not to have detected the doctrine of semi-decussation in the Query, and to have believed that individual nerves, not half-nerves, from the two sides of both eyes, united before they reached the brain, and there produced a joint and single impression; and Dr. Alison has either taken up Dr. Reid's opinion, or misunderstood the Query, and also the theory of semi-decussation. " It is well-known," he says, " that an explanation (of single vision by means of double images) was proposed by Newton, fully considered by Reid, and since supported by Wollaston (often called the theory of Wollaston, but quite incorrectly), proceeding on the supposition of *a semi-decussation of the human optic nerves* at their commissure, *whereby the fibres from the right half of the retina go to the right optic lobe in the brain*, and *vice versa*." This is the theory of Rohault, and not of Newton and Wollaston, in which the *half-fibres*, from the right half of the retina of each eye, unite into one fibre at their commissure G H in *Fig.* 12, and then go to the right optic lobe.

" appear full of spots or pimples, which are a little prominent, especially if the nerve be pressed or warmed at a candle ; that these shoot into the very eye, and may be seen withinside where the retina grows to the nerve ; and that they continue to the very juncture E F G H.   But at the juncture they end on a sudden into a more tender white pap, like the anterior part

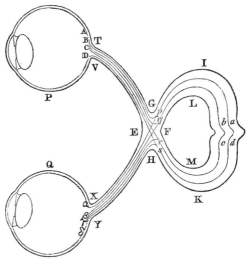

FIG. 16.

of the brain, and so the nerve continues after the juncture into the brain, filled with a white tender pap, in which can be seen no distinction of parts as betwixt the said juncture and the eye."

" Now I conceive," says he, " that every point in the retina of one eye hath its correspondent point in the other, from which two very slender pipes, filled with a most limpid liquor, do without any interruption, or any other unevenness or irregu-

larity in their process, go along the optic nerves to the juncture
E F G H, where they meet either betwixt G F or F H, and there
unite into one pipe as big as both of them ; and so continue
in one passing either betwixt I L or M K into the brain, where
they are terminated perhaps at the next meeting of the nerves
between the *cerebrum* and *cerebellum*, in the same order that
their extremities were situated in the retinas.   And so there
are a vast multitude of these slender pipes which flow from the
brain, the one-half through the right-side nerve I L, till they
come at the juncture G F, where they are each divided into two
branches, the one passing by G and T to the right side of the
right eye A B, the other half shooting through the space E F, and
so passing by X to the right side of the left eye $a\beta$.   And, in
like manner, the other half shooting through the left-side nerve
M K, divide themselves at F H, and their branches passing by E V
to the right eye, and by H Y to the left, compose that half of
the retina in both eyes which is towards the left side C D
and $\gamma\delta$."

From this theory of the *semi-decussation* of the *optic nerves*,
Newton draws the following conclusions :—

" Hence it appears," says he,—

" 1. Why the two images of both eyes make but one image,
$a\,b\,c\,d$, in the brain.

" 2. Why, when one eye is distorted, objects appear double,
for if the image of any object be made upon A in the one eye,
and $\beta$ in the other, that object shall have two images in the
brain at $a$ and $b$.   Therefore, the pictures of any objects ought
to be made upon the corresponding points of the two retinas ;
if upon A in the right eye, then upon $a$ in the left ; if upon B,
then also upon $\beta$.   And so shall the motions concur after they
have passed the juncture G H, and make one image at $a$ or $b$
more vivid than one eye alone could do.

" 3. Why, though one thing may appear in two places by
distorting the eyes, yet two things cannot appear in one place.
If the picture of one thing fall upon A, and of another upon $a$,

they may both proceed to $p$, but no farther. They cannot both be carried on the same pipe $p\,a$ into the brain ; that which is strongest, or most helped by phantasy, will there prevail, and blot out the other.

"4. Why, if one of the branches of the nerve beyond the juncture, as at G F or F H should be cut, that half of both eyes towards the wounded nerve would be blind, the other half remaining." [1]

This ingenious theory, decidedly superior to that of Briggs, was to a considerable extent anticipated by M. Rohault, in his *Traité de Physique*, published in 1671, more than ten years before Newton's attention was called to the subject. Rohault gives the very same figure as the preceding one, with this difference, that the nerves neither cross nor split into two at G H. He supposes that the two optic nerves have their corresponding or sympathetic fibres, which unite in one point in the brain ; and he thus explains single vision with two eyes, their duplicity by distortion, and the impossibility of two things appearing in one place. [2]

During the 120 years that have elapsed since the publication of Newton's Optics, we hear nothing more of the Theory of Vision in the 15th Query, and in the manuscript above referred to, till the year 1824, when Dr. Wollaston published in the *Philosophical Transactions* of that year, a paper *On Semi-decussation of the Optic Nerves*, in which he reproduces the very theory of Newton, in order to account for the curious disease of *hemiopsy*, or *amaurosis dimidiata*,[3] in which the patient sees with each eye only half of an object, being blind to the other

[1] Sir Isaac draws other four conclusions from his theory, but they will find a fitter place in the APPENDIX, No. VII.

[2] A Latin translation of Rohault's work was published in 1708, by Dr. Clarke, " with annotations chiefly from the philosophy of Newton, and yet no notice is taken of Newton's Theory, as contained in his 15th Query, although Dr. Clarke had translated the *Optics* into Latin. He adds a note stating that the conjecture respecting the fibres of the optic nerve had not yet been confirmed by dissection. Part I. cap. 31, p. 225, *note*.

[3] The *suffusio dimidians* of other authors.

half. This sympathy between the two eyes may certainly arise from structure, and depend upon " connexion of nervous fibres," and if it does, is very well explained either by the hypothesis of Rohault or of Newton ; but we cannot attach any value to the invention of structural hypotheses when the phenomena may be explained by that habitual sympathy of double organs with which we are so well acquainted. This observation is still more applicable to the remark of Wollaston, that by his theory " we clearly gain a step in the solution, if not a full explanation of the long agitated question of single vision with two eyes," because this great fact in vision can be perfectly explained, as we shall presently see, without any hypothesis whatever.

But not only is this theory of semi-decussation uncalled for, it is contradicted by numerous facts. It has been examined with great ability by Mr. Twining, of the Indian Medical Service,[1] who concludes " from anatomical observations respecting the structure of the optic nerves and thalami, and the effects of disease on those parts, that no decussation or semi-decussation of the optic nerves exists in the human subject. No anatomist, indeed, has pretended to say that there is any trace of semi-decussation ; and it has been proved that the decussation or crossing at G H, *Fig.* 16, is only partial, the inner bundles decussating, while the outer bundles remain on the side on which they previously lay."[2]

There is no branch of physical science upon which such unsound views have prevailed as in that which relates to the optical functions of the eye ; and in studying the speculations of modern metaphysicians and physiologists, we feel as if we were grappling with the chimeras of Aristotle or Descartes. While Dr. Reid maintains that objects appear single when their images are formed upon corresponding points of the retina,

[1] See *Transactions of the Medical and Physical Society of Calcutta*, vol. ii. p. 151 ; or *Edinburgh Journal of Science*, July 1828, vol. ix. p. 143.

[2] Wagner's *Handwörterbuch der Physiologie*, vol. iii. part ii. p. 297.

and double in all other circumstances, he gives *no explanation whatever* of single vision : he merely attaches the name of corresponding points to those upon which the image falls when it is seen single ! And when Dr. Brown tells us that it is from association alone we see objects single and erect, by means of double and inverted pictures, he merely asserts his ignorance of the cause ; and his assertion is contrary to the most notorious facts and to all experience, as Dr. Reid has shown.[1]  Nor does Dr. Alison, one of the latest writers on the subject, bring us a single step nearer the truth.  After controverting the views of Brown and Reid, he apprehends that he has established the following two facts, the one explaining single, and the other erect vision :[2]—

1. That images formed on corresponding points of the retinæ of the human eyes, and on those only, naturally affect our minds in the same manner as a single image formed on the retina of one eye ; and,

2. That impressions made on different points of the retina

---

[1] If by the sense of touch we could make the *two* images appear *one*, then we should also see an object single when it is doubled by looking either at a nearer or a more distant object, or when it is made 100 by a multiplying glass ; but if a man were to live 1000 years, he would still see the *two* or the hundred images, though he knew there was only one object.  In order to illustrate his opinion, Dr. Brown says that the two English words *he conquered*, excite the same idea as the one Latin word *vicit*.  In reply to this Dr. Whewell says, " that to make this pretended illustration of any value, it ought to be true that when a person has thoroughly learned the Latin language, he can no longer distinguish any separate meaning in *he* and in *conquered*."  With this assertion we cannot concur.  The two words *he conquered*, undoubtedly convey the same meaning as *vicit*.  If we unite the two words thus, *heconquered* or *conqueredhe*, we cannot doubt that the word *he* is as truly included in the termination *it* of *vicit*, as *he* is in the single word *heconquered*, unless it is alleged that *vicit* may also mean *she conquered*.

Dr. Brown's real mistake consists in not taking *two exactly similar words*, as *vicit*, *vicit*, like what he considers as the *two exactly* similar images.  The two words pronounced in succession convey certainly only one idea, but the mind recognised the same in succession or its *duplicity*, just as it would do the two similar and united images, if one of them were slipped from its superposition on the other by pressing aside one of the eye-balls.

Dr. Brown's views are affected with another error, namely, in the assumption that the pictures in each eye are exactly similar.

[2] *Edinburgh Transactions*, vol. xiii. p. 479.

of the eye, are *naturally* followed by inferences as to the relative position of the objects producing these impressions, *exactly opposite* to those which follow impressions made on different points of the surface of the body.[1]

We are unable to controvert these two palpable facts. They are truisms which explain nothing ; and if Nature had been so perverse as to produce *three* pictures in place of *one* from two eyes, and had turned round an erect picture 90° in place of 180°, which it does in inverting it, that is, had represented a man upon the retina lying horizontally in place of vertically and inverted, the explanation of Dr. Alison would have been, that in the first case it was *natural*, and that in the other it was *naturally*, and *exactly half opposite* to other impressions on the surface of the body.[2]

From these speculations we venture to solicit the attention of the reader to the true explanation of single and erect vision, and of all the other normal visual phenomena with which we are acquainted, an explanation which has been overlooked by our most distinguished optical writers.

1. The retina[3] is the seat of visual sensation and of vision ; and there is a law of visual sensation as well as a law of vision, which can be determined only by experiment.

2. In order to determine the law of visual sensation, or the mental information given by the action of a physical point of

---

[1] There is no opposition between the impressions on the concave retina and on a concave surface of the body. If we hold up the hand vertically, and bend it into a concavity, an impression made on the *upper* part of the concavity, will be felt as coming from below, and an impression on the lower part of the concavity will be felt as coming from above, exactly as in the case of the concave retina.

[2] We have not noticed the additional explanation adopted by Dr. Alison, " that impressions on the *upper* part of the *retina* are impressions on the *lower* part of the *optic lobes, i.e.,* of the *sensorium ;*" because he has not told us what requires as much explanation as inverted vision, namely, why the lower part of the sensorium makes the object seem lower ! Is the sensorium a plane, or a convexity, or a concavity ? If it is a concavity, a physical impression on the *lower* part *will* correspond to the *top* of the object, and an impression on the *upper* part with the *bottom* of it.

[3] I omit all consideration of the question, whether the choroid coat or retina is the seat of vision, or whether the *foramen centrale* is or is not an opening in the retina.

light upon the retina, let us make a hole of the smallest size, that of the *minimum visibile*, for example, on a sheet of black paper, and let a ray of the sun's light pass through it and fall upon the eye. This cone of rays, with the pupil for its base, will be refracted by the humours of the eye into a smaller cone, the apex of which falls upon the retina. This apex, or point, is the image of the hole in the paper, and is formed by a cone of rays whose angle we may suppose to be 12°, so that the impression is made by rays falling at all angles on the retina from 0° to 6° on each side of the perpendicular or axis of the cone. If, while looking at the hole in the paper, we stop all the different rays in succession from 0° to 6°, we shall find that the hole is seen by them all *in one direction*, and that this direction is the axis of the cone, and, as nearly as can be ascertained, the real direction of the hole, or the axis of the incident cone of rays. Hence it follows, that the impression of a ray of light upon the retina, whatever be the angle of its incidence, gives the sensation of having proceeded in a direction perpendicular to the retina, a direction as will be afterwards seen coinciding nearly with the real direction of the hole from which it issues. This is the law of visible direction.

3. In order to determine the law of vision, look at the hole in the paper with both eyes, and it will be found, by opening and shutting each eye alternately, that a single image of the hole is seen, and always in the same place, namely, at the point where the optical axes of the two eyes meet, and consequently at the distance from the eye where these axes meet. The single image seen by both eyes is formed by the superposition or coincidence of the two images. This is the law of visible distance, and the law of single vision ; but the law of single vision is true only for visible points. If we had the *hundred* eyes of Argus in place of *two*, the hundred images of a point would coincide in *one* at the point where the hundred images converge.

4. The law of vision for visual *objects* is entirely different

from that for points.   A visual object cannot be seen single at
once.   Let the object, for example, be a *line* $\frac{1}{10}$th of an inch
long.   The two images of it cannot be seen coincident by both
eyes.   When the right hand extremities of the images are coincident or single, the left hand extremities are not, and *vice versa*.
When the object is a *lineal* space or *superficies*, only one point
of it is seen single and distinct, the two eyes converging their
optic axes on every point of it in succession, and thus obtaining the idea of space.   When the object is a *solid*, such as a
cube, only one point of it is seen single and distinct, the two
eyes converging their optical axes to the near and remote parts
of it in succession, and thus obtaining an idea of the different distances of its parts by the varying angle of the optic
axes.   This law of vision for solids, includes the theory of the
stereoscope. [1]

We have stated that the law of sensation gives a visible
direction, which is *nearly* coincident with the real direction of
objects.   The celebrated D'Alembert maintained that the action
of light upon the retina is conformable to the laws of Mechanics,[2]
and therefore that the visible direction of an object should be a
line perpendicular to the curvature of the retina at the excited
point ; but he rejected this law as contrary to observation.   By
using, however, more correct refractive powers for the humours
of the eye, and more accurate measures of its parts, we have
shown that the visible and true direction of points nearly coincide. [3]

By means of these laws all the phenomena of erect vision from
an inverted image,—of the single vision of points,—of the
vision of plane surfaces and solids,—and of the conversion of

[1] See *Edinburgh Transactions,* vol. xv. p. 360 ; *North British Review,* vol. xvii. p.
165 ; and my Treatise on the Stereoscope.

[2] When a ray falls obliquely upon the retina (or any other surface of sensation) its
action may be decomposed into two, the one lying in the surface of the membrane, and
acting laterally upon the papillæ, and the other perpendicular, and acting in the direction of the axis of the papillæ, and therefore passing to the brain.

[3] See *Edinburgh Transactions,* vol. xv. pp. 350-353.

two plane pictures into solids or objects in relief, may be calculated with as much accuracy as we can compute the positions of the heavenly bodies.

Among the minor optical labours of Sir Isaac Newton, we must rank some curious observations on the action of strong light upon his own eyes, which have been only recently published by Lord King in his Life of Locke. In his work on Colours, Mr. Boyle has described a curious case, in which a gentleman " eminent for his profound skill in almost all kinds of philological learning, had injured his eyes by looking too fixedly upon the sun through a telescope, without any coloured glass to take off from the dazzling splendour of the object. The excess of light did so strongly affect his eye, that *ever since* when he turns it towards a window or any white object, he fancies he sees a globe of light of about the bigness the sun then appeared to him, to pass before his eyes ; and having inquired of him how long he had been troubled with this indisposition, he replied, that it was already *nine* or *ten* years since the accident that occasioned it first befell him." [1] This remarkable case having attracted the attention of Locke, he requested Sir Isaac to give him his opinion on the subject. In his reply, dated Cambridge, June 30, 1691, Sir Isaac sent him the following very interesting observations, made by himself. [2]

" The observation you mention in Mr. Boyle's book of colours, I once made upon myself with the hazard of my eyes. The manner was this : I looked a very little while upon the sun in the looking-glass with my *right eye*, and then turned my eyes into a dark corner of my chamber, and winked, to observe the impression made, and the circles of colours which encompassed it, and how they decayed by degrees, and at last vanished. This I repeated a second and a third time. At the third time, when the phantasm of light and colours about it were almost vanished, intending my fancy upon them to see their last appearance, I

1 *Experiments and Considerations touching Colours*, chap. ii. § 9, p. 19.   Lond. 1664.
King's *Life of Locke*, vol. i. pp. 404-408.   Edit. 1830.

found, to my amazement, that they began to return, and by little
and little to become as lively and vivid as when I had newly
looked upon the sun.   But when I ceased to intend my fancy
upon them, they vanished again.   After this, I found, that, as
often as I went into the dark, and intended my mind upon them,
as when a man looks earnestly to see anything which is difficult
to be seen, I could make the phantasm return without looking
any more upon the sun ; and the oftener I made it return, the
more easily I could make it return again.   And at length, by
repeating this without looking any more upon the sun, I made
such an impression on my eye, that, if I looked upon the clouds,
or a book, or any bright object, I saw upon it a round bright
spot of light like the sun, and, which is still stranger, though I
*looked upon the sun with my right eye only, and not with my
left, yet my fancy began to make an impression upon my left
eye, as well as upon my right.*   For if I shut my right eye, or
looked upon a book or the clouds *with my left eye, I could see
the spectrum of the sun almost as plain as with my right eye,* if
I did but intend my fancy a little while upon it ; for at first,
if I shut my right eye, and looked with my left, the spectrum
of the sun did not appear till I intended my fancy upon it; but
by repeating, this appeared every time more easily.   And now,
in a few hours' time, I had brought my eyes to such a pass,
that I could look upon no bright object with either eye, but I
saw the sun before me, so that I durst neither write nor read ;
but to recover the use of my eyes, shut myself up in my chamber
made dark, for three days together, and used all means to divert
my imagination from the sun.   For if I thought upon him, I presently saw his picture, though I was in the dark.   But by keeping
in the dark, and employing my mind about other things, I began
in three or four days to have some use of my eyes again ; and,
by forbearing to look upon bright objects, recovered them pretty
well, though not so well, but that, for some months after, the
spectrum of the sun began to return as often as I began to me-
ditate upon the phenomena, even though I lay in bed at mid-

night with my curtains drawn. But now I have been very well *for many years*, though I am apt to think, if I durst venture my eyes, I could still make the phantasm return by the power of my fancy. This story I tell you, to let you understand, that in the observation related by Mr. Boyle, the man's fancy probably concurred with the impression made by the sun's light, to produce that phantasm of the sun which he constantly saw in bright objects. And so your question about the cause of this phantasm involves another about the power of fancy, which, I must confess, is too hard a knot for me to untie. To place this effect in a constant motion is hard, because the sun ought then to appear perpetually. It seems rather to consist in a disposition of the sensorium to move the imagination strongly, and to be easily moved, both by the imagination and by the light, as often as bright objects are looked upon."

These observations possess in many respects a high degree of interest. The fact of the transmission of the impression from the retina of the one eye to that of the other, or of its production in that eye merely by fancy, is particularly important ; and it deserves to be remarked as a singular coincidence, that we had occasion to observe, and to describe the same phenomena above forty years ago,[1] and long before the observations of Sir Isaac were communicated to the scientific world. Æpinus of St. Petersburg observed the circles of colours described by Newton, when produced by looking at the setting sun for fifteen seconds. In the experiments alluded to, we looked at the brilliant image of the sun formed by a concave speculum of 30 inches focus with the right eye tied up, and upon turning the left eye to a white ground, we observed *six* successions of different colours with their complementary tints when the left eye was shut. Upon uncovering the right eye, and turning it to a white ground, we were surprised to observe the reverse spectra, as if the impression had been conveyed from the left to the right eye, as in Sir Isaac's case. A spectrum of a darkish

[1] Art. ACCIDENTAL COLOURS, in the *Edinburgh Encyclopædia*, vol. i. pp. 91, 92.

hue floated before the left eye for many hours, and this was succeeded by severe pains shooting through every part of the head. A slight inflammation, affecting both eyes, continued for several days, and it was not till several years had elapsed that our eyes had recovered their former power.

Among the inventions of Sir Isaac Newton, we may enumerate his reflecting sextant for observing the moon's distance from the fixed stars at sea. The description of this instrument was communicated to Dr. Halley in the year 1700; but, either

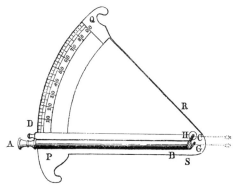

FIG. 17.

from having mislaid the manuscript, or from attaching no value to the invention, he never submitted it to the Royal Society, and it remained among his papers till after his death in 1742, when it was read on the 28th October. The following is Sir Isaac's own description of it, as copied from the original manuscript :[1]—

" In the annexed figure, P Q R S denotes a plate of brass, accurately divided in the limb D Q into $\frac{1}{2}$ degrees, $\frac{1}{2}$ minutes, and $\frac{1}{12}$ minutes by a diagonal scale ; and the $\frac{1}{2}$ degrees, and $\frac{1}{2}$

[1] See *Phil. Trans.* 1742-43, vol. xlii. p. 155.

minutes, and $\frac{1}{12}$ minutes, counted for degrees, minutes, and $\frac{1}{6}$ minutes.   A B is a telescope three or four feet long, fixed on the edge of that brass plate.   G is a speculum fixed on the brass plate perpendicularly as near as may be to the object-glass of the telescope, so as to be inclined forty-five degrees to the axis of the telescope, and intercept half the light which would otherwise come through the telescope to the eye.   C D is a moveable index turning about the centre C, and, with its fiducial edge, showing the degrees, minutes, and $\frac{1}{6}$ minutes on the limb of the brass plate P Q ;  the centre C must be over against the middle of the speculum G.   H is another speculum, parallel to the former, when the fiducial edge of index falls on $0^\circ \ 0' \ 0''$ ;  so that the same star may then appear through the telescope in one and the same place, both by the direct rays and by the reflexed ones ;  but if the index be turned, the star shall appear in two places, whose distance is showed on the brass limb by the index.

" By this instrument the distance of the moon from any fixed star is thus observed ;  view the star through the perspicil by the direct light, and the moon by the reflexed (or on the contrary) ;  and turn the index till the star touch the limb of the moon, and the index shall show on the brass limb of the instrument the distance of the star from the moon's limb ;  and though the instrument shake by the motion of the ship at sea, yet the moon and star will move together as if they did really touch one another in the heavens ;  so that an observation may be made as exactly at sea as at land.

" And by the same instrument, may be observed exactly the altitudes of the moon and stars, by bringing them to the horizon ; and thereby the latitude and times of observation may be determined more exactly than by the ways now in use.

" In the time of the observation, if the instrument move angularly about the axis of the telescope, the star will move in a tangent of the moon's limb, or of the horizon ;  but the observation may notwithstanding be made exactly, by noting when the line, described by the star, is a tangent to the moon's limb, or to the horizon.

" To make the instrument useful, the telescope ought to take in a large angle ; and, to make the observation true, let the star touch the moon's limb, not on the outside, but on the inside."

This ingenious contrivance is obviously the very same as that which Mr. Hadley produced in 1731 ;[1] and which, under the name of Hadley's Quadrant, has been of so great service in navigation. But though the merit of this invention is thus transferred to Newton, we must not omit to state, that the germ of it, and something more, had been previously published by Hooke. In giving an account of the inventions of members of the Royal Society, Sprot mentions " a new instrument for taking angles by reflexion, by which means the eye at the same time sees the two objects both as touching on the same point, though distant almost to a semicircle, which is of great use in promoting exact observations at sea."[2] Hooke was the member who made this invention, and there is a drawing and description of it in his Posthumous Works.[3] About the end of the year 1730, Thomas Godfrey of Philadelphia invented an instrument similar to Hadley's ; and the Royal Society, having found that Hadley's invention could be traced to the summer of 1730, decided that Hadley and Godfrey were independent inventors. The enlargement of this valuable instrument, so as to measure an angle of 120°, was first proposed by Captain Campbell in 1757.[4]

On the 6th February 1672, Sir Isaac communicated to Mr. Oldenburg his " design of a microscope by reflexion, which

[1] *Phil. Trans.* 1731, p. 147.

[2] Sprot's *Hist. of the Royal Society*, p. 246. Lond. 1667.

[3] *The Posthumous Works of* Robert Hooke, M.D., p. 503, tab. xi. fig. 2. Lond. 1705. In the description given of it by Waller, his biographer, the invention is mentioned as " an instrument for taking angles at one prospect, which he found described on a loose paper."

[4] Grant's *Hist. of Physical Astronomy*, p. 487 ; and *Nautical Mag.* vol. i. p. 351.

should have, instead of an object-glass, a reflecting piece of
metal, and which seemed as capable of improvement as telescopes, and perhaps more so, because but one reflective piece of
metal is requisite in them." This microscope is shown in the
annexed diagram, copied from the original, where A B is the
object-metal, C D the eye-glass, F their common focus, and O the
other focus of the metal in which the object is placed. This
ingenious idea has been greatly improved in modern times by
Professor Amici, Professor Potter, and Dr. Goring,[1] who make
A B a portion of an ellipsoid, whose foci are O and F, and who
fix a small plain speculum between O and A B, in order to

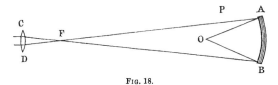

FIG. 18.

reflect into the speculum the object which is placed on one side
at P, for the purpose of being illuminated.[2]

In another letter to Mr. Oldenburg, dated July 11th in the
same year, he suggests an improvement of microscopes by refraction, " which I do," he says, " more willingly, because Mr.
Hooke hath made such excellent use of that instrument ; and
I shall be glad to contribute any thing to your promotion of
these his ingenious endeavours, or add to his inventions of that
kind. The way is, by illuminating the object in a darkened
room with light of any convenient colour not too much compounded ; for by that means the microscope will, with distinctness, bear a deeper charge and larger aperture, especially if its
construction be such as I may hereafter describe."[3] This happy

[1] See *Edinburgh Journal of Science*, vol. vi. p. 61 ; *Encyclopædia Brit.*, Art. *Microscope*, vol. xv. p. 41.

[2] Newtoni *Opera*, tom. iv. p. 300.

[3] Sir Isaac does not seem to have afterwards described this construction.

idea we have some years ago succeeded in realizing, by illuminating microscopic objects with the light of a monochromatic
lamp, which discharges a copious flame of pure yellow light of
definite refrangibility.[1]   Since the time of Newton, the microscope has undergone the greatest improvement,—the single
microscopes made of diamond and the other precious stones,—
the microscopic doublets, and the magnificent compound microscopes of Ross, Powell, and Nachet fitted up as polarizing
microscopes.

In order to remedy the evil of want of light in his reflecting
telescope, arising from the weak reflecting power of speculum
metal, and from its tarnishing by exposure to the air, Sir Isaac
proposed to substitute for the small oval speculum a triangular
prism of glass or crystal A B C, *Fig.* 19.   Its side A B *b a* he
supposes to perform the office of that
metal, by reflecting towards the eye-
glass the light which comes from the
concave speculum D F, *Fig.* 20, the
light reflected from which he supposes
to enter into this prism at its side
C B *b c*, and lest any colours should
be produced by the refraction of these
planes, it is requisite that the angles
of the prism at A *a* and B *b* be precisely equal.   This may be done most

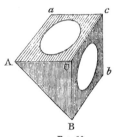

FIG. 19.

conveniently, by making them half right angles, and consequently the third angle at C *c* a right one.   The plane A B *b a*
will reflect all the light incident upon it, " especially if the
prism be made of crystal ;" but in order to exclude unnecessary
light, it will be proper to cover it all over with some black
substance, excepting two circular spaces of the planes A *c* and
B *c*, through which the useful light may pass.   The length of
the prism should be such that its sides A *c* and B *c* may be

[1] See *Edinburgh Transactions,* vol. ix. p. 433 ; and the *Edinburgh Journal of Science,*
July 1829, No. I. new series, p. 108.

" four-square," and so much of the angles B and *b* as are superfluous ought to be ground off, to give passage for as much light
as is possible from the object to the speculum.

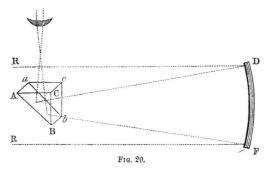

Fig. 20.

One great advantage of this prism, which cannot be obtained
from the oval metal, is that, without using two glasses, the
object may be erected, and the magnifying power of the tele-

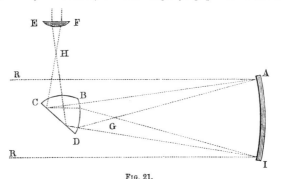

Fig. 21.

scope varied at pleasure, by merely varying the distances of
the speculum, the prism, and the eye-glass.    This will be understood from *Fig.* 21, where A I represents the great concave

speculum, E F the eye-glass, and B C D the prism of glass,
whose sides B C and B D are not flat, but spherically convex.
The rays which come from G, the focus of the great speculum
A I, will, by the refraction of the first side B D, be reduced to
parallelism, and after reflexion from the base C D, will be made
by the refraction of the next side B C to converge to the focus
H of the eye-glass E F. If we now bring the prism B C D
nearer the image at G, the point H will recede from B D, and
the image formed there will be greater than that at G ; and if
we remove the prism B C D from G, the point H will approach
to B C, and the image at H will be less than at G. The prism
B C D performs the same part as a convex lens, G and H being
its conjugate foci, and the relative size of the images formed
at these points being proportional to their distance from the
lens. These different contrivances were suggested by some
criticisms upon his reflecting telescope by M. Auzout ; and
Newton does not seem to have executed them, as he recommends " that the first trials be made with prisms whose sides
are all of them plane." [1]   As more than one-half of the light
is lost by reflexion from the small mirror, we have proposed
to substitute for it an achromatic prism to refract the rays to
the side of the tube. [2]   An advantage would be gained by the
use of a plane speculum of *silver*, which reflects much more
light than speculum metal.   The objection to reflecting prisms
arises from the imperfection of the glass, and the difficulty of
obtaining three perfectly flat surfaces, and two angles perfectly
equal.   This construction would be a good one for varying
optically the angular distance of a pair of wires placed in the
focus of the eye-glass E F ; and by bisecting the lenticular
prism B C D, and giving the halves a slight inclination, we
should be able to separate and to close the two images or discs
which the two halves would produce, and thus form a double
image micrometer.

[1] See Newtoni *Opera*, tom. iv. p. 276.
[2] *Treatise on Optics*, edit. of 1853, p. 494.

In concluding our account of Newton's optical discoveries, some notice of the principal work which contains them will suitably terminate the present chapter. This work, entitled *Opticks, or a treatise on the Reflexions, Refractions, Inflexions, and Colours of Light*, was published in London, without a date, on the 16th February 1704. Newton, from the President's chair, presented it to the Royal Society. Dr. Halley was desired to peruse it and make an abstract of it, and the thanks of the Society were given to the author " for the book, and for being pleased to publish it." In the second edition, with the date of July 16, 1717, the date of April 1, 1704, is added to the advertisement of the first edition, a step of which, as Mr. Edleston observes, " the dispute with Leibnitz had probably taught our philosopher the importance." [1]

In the advertisement to the first edition, we are informed by the author, that " a part of the ensuing discourse about light was written at the desire of some gentlemen of the Royal Society in the year 1675, and then sent to their Secretary and read at their meetings, and the rest was added about twelve years after, to complete the theory, except the third book, and the last proposition of the second, which were since put together out of scattered papers. To avoid being engaged in disputes about these matters, I have hitherto delayed the printing, and should still have delayed it, had not the importunity of friends prevailed upon me. *If any other papers writ on this subject are got out of my hands, they are imperfect,* and were perhaps written before I had tried all the experiments here set down, and fully satisfied myself about the laws of refractions and compositions of colours. I have here published what I think proper to come abroad, wishing that it may not be translated into another language without my consent." In the advertisement to the second edition, which appeared in 1717, he mentions that he could have added at the end of the

[1] It is a curious fact, that " there is the same peculiarity about the preface to the Principia."—Edleston's *Correspondence*, &c. &c., pp. lviii. and lxxi.

third book some questions (namely the thirty-one celebrated queries) ; " and," he adds, " to show that I do not take gravity for an essential property of bodies, I have added one question concerning its cause, choosing to propose it by way of a question, because I am not yet satisfied about it for want of experiments."

At the request of Newton, Dr. Samuel Clark prepared a Latin edition of his Optics, which appeared in 1706, and he was generously presented by Sir Isaac with £500, or £100 for each of his five children, as a token of the approbation and gratitude of the author. Demoivre is said to have secured and taken charge of this translation, and to have spared neither time nor trouble in the task. Newton met him every evening at a coffee-house,[1] and when they had finished their work, he took Demoivre home with him to spend the evening in philosophical conversation.[2] Both the English and the Latin editions have been frequently reprinted, both in England and on the Continent, and perhaps there never was a work of profound science more widely circulated.[3]

The only other optical work by Newton was his *Lectiones Opticæ*, a course of lectures on optics, which he read as Lucasian Professor in the public schools of the University of Cambridge in the years 1669, 1670, and 1671. It was not published till after his death ;—an English edition in 1728, in octavo,[4] and the Latin original in 1729 in quarto.

This valuable work is divided into two parts, and contains many beautiful propositions, and interesting and instructive experiments, which are not to be met with in any modern treatise on optics.

In the *first* part, which is entitled, *On the Refraction of the*

---

[1] " Probably Slaughters' Coffee-house in St. Martin's Lane. —Edleston's *Correspondence*, p. lxxiv.

[2] Eloge, by Fontenelle.—*Mém. Acad. Par.* 1727.   Hist. p. 121.

[3] The English edition was reprinted at London in 1717, 1721, and 1730, and the Latin one at London in 1719, 1721, 1728, at Lausanne in 1740, and at Padua in 1773.

[4] *Biographia Brit.* Art. *Newton*, vol. vii. p. 779.

*Rays of Light,* he treats in *four* sections :—1. Of the different refrangibility of the rays of light ; 2. Of the measure of refractions ; 3. Of the refractions of plane surfaces ; and 4. Of the refractions of curved surfaces.

In the *second* part, which is entitled, *On the Origin of Colours,* he treats in five sections :—1. On the doctrine of colours, and its proof by experiments with the prism ; 2. On the various phenomena of colours, and on the phenomena of light thrown upon a wall by the prism ; 3. On the phenomena of light received in the eye from a prism ; 4. On the phenomena of light transmitted through a refracting medium terminated by parallel planes ; and, 5. On the phenomena of light transmitted through media terminated spherically, and on the rainbow.[1]

The manuscript from which the Latin edition was printed, was that which had been given by Newton himself to David Gregory, Savilian Professor of Astronomy at Oxford ; but after the edition had been printed, the editor learned that a more perfect manuscript, containing several corrections and emendations in Newton's own handwriting, had been preserved in the archives of the University of Cambridge. These emendations, occupying five quarto pages, were therefore printed at the end of the work, and we observe that Bishop Horsley has introduced them into the text in the third volume of his edition of Newton's works.

[1] An analysis of the *Lectiones Opticæ* has been given by the author of the Life of Newton in the *General Dictionary*, vol. ii. p. 779, note ; but it is by some mistake confined to the *first* Part, as if there were no *second* Part. The same mistake is committed in the *Biographia Britannica*, vol. v. p. 3215, note, where it is obvious that the author knew nothing of the *second* Part, as he calls the last portion of the *first* Part the " Last Section of these Lectures."

## CHAPTER XI.

Astronomical Discoveries of Newton—Combined Exertion necessary for the Completion of great Discoveries—Sketch of the History of Astronomy previous to the Time of Newton—Discoveries of Nicolas Copernicus, born 1473, died 1553—He places the Sun in the centre of the System—His Work on the Revolutions of the Heavenly Bodies, printed at the expense of Cardinal Schonberg, and dedicated to Pope Paul III.—Tycho Brahe, born 1546, died 1601—His Observatory of Uraniburg—Is visited by James VI.—Is persecuted by the Danish Minister—Retires to Germany—His Discoveries and Instruments—The Tychonic System—John Kepler, born 1571, died 1631—His Speculation on the Six Regular Solids—Discovers the Ellipticity of Mars' Orbit—His Laws of the Planetary Motions—His Ideas of Gravitation—His Religious Character—Galileo, born 1564, died 1642—The First to apply a Telescope to the Heavens—Discovers the Four Satellites and Belts of Jupiter—His Researches in Mechanics—Is summoned before the Inquisition for Heresy—Retracts his Opinions, but persists in teaching the Doctrine of the Earth's Motion—Is again summoned before the Inquisition—His Sentence to Imprisonment for Life—Becomes Blind—His scientific Character—Labours of Bouillaud, and of Borelli—Suggestion of Dr. Hooke on Gravity—His Circular Pendulum—His Experiments with it—His Views respecting the Cause of the Planetary Motions.

FROM the optical researches of Newton, brilliant though they be, we turn with fresh wonder to the contemplation of his astronomical discoveries—those transcendent deductions of human reason,* by which he has added to the scientific glory of his country, achieved for himself an immortal name, and vindicated the intellectual dignity of his species. Pre-eminent as his triumphs have been, it would be unjust to affirm that they were won by his single arm. The torch of many a preceding age had cast its light into the labyrinths of the material universe, and the grasp of many a powerful hand had thrown down the most impregnable of its barriers. An alliance indeed of many kindred spirits had been long struggling in the combat, and

Newton was but the leader of the mighty phalanx—the director of their combined genius—the general who won the victory, and wears its laurels.

The history of science presents us with no example of an individual mind throwing itself far in advance of its contemporaries. It is only in his career of crime and ambition that reckless man takes the start of his species, and, uncurbed by moral and religious ties, represses the claims of truth and justice, and founds an unholy empire upon the ruins of ancient and venerable institutions. The achievements of intellectual power, though frequently begun by one mind, and completed by another, have ever been the results of united labour. Slow in their growth, they gradually approximate to a more perfect condition : The variety in the objects and phenomena of nature, summons to research a variety of intellectual gifts : Observation collects her materials, and patiently plies her humble avocation : Experiment, with her quick eye and ready hand, develops new facts : The lofty powers of analysis and combination generalize insulated results, and establish physical laws ; and in the ordeal of contending schools and rival inquirers, truth is finally purified from error. How different is it with those systems which the imagination rears—those theories of wild import which are directed against the liberties, the consciences, and the hopes of man ! The fatal poison tree distils its virus in the spring as well as in the summer and the autumn of its growth ; but the fruit which sustains life must have its bud prepared before the approach of winter, its blossom expanded in the spring, and its juice elaborated by the light and heat of a summer and an autumnal sun.

In the century which preceded the birth of Newton, the science of astronomy advanced with the most rapid pace. Emerging from the darkness of the middle ages, the human mind seemed to rejoice in its new-born strength, and to apply itself with elastic vigour to unfold the mechanism of the heavens. Ancient astronomers, indeed, had cleared and paved the way for the onward march of their science. A century and a half before Christ, Hipparchus, in his observatory at Rhodes, made the first catalogue of the stars, and representing the motions of the sun and moon by epicycles revolving upon circular orbits, he compiled tables for calculating their places in the heavens. Guided by the genius of Hipparchus, Claudius Ptolemy, a century and a half after Christ, though he placed the earth in the centre of the system, improved the theories of the sun, moon, and planets—discovered the principal inequality in the moon's orbit—gave a theory of astronomical refractions more complete than that of any astronomer before Cassini, and bequeathed to posterity the valuable legacy of his *Almagest*, and his Five Books of *Optics*.[1]

After centuries of darkness, Bagdad, the capital of Arabia, became the focus of science. The ancient astronomy was preserved and cultivated, but though new and more accurate observations were made, the science lay prostrate amid the cumbrous appendages of cycles and epicycles.

In the thirteenth century, the noble-minded Alphonso x., sovereign of Castile, published, at a great expense, new astronomical tables, computed by the most distinguished professors in the Moorish universities ; and, as if he had obtained a glimpse of a simpler arrangement, he denounced the rude mechanism of epicycles in language less reverent in its expression than in its truth. Were the heavens thus constituted, he said, I could have given the deity good advice had he consulted me at their creation. Notwithstanding these obstructions, Astronomy advanced, though with faltering steps, unable to escape from the trammels of authority, and free itself from those vulgar prejudices which a false interpretation of Scripture had excited against a belief in the motion of the earth.

In this almost stationary condition, however, the science of the heavens was not suffered to remain. Nicolas Copernicus arose—a philosopher fitted to develop the true system of the

[1] See Art. OPTICS in *Edin. Encyclopædia*, vol. xv. p. 462.

universe, and a priest willing to give absolution for the sin of placing the great luminary in the centre of the system. This distinguished individual, a native of Thorn in Prussia, though of Bohemian origin, was born on the 19th January 1472. He at first followed his father's profession of medicine, but finding it uncongenial with his love of astronomy, he went to Bologna to study that science under Dominic Mario. In this situation he was less the disciple than the assistant and friend of Mario, and we find that he had made observations on the moon at that place in 1497. About the year 1500, he went to Rome, where he taught mathematics publicly to a large assemblage of youth, and of persons of distinction ; and in the month of November of the same year, he observed an eclipse of the moon, and made other observations which formed the basis of his future researches. While thus occupied, the death of one of the Canons of the Cathedral Church of Ermeland, at Frauenburg, enabled his uncle, who was Bishop of that See, to nominate him to the vacant office. In this secluded spot,—in the residence of the Canons, situated on the brow of a hill, Copernicus carried on his astronomical observations. During his sojourn at Rome, the Bishop of Fossombrossa, who presided over the council for reforming the calendar, had requested his assistance in that important undertaking. Upon this congenial task he entered with youthful zeal. He charged himself with the duty of determining the length of the year, and the other elements which were required by the council ; but the observations became irksome, and interfered with the completion of those interesting views which had already dawned upon his mind.

Convinced that the simplicity and harmony which appeared in the other works of creation should characterize the arrangements of the planetary system, he could not regard the hypothesis of Ptolemy as a representation of nature. This opinion was strengthened by actual observation. The variable appearance of the superior planets, of Mars, for example, in opposition

and conjunction,—in the one case shining with the effulgence
of Jupiter, and in the other with the light of a secondary star,
was irreconcilable with the dogma that the planet moved round
the earth.  That it moved round the sun was the conclusion
to which he was then led ; and the grand idea of the bright orb
of day being the centre of the planetary system burst upon his
mind, though perhaps with all the dimness of a dream—the first
phase of every great discovery.  In the opinions of the Egyptian
sages,—in those of Pythagoras, Philolaus, Aristarchus, and
Nicetas of Syracuse, he recognised his first conviction that the
earth was not the centre of the universe ; and in the works of
Martianus Capella, he found it to be the opinion of the Egyp-
tians that Mercury and Venus revolved about the sun during
his annual motion round the earth.  Thus confirmed in his
views, the difficulties which had previously surrounded them
were gradually dispelled, and after thirty-six years of intense
study, in which the labours of the observer, and the calculations
of the mathematician, were combined with the sagacity of the
philosopher, he was permitted to develop the true system of
the heavens.

Iu his eye the sun stood immovable in the centre of the
universe, while the earth revolved annually round him between
the orbits of Venus and Mars, producing by its rotation upon
its axis in twenty-four hours all the diurnal phenomena of the
celestial sphere—Mercury and Venus moving round the sun
within the earth's orbit, and all the rest of the planets without
it, while the moon revolved monthly round the earth during its
annual motion.  In the system thus constituted, all the phenomena of the celestial motions received an immediate explanation.
The alternation of day and night—the vicissitudes of the seasons—the varying brightness of the planets—their stations and
retrogradations, and even the precession of the Equinoxes,
became the necessary results of the Copernican System.

The circulation of these great truths, and of the principles
on which they rest, became the leading object of Copernicus's

life.  The Canon of Ermeland, however, saw the difficulties of
his position, and exhibited the most consummate prudence in
surmounting them.  Aware of the prejudice and even of the
hostility with which his discoveries would be received, he
resolved neither to startle the one nor provoke the other.  He
committed his opinions to the slow current of personal communication.  The points of opposition which they presented to
received doctrine were thus gradually worn down, and they
insinuated themselves into ecclesiastical minds by the very
reluctance of their author to bring them into notice.  In 1536,
Cardinal Nicolas Schonberg, Bishop of Capua,[1] and Tidemann
Gyse, Bishop of Culm, exerted all their influence to induce
Copernicus to lay his system before the world ; but their
entreaties were in vain, and it was not published till 1539,
when an accidental circumstance contributed with other causes
to alter his resolution.[2]  Having heard of the system of Copernicus, George Rheticus, Professor of Mathematics at Wirtemberg, resigned his chair, and repaired to Frauenburg to make
himself master of his discoveries.  After studying and adopting
them, this zealous disciple prevailed upon Copernicus to permit
their publication ; and they seemed to have arranged a plan
for giving them to the world without alarming the vigilance of
the Church.  Under the disguise of a student of mathematics,
Rheticus published in 1540 an account of the manuscript
volume of Copernicus.  The pamphlet was received without
any expression of censure, and its author was thus encouraged
to reprint it at Basle with his own name.  The success of these
publications, and the flattering manner in which the new astronomy was received, combined with the solicitations and even
reproaches of his friends, overcame the scruples of Copernicus,
and induced him to place his manuscript in the hands of
Rheticus.  It was accordingly printed at the expense of
Cardinal Schonberg, and was published at Nuremberg in 1543,

---

[1] The Cardinal's letter is published in the work of Copernicus afterwards mentioned.
[2] These facts are recorded by Copernicus himself in the preface to his work.

under the title of " *On the Revolutions of the Celestial Bodies.*"[1]
Its illustrious author, however, did not live to peruse it.  A
complete copy was handed to him on his dying day, and he
saw and touched it a few hours before he expired.[2]  In an
introductory address " on the hypotheses of his work," Copernicus propitiates such of his readers as may be alarmed at their
novelty, by assuring them that it is not necessary that astronomical hypotheses be either true or probable, and that they
accomplish their object if they reconcile the calculus with
observation.[3]  With the same view he inscribed his preface to
the Holy Pontiff himself,[4] and boldly alludes to the hostility to
which his opinions will expose him.  " I have preferred," says
he, " dedicating my lucubrations to your Holiness rather than
to any other person, because, in the very remote corner of the
world in which I live, you are so distinguished by your rank
and your love of learning and mathematics, that you will easily
repress the virulence of slander, notwithstanding the proverb
that there is no remedy against the wound of the sycophant."
And " should there be any babblers who, ignorant of all mathematics, presume to judge of these things, on account of some
passage of Scripture wrested to their own purpose, and dare to
blame and cavil at my work, I will not scruple to hold their
judgment in contempt. . . . . Mathematics are written for
mathematicians, and I am much mistaken if such men will not
regard my labours as conducive to the prosperity of the ecclesiastical republic over which your Holiness presides."  Thus
recommended to the sovereign authority of the Church, and
vindicated against the charge of being hostile to Scripture, the

[1] Nicolai Copernici Torinensis *De Revolutionibus orbium cœlestium*, Lib. vi. Fol.  A
second edition in folio appeared at Basle in 1566, and a third edition in quarto was published at Amsterdam in 1617, with notes, by Nicolas Muler, under the title of *Astronomia Instaurata*, &c.
[2] Copernicus died in 1543, at the age of 70.
[3] Neque enim necesse est, eas hypotheses esse veras, imo ne verisimiles quidem, sed
sufficit hoc unum, si calculum observationibus congruentem exhibeant."—*Ad Lectorem.*
[4] Paul III., a member of the Farnese family, who held the Pontificate from 1534 to
1550.  The year in which this preface was written is not known.

Copernican system met with no ecclesiastical opposition, and
gradually made its way in spite of the ignorance and prejudices
of the age.

Although the true solar system was thus established, yet
much remained to be done by the practical astronomer before
the motions of the planets could be subjected to mechanical
laws.  Copernicus had not rejected the machinery of epicycles ;
and the distances of the planets and the form of their orbits
were very imperfectly known.  A skilful observer, therefore,
expert in mechanism, and girt for nocturnal labour, was now
required to prepare for Kepler distances and periods, and for
Newton the raw material of his philosophy.

The astronomer thus required appeared in the person of
Tycho Brahe, who was born at Knudstrup, in Scania, on the
14th December 1546, three years after the death of Copernicus.  When a student at Copenhagen, the great solar eclipse
of the 21st August 1560, arrested his attention, and having
found that all its phases had been accurately predicted, he
resolved to acquire the knowledge of a science so infallible in
its results.  Though destined for the profession of the law, he
refused to enter upon its study ; and when urged to it by the
entreaties and reproaches of his friends, he escaped from their
importunities by travelling into Germany.  During his visit to
Augsburg, he resided in the house of Peter Hainzell, the burgo-
master, whom he inspired with such a love of astronomy, that
he erected an excellent observatory at his own expense, and
thus enabled his youthful instructor to commence that splendid
career of observation which has placed him in the first rank of
practical astronomers.

On his return to Copenhagen in 1570, he was welcomed by
the King and the nobility as an honour to the nation, and his
maternal uncle at Herritzvold, near his native place, offered
him a retreat from the gaieties of the capital, and every accom-
modation for pursuing his astronomical studies.  Love and
alchemy, however, distracted his thoughts ; and he found the

peasant girl, whom he fancied, of easier attainment than the philosopher's stone. His noble relatives were deeply offended with the marriage, and it required all the influence of the King to allay the quarrel which it occasioned. In 1572 and 1573, he had observed the remarkable star in Cassiopeia, which rivalled Venus in her greatest brightness, and which, after being the wonder of astronomers for sixteen months, disappeared in March 1574 ; but he refused, for a long time, to publish his observations upon it, lest he should thus cast a stain upon his nobility !

Fickle in purpose, and discontented with Denmark, Tycho set out in search of a more suitable residence ; but when the King heard of his plans, he resolved to detain him by acts of kindness and liberality. He was therefore presented to the canonry of Roschild, with an annual income of 2000 crowns, and an additional pension of 1000 ; and the island of Huen was offered to him as the site of an observatory, to be furnished with instruments of his own choice. The generous offer was instantly accepted. The celebrated observatory of Uraniburg —the city of the Heavens—was completed at the expense of £20,000, and from its hallowed towers Tycho continued for twenty-one years to enrich astronomy with the most valuable observations. From every kingdom in Europe admiring disciples repaired to this sanctuary of the sciences, to acquire a knowledge of the heavens ; and kings and princes felt themselves honoured as the guests of the great astronomer.

Among the princes who visited Uraniburg, we are proud to enumerate James VI. of Scotland. In 1590, during his visit to Denmark to celebrate his marriage with the Princess Anne, he spent eight days with Tycho, accompanied by his counsellors and a large suite of nobility. He studied the construction and use of the astronomical instruments ; he inspected the busts and pictures in the Museum, and when he found among them the portrait of his own distinguished preceptor, George Buchanan, he could not refrain from the strongest expressions of delight.

Upon quitting Uraniburg, James not only presented Tycho with a magnificent donation, but afterwards gave him his Royal license to publish his works in England.

The equanimity of Tycho was not disturbed by these marks of respect and admiration ; but while they animated his zeal and stimulated his labours, they were destined to be the instruments of his ruin. By the death of Frederick II. in 1588, Tycho lost his most valued friend ; and though his son and successor, Christian IV., visited Uraniburg, and seemed to take an interest in astronomy, his wishes to foster it, if he did cherish them, must have been overruled by the influence of his counsellors. The parasites of royalty found themselves eclipsed by the brightness of Tycho's reputation. They envied the munificent provision which Frederick had made for him ; and instigated by a physician who was jealous of his reputation, as a successful practitioner of medicine, they succeeded in exciting against Tycho the hostility of the Court. Walchendorp, the President of the Council, was the tool of his enemies, and on the ground of an exhausted treasury, and the inutility of the studies of Tycho, he was deprived of his canonry, his pension, and his Norwegian estate.

Thus stripped of his income, and degraded from his office, Tycho, with his wife and family, sought for shelter in a foreign land. His friend, Count Henry Rantzau, offered him the hospitality of his Castle of Wandesberg, near Hamburg, and having embarked his family and his instruments on board a small vessel, the exiled patriarch left his ungrateful country never to return. In the Castle of Wandesberg he enjoyed the kindness and conversation of his accomplished host, by whom he was introduced to the Emperor Rodolph, who, to a love of science, added a passion for alchemy and astrology. The reputation of Tycho having already reached the Imperial ear, the recommendation of Rantzau was hardly necessary to insure him his warmest friendship. On the invitation of the Emperor, he repaired in 1599 to Prague, where he met with

the kindest reception.  A pension of three thousand crowns
was immediately settled upon him, and a commodious observatory erected for his use.   Here he renewed with delight
his interrupted labours, and rejoiced in the resting-place which
he had so unexpectedly found for his approaching infirmities.
These prospects of returning prosperity were enhanced by
the pleasure of receiving into his house two such pupils
as Kepler and Longomontanus ; but the fallacy of human
anticipations was here, as in so many other cases, strikingly
displayed.   His toils and his disappointments had made severe
inroads upon his constitution.   Though surrounded with affectionate friends and admiring disciples, he was still an exile in
a foreign land.   Though his country had been base in its in-
gratitude, it was yet the land which he loved—the scene of his
earliest affections—the theatre of his scientific glory.   These
feelings constantly preyed upon his mind, and his unsettled
spirit was ever hovering among his native mountains.   In this
condition he was attacked with a disease of the most painful
kind, and though the paroxysms of its agonies had lengthened
intermissions, yet he saw that death was approaching him.  He
implored his pupils to persevere in their scientific labours.  He
conversed with Kepler on some of the profoundest questions
in astronomy, and with these secular occupations he mingled
frequent acts of piety and devotion.   In this happy frame of
mind he expired without pain on the 24th October 1601, at
the age of fifty-five, the unquestionable victim of the councils
of Christian IV.

Among the great discoveries of Tycho, his improvements of
the lunar theory are perhaps the most important. He discovered
the inequality, called the variation, amounting to thirty-seven
minutes, and depending on the distance of the moon from the
sun.   He discovered also the annual inequality of the moon
depending on the position of the earth in its orbit, and affecting
also the place of her apogee and node.   He determined likewise the greatest and the least inclination of the moon's orbit,

and he represented this variation by the motion of the pole of
the orbit in a small circle.  Tycho had the merit, too, of being
the first to correct by the refraction of the atmosphere the
apparent places of the heavenly bodies ; but, what is very
unaccountable, he made the refraction which he found to be
34' in the horizon, to vanish at 45°, and he maintained that
the light of the moon and stars was refracted differently by the
atmosphere !  By his observations on the comet of 1577 he
proved that it was three times as distant as the moon, and
that since these bodies moved in all directions, the doctrine of
solid orbs could not be true.  By means of large and accurately
divided instruments, some of which were altitude and azimuth
ones, having their divided circles six and nine feet in diameter,
and others mural quadrants, sextants, and armillary spheres, he
made a vast collection of observations, which led Kepler to the
discovery of his celebrated laws, and formed the basis of the
Rudolphine Tables.  But the most laborious of his undertakings
was his catalogue of 777 stars, for the epoch of 1600, A.D.[1]—
a catalogue afterwards enlarged by Kepler from Tycho's observations, and published in 1627.[2]  The skill of Tycho in
observing phenomena, surpassed his genius for discovering their
cause, and it was perhaps from a mistaken veneration for the
Scriptures, rather than from the vanity of giving his name to
a new system, that he rejected the Copernican hypothesis.  In
the system which bears his name, the earth is stationary in the
centre of the universe, while the sun, with all the other planets
and comets revolving around him, performs his daily revolution
about the earth.

Notwithstanding the great accessions which astronomy had
received from Copernicus and Tycho, yet no progress had been
made in developing the general laws of the Solar System,
and scarcely an idea had been formed of the invisible power
by which the planets were retained in their orbits.  The

[1] *Astronomiæ Instauratæ Progymnasmata.*  1602.
[2] Published at the end of the *Rudolphine Tables.*

materials, however, were prepared, and Kepler arose to lay the foundations of a structure which Newton was destined to complete. John Kepler was born at the imperial city of Wiel, in Wirtemberg, on the 21st December 1571. Although his early education was neglected, he made considerable progress in his studies at the preparatory school of Maulbronn, and when he took his degree of Master of Arts at the University of Tübingen in 1591, he held the second place at the examination. While he was the mathematical pupil of Mæstlin, he not only adopted his views of the Copernican System, but wrote an essay on the " Primary Motion," as produced by the earth's daily rotation. When the astronomical chair at Gratz, in Styria, fell vacant in 1594, Kepler accepted the appointment, although he knew little of mathematics. His attention, however, was necessarily turned to astronomy, and in 1595, when he enjoyed some professional leisure, he directed the whole energy of his mind to the number, the dimensions, and the motions of the orbits of the planets. After various fruitless attempts to discover some relation between the distances and magnitude of the planets, by assuming the existence of new planets in the wider spaces, he at last conceived the extraordinary idea that the distances of the planets were regulated by the six regular geometrical solids. " The *Earth's* orbit," says he, " is the *sphere*, the measurer of all. Round it describe a *dodecahedron*, the circle including this will be (the orbit of) *Mars*. Round Mars describe a *tetrahedron*, the circle including this will be *Jupiter*. Describe a *cube* round Jupiter, the circle including this will be *Saturn*. Then inscribe in the (orbit of the) Earth an *icosahedron*, the circle described in it will be *Venus*. Describe an *octohedron* round Venus, the circle inscribed in it will be *Mercury*." This singular law, rudely harmonizing with some of Copernicus's measures, would have failed, for want of solids, in its application to *Uranus* and *Neptune ;* but it took possession of Kepler's mind, and he declared that he " would not barter the glory of

its invention for the whole Electorate of Saxony."[1]  When
Galileo's opinion of this hypothesis was requested by Kepler,
he praised the ingenuity which it displayed ; but when a copy
of the *Prodromus* was presented to Tycho, he advised his
young friend " first to lay a solid foundation for his views by
actual observation, and by ascending from these to strive to
reach the cause of things ;" and there is reason to believe, that
by the magic of the whole Baconian philosophy thus compressed
by anticipation into a nutshell, Kepler abandoned for a while
his visionary speculations.

When driven by religious persecution from the states of
Styria, he accepted an invitation from Tycho to settle at Prague
as his assistant.  Here he was introduced to the Emperor
Rodolph, and upon Tycho's death in 1601, he was appointed
mathematician to the Emperor, a situation which he held
during the successive reigns of Matthias and Ferdinand.

After devoting much of his time to the subjects of refraction
and vision, and adding largely to our knowledge of both these
branches of Optics,[2] he resumed his inquiries respecting the
orbits of the planets.  Possessed of the numerous and valuable
observations of Tycho, he endeavoured to represent them by
the hypothesis of a uniform motion in circular orbits ; but in
examining the orbit of Mars, he found the deviations from a
circle too great to be owing to errors of observation.  He
therefore compared the observations with various other curves,
and was led to the fine discovery that *Mars revolved round the
sun in an elliptical orbit in one of the foci of which the sun
himself was placed.*  By means of the same observations he
computed the dimensions of the planet's orbit, and by comparing the times in which Mars passed over different parts of
it, he found that they were to one another as the areas de-

[1] These researches were published in his *Prodromus Dissertationum Cosmographi-
corum, &c.*  Tubingæ, 1596, 4to.

[2] Kepler was foiled in his attempt to find out the law of refraction, afterwards discovered by Snellius.  His optical discoveries will be found in his *Paralipomena ad Vitel-
lionem,* Francof. 1604 ; and in his admirable *Dioptrica,* Franc. 1611.

scribed by the lines drawn from the centre of the planet to the centre of the sun, or, in more technical language, *that the radius vector, or line joining the sun and planet, describes equal areas in equal times.* These two brilliant discoveries, the first ever made in physical astronomy, were extended to all the other planets of the system, and were given to the world in his Commentaries on the Motions of the Planet Mars.[1]

Thus successful in his researches, and overjoyed with the result of them, Kepler renewed his attempts to discover the mysterious relation which he believed to exist between the mean distances of the planets from the sun.  Distrusting his original hypothesis of the geometrical solids, he compared the planetary distances with the intervals of musical notes, but though he was supported in this notion by the opinions of Pythagoras, and even of Archimedes, his comparisons were fruitless, and he was about to abandon an inquiry which had more or less occupied his mind during seventeen years of his life.

After Kepler had refused to accept the mathematical chair at Bologna, which was offered to him in 1617, he seems to have resumed his speculations " on the exquisite harmonies of the celestial motions."  On the 8th March 1618, he conceived the idea of comparing the powers of the different numbers which express the distances of the planets, with the powers of the different numbers which express their periods round the sun.  He compared, for example, the squares and the cubes of the distances with the same powers of the periodic times, and he even made the comparison between the squares of the periodic times and the cubes of the distances ; but having, in the hurry and impatience of research, been led into an error of calculation, he rejected the last of these relations,—the relation that was true,—as having no existence in nature.  Before a week, however, had elapsed, his mind reverted to the law which he had

---

[1] *Nova Astronomia seu Physica Celestis tradita Commentariis de Motibus Stellæ Martis.*  Pragæ, 1609, fol.

rejected, and, upon repeating his calculations, and discovering
his error, he recognised with rapture the great truth of which
he had for seventeen years been in search, *that the periodic
times of any two planets in the system are to one another as the
cubes of their distances from the sun.* This great discovery was
published in 1619 in his " Harmony of the World,"[1] which
was dedicated to James VI. of Scotland, and which is marked
with all the peculiarities of the author.    The passage which
describes the feelings under which he recognised the truth of
his third law, is too instructive to be omitted from his history :—" What sixteen years ago I urged as a thing to be
sought—that for which I joined Tycho Brahe—for which I
settled in Prague—for which I have devoted the best part of
my life to astronomical contemplations—at length I have brought
to light, and have recognised its truth beyond my most sanguine
expectations. . . . . It is now eighteen months since I got the
first glimpse of light, three months since the dawn ; a very few
days since the unveiled sun, most admirable to gaze on, burst
out upon me . . . . the die is cast—the book is written, to
be read either now or by posterity, I care not which.    It may
well wait a century for a reader, as God has waited six thousand
years for an interpreter of his works."[2]
     As the planes of the orbits of all the planets, as well as the
line of their apsides passed through the sun, Kepler could not
fail to suspect that some power resided in that luminary, by
which the motions of the planets were produced, and he went
so far as to conjecture that this power diminishes as the square
of the distance of the body on which it was exerted ; but he
immediately rejects this law in favour of that of the simple
distances.    In the Introduction to his Commentaries on Mars,
he distinctly recognises the mutual gravitation of matter, in the
descent of heavy bodies to the centre of the earth, as the centre
of a round body of the same nature with themselves.    He

[1] *Harmonia Mundi*, lib. v.   Linzii, 1619, fol.
[2] Ibid. p. 178.

maintained, that two stones situated beyond the influence of a third body would approach like two magnets, and meet at a point, each describing a space proportional to the mass of the other.   He maintained also, that the tides were occasioned by the moon's attraction, and that the lunar inequalities were owing to the joint action of the sun and earth.   Our country-man, Dr. Gilbert, in his celebrated book *De Magnete,* published in 1600, had about the same time announced similar opinions on gravitation.   He compares the earth's action upon the moon to that of a great loadstone ; and in his posthumous work which appeared half a century afterwards, he maintains that the earth and moon act upon each other like two magnets, the influence of the earth being the greater on account of its superior mass. But though these opinions were a step in celestial physics, yet the identity of the gravity which is exhibited on the earth's surface by falling bodies, with that which guided the planets in their orbits, was not revealed either to the English or the Ger-man philosopher.   It required more patience and thought than either could command, and its discovery was reserved for the exercise of higher powers.

The misery in which Kepler lived, stands in painful contrast with his arduous labours as an author, and his noble services to science.   His small pension was ever in arrears, and when he retired to Silesia to spend the remainder of his days in re-tirement, his pecuniary difficulties became more embarrassing than before.   He was compelled to apply personally for his arrears ; and, in consequence of the great fatigue which he suffered in his long journey to Ratisbon on horseback, he was seized with a fever which carried him off on the 30th Novem-ber 1630, in the fifty-ninth year of his age.   Thus perished one of the noblest of his race, a victim of poverty, and a martyr to science.

In a work which is to record the religious character of New-ton, it would be unjust to withhold from Kepler the credit which is due to his piety and faith.   The harmony of the universe, which he strove to expound, excited in him not only admiration, but love.  He felt his own humility the farther he penetrated into the mysteries of the universe, and sensible of the incompetency of his unaided powers for such transcendent researches, and recognising himself as but the instrument of the Almighty in making known his wonders, he never entered upon an inquiry without praying for assistance from above. Nor was this frame of mind inconsistent with the tumultuous delight with which he surveyed his discoveries.   His was the unpretending ovation of success, not the ostentatious triumph of ambition ; and if a noble pride occasionally mingled with his feelings, it was the pride of being the chosen messenger of physical truth, not the vanity of being the favoured possessor of superior genius.   With such a frame of mind, Kepler was necessarily a Christian.   The afflictions with which he was tried confirmed his faith and brightened his hopes.   He bore them in all their variety and severity with Christian patience ; and though he knew that this world was to be the theatre of his glory, yet he felt that his rest and his reward could be found only in another.

It is a remarkable fact in the history of astronomy, that three of its most distinguished cultivators were contemporaries. Galileo was the contemporary of Tycho during thirty-seven years, and of Kepler during the fifty-nine years of his life. Galileo was born seven years before Kepler, and survived him nearly the same time.   We have not learned that the intellectual triumvirate of the age enjoyed any opportunity for mutual congratulation.   What a privilege would it have been to have contrasted the aristocratic dignity of Tycho with the reckless ease of Kepler, and the manly and impetuous mien of the Italian sage !

While his two predecessors were laying deeply and surely the foundations of physical astronomy, Galileo was preparing himself for extending widely the limits of the Solar system, and exploring the structure of the bodies that compose it.   He was

born at Pisa on the 15th February 1564, and was descended
from the noble family of Bonajuti.    Although he exhibited an
early passion for geometry, and had studied without a master
the writings of Euclid and Archimedes, yet even after he was
called to the mathematical chair at Pisa in the twenty-fifth
year of his age, he was more distinguished for his hostility to
the Aristotelian philosophy than for his progress in original
inquiry.    In 1592 he was promoted to the same chair in
Padua, where he remained for eighteen years, adorning the
university by his talents, and diffusing around him a taste for
science.    With the exception of some minor contrivances, Galileo
had made no discovery till he entered his forty-fifth year, *an
age at which Newton had completed all his discoveries.*    In
1609, the memorable year in which Kepler published his
" New Astronomy," Galileo paid that visit to Venice during
which he heard of the telescope of Lippershey.[1]    The idea of
so extraordinary an instrument at once filled his mind, and
when he learned from Paris that it had an existence, he resolved instantly to realize it.    The simple idea, indeed, was the
invention, and Galileo's knowledge of optics was sufficient to
satisfy him that a convex lens at one end of a tube, with a
concave one at the other, would bring objects nearer to his eye.
The lenses were placed in the tube, the astronomer looked into
the concave lens, and saw the objects before it " pretty large
and pretty near him."    This little toy, which magnified only
*three* times lineally, and *nine* times superficially, he carried in
triumph to Venice, where the chief magistrate obtained it in
barter for the life possession of his professorship, and 480
florins as an increase of salary.    The excitement produced on
this occasion at Venice was of the most extraordinary kind ;
and, on a subsequent occasion, when Sirturi[2] had made one of
the instruments, the populace followed him with eager curiosity,
and at last took possession of the tube, till they had each

[1] Professor Moll, *Journal of Royal Institution*, 1831, vol. i. p. 496.
[2] Sirturus, *De Telescopio.* Francofurtæ, 1618.

witnessed its wondrous effects.    Galileo lost no time in availing
himself of his new power.    He made another telescope which
magnified about eight or nine times, and, sparing neither labour
nor expense, he finally constructed an instrument so excellent,
as " to show things almost a thousand times larger (in surface),
and above thirty times nearer to the eye."

There is, perhaps, no invention in science so extraordinary
in its nature, and so boundless in its influence, as that of the
telescope.    To the uneducated man the power of bringing
distant objects near to the eye must seem almost miraculous ;
and to the philosopher even who comprehends the principles
upon which it acts, it must ever appear one of the most elegant
applications of science.    To have been the first astronomer in
whose hands such a power was placed, was a preference to
which Galileo owed much of his reputation.

Before the telescope was directed to the heavens, it was impossible to distinguish a planet from a star.    Even with his
first instrument, Galileo saw that Jupiter had a round appearance like the sun and moon ; but, on the 7th January 1610,
when he used a telescope of superior power, he saw three little
bright stars very near him, *two* to the *right*, and *one* to the
*left* of his disc.    Though ranged in a line parallel to the ecliptic, he regarded them as ordinary stars ; but having, on the
8th of January, accidentally[1] directed his telescope to Jupiter,
he was surprised to see the three stars to the west of the planet,
and nearer one another than before,—a proof that they had a
motion of their own.    This fact did not excite his notice ; and
it was only after observing various changes in their relative
position, and discovering a fourth on the 13th of January,
that he was enabled to announce the discovery of the four
satellites of Jupiter.[2]

In continuing his observations with the telescope, Galileo

---

[1] " Nescio quo fato ductus."—*Sidereus Nuncius*, p. 20.

[2] The satellites were observed by our celebrated countryman, Harriot, on the 17th
October 1610.—See *Martyrs of Science*, Life of Galileo, pp. 40, 41.

discovered that Venus had the same crescent phases as the waxing and the waning moon ;—that the sun had spots on his surface which proved that he revolved round his axis ;—that Saturn was not round, but had handles attached to his disc ;— that the surface of the moon was covered with mountains and valleys, and that parts of the margin of her disc occasionally appeared and disappeared ;—that the milky way consisted of numerous stars, which the unassisted eye was unable to per- ceive ; and that the apparent size of the stars arose from irradiation, or a spurious light, in consequence of which they were not magnified by the telescope.  These various discoveries furnished new arguments in support of the hypothesis of Co- pernicus ; and we may now consider it as established by incon- trovertible evidence, which ignorance or fanaticism only could resist, that the sun is placed in the centre of the System, in the focus of the elliptical, or in the centre of the nearly circular, orbits of the planets, and that by some power, yet to be discovered, he guides them in their course, while the Earth and Jupiter exercise a similar influence over the satellites which accompany them.

But it is not merely from his astronomical discoveries, brilliant as they are, that Galileo claims a high place in the history of Newton's discoveries.  His profound researches on mechanical science—his determination of the law of acceleration in falling bodies—and his researches respecting the resistance and cohesion of solid bodies, the motion of projectiles, and the centre of gravity of solids, have ranked him among the most distinguished of our mechanical philosophers.  The great step, however, which he made in mechanics, was his discovery of the general laws of motion uniformly accelerated, which may be regarded as the basis of the theory of universal gravitation.[1]

The current of Galileo's life had hitherto flowed in a smooth and undisturbed channel.  His discoveries had placed him at

[1] See *Edinburgh Encyclopædia*, Art. MECHANICS, vol. xiii. p. 502, where we have given a copious abstract of the mechanical discoveries of Galileo.

the head of the great men of the age, and with an income
above his wants, he possessed both the means and the leisure
for prosecuting his studies.  Anxious, however, to propagate
the great truths which he discovered, and by force of reason to
make proselytes of his enemies, he involved himself in disputes
which tried his temper and disturbed his peace.  When argument failed to convince his opponents, he wielded against them
the powerful weapons of ridicule and sarcasm, and he thus
marshalled against himself and his opinions the Aristotelian
professors, the temporizing Jesuits, the political churchmen,
and that timid section of the community who tremble at innovation, whether it be in religion or in science.  The party of
Galileo who abetted him in his crusade against error, though
weak in numbers, were strong in position and in zeal.  His
numerous pupils occupying the principal chairs in the Italian
universities, formed a devoted band who cherished his doctrines
and idolized his genius.  The enemies of religion followed the
intellectual banner, and many princes and nobles, who had
smarted under ecclesiastical jurisdiction, were willing to see it
shorn of its power.

While these two parties were standing on the defensive,
Galileo hoisted the first signal for war.  In a letter to his
friend and pupil, the Abbé Castelli, he proved that the Scriptures were not intended to teach us science and philosophy, and
that the expressions in the Bible were as irreconcilable with
the Ptolemaic as with the Copernican system.  In reply to this
letter, Caccini, a Dominican friar, attacked Galileo from the
pulpit, and so violent was his language, that Maraffi, the general
of the Dominicans, expressed his regret that he should be implicated " in the brutal conduct of thirty or forty thousand
monks."  Encouraged by this apology, Galileo launched another
pamphlet, addressed to the Grand Duchess of Tuscany, in which
he supports his views by quotations from the Fathers, and by
the conduct of the Roman Pontiff himself, Paul III., in accepting
the dedication of Copernicus's work.  It was in vain to meet

such arguments by any other weapon than that of the civil power.  It was deemed necessary either to crush the heresy, or retire from the contest ; and the Church party determined to appeal to the Inquisition.

Various circumstances concurred to excite the suspicions of Galileo, and, about the end of 1615, he set off for Rome, where he was lodged in the palace of the Tuscan ambassador. While Galileo was enjoying the hospitality of his friend, Caccini was preparing the evidence of his heresy, and in due time he was charged by the Inquisition with maintaining the motion of the earth and the stability of the sun,—with teaching and publishing this heretical doctrine, and with attempting to recon- cile it to Scripture.  On the 25th February 1615, the Inquisi- tion assembled to take these charges into consideration, and having no doubt of their truth, they desired that Galileo should be enjoined by Cardinal Bellarmine to renounce the obnoxious doctrines, and to pledge himself that he would neither teach, publish, nor defend them in future.  In the event of his refusing to obey this injunction, it was decreed that he should be thrown into prison.  Galileo acquiesced in the sentence, and on the following day he renounced before the Cardinal his heretical opinions, abandoning the doctrine of the earth's motion, and pledging himself neither to defend nor teach it either in his writings or his conversation.

Although Galileo had made a narrow escape from the grasp of the Inquisition, he left Rome in 1616 with a suppressed hostility against the Church ; and his resolution to propagate the heresy seems to have been coeval with the vow by which he renounced it.  Although he affected to bow to the decisions of theology, he never scrupled, either in his writings or in his conversation, to denounce them with the severest invective. The Lyncean Academy, ever hostile to the Church, encouraged him in this unwise procedure, and it was doubtless at their instigation that he took the daring step which brought him a second time to the bar of the Inquisition.  Forgetting the

pledges under which he lay,—the personal kindness of the
Pope,—and the pecuniary obligations which he owed him, he
resolved to compose a work in which the Copernican system
should be indirectly demonstrated. This work, entitled, *The
System of the World of Galileo Galilei*, &c., was completed in
1630, but was not published till 1632, owing to the difficulty
of obtaining a license to print it. It was dedicated to the
Grand Duke of Tuscany ; and while the decree of the Inquisition
was referred to in insulting and ironical language, the Ptolemaic
system, the doctrine of the Church, was assailed by arguments
which admitted of no reply. The Copernican doctrines, thus
eloquently maintained, were eagerly received and widely disseminated, and the Church of Rome felt the shock thus given
to its intellectual supremacy. Pope Urban VIII., though attached
to Galileo, and friendly to science, was driven into a position
from which he could not recede. The guardian of its faith, he
mounted the ramparts of the Church to defend the weakest of
its bastions, and, with the artillery of the Inquisition, he silenced
the batteries of its assailants. The Pope brought the obnoxious
work under the eye of the Inquisition, and Galileo, advanced
in years, and infirm in health, was summoned before its stern
tribunal. He arrived in Rome on the 14th of February 1663,
and soon after his arrival he was kindly visited by Cardinal
Barberino, the Pope's nephew, and other friends of the Church,
who, though they felt the necessity of its interference, were yet
anxious that it should be done with the least injury to Galileo
and to science.

    Early in April, when his examination in person took place,
he was provided with apartments in the house of the Fiscal of
the Inquisition ; and to make this nominal confinement as
agreeable as possible, his table was provided by the Tuscan
ambassador, and his servant was allowed to sleep in an adjoin-
ing apartment. Even with these indulgences, however, Galileo
could not brook the degradation under which he lay. A return
of his complaint ruffled his temper, and made him impatient

for his release ; and the Cardinal Barberino having been made acquainted with his feelings, liberated the philosopher on his own responsibility, and on the 30th of April, after ten days' confinement, restored him to the hospitable roof of the Tuscan ambassador.

It has been stated on authority which is considered unquestionable, that during his personal examination Galileo was put to the torture, and that confessions were thus extorted which he had been unwilling to make.   He acknowledged that the obnoxious dialogues were written by himself ;—that he had obtained a license to print them without informing the functionary who gave it—and that he had been prohibited from publishing such opinions ; and in order to excuse himself, he alleged that he had forgotten the injunction under which he lay not to teach, in any manner, the Copernican doctrines. After duly considering the confessions and excuses of their prisoner, the Inquisition appointed the 22d of June as the day on which their sentence was to be pronounced.   In obedience to the summons, Galileo repaired to the Holy Office on the morning of the 21st.   Clothed in a penitential dress, he was conducted, on the 22d, to the convent of Minerva, where the Inquisition was assembled, and where an elaborate sentence was pronounced, which will ever be memorable in the history of science.   Invoking the name of our Saviour and of the Holy Virgin, Galileo is declared to be a heretic, in consequence of believing that the sun was the centre of the earth's orbit, and did not move from east to west, and defending the opinion that the earth moved and was not the centre of the world.   He is therefore charged with having incurred all the censures and penalties enacted against such offences : but from all these he is to be absolved, provided that with a sincere heart, and faith unfeigned, he abjures and curses the heresies he has maintained, as well as every other heresy against the Catholic Church.   In order to prevent the recurrence of such crimes, it was also decreed that his work should be prohibited by a formal edict,—

that he should be imprisoned during the pleasure of the Inquisition,—and that during the next three years he should recite weekly the seven penitential psalms.  This sentence was subscribed by seven cardinals, and on the same day Galileo signed the abjuration which the sentence imposed.

Clothed in the sackcloth of a repentant criminal, Galileo, at the age of seventy, fell upon his knees before the assembled cardinals, and laying his right hand on the Holy Evangelists, he invoked the Divine assistance, in abjuring and detesting and vowing never again to teach the doctrine of the earth's motion and of the sun's stability.  He pledged himself never again to propagate such heresies either in his conversation or in his writings, and he vowed that he would observe all the penances which had been inflicted upon him.  What a mortifying picture does this scene present to us of moral infirmity and intellectual weakness !  If we brand with infamy the unholy zeal of the inquisitorial conclave, what must we think when we behold the venerable sage, whose grey hairs were entwined with the chaplet of immortality, quailing under the fear of man, and sacrificing the convictions of his conscience, and the deductions of his reason, at the altar of a base superstition ?  Had Galileo added the courage of the martyr to the wisdom of the sage,— had he carried the glance of his eye round the circle of his judges, and with uplifted hands called upon the living God to witness the truth and immutability of his opinions, he might have disarmed the bigotry of his enemies, and science would have achieved a memorable triumph.

The sentence of abjuration was publicly read at several universities.  At Florence it was promulgated in the Church of Santa Croce, and the friends and disciples of Galileo were summoned to the ceremonial, in order to witness the degradation of their master.  But though the Church was thus anxious to maintain its authority, Galileo was personally treated with consideration, and even kindness.  After remaining only four days in the dungeons of the Inquisition, he was, at the request of the

Tuscan ambassador, allowed to reside with him in his palace, and when his health began to suffer, he was permitted to leave Rome and to reside with his friend Piccolomini, Archbishop of Sienna, under whose hospitable roof he completed his investigations respecting the resistance of solids. At the end of six months he was allowed to return to Florence, and before the close of the year he re-entered his house at Arcetri, where he spent the remainder of his days.

Although still a prisoner, Galileo had the happiness of being with his family and living under his own roof ; but like the other " spots of azure in his cloudy sky," it was ordained to be of short duration. It was now that he was justly characterized by the poet as " the starry Galileo with his woes." His favourite daughter Maria, who, along with her sister, had joined the convent of St. Matthew, near Arcetri, hastened to the filial duties which she had so long been prevented from discharging. She assumed the task of reciting weekly the seven penitential psalms which formed part of her father's sentence ; but she had scarcely commenced her domestic toils when she was seized with a dangerous illness, which in a few weeks proved fatal. Galileo was laid prostrate by this heavy and unexpected blow. He was inconsolable for the loss of his daughter, and disease in various forms shook the frail tenement which philosophy had abandoned. Time, however, the only anodyne of sorrow, produced its usual effects, and Galileo felt himself able to travel to Florence for medical advice. The Pope refused him permission, and he remained at Arcetri from 1634 to 1638, preparing for the press his " Dialogues on Motion," and corresponding with the Dutch government on his proposal to find the longitude by the eclipses of Jupiter's satellites. Galileo, whose eyes had been gradually failing him since 1636, was struck with total blindness in 1638. " The noblest eye," as his friend Father Castelli expressed it, " was darkened—an eye so privileged and gifted with such rare powers, that it may truly be said to have seen more than the eyes of all that are gone, and have opened the eyes of all that were to come." To the want of sight was soon added the want of hearing, and in consequence of the mental labour to which he had been subjected, " his head," as he himself said, " became too busy for his body ;" and hypochondriacal attacks, want of sleep, acute rheumatism, and palpitation of the heart, broke down his constitution. His last illness, after two months' continuance, terminated fatally on the 8th January 1642, when he was in the 78th year of his age.

" The scientific character of Galileo," as we have elsewhere[1] had occasion to remark, " and his method of investigating truth, demand our warmest admiration. The number and ingenuity of his inventions, the brilliant discoveries which he made in the heavens, and the depth and beauty of his researches respecting the laws of motion, have gained him the applause of every succeeding age, and have placed him next to Newton in the lists of original and inventive genius. To this high rank he was doubtless elevated by the inductive processes which he followed in all his inquiries. Under the sure guidance of observation and experiment, he advanced to general laws ; and if Bacon had never lived, the student of nature would have found in the writings and labours of Galileo not only the boasted principles of the Inductive philosophy, but also their practical application to the highest efforts of invention and discovery."

Among the astronomers who preceded Newton in astronomical inquiries, and contributed some ideas to the establishment of the true system of the planets, we must place the names of Bouillaud,[2] Borelli, Hooke, Huygens, Wren, and Halley. After refuting the magnetic notions of Kepler, Bouillaud maintained that the force of attraction must vary reciprocally as the square, and not, as Kepler asserted, in the simple ratio of the distance ;

---

[1] *Life of Galileo*, chap. vi. in the *Martyrs of Science.*

[2] Ismaelis Bullialdi *Astronomia Philolaica.*—Paris, 1645, p. 23. Sir Isaac admitted that Bullialdus here gives the true " proportion on gravity."—*Letter to Halley*, June 20, 1686, postscript.

but Delambre does not allow him any credit in this respect, and remarks that he has done nothing more for astronomy than to introduce the word evection into its language.

The influence of gravity as a central force in the planetary motions has been very distinctly described by Borelli, Professor of Mathematics at Pisa, in his work on the theory of Jupiter's Satellites.[1]  He considers the motions of the planets round the sun, and of the satellites round their primaries, as produced by some virtue residing in the central body.  In speaking of the motion of bodies in circular orbits, he compares the tendency of the body to recede from·the centre of motion to that of a stone whirled in a sling.  When this force of recession is equal to the tendency of the body to the centre, a balance is effected between these tendencies, and the body will continually revolve round the centre, and at a determinate distance from it.  Delambre attaches no value to these speculations of Borelli.  He has in his opinion pointed out no physical cause,[2] and has merely made a series of reflections which every astronomer would necessarily make who was studying the theory of the satellites.  He gives him the credit, however, of being one of the first who conjectured that the comets described round the sun elliptical or parabolic orbits.[3]

The speculations of our distinguished countryman, Dr. Hooke, respecting the cause of the planetary motions, exceeded greatly

[1] *Theoricæ Medicæorum Planetarum ex causis physicis deductæ.* A Alphonso Borellio.—Florentiæ, 1666.

[2] Newton (in his posthumous work, *De Systemate Mundi,* § 2, *Opera,* tom. iii. p. 180, and in his postscript in his letter to Halley, June 26, 1688, where he says " that Borelli did something") and Huygens have attached greater value to the views of Borelli.  The last of these philosophers thus speaks of them :—" Refert Plutarchus in libro supramemorato de Facie in Orbe Lunæ, fuisse jam olim qui putaret ideo manere lunam in orbe suo, quod vis recedendi a terra, ob motum circularem, inhiberetur pari vi gravitatis, qua ad terram accedere conaretur.  Idemque ævo nostro, non de luna tantum sed et planetis ceteris statuit Alphonsus Borellius, ut nempe primariis eorum gravitas esset solem versus ; lunis vero ad Terram Jovem et Saturnum quos comitantur.  Multoque diligentius, subtiliusque idem nuper explicuit Isaacus Newtonus, et quomodo ex his causis nascantur Planetarum orbes Elliptici, quos Keplerus excogitaverat ; in quorum foco altero Sol ponitur.  Christiani Hugenii *Cosmotheoros,* lib. ii. *ad finem.* OPERA, tom. ii. p. 720.

[3] Angelo Fabroni, *Lettere inedite d'uomini illustri,* tom. i p. 173.

in originálity and value the crude views of Borelli, and form a
decided step in physical astronomy.  On the 21st of March
1666, he communicated to the Royal Society an account of a
series of experiments to determine if bodies experienced any
change in their weight at different distances from the surface of
the earth " either upwards or downwards."  Kepler had maintained that this force, namely, that of gravity, was a property
inherent in all celestial bodies, and Hooke proposed " to consider
whether this gravitating or attractive power be inherent in the
parts of the earth ; and, if so, whether it be magnetical, electrical, or of some other nature distinct from either."  The
experiments which he made with the instrument described in
this communication, were far from being satisfactory, and he
was therefore led to the ingenious idea of measuring the force
of gravity " by the motion of a swing clock," which would go
slower at the top of a hill than at the bottom. [1]

About two months afterwards, namely, on the 22d May 1666,
Hooke communicated to the Society a paper " On the inflexion
of a direct motion into a curve by a supervening attractive
principle." [2]   After maintaining that the celestial bodies moving
in circular and elliptical orbits " must have some other cause
beside the first impressed impulse to bend their motion into
these curves," he considers the only two causes which appear to
him capable of producing such an effect.   The *first* of these
causes, which he considers an improbable one, is that the tendency to a centre is produced by a greater density of the ether
in approaching to the sun.  " But the *second* cause," he adds, " of
inflecting a direct motion into a curve may be from an attractive
property of the body placed in the centre, whereby it continually
endeavours to attract or draw it to itself.  For if such a principle
be supposed, all the phenomena of the planets seem possible to
be explained by the common principle of mechanic motions ; and
possibly the prosecuting this speculation, may give us a true
hypothesis of their motion, and from some few observations their

[1] Birch's *Hist. of Royal Society,* vol. ii. pp. 69-72.        [2] *Ibid.* vol. ii. pp. 90-92.

motions may be so far brought to a certainty that we may be
able to calculate them to the greatest exactness and certainty
that can be desired." After describing the circular pendulum[1]
for illustrating these views, he adds that " by this hypothesis
the phenomena of the comets, as well as of the planets, may be
solved ; and the motions of the secondary as well as of the
primary planets. The motions also of the progression of the
apsides are very evident, but as for the motion of libration or
latitude that cannot be so well made out by this way of pendulum ; but by the motion of a wheel upon a point is most easy."

By means of the circular pendulum already mentioned, it
was found that " if the impetus of the *endeavour by the tangent*
at the first setting out was stronger *than the endeavour to the
centre*, there was then generated an elliptical motion whose
*longest* diameter was parallel to the direct endeavour of the
body in the first point of impulse. But if that impetus was
weaker than the endeavour to the centre, there was generated
such an elliptical motion whose *shorter* diameter was parallel
to the direct endeavour of the body in the first point of impulse." Another experiment was made by fastening a small
pendulous body by a shorter string on the lower part of the
wire which suspended the larger ball, " that it might freely
make a circular or elliptical motion round about the bigger,
whilst the bigger moved circularly or elliptically about another
centre." The object of this arrangement was to explain the
manner of the moon's motion about the earth ; but neither of
the balls moved in such perfect circles and ellipses as when
they were suspended singly. " A certain point, however,
which seemed to be the centre of gravity of the two bodies,
however pointed (considered as one), seemed to be regularly
moved in such a circle or ellipsis, the two balls having other
peculiar motions in small epicycles about the same point."[2]

---

[1] This pendulum consisted of a wire fastened to the roof of the room, with a large
wooden ball of *lignum vitæ* at the end of it.—Waller's *Life of Hooke,* p. xii.

[2] Waller's *Life of Hooke,* p. xii. ; and Birch's *Hist.*, vol. ii. p. 92.

At a later period of his life, Hooke resumed the consideration of the subject of the planetary motions, and, in a work
which appeared in 1674,[1] he published some interesting observations on gravity, which we shall give in his own words.—
" I shall hereafter," he says, " explain a system of the world
differing in many particulars from any yet known, but answer-
ing in all things to the common rules of mechanical motions.
This depends upon three suppositions : *First*, That all celestial
bodies whatsoever have an attraction or gravitating power towards their own centres, whereby they attract not only their
own parts, and keep them from flying from them, as we may
observe the Earth to do, but that they also do attract all the
other celestial bodies that are within the sphere of their activity,
and consequently that not only the Sun and Moon have an influence upon the body and motion of the Earth, and the Earth
upon them, but that Mercury, Venus, Mars, Jupiter, and Saturn
also, by their attractive powers, have a considerable influence
upon its motion, as in the same manner the corresponding
attractive power of the Earth hath a considerable influence
upon every one of their motions also.   The *second* supposition
is this, that all bodies whatsoever that are put into a direct
and simple motion, will so continue to move forward in a
straight line till they are, by some other effectual powers, deflected, and sent into a motion describing a circle, ellipsis, or
some other more compound curve line.   The *third* supposition
is, that these attractive powers are so much the more powerful
in operating by how much the nearer the body wrought upon
is to their own centres.   Now, what these several degrees are,
I have not yet experimentally verified, but it is a motion which,
if fully prosecuted, as it ought to be, will mightily assist the
astronomers to reduce all the celestial motions to a certain rule,
which I doubt will never be done without it.   He that understands the nature of the circular pendulum, and of circular

1 *An Attempt to prove the Motion of the Earth, from Observations made by* Robert
Hooke, 4to.  See *Phil. Trans.* No. 101, p. 12.

motion, will easily understand the whole of this principle, and will know where to find directions in nature for the true stating thereof. This I only hint at present to such as have ability and opportunity of prosecuting this inquiry, and are not wanting of industry for observing and calculating, wishing heartily such may be found, having myself many other things in hand which I would first complete, and therefore cannot so well attend it. But this I durst promise the undertaker, that he will find all the great motions of the world to be influenced by this principle, and that the true understanding thereof will be the true perfection of astronomy." [1]

In this remarkable passage, the doctrine of universal gravitation, and the general law of the planetary motions, are clearly laid down. The diminution of gravity as the square of the distance, is alone wanting to complete the basis of the Newtonian philosophy ; but even this desideratum was in the course of a few years supplied by Dr. Hooke. In a letter which he addressed to Newton in 1679, relative to the curve described by a projectile influenced by the Earth's daily motion, he asserted, that if the force of gravity decreased as the square of the distance, the curve described by a projectile would be an ellipse, whose focus was the centre of the earth. But however great be the merit which we may assign to Hooke's experimental results and sagacious views, they cannot be regarded either as anticipating the discoveries of Newton, or diminishing his fame. Newton had made the same discoveries by independent researches, and there is no reason to believe that he derived any ideas from his contemporaries.

[1] In quoting this passage, which Delambre admits to be very curious, we think he scarcely does justice to Hooke, when he says that what it contains is found expressly in Kepler. It is quite true that Kepler mentioned as probable the law of the squares of the distances, but he afterwards, as Delambre admits, rejected it for that of the simple distances. Hooke, on the contrary, announces it as a truth.—See *Astronomie du 18me Siècle*, pp. 9, 10. Clairaut has justly remarked, that the example of Hooke and Kepler shows how great is the difference between a truth conjectured or asserted, and a truth demonstrated.

# CHAPTER XII.

The First Idea of Gravity occurs to Newton in 1665—His first Speculations upon it—He abandons the subject from having employed an erroneous measure of the Earth's Radius—He resumes the subject in consequence of a discussion with Dr. Hooke, but lays it aside, being occupied with his Optical Experiments—By adopting Picard's Measure of the Earth he discovers the Law of Gravity, and the cause of the Planetary Motions—Dr. Halley goes to Cambridge, and urges him to publish his Treatise on Motion—The germ of the Principia which was composed in 1685 and 1686—Correspondence with Flamsteed—Manuscript of Principia sent to the Royal Society—Halley undertakes to publish it at his own expense—Dispute with Hooke, who claims the discovery of the Law of Gravity—The Principia published in 1687—The New Edition of it by Cotes begun in 1709, and published in 1713—Character and Contents of the Work—General account of the discoveries it contains—They meet with opposition from the followers of Descartes—Their reception in Foreign Countries—Progress of the Newtonian Philosophy in England and Scotland.

SUCH is a brief and general view of the labours and lives of those illustrious men who prepared the science of Astronomy for the application of Newton's genius. Copernicus had determined the form of the Solar System, and the relative position and movements of the bodies that composed it. Kepler had proved that the-planets revolve in elliptical orbits ; that their *radii vectores* describe areas proportional to the times ; and that the squares of their periodic times are as the cubes of their distances from the sun. Galileo had added to the universe a whole system of secondary planets. Huygens had given to Saturn a satellite, and the strange appendage of a ring ; and while some astronomers had maintained the doctrine of universal gravitation, others had referred the motions to an attractive force, diminishing with the square of the distance, and producing a curvilineal motion from one in a straight line.[1]

We have already seen that, in the autumn of 1665, Newton was led to the opinion that the same power by which an apple falls from a tree extends to the moon, and retains her in her orbit ; but upon making the calculation, he found such a discrepancy between the two forces that he abandoned the subject, suspecting that the power which retained the moon in her orbit might be partly that of gravity, and partly that of the vortices of Descartes.[2] This discrepancy arose from the adoption of an erroneous measure of the semi-diameter of the earth, of which the moon's distance was taken as a multiple. Unacquainted with the more accurate determinations of Snellius[3] and Norwood,[4] the last of which would have given Newton the exact quantity which he required, he adopted the measure of sixty miles for a degree of latitude, which had been employed by the old geographers and seamen, and in which, as Mr. Rigaud conjectures, he may have placed the more confidence, as it agreed with the result of the observations which Edward Wright, a Cambridge mathematician, had published in 1610.

It does not distinctly appear at what time Newton became acquainted with the more accurate measurement of the earth, executed by Picard in 1670, and was thus led to resume his investigations. Picard's method of measuring his degree, and the precise result which he obtained, were communicated to the Royal Society on the 11th January 1672,[5] and the result of his

[1] In 1673, Huygens had announced the relations between attractive force and velocity in circular motion.

[2] Whiston's *Memoirs of his own Life*, p. 37.

[3] *Eratosthenes Batavus*, 1617.                    [4] *Seaman's Practice*, 1636.

[5] Mr. Rigaud remarks, that " we do not know when Norwood's determination became known to Newton, but we are certain that he was well aware of Snellius's measures quite as soon as he was of Picard's,—probably much sooner, since the specific mention of them is made in Varenius's *Geography* (cap. iv. pp. 24-26, 1672), of which he edited a new edition at Cambridge in 1672."—*Historical Essay*, p. 12. " Had he adopted," as Mr. Rigaud adds, " 28,500 Rhinland perches, the length of a degree given by Snellius, he would have obtained for the moon's deflexion, in a minute, 15·5 feet."

observations and calculations were published in the Philosophical Transactions for 1675. But whatever was the time when Newton became acquainted with Picard's measurement, it seems to be quite certain that he did not " resume his former thoughts concerning the moon " till 1684. Pemberton tells us, that " some years after he laid aside" his former thoughts, " a letter from Dr. Hooke put him on inquiring what was the real figure in which a body, let fall from an high place, descends, taking the motion of the earth round its axis into consideration ;" and that this gave occasion to his resuming his former thoughts concerning the moon, and determining, from Picard's recent measures, that " the moon appeared to be kept in her orbit purely by the power of gravity."[1]   But though Hooke's letter of 1679 was the occasion of Newton's resuming his in-

[1] Among the manuscripts of Conduitt, I found the following statement regarding Newton's " resuming his former thoughts concerning the moon :"—

" In 1673, Dr. Hooke wrote to him to send him something new for the *Transactions*, whereupon he sent him a little dissertation to confute the common objection that if it were true that the earth moved from east to west, all falling bodies would be left to the west ; and maintained that, on the contrary, they would fall a little eastward, *and having described a curve with his hand to represent the motion of a falling body, he drew a negligent stroke with his pen, from whence Dr. Hooke took occasion to imagine that he meant the curve would be a spiral*, whereupon the Doctor wrote to him that the curve would be an ellipsis, and that the body would move according to Kepler's notion, which gave Sir Isaac Newton an occasion to examine the thing thoroughly ; and for the foundation of the calculus he intended, he laid down this proposition, that the areas described in equal times were equal, which, though assumed by Kepler, was not by him demonstrated, of which demonstration the first glory is due to Newton."

Immediately after this statement, Conduitt adds : " Pemberton, in his preface, mentions this in another manner," and he quotes part of that preface.

The above extraordinary story of Hooke's having considered a negligent stroke of Newton's pen as a spiral, and on that ground having charged him with maintaining that falling bodies would describe such a curve, could not have been given on Newton's authority, but must have been invented by an enemy of Hooke's. Newton himself admits, in his letter to Halley, July 27, 1686, that Hooke's " correcting his spiral occasioned his finding the theorem by which he afterwards examined the ellipsis."

In the preceding extract, the date 1673 is obviously erroneous. The document was copied for me by the late Henry Arthur Wallop Fellowes, the elder brother of the Earl of Portsmouth, who kindly assisted me in the examination of Newton's papers, and who placed at the top of the document the words (P. 49 in Jones), which I cannot explain.

quiries, it does not fix the time when he employed the measures
of Picard.  In a letter from Newton to Halley in 1686, he
tells him that Hooke's letters in 1679 were the cause of his
" finding the method of determining the figures, which, when
I had tried in the ellipsis, I threw the calculations by, being
upon other studies : and so it rested for about five years, till,
upon your request, I sought for the papers."     Hence Mr.
Rigaud considers it clear, that the figures here alluded to were
the paths of bodies acted upon by a central force, and that the
same occasion induced him to resume his former thoughts concerning the moon, and to avail himself of Picard's measures to
correct his calculations.     It was, therefore, in 1684, that
Newton discovered that the moon's deflexion in a minute was
sixteen feet, the space through which a body falls in a second
at the surface of the earth.     As his calculations drew to a close,
he is said to have been so much agitated that he was obliged to
desire a friend to finish them.[1]

Sir Christopher Wren and Hooke and Halley had each of
them, from independent considerations, concluded that " the
centripetal force decreased in the proportion of the squares of
the distances reciprocally."[2]     Halley had in 1683-4 derived
this law " from the consideration of the sesquialterate proportion of Kepler," but was unsuccessful in his attempts to demonstrate by it the laws of the celestial motions.     Sir Christopher
Wren had, " very many years" before 1686, attempted by the
same law " to make out the planet's motion by a descent towards the sun, and an impressed motion," but had " given it
over, not finding the means of doing it ;" and Dr. Hooke, as
we have already seen, though he adopted the law of the squares,
never fulfilled his promise of proving that it could be applied
to the motions of the planets.[3]     It is therefore to Newton alone

[1] Robison's *Works*, vol. ii. p. 94, 1822.  Tradition is, we believe, the only authority
for this anecdote.  It is not supported by what is known of Newton's character.
[2] *Principia*, lib. i. Prop. iv. Schol.
[3] These various facts are stated in a letter from Halley to Newton, dated June 29,

that we owe the demonstration of the great truth, that the moon is kept in her orbit by the same power by which bodies fall on the earth's surface.

The influence of such a result upon such a mind, may be more easily conceived than described. If the force of the earth's gravity bends the moon into her orbit, the satellites of the other planets must be guided by the same power in their primaries, and the attractive force of the sun must in like manner control the movements of the comets and the planets which surround him. In the application of this grand truth to the motions of the Solar System, and to the perturbations arising from the mutual action of the bodies that compose it, Newton must have rejoiced in the privilege of laying the foundation of so magnificent a work, while he could not fail to see that the completion of it would be the achievement of other minds, and the glory of another age. But, however fascinating must have been the picture thus presented to his mind, it was still one of limited extent. He knew not of the existence of binary and multiple systems of stars, to which the theory of

1686. " According to your desire in your former, I waited upon Sir Christopher Wren, to inquire of him if he had the first notion of the reciprocal duplicate proportion from Mr. Hooke. His answer was, that he himself very many years since had had his thoughts upon making out the planet's motions by a composition of a descent towards the sun and an impressed motion; but that at length he gave over, not finding the means of doing it. Since which time Mr. Hooke had frequently told him that he had done it, and attempted to make it out to him, but that he never was satisfied that his demonstrations were cogent. And this I know to be true, that in January 1683-4, I, having from the consideration of the sesquialterate proportion of Kepler, concluded that the centripetal force decreased in the proportion of the squares of the distances reciprocally, came on Wednesday to town (from Islington) where I met with Sir Christopher Wren and Mr. Hooke, and falling in discourse about it, Mr. Hooke affirmed that upon that principle all the laws of the celestial motions were to be demonstrated, and that he himself had done it. I declared the ill success of my attempts, and Sir Christopher, to encourage the inquiry, said that he would give Mr. Hooke some two months' time to bring him a convincing demonstration thereof, and besides the honour he of us that did it should have from him the present of a book of forty shillings. Mr. Hooke then said he had it, but that he would conceal it for some time, that others trying and failing might know how to value it when he should make it public. However, I remember that Sir Christopher was little satisfied that he could do it, and though Mr. Hooke then promised to show it him, I do not find that in that particular he has been so good as his word."

universal gravitation would be extended.  He could not have
anticipated that Adams and Leverrier would have tracked an
unseen planet to its place by the perturbations it occasioned :
Nor could he have conjectured that his own theory of gravitation might detect the origin and history of nearly thirty planetary bodies, revolving within a sphere apparently destined for
one.  It was enough for one man to see what Newton saw.
The service in the Temple of Science must be performed by
many priests ; and fortunate is he who is called to the humblest
task at its altar.  The revelations of infinite wisdom are not
vouchsafed to man in a day.  A light so effulgent would para-
lyse the noblest intellect.  It must break in upon it by degrees ;
and even each separate ray must be submitted to the ordeal of
various minds,—to the apprentice skill of one age, and to the
master genius of another.

It is not easy to determine the exact time when Newton first
adopted the great truth, " that the forces of the planets from
the sun are reciprocally duplicate of their distances from him,"
but there is sufficient evidence to show that it must have been
as early as 1666, and therefore contemporaneous with his
speculations on Gravity in his garden at Woolsthorpe.  " In
one of my papers," says he,[1] " writ (I cannot say in what year),
but I am sure some time before I had any correspondence with
Oldenburg,[2] and that's *above fifteen years ago* (1671), the pro·
portion of the forces of the planets from the sun, reciprocally
duplicate of their distances from him, is expressed, and the proportion of our gravity to the moon's *conatus recedendi a centro
terræ*, is calculated, though not accurately enough.   That when
Hugenius put out his Horologium Oscillatorium, a copy being
presented to me, in my letter of thanks to him I gave those
rules in the end thereof a particular commendation for their
usefulness in philosophy, and added, *out of my aforesaid* paper,

[1] Letter to Halley, June 20, 1686.  See also Rigaud's *Hist. Essay*, pp. 51, 52.
[2] It appears from Birch, in his *Hist. of the Royal Society*, vol. iii. p. 1, that Newton
had written to Oldenburg a letter, dated January 6, 1673.

an instance of their usefulness in comparing the forces of the
moon from the earth, and the earth from the sun ; in determining a problem about the moon's phase, and putting a limit
to the sun's parallax, which shows that I had then my eye
upon comparing the forces of the planets arising from their
circular motion, and understood it ; so that a while after when
Mr. Hooke propounded the problem solemnly in the end of his
attempt to prove the motion of the earth, if I had not known
the duplicate proportion before, I could not but have found it
now." In another letter to Halley, written about three weeks
afterwards,[1] he distinctly states, that " for the duplicate proportion I can affirm that I gathered it from Kepler's theorem
*about twenty* years ago," that is, in 1666. Hence it is obvious
that the written paper referred to by Newton was, as Mr.
Rigaud says, " the result of his early speculations at Woolsthorpe," and that " the deduction from Kepler, which is said
to have preceded the calculation[2] by a twelvemonth, took place
in 1665."

Such was the state of Newton's knowledge regarding the law
of gravity, when, in January 1684, Halley, Wren, and Hooke
were discussing together the subject in London. Halley had
learned from this interview that neither of his friends possessed
a " convincing demonstration" of this law, and finding, after a
delay of some months, that Hooke " had not been so good as
his word," in showing his demonstration to Wren, he set out
for Cambridge in the month of August 1684, to consult Newton
on the subject.[3] Without mentioning either his own specula-

[1] July 14, 1686.  Rigaud's *Hist. Ess.* App. pp. 39, 40.

[2] The erroneous calculations from his having used an incorrect measure of the earth's diameter.

[3] In both the editions of the *Commercium Epistolicum*, drawn up by a committee of Newton's best friends, there occurs the following passage, which has misled several of Newton's biographers.  "Anno . . . 1683, in . . . Actis Lipsicis pro mense Octobri, calculi differentialis elementa primum edidit D. Leibnitius, literis A. G. L. designatus. Anno autem 1683 ad finem vergente, D. Newtonus propositiones principales, earum quæ in Philosophiæ Principiis Mathematicis habentur Londinum misit," &c., No. LXXI. It is certain that 1684 should have been substituted for 1683. Mr. Rigaud, who justly

tions, or those of Hooke and Wren, he at once indicated the object of his visit by asking Newton what would be the curve described by the planets on the supposition that gravity diminished at the square of the distance. Newton immediately answered, *an Ellipse*. Struck with joy and amazement, Halley asked him how he knew it ? Why, replied he, I have calculated it ; and being asked for the calculation, he could not find it, but promised to send it to him. After Halley left Cambridge, Newton endeavoured to reproduce the calculation, but did not succeed in obtaining the same result. Upon examining carefully his diagram and calculation, he found that in describing an ellipse coarsely with his own hand, he had drawn the two axes of the curve instead of two conjugate diameters somewhat inclined to one another. When this mistake was corrected he obtained the result which he had announced to Halley.[1]

remarks that this could not have been an error of the press, as "the argument with reference to Leibnitz would fall to the ground if 1684 were substituted for it," has endeavoured successfully to find out the cause of the mistake. In the Macclesfield Collection he found *two* Memoranda on the first communication of the Principia to the Royal Society, said to be "from an original paper of Newton," which we presume means in Newton's handwriting. In the first the date of 1683 is given, and in the second the correct date of 1684, "the 3 having been evidently altered to 4," by Newton himself, so that the editors of the *Commercium Epistolicum* made a grave mistake in adopting the date 1683.

Since the publication of Mr. Rigaud's Historical Essay, Mr. Edleston has thrown a new light on this subject. The two Memoranda mentioned by Mr. Rigaud are the commencement of a critique by Newton himself on three papers by Leibnitz in the Leipsic Acts for January and February 1689. The critique, which Mr. Edleston thinks was probably written in 1712, occupied nearly six pages, and is preserved among the Lucasian Papers. The first sentence is given in *four* different forms. In the two first the date 1684 is used, and in the two last 1683. "Newton," says Mr. Edleston, "first of all clearly wrote 1684, then altered the 4 to a 3, afterwards crossed all the figures out, *and wrote distinctly* 1683. . . . . Newton, therefore, after endeavouring to recollect the exact year in which he sent up the fundamental proposition of the *Principia* to London, antedated the event by a twelvemonth," so that no blame can be cast upon the editors of the *Commercium Epistolicum*, for the erroneous date which they adopted. The critique is given by Mr. Edleston in his APPENDIX, p. 307. See Rigaud's *Hist. Essay*, pp. 16-18, and his APPENDIX, No. xix.

[1] We have given this account of Halley's interview with Newton, nearly as we find it in Conduit's manuscript, in which *May* is erroneously mentioned as the time of Halley's visit. Halley's own account is more brief :—"The August following when I did myself

Halley returned to London with the double satisfaction that a grand truth had been demonstrated which he himself had anticipated, and that he had the honour of bringing it to light. He was indeed proud of the success of his mission, and after the Principia had excited the admiration of Europe, he used frequently to boast to Conduit that he had been the Ulysses who produced this Achilles.[1] In the month of November, Newton fulfilled the promise he made to Halley, by sending him through Mr. Paget[2] a copy of the demonstration which he had brought to perfection ; and very soon after receiving it, Halley took another journey to Cambridge, " to confer with Newton about it." Immediately after his return to London, namely, on the 10th December, he informed the Royal Society " that he had lately seen Mr. Newton at Cambridge, who had showed him a curious treatise *De Motu*," which at Dr. Halley's desire he promised to send to the Society to be entered upon their register. " Mr. Halley was desired to put Mr. Newton in mind of his promise for the securing this invention to himself, till such time as he could be at leisure to publish it," and Mr. Paget was desired to join with Mr. Halley.

the honour to visit you, I then learned the good news that you had brought the demonstration to perfection, and you were pleased to promise me a copy thereof, which I received with a great deal of satisfaction from Mr. Paget."—*Letter to Newton*, June 29, 1686.

[1] " Dr. Halley has often valued himself to me," says Conduitt, " for being the Ulysses which produced this Achilles."

[2] Mr. Paget was Mathematical Master in Christ's Hospital. He was a friend of Newton's, and was recommended by him to Flamsteed on the 3d April 1682, as a competitor for the Mastership. Flamsteed joined in the recommendation, and after his appointment found him " an able mathematician." He gave such satisfaction to the Governors, indeed, that they sent Flamsteed " a staff," and made him one of their number. Flamsteed has left it on record that this accomplished young man, before seven years had expired, became a drunkard, neglected his duties, lost his character, and banished himself to India. What a lesson to the young who are accidentally associated with great men after whom posterity inquires ! As the bearer of the germ of the Principia to Halley, Paget's name has for nearly two centuries been mentioned with honour. As a protégé of Newton and Flamsteed, who failed in justifying their recommendation, a blot has been left upon his name, which but for that honour would never have been known. See Baily's *Flamsteed*, p. 125.

That Halley and Paget would, without delay, remind Newton of his promise, and that Newton would fulfil it, there can be no doubt ; and we accordingly find that about the middle of February he had sent to Mr. Aston, one of the Secretaries of the Royal Society, his " notions about motion." Mr. Aston, as a matter of course, would thank Newton for the communication, and mention the fact of its being registered ; and that all this was done, appears from a letter of Newton's to Aston of the 23d February 1685, written on another subject, but thanking him for " having entered on the register his notions about motion." Newton added, " I designed them for you before now, but the examining several things has taken a greater part of my time than I expected, and a great deal of it to no purpose. And now I am to go into Lincolnshire for a month or six weeks. Afterwards I intend to finish it as soon as I can conveniently."

The treatise *De Motu*, thus registered in the books of the Royal Society, was the germ of the Principia, and was obviously intended to be a brief exposition of the system which that work was to establish. It occupies twenty-four octavo pages, and consists of four theorems and seven problems, four of the theorems and four of the problems containing the more important truths which are demonstrated in the second and third sections of the First Book of the Principia. [1]

[1] Mr. Rigaud has published it in his Historical Essay. He is of opinion that it is not the same paper, a copy of which was brought to Halley by Mr. Paget in November 1684, on the ground that that paper was never mentioned to the Royal Society by Halley, and that Halley did not see the " curious treatise *De Motu* till his second visit to Cambridge, in November or December 1684." Mr. Edleston, however, is of opinion that the treatise De Motu was part of the lectures delivered by Newton as Lucasian Professor, which commenced in October 1684, and a copy of which is preserved in the University library ; and that the paper sent to Halley in November was the germ of this treatise, and the one registered by Mr. Aston. In a letter from Cotes to Jones, published in Edleston's *Correspondence*, p. 209, it is stated that the manuscript at Cambridge was " the first draught of the Principia," as Newton read it in his lectures,—a statement to which Mr. Edleston refers in support of his opinion. There are certainly expressions in the letters both of Newton and Halley unfavourable to both these opinions, but we think that the following view of the question is the most probable. Halley went to Cambridge to learn

The years 1685 and 1686 will ever be memorable in the life of Newton, and in the history of science.  It was in these two years, and in the early months of 1687, that he composed the Principia and gave it to the world, and all the details connected with this great event have been carefully preserved for the instruction and gratification of posterity.  The personal history of the philosopher, therefore, during this period, the nature of his correspondence and inquiries, and all the mechanical and even commercial circumstances under which his great work was written, and printed and published, are subjects which cannot be overlooked in any extended account of his life and writings. Although Newton had identified the law of gravity on the earth with the same law at the moon, yet he required the aid of the practical astronomer in enabling him to apply his theory to the motions of the planets and comets of the system.  Fortunately for Newton, Flamsteed was the Astronomer-Royal at Greenwich.

In November and December 1680, when the great comet appeared, Flamsteed observed it with peculiar care, and, before it had ceased to be visible, he put all its observed places into

if Newton had a demonstration of a proposition that a force varying reciprocally with the square of the distance would produce a motion in an ellipsis.  Newton told him that he " had brought this demonstration to perfection," but that having mislaid it, he would send him " a copy thereof."  This copy was sent to Halley in November obviously for his own information.  Halley does not lay it before the Society, but is so pleased with *it*, that he goes again to Cambridge in order to " confer with Newton about *it*."  He now saw the treatise De Motu which Newton promised to send to the Society, and which was registered.  Now when Halley says (letter to Newton, June 29. 1686) that he went to Newton to confer with him about *it*, that is, the demonstration, and adds immediately, " since which time *it* has been entered upon the register books of the Society," he can only mean that the demonstration was entered *as part* of the treatise De Motu, of which it was certainly the leading feature.  If the two *its* mean the same thing, then Halley received in November the same treatise that was afterwards sent to Aston in the following February, which is scarcely admissible even upon Mr. Edleston's conjecture that Halley did produce the paper on the 10th December, though the fact is not recorded in the journal book.  In Newton's letter to Halley, July 14, 1686, he says, that having tried the calculation *in the Ellipsis*, he had thrown them by for about five years, till upon Dr. Halley's request " he sought for that paper (namely, the calculation in the Ellipsis), and not finding it, did *it* again, and reduced it into the propositions (we read proposition) showed you by Mr. Paget."—See Rigaud's *Hist. Essay*, p. 14, and Edleston's *Correspondence*, pp. lv. and 209.

a little table, which, with his thoughts on the subject of comets, he communicated to Mr. Crompton, Fellow of Jesus College, Cambridge. In this letter, Flamsteed asserted that " the *two* comets (as they were generally thought) were only one and the same ; and he described the line of their motions before and after it passed the sun." Mr. Crompton showed this letter to Newton, who, in return, addressed a long letter to him, to be sent to Flamsteed, containing observations on Flamsteed's " hypothetical notions," and endeavouring to prove " that the comets of November and December were different comets. The commencement of Newton's letter is very characteristic, and though it is intended to be kind in its expressions, we can conceive a mind like that of Flamsteed regarding it, as he did many years afterwards, as " magisterially ridiculing the opinion for which he thought the arguments convincing and unanswerable."[1] " I thank Mr. Flamsteed," says Newton, " for this kind mention of me in his letters to Mr. Crompton, and, as I commend his wisdom in deferring to publish his hypothetical notions till they have been well considered both by his friends and himself, so I shall act the part of a friend in this paper, not objecting against it by way of opposition, but in describing what I imagine might be objected by others, and so leaving it to his consideration. If hereafter he shall please to publish his theory, and think any of the objections I propound need an answer, to prevent their being objected by others, he may describe the objections as raised by himself or his friends in general, without taking any notice of me." After this kind introduction, Newton proceeds, in a long and elaborate letter, to controvert Flamsteed's opinions, and, from the evidence of several Cambridge scholars, to show that there were *two* comets, and not *one ;* and also in opposition to Flamsteed, that " more comets go northward than southward." Flamsteed replied to this letter on the 7th March 1681, in such complimentary terms, that he could not have taken any offence at

[1] See Baily's *Flamsteed,* p. 50, *note.*

Newton's remarks upon his views.[1]  He seems to have answered several of Newton's objections, and removed some of his difficulties, but to have failed in satisfying him that there was only one comet in 1680.  Newton had been on a visit in the country during almost the whole of March, and, after his return to Cambridge, was prevented, " by some indisposition and other impediments," from replying to Flamsteed till the 16th of April.  In this letter " he forbears to urge further" any objections to Flamsteed's hypothesis, and confines himself " to the question of two comets," which he discusses at great length, pertinaciously maintaining an opinion, which, a few years afterwards, he was obliged to abandon.[2]

When, after his return from Lincolnshire to Cambridge, Newton was occupied with the composition of the Principia, he renewed his correspondence with Flamsteed.  Some of their

[1] Mr. Baily, whose views respecting the quarrel which subsequently arose between Newton and Flamsteed, we shall afterwards have occasion to controvert, acknowledges that he cannot find in these two letters of Newton " any foundation for Flamsteed's censure."  It is very obvious, indeed, from the highly complimentary terms in which Flamsteed at this time wrote to Newton, that he did not consider Newton as "magisterially ridiculing his opinions."

[2] At this time, and even in 1684, when he wrote his treatise De Motu, Newton had very erroneous views regarding the motions of comets ; and it was not till September 19, 1685, that he acknowledged, in a letter to Flamsteed, that " it seemed very probable that the comets of November and December were the same comet."  In the first edition of the Principia, p. 494, he went farther, and acknowledged that Flamsteed was right. In giving an account of the treatise De Motu, Mr. Rigaud thus speaks of Newton's views respecting the motions of comets :—" He certainly at this time had not resolved the difficult question of the paths of comets.  In the Arithmetica Universalis (Prob. 56), he had proceeded on their supposed uniform rectilinear motion, and, in the present case, he still holds expressly to that earlier theory.  How, under such conditions (if strictly adhered to), they could return, is not easy to understand ; but waiving this question, his reasoning seems to show that if they did, they might be recognised by a similarity in their motions.  To determine this, he proposes to reduce the places of the comet to analogous points in an imaginary ellipse, of which the focus is occupied by the sun ; and these places having been calculated by means of the auxiliary curve, were to be verified by their application to the rectilinear path.  It seems wonderful, when we consider his extraordinary acuteness, that such an hypothesis did not immediately lead him to the truth ; but as he so repeatedly and so distinctly describes the supposed motion of the comet to be in a straight line, it is impossible not to conclude, that even his most powerful mind required the assistance of time to emancipate itself from preconceived opinions."—Rigaud's Hist. Essay, p. 29.

letters are lost;[1] but it is obvious, from one of Newton's, dated
September 19, 1685, that he had received many useful communications from Flamsteed, and especially regarding Saturn,
" whose orbit, as defined by Kepler," Newton " found too little
for the sesquialterate proportions." In the other letters written
in 1685 and 1686, he applies to Flamsteed for information
respecting the orbits of the satellites of Jupiter and Saturn ;—
respecting the rise and fall of the spring and neap tides at
the solstices and the equinoxes ;—respecting the flattening of
Jupiter at the poles, which, if certain, he says, would conduce
much to the stating the reasons of the procession of the equinoxes ;—and respecting the differences between the observed
places of Saturn and those computed from Kepler's tables about
the time of his conjunction with Jupiter. On this last point
the information supplied by Flamsteed was peculiarly gratifying to Newton ; and it is obvious from the language of this
part of his letter, that he had still doubts of the universal
application of the sesquialteral proportion. " Your information," says he, " about the errors of Kepler's tables for Jupiter
and Saturn, has eased me of several scruples. I was apt to
suspect there might be some cause or other unknown to me
which might disturb the sesquialteral proportions, for the in-
fluences of the planets one upon another seemed not great
enough, though I imagined Jupiter's influence greater than your
numbers determine it. It would add to my satisfaction if you
would be pleased to let me know the long diameters of the
orbits of Jupiter and Saturn, assigned by yourself and Mr.
Halley in your new tables, *that I may see how the sesquialteral
proportion fills the heavens, together with another small proportion which must be allowed for.*"[2]

[1] The dates of these letters, which are published in the *General Dictionary*, vol. vii.
pp. 793-797, are September 19, 1685 ; September 25, 1685 ; October 14, 1685 ; December 30, 1685 (?) ; January (?) 1686 ; September 3, 1686. Excepting the second, which
is from Flamsteed, they are all from Newton. See Vol. II. Chap. XVIII.

[2] This letter has no date, but Flamsteed says that it was written about 1685, or
January 1685-86.

Upon Newton's return from Lincolnshire in the beginning of April 1685, he seems to have devoted himself to the preparation of his work, and to fulfil his intention, as expressed to Aston, " of finishing it as soon as he conveniently could." In the spring he had determined the attractions of masses, and thus completed the demonstration of the law of universal gravitation ; and in summer he had finished the *Second* Book of the Principia,[1] the *First* Book being the Treatise *De Motu*, which he had already enlarged and completed. Excepting in the correspondence with Flamsteed, to which we have already referred, we hear nothing more of the preparation of the Principia till the 21st of April 1686, when Halley read to the Royal Society his " Discourse concerning Gravity, and its Properties," in which he states " that his worthy countryman, Mr. Isaac Newton, has an incomparable *Treatise of Motion almost ready* for the press ;" and that the reciprocal law of the squares " is the principle on which Mr. Newton has made out all the phenomena of the celestial motions so easily and naturally, that its truth is past dispute."[2] The intelligence thus given by Halley was speedily confirmed. At the very next meeting of the Society on the 28th of April, " Dr. Vincent presented to the Society a manuscript treatise entitled *Philosophiæ Naturalis Principia Mathematica*, and dedicated to the Society by Mr. Isaac Newton." Although this manuscript contained only the First Book, yet such was the confidence which the Society placed in its author, that an order was given " that a letter of thanks be written to Mr. Newton ; that the printing of his book be referred to the consideration of the Council ; and that in the meantime the book be put into the hands of Mr. Halley, to make a report thereof to the Council." Although there could be no doubt of the meaning of this report, yet no progress was made in the publication of the work. At the next meeting of the Society on the 19th May, some dissatisfaction seems

<hr/>

[1] Edleston's *Correspondence*, &c., p. xxix. ; and Newton's letter to Halley, June 20, 1686.　　　[2] *Phil. Trans.* 1686, pp. 6-8.

to have been expressed at the delay, as it was ordered " that Mr. Newton's work should be printed `forthwith` in quarto, and that a letter should be written to him to signify the Society's resolutions, and to desire his opinion as to the print, volume, cuts, and so forth." Three days afterwards, namely, on the 22d of May, Halley communicated the resolution to Newton, and stated to him that the printing was to be at the charge of the Society. As the manuscript, however, had not been referred to the consideration of the Council, as previously ordered, and as no sum exceeding five pounds could be paid without its authority, a farther delay took place. At the next meeting of the Council on the 2d of June, it was again ordered " that Mr. Newton's book be printed ;" but instead of sanctioning the resolution of the general meeting to print it at their charge, they added, " that Mr. Halley undertake the business of looking after it, and printing it at his own charge, which he engaged to do."

In order to explain to Newton the cause of the delay, Halley, in his letter of the 22d May, alleges that it arose from " the President's attendance upon the King, and the absence of the Vice-Presidents, whom the good weather had drawn out of town ;" but there is reason to believe that this was not the real cause, and that the delay arose from the unwillingness of the Council to undertake the publication in the present state of their finances.[1]

Such was the emergency in which Halley undertook the labour of editing, and the expense of printing, the *Principia*, and thus earned the gratitude of Newton and of posterity. We cannot admit that the low state of their funds was any apology for the conduct of the Council in refusing to carry into effect the resolution of a general meeting of the Society. Why did

---

[1] We here express the opinion of Mr. Rigaud, who, after a careful and repeated examination of the Royal Society's minutes, from 1686 to 1699, " ventures to say," that " there is no notice of any pecuniary aid having been extended to the *Principia*." Halley was a married man with a family, and at " a considerable pecuniary risk provided for the disbursement, precisely at that period of his life when he could least afford it."—Rigaud's *Hist. Essay*, pp. 33-37.

they not borrow the necessary sum on the security of their future income, or subscribe individually to fulfil an honourable obligation, and discharge an important duty? If the nobility and gentry who then composed the Royal Society devolved upon their secretary the payment of expenses which, as a body, they had agreed to defray, let it not be said that it was to the Royal Society that we are indebted for the publication of the *Principia*. It is to Halley alone that science owes this debt of gratitude : It was he who tracked Newton to his College, who drew from him his great discoveries, and who generously gave them to the world.

In Halley's letter of the 22d May, announcing to Newton the resolution of the Society, he found it necessary to inform him of the conduct of Hooke when the manuscript of the Principia was presented to the Society. Sir John Hoskyns, the particular friend of Hooke, was in the chair, when Dr. Vincent presented the manuscript, and passed a high encomium on the novelty and dignity of the subject. Another member remarked that Newton had carried the thing so far that there was no more to be added, to which Sir John replied, that it was so much the more to be prized, as it was both invented and perfected at the same time. Mr. Hooke was offended because Sir John did not mention what he had told him of his own discovery ; and the consequence was, as Halley says, " that these two, who, till then, were inseparable cronies, have since scarce seen one another, and are utterly fallen out." After the meeting broke up and adjourned to the coffee-house, Mr. Hooke endeavoured to persuade the members " that he had some such thing by him, and that he gave Newton the first hint of this invention." Although this scene passed at the Royal Society, Halley only communicated to Newton the fact, " that Hooke had some pretensions to the invention of the rule for the decrease of gravity being reciprocally as the squares of the distances from the centre," acknowledging at the same time, · that though Newton had the notion from him,

" yet the demonstration of the curves generated thereby belonged wholly to Newton." " How much of this," Halley adds, " is so, you know best, as likewise what you have to do in this matter ; only Mr. Hooke seems to expect you should make some mention of him in the preface which 'tis possible you may see reason to prefix. I must beg your pardon that 'tis I that send you this ungrateful account ; but I thought it my duty to let you know it, that so you might act accordingly, being in myself fully satisfied that nothing but the greatest candour imaginable is to be expected from a person who has of all men the least need to borrow reputation." In thus appealing to Newton's candour, Halley obviously wished that some acknowledgment of Hooke should be made. He knew indeed, that before Newton had announced the inverse law, Hooke and Wren and himself had spoken of it and discussed it, and therefore justice demanded that though none of them had given a demonstration of the law, Hooke especially should receive credit for having maintained it as a truth of which he was seeking the demonstration.

Newton's reply to Halley,[1] written after a month's delay, is a remarkable production. He acknowledges that Hooke told him of the duplicate proportion, but that his views were erroneous, as he conceived it " to reach down from hence to the centre of the earth." He confesses " that he himself *had never extended the duplicate proportion lower than to the superficies of the earth,*" and that " *before a certain demonstration he found last year* (1685) *he suspected it did not reach accurately enough down so low.*" In the rest of the letter he shows very satisfactorily, from letters to Oldenburg and Huygens, and even from this theory of gravity, that he must have been acquainted with the duplicate proportion before his conversation with Hooke.

When Newton had finished· this letter, he was informed " by one who had it from another lately present at one of the

[1] June 20, 1686. APPENDIX, No. IX.

Society's meetings, that Mr. Hooke had there made a great
stir, pretending that Newton had all from him, and desiring
they would see that he had justice done him." Roused by
what he considered " a very strange and undeserved carriage
towards him," he writes an angry postscript to his letter,
putting forward the claims of Borelli and Bullialdus to the
duplicate proportion, and ungenerously charging Hooke with
having derived his knowledge of it from them, and even with
having been led to it by perusing his own letter to Huygens,
which might have come into his possession after the death of
Oldenburg. " My letter," says he, " to Huygens was directed
to Mr. Oldenburg, who used to keep the originals. His papers
came into Mr. Hooke's possession. Mr. Hooke, knowing my
hand, might have the curiosity to look into that letter, and
thence take the notion of comparing the forces of the planets
from their circular motion ; and so what he wrote to me afterwards about the rate of gravity might be nothing but the fruit
of my own garden. And it's more than I can affirm, that the
duplicate proportion was not expressed in that letter." [1]  This
reasoning is certainly far from being sound. If Hooke had the
law of gravity from Borelli and Bullialdus, Newton might have
had it from them also ; and if Hooke obtained it by the process indicated in the letter to Huygens, which he probably
never saw, it follows that Hooke's views were as sound as those
expressed in that letter, and that he then knew as much about
the law as Newton did. But there is no evidence whatever
that Hooke saw the letter.

Halley was much annoyed with the contents of this postscript, and lost no time in replying to it. He gives Newton an
account of the interview between Hooke, Wren, and himself,
previously described, and which led him to go to Cambridge.
He tells him that Hooke's manner of claiming the discovery
has been represented in worse colours than it ought, " for he

[1] It was not expressed in the letter, as Newton afterwards admits. See APPENDIX,
No. X. Letter, July 27, 1686.

neither made application to the Society for justice, nor pretended you had all from him ;" and he gives " the truth," by
telling what really happened at the meeting of the Society, and
of the little quarrel between Hooke and his friend Sir John
Hoskyns.  Halley concludes his letter by begging Newton
" not to let his resentments run so high" as to deprive the
world of his Third Book, on the theory of comets.

Though ruffled for a moment, Newton's excellent temper
soon recovered its serenity.  When he understood from Halley
that Hooke had been in some respects misrepresented to him,
he " wished that he had spared the postscript in his last ;"
and he goes on to acknowledge that Hooke's " letters occasioned his finding the method of determining figures which he
tried in the ellipsis ;"—that Hooke told him of the experiment
with " Halley's pendulum clock at St. Helena, as an argument
that gravity was lessened at the equator by the diurnal motion ;"
—and that he also told him a third thing which was new to
him, and which he would acknowledge if he made use of it,
namely, " the deflexion of fallen bodies to the south-east in
our latitude."  Having thus sincerely told Mr. Halley the case
between him and Mr. Hooke, " he considered how best to
compose the present dispute," which he thought might be done
by the enclosed scholium to the fourth proposition.  " The
inverse law of gravity holds in all the celestial motions, as was
discovered also independently by my countrymen, Wren, Hooke,
and Halley."

On the 30th June, the President was desired by the Council
to license Mr. Newton's book, entitled *Philosophiæ Naturalis
Principia Mathematica*, and after Halley had obtained the
author's leave about the middle of July to substitute wooden
cuts for copperplates, the printing of it was commenced and
went on with considerable regularity.  The Second Book,
though ready for the press in autumn, was not sent till March
1687.  The Third Book was presented to the Society on the
6th of April, and the whole work published about midsummer

of 1687.[1]   It was dedicated to the Royal Society as flourish-
ing under his august Majesty James VII.,[2] and there was prefixed to it a set of beautiful Latin hexameters, addressed by
Halley to its immortal author.[3]   They began thus—

> En tibi norma poli, et divæ libramina molis,
> Computus atque Jovis ; quas, dum primordia rerum
> Pangeret, omniparens leges violare creator
> Noluit, æternique operis fundamina fixit,

and ended with the following lines—

> Talia monstrantem mecum celebrate camœnis,
> Vos qui cœlesti gaudetis nectare vesci,
> NEWTONUM clausi reserantem scrinia veri ;
> NEWTONUM Musis charum, cui pectore puro
> Phœbus adest, totoque incessit numine mentem,
> Nec fas est propius mortali attingere divos.

This great work, as might have been expected, excited a
warm interest in every part of Europe.   The impression was

[1] The manuscript of the Principia, without the preface, bound in one volume, is in
the possession of the Royal Society.   Mr. Edleston is of opinion that the manuscript is
not in Newton's autograph, and he believes it to be of the same hand as the first draught
of the Principia in the University library, the author's own handwriting being easily
recognised in the additions and alterations in both manuscripts.   Edleston's *Correspondence, &c.*, pp. lvii. lviii.   In a very interesting letter from Dr. Humphrey Newton to
Conduitt, which is printed in our second volume, he informs him, that " he copied
out the Principia before it went to press."   Pemberton states that the Principia was
written in a year and a half.   In reference to this point I found the following memorandum in Sir Isaac's handwriting :—
" In the tenth proposition of the second book, there was a mistake in the first edition,
by drawing the tangent of the arch G H from the wrong end of the arch, which caused an
error in the conclusion ; but in the second edition I rectified the mistake.   And there
may have been some other mistakes occasioned by the shortness of the time in which
the book was written, and by its being copied by an amanuensis who understood not
what he copied, besides the press faults ; for I wrote it in seventeen or eighteen months,
beginning in the end of December 1684, and sending it to the Royal Society in May 1686,
excepting that about ten or twelve of the propositions were composed before, viz., the
1st and 11th in December 1679, the 6th, 7th, 8th, 9th, 10th, 12th, 13th, and 17th, Lib. I.,
and the 1st, 2d, 3d, and 4th, Lib. II., in June and July 1684."
[2] A copy of the Principia was presented to the King by Halley, accompanied with a
paper giving a general account of the Book, and more especially an explanation of the
tides, a subject in which the King was likely to take a deep interest, from his having as
Lord High Admiral commanded the British fleet in the war with the United Provinces.
See *Phil. Trans.* vol. xix. p. 445, and Rigaud's *Hist. Essay,* APP. p. 77.
[3] See APPENDIX, No. XI.

quickly sold.[1] A copy of the Principia could scarcely be procured in 1691, and at that time an improved edition was in contemplation. Newton himself, though pressed by his friends, had refused to undertake it, and M. Facio D'Huillier, who had studied it with the most minute attention, had intimated to Huygens his design of publishing a new edition.[2] In 1694, Newton resumed the study of the lunar and planetary theories, with the view of rendering more perfect a new edition of his book ; but the difficulty which he experienced in getting the necessary observations from the Astronomer-Royal, interfered with his investigations, and contributed more than any other cause to prevent him from bringing them to a close. Flamsteed did not sufficiently appreciate the importance of Newton's labours ; but while we deeply regret that he should have treated so ungraciously the importunities of his friend, we are disposed to find some apology for his conduct in the infirmities of his health and of his temper.

Mr. Edleston has stated, with much appearance of truth, that the steps taken by Newton's friends at the close of 1695, may have interfered as much as the infirmities of Flamsteed with the completion of the lunar theory ;[3] but whether or not this was the case, there can be no doubt that his appointment to the Wardenship of the Mint in 1696, and to the Mastership in 1699, deferred to a distant day the appearance of a new edition of the Principia. Even in November 1702, when he was visited by Bd. Greves, who saw in his hands an interleaved and corrected copy of the Principia, he would not acknowledge that he had any intention to reprint it.[4] The preparation of his Optics, which was published in April 1704, must have interfered with his revision of the Principia, and it appears, from his letter to Flamsteed, in November 1694, that he was then

---

[1] The number of copies printed is not known.  The original price seems to have been ten shillings.

[2] See Rigaud's *Hist. Essay*, pp. 89-95.

[3] *Correspondence*, &c., *Præf.* p. xi.        [4] Ibid. *Præf.* p. xiv.

occupied in preparing a new edition of his great work.[1]   His
duties at the Mint allowed him but little time for the 'performance of so laborious a task ; and when his consent was at
last obtained to put the work to press, they greatly interrupted
its progress.

Dr. Bentley, the distinguished Master of Trinity College, had
for a long time solicited and even urged Newton to give his
consent to the re-publication of the Principia.[2]   In the middle
of 1708 he succeeded in removing his scruples, but it was not
till the spring of 1709 that he prevailed upon him to intrust
the superintendence of it to a young mathematician of great
promise, Roger Cotes, Fellow of Trinity College, who had been
recently appointed Professor of Astronomy and Experimental
Philosophy.   On the 21st May 1709, after having been that
day with Newton, Bentley announced this arrangement to
Cotes.   " Sir Isaac Newton," he said, " will be glad, to see you
in June, and then put into your hands one part of his Book
corrected for the press."   About the middle of July, Cotes went
to London, in the expectation doubtless to bring down with
him to Cambridge the corrected portion of the Principia.
Newton, however, had some farther improvements to make
upon it, and promised to send it down in about a fortnight.
Cotes was impatient to begin his work, and when a whole
month had passed without any intelligence from Newton, he
addressed to him the following letter :—

" CAMBRIDGE, *August* 18*th*, 1709.

" S$^R$,—The earnest desire I have to see a new Edition of
y$^r$ Princip. makes me somewhat impatient till we receive your
Copy of it which You was pleased to promise me about the

---

[1] Baily's *Flamsteed*, p. 138.

[2] It would appear from a conversation between Sir Isaac and Conduitt, that Bentley
was at the expense of printing the second edition of the Principia, and received the
profits of the work.   " I asking him (Newton)," says Conduitt, " how he came to let
Bentley print his Principia, which he did not understand—' Why,' said he, ' he was
covetous, and I let him do it to get money.' "—Conduitt's MS. See Vol. II. ch. xxi.

middle of the last Month, You would send down in about a
Fourtnights time.   I hope you will pardon me for this uneasi-
ness from which I cannot free myself & for giving You this
Trouble to let You know it.   I have been so much obliged to
You by Y\ʳself & by Yʳ Book yᵗ (I desire you to believe me) I
think myself bound in gratitude to take all the Care I possibly
can that it shall be correct . . . . . I take this Opportunity
to return You my most hearty thanks for Yʳ many Favours
and Civilitys to me who am
                Your most obliged humble Servant,
                                        ROGER COTES.

"For SIR ISAAC NEWTON at His House in
    Jermin Street near Sᵗ. James's Church
    Westminster."

No answer was returned to this letter from Cotes, and a
long month had passed away when one evening his next-door
neighbour, William Whiston, about the end of September, put
into his hands "the greatest part of the copy of the Principia,"
ending with the thirty-second Proposition of the Second Book.
In a letter dated October 11, Newton intimated to Cotes that
he had sent him by Mr. Whiston "the greatest part of the
copy of his Principia, in order to a new edition," thanked him
for his letter of the 18th of August, and requested him not to
be at the trouble of examining all the Demonstrations, but "to
print by the copy sent him, correcting only such faults as occur
in reading over the sheets," which would entail upon him
" more labour than it was fit to give him."   These were the
two first letters of that celebrated correspondence between
Newton and Cotes, which has lain in Trinity College Library
for nearly a century and a half, in spite of the wishes expressed
by Dr. Monk,[1] and felt by other admirers of the Principia,
" that one of the many accomplished Newtonians who are
resident in that society would favour the world by publishing

[1] Monk's *Life of Bentley*, p. 180.

the whole collection." Through the liberality of the present
Master and Seniors of Trinity College, this has at last been
done, and in a manner highly creditable to the learning and
talents of Mr. Edleston, by whom the correspondence is edited.[1]
The printing of the Principia went on very slowly, and was not
finished till the first week of March 1713. Cotes expressed a
wish that Dr. Bentley should write the preface to it, but it was
the opinion of Sir Isaac and the Master of Trinity, that the
preface should come from the pen of Cotes himself. This he
readily undertook, but previous to writing it he addressed the
following letter to Dr. Bentley, in order to learn " with what
view he thought proper to have it written."

TO DR. BENTLEY.

" *March* 10*th*,1712-13.

" S$^R$,—I received what you wrote to me in S$^r$ Isaac's letter.
I will set about the Index in a day or two. As to the Preface,
I should be glad to know from S$^r$ Isaac with what view he
thinks proper to have it written. You know the book has
been received abroad with some disadvantage, and the cause of
it may easily be guessed at. The Commercium Epistolicum,
lately published by order of the Royal Society, gives such in-
dubitable proofs of Mr. Leibnitz's want of candour, that I shall
not scruple in the least to speak out the full truth of the matter
if it be thought convenient. There are some pieces of his looking this way which deserve a censure, as his *Tentamen de
Motuum Cœlestium causis*.[2] If S$^r$ Isaac is willing that some-

---

[1] These letters, relating to questions connected with the new edition of the Principia,
are *seventy-two* in number, and extend from May 21, 1709, to March 31, 1713. Mr.
Edleston has added other *fifty*, connected with the Principia, from Newton, Cotes,
Keill, Jones, Brook Taylor, and others, and in an Appendix he has published *thirty-four*
letters, chiefly from Newton, and collected principally from original sources. Mr.
Edleston has enriched this valuable work with an excellent synoptical view of Newton's
life, and a large number of notes of the highest interest.

[2] The critique by Newton, already mentioned, bore upon this paper by Leibnitz ; see
p. 258, Note.

thing of this nature may be done, I should be glad of it, whilst I am making the Index, he would be pleased to consider of it, and put down a few notes of what he thinks most material to be insisted on.    This I say upon supposition that I write the Preface myself.    But I think it would be much more adviseable that you or he or both of you should write it whilst you are in town.    You may depend upon it that I will own it, and defend it as well as I can, if hereafter there be occasion.—I am, S$^r$, " &c.

Immediately after the arrival of this letter on the 12th, Sir Isaac happened to call upon Dr. Bentley, and they agreed to meet in the evening at Sir Isaac's house, to write a reply to it. They objected to any joint preface " to be fathered by Cotes :" they suggested as the subject of the Preface an account of the work itself, and of the improvements of the new edition, and they answered that he has Sir Isaac's consent " to add what he thought proper about the controversy of the first invention, you yourself being full master of it, and want no hints to be given you."    Cotes was also instructed " to spare the *name* of M. Leibnitz, and abstain from all words and epithets of reproach." In reply to this letter on the 18th March, Cotes sketched the plan of the Preface in conformity with the directions already given him, and asks Newton for permission to appeal to the judgment of the Society in the Commercium Epistolicum.    To this Newton answers, that if any farther Preface is written, " he must not see it, as he finds he shall be examined about it."    The plan of the Preface is therefore altered, and the proposed notice of the dispute respecting the discovery of fluxions is abandoned.    Cotes confines himself to an exposition of " the manner of philosophizing made use of " in the Principia, and to an examination of the objections of Leibnitz and of the theory of vortices.

The general Preface thus drawn up by Cotes, is dated 13th May 1713, and in a subsidiary Preface, dated March 2d, Sir Isaac himself mentions the leading alterations which have been

made in the New Edition. " In the second section of the First
Book," he says, " the determination of the force by which bodies
may revolve in given orbits, is simplified and enlarged. In the
seventh section of the Second Book, the theory of the resistance
of fluids is more accurately investigated, and confirmed by new
experiments ; and in the Third Book the theory of the moon,
and the precession of the equinoxes, are more fully deduced
from their principles, and the theory of comets is confirmed by
several examples, and their orbits more accurately computed."

On the 25th of June, Cotes[1] announces to its author, through
Dr. Samuel Clarke, " that the book is finished," and on the
27th of July, Newton waited on the Queen to present a copy
of the Principia to her Majesty.

Such is a brief notice of the composition and printing of the
first and second editions of a work which will be memorable
not only in the annals of one science or of one country, but
which will form an epoch in the history of the world, and will
ever be regarded as the brightest page in the records of human
reason,—a work, may we not add, which would be read with
delight in every planet of our system,—in every system of the
universe. What a glorious privilege was it to have been the
author of the Principia ! There was but one earth upon whose
form and tides and movements the philosopher could exercise
his genius,—one moon, whose perturbations and inequalities
and actions he could study,—one sun, whose controlling force
and apparent motions he could calculate and determine,—one
system of planets, whose mutual disturbances could tax his
highest reason,[2]—one system of comets, whose eccentric paths
he could explore and rectify,—and one universe of stars, to

[1] Some account of this interesting and distinguished person, whose name is so indissolubly associated with that of Newton, and with the Principia, will be found in APPEN-
DIX, No. XII.

[2] The celebrated Lagrange, who frequently asserted that Newton was the greatest
genius that ever existed, used to add—and the most fortunate, for we cannot find *more*
*than once* a system of the world to establish.—Delambre, *Notice sur la Vie de Lagrange,*
*Mém. de l'Institut.* 1812, p. lxv.

whose binary and multiple combinations he could extend the
law of terrestrial gravity.   To have been the chosen sage summoned to the study of that earth, these systems, and that universe,— the favoured lawgiver to worlds unnumbered, the high-
priest in the temple of boundless space,—was a privilege that
could be granted but to one member of the human family ;—
and to have executed the task was an achievement which in its
magnitude can be measured only by the infinite in space, and
in the duration of its triumphs by the infinite in time.   That
Sage—that Lawgiver—that High-priest was Newton.   Let us
endeavour to convey to the reader some idea of the revelations
which he made, and of the brilliant discoveries to which they
conducted his successors.

The Principia consists of three Books.   The *First* and *Second*,
which occupy three-fourths of the work, are entitled, *On the
Motion of Bodies ;* the First treating of their motions in free
space, and the Second of their motions in a resisting medium.
The *Third* bears the title, *On the System of the World.*

The *First* Book, besides the definition and axioms, or laws
of motion, with which it begins, consists of *fourteen* sections, in
the first of which the author explains the method of prime and
ultimate ratios, used in his investigations, and which is similar
to the method of fluxions, more fully explained in the Second
Book.   The other sections treat of centripetal forces, and motions in fixed and moveable orbits.

The *Second* Book consists of nine sections, and treats of bodies
moving in resisting media, or oscillating as pendulums.

The *Third* Book is introduced by the " Rules of Philosophizing."   It consists of *five* sections, on the Causes of the
System of the World,—on the Quantity of Lunar Errors,—on
the Quantity of the Tides,—on the Precession of the Equinoxes,
—and on Comets ; and it concludes with a general scholium,
containing reflections on the constitution of the universe, and
on the " Eternal, Infinite, and perfect Being" by whom it is
governed.

The great discovery which characterizes the Principia, is that of the principle of universal gravitation, *that every particle of matter in the universe is attracted by, or gravitates to every other particle of matter, with a force inversely proportional to the squares of their distances.* In order to establish this principle, Newton begins by considering the curves, which are generated by the composition of a direct impressed motion with a gravitation or tendency towards a centre ; and having demonstrated, that in all cases the areas described by the revolving body are proportional to the times of their description, he shows how to find, from the curves described, the law of the force. In the case of a circular orbit passing through the centre of tendency, the force or tendency towards the centre will be in every point as the fifth power of the distance. If the orbit is the proportional spiral, the force will be reciprocally as the cube of the distance. If it is an ellipse, the force towards the centre of it will be directly as the distance. If it is any of the conic sections, the centripetal force, or tendency towards the focus, will, in all points, be reciprocally as the square of the distance from the focus. If the velocity of the impressed motion is of a certain magnitude, the curve described will be a hyperbola,—if different to a certain degree, it will be a parabola,—and if slower, an ellipse, or a circle in one case.

In order to determine whether the force of gravity resided in the centres of the sun and planets, or in each individual particle of which they are composed, Newton demonstrated that if a spherical body acts upon a distant body with a force varying as the distance of this body from the centre of the sphere, the same effect will be produced as if each of its particles acted upon the distant body according to the same law. And hence it follows, that the spheres, whether they are of uniform density, or consist of concentric layers, with densities varying according to any law whatever, will act upon each other in the same manner as if their force resided in their centre alone. But as the bodies of the solar system are very nearly spherical,

they will all act upon one another, and upon bodies placed on
their surface, as if they were so many centres of attraction ;
and therefore we obtain the law of gravity which subsists between spherical bodies, namely, that one sphere will act upon
another with a force directly proportional to their quantities of
matter, and inversely, as the square of the distance between the
centres of the spheres.   From the equality of action and reaction, to which no exception can be found, Newton concluded
that the sun gravitated to the planets, and the planets to their
satellites, and the earth itself to the stone which falls upon its
surface ; and consequently that the two mutually gravitating
bodies approached to one another with velocities inversely proportional to their quantities of matter.

Having established this universal law, Newton was enabled
not only to determine the weight which the same body would
have at the surface of the sun and the planets, but even to
calculate the quantity of matter in the sun and in all the
planets that had satellites, and even to determine the density
or specific gravity of the matter of which they were composed,—results which Adam Smith pronounced to be " above
the reach of human reason and experience."   In this way he
found that the weight of the same body would be twenty-three
times greater at the surface of the sun than at the surface of
the earth, and that the density of the earth was four times
greater than that of the sun, the planets increasing in density
as they are nearer the centre of the system.

If the peculiar genius of Newton has been displayed in his
investigation of the law of universal gravitation, it shines with
no less lustre in the patience and sagacity with which he traced
the consequences of this fertile principle.

The discovery of the spheroidal form of Jupiter by Cassini
had probably directed the attention of Newton to the determination of its cause, and consequently to the investigation of the
true figure of the earth.   The spherical form of the planets
had been ascribed by Copernicus to the gravity or natural

appetency of their parts ; but upon considering the earth as a
body revolving upon its axis, Newton quickly saw that the
figure arising from the mutual attraction of its parts must be
modified by another force arising from its rotation.   When a
body revolves upon an axis, the velocity of rotation increases
from the poles where it is nothing, to the equator where it is a
maximum.   In consequence of this velocity the bodies on the
earth's surface have a tendency to fly off from it, and this tendency increases with the velocity.   Hence arises a centrifugal
force, which acts in combination with the force of gravity, and
which Newton found to be the 289th part of the force of
gravity at the equator, and decreasing as the cosine of the latitude, from the equator to the poles.   The great predominance
of gravity over the centrifugal force prevents the latter from
carrying off any bodies from the earth's surface, but the weight
of all bodies is diminished by the centrifugal force, so that the
weight of any body is greater at the poles than it is at the
equator.   If we now suppose the waters at the pole to communicate with those at the equator by means of a canal, one
branch of which goes from the pole to the centre of the earth,
and the other from the centre of the earth to the equator,
then the polar branch of the canal will be heavier than the
equatorial branch, in consequence of its weight not being
diminished by the centrifugal force ; and, therefore, in order
that the two columns may be in equilibrio, the equatorial one
must be lengthened.   Newton found that the length of the
polar must be to that of .the equatorial canal as 229 to 230,
or that the earth's polar radius must be seventeen miles less
than its equatorial radius ; that is, that the figure of the earth
is an oblate spheroid, formed by the revolution of an ellipse
round its lesser axis.   Hence it follows, that the intensity of
gravity at any point of the earth's surface is in the inverse
ratio of the distance of that point from the centre, and consequently that it diminishes from the equator to the poles,—a
result which he confirmed by the fact, that clocks required to

have their pendulums shortened, in order to beat true time, when carried from Europe towards the equator.[1]

The next subject to which Newton applied the principle of gravity, was the tides of the ocean. The philosophers of all ages had recognised the connexion between the phenomena of the tides and the position of the moon. The College of Jesuits at Coimbra, and subsequently Antonio de Dominis and Kepler, distinctly referred the tides to the attraction of the waters of the earth by the moon, but so imperfect was the explanation which was thus given of the phenomena, that Galileo ridiculed the idea of lunar attraction, and substituted for it a fallacious explanation of his own. That the moon is the principal cause of the tides is obvious from the well-known fact, that it is high water at any given place a short time after she is in the meridian of that place ; and that the sun performs a secondary part in their production, may be proved from the circumstance, that the highest tides take place when the sun, the moon, and the earth are in the same straight line, that is, when the force of the sun conspires with that of the moon ; and that the lowest tides take place when the lines drawn from the sun and moon to the earth are at right angles to each other, that is, when the force of the sun acts in opposition to that of the moon. The most perplexing phenomenon in the tides of the ocean, and one which is still a stumbling-block to persons slightly acquainted with the theory of attraction, is the existence of high water on the side of the earth opposite to the moon, as well as on the side next the earth. To maintain that the attraction of the moon at the same instant draws the waters of the ocean towards herself, and also draws them from the earth in an opposite direction, seems at first sight paradoxical ; but the difficulty vanishes when we consider the earth, or rather the centre of the earth, and the water on each side of it, as three distinct bodies,

---

[1] This was first observed by Richer, who found that a clock regulated to mean time at Paris lost 2' 28'' daily at Cayenne.

placed at different distances from the moon, and consequently attracted with forces inversely proportional to the squares of their distances. The water nearest the moon will be much more powerfully attracted than the centre of the earth, and the centre of the earth more powerfully than the water farthest from the moon. The consequence of this must be, that the waters nearest the moon will be drawn away from the centre of the earth, and will consequently rise from their level, while the centre of the earth will be drawn away from the waters opposite the moon, which will, as it were, be left behind, and consequently be in the same situation as if they were raised from the earth in a direction opposite to that in which they are attracted by the moon. Hence the effect of the moon's action upon the earth is to draw its fluid parts into the form of an oblong spheroid, the axis of which passes through the moon. As the action of the sun will produce the very same effect, though in a smaller degree, the tide at any place will depend on the relative position of these two spheroids, and will be always equal either to the sum, or to the difference of the effects of the two luminaries. At the time of new and full moon, the two spheroids will have their axes coincident ; and the height of the tide, which then will be a *spring* one, will be equal to the sum of the elevations produced in each spheroid considered separately, while at the first and third quarters the axes of the spheroids will be at right angles to each other, and the height of the tide, which will then be a *neap* one, will be equal to the difference of the elevations produced in each separate spheroid. By comparing the spring and neap tides, Newton found that the force with which the moon acted upon the waters of the earth, was to that with which the sun acted upon them as 4·48 to 1 ;—that the force of the moon produced a tide of 8·63 feet ;—that of the sun one of 1·93 feet ; —and both combined, one of $10\frac{1}{2}$ feet,—a result which, in the open sea, does not deviate much from observation. Having thus ascertained the force of the moon on the waters of our

globe, he found that the quantity of water in the moon was to
that in the earth as 1 to 40, and the density of the moon to
that of the earth as 11 to 9.

The motions of the moon, so much within the reach of our
own observation, presented a fine field for the application of
the theory of universal gravitation. The irregularities exhibited
in the lunar motions had been known in the time of Hipparchus
and Ptolemy. Tycho had discovered the great inequality called
the *variation*, amounting to 37′, and depending on the alternate
acceleration and retardation of the moon by the action of the
sun in every quarter of a revolution ; and he had also ascertained the existence of the annual equation. Of these two
inequalities, Newton gave a most satisfactory explanation,
making the first 36′ 10″, and the other 11′ 51″, differing only
a few seconds from the numbers adopted by Tobias Mayer in
his celebrated Lunar Tables. The force exerted by the sun
upon the moon may be always resolved into two forces, one
acting in the direction of the line joining the moon and the
earth, and consequently tending to increase or diminish the
moon's gravity to the earth ; and the other in a direction at
right angles to this, and consequently tending to accelerate or
retard the motion in her orbit. Now, it was found by Newton
that this last force was reduced to nothing, or vanished at the
syzygies or quadratures, so that at these four points the described areas are proportional to the times. The instant, however, that the moon quits these positions, the force under
consideration, which we may call the tangential force, begins,
and it reaches its maximum in the four octants. The force,
therefore, compounded of these two elements of the solar force,
or the diagonal of the parallelogram which they form, is no
longer directed to the earth's centre, but deviates from it at a
maximum about thirty minutes, and therefore affects the angular motion of the moon, the motion being accelerated in
passing from the quadratures to the syzygies, and retarded in
passing from the syzygies to the quadratures. Hence the

velocity is in its mean state in the octants, a maximum in the syzygies, and a minimum in the quadratures.

Upon considering the influence of the solar force in diminishing or increasing the moon's gravity to the earth, Newton saw that her distance and periodic time must, from this cause, be subject to change, and in this way he accounted for the annual equation observed by Tycho. By the application of similar principles, he explained the cause of the motion of the apsides, or of the greater axis of the moon's orbit, which was an angular progressive motion of 3° 4' nearly in the course of one lunation;[1] and he showed that the retrogradation of the nodes, amounting to 3' 10" daily, arose from one of the elements of the solar force being exerted in the plane of the ecliptic, and not in the plane of the moon's orbit,—the effect of which was to draw the moon down to the plane of the ecliptic, and thus cause the line of the nodes, or the intersection of these two planes, to move in a direction opposite to that of the moon.

The lunar theory thus sketched by Newton, required for its completion the labours of another century. The imperfections of the fluxionary calculus prevented him from explaining the other inequalities of the moon's motions, and it was reserved to Euler, D'Alembert, Clairaut, Mayer, and Laplace, to bring the lunar tables to a high degree of perfection, and to enable the navigator to determine his longitude at sea with a degree of precision which the most sanguine astronomer could scarcely have anticipated.

By the consideration of the retrograde motion of the moon's nodes, Newton was led to one of the most striking of all his discoveries, namely, the cause of the remarkable phenomenon of the precession of the equinoctial points, which moved 50" annually, and completed the circuit of the heavens in 25,920

---

[1] Newton made it only 1° 31' 28", just one-half of its real value. Clairaut obtained the same result, but afterwards, by a more accurate calculation, found it to be 3° 4', agreeing exactly with observation.

years.   Kepler had declared himself incapable of assigning any
cause for this motion, and we do not believe that any other
astronomer ever made the attempt.   From the spheroidal form
of the earth, it may be regarded as a sphere with a spheroidal
ring surrounding its equator, one half of the ring being above
the plane of the ecliptic, and the other half below it.   Considering this excess of matter as a system of satellites adhering
to the earth's surface, Newton now saw that the combined
actions of the sun and the moon upon these satellites tended to
produce a retrogradation in the nodes of the circles which they
described in their diurnal rotation, and that the sum of all the
tendencies being communicated to the whole mass of the planet,
ought to produce a slow retrogradation of the equinoctial points.
The effect produced by the motion of the sun he found to be
*forty* seconds, and that produced by the action of the moon *ten*
seconds.

Although there could be little doubt that the comets were
retained in their orbits by the same laws which regulated the
motions of the planets, yet it was not easy to put this opinion
to the test of observation.   The visibility of comets only in a
small part of their orbits rendered it difficult to ascertain their
distance and periodic times, and as their periods were probably
of great length, it was impossible to obtain approximate results
by repeated observation.   Newton, however, though he at first
imagined that comets moved in straight lines, removed this
difficulty, by showing how to determine the orbit of a comet,
namely, the form and position of the orbit, and the periodic
time, by three observations.   This method consists of an easy
geometrical construction, founded on the supposition that the
paths of comets are so nearly parabolic, that the parabola may
be used without any sensible error, although he considers it
more probable that their orbits are elliptical, and that after a
long period they may return.   By applying this method to the
comet of 1680, he calculated the elements of its orbit, and
from the agreement of the computed places with those which

were observed, he justly inferred that the motions of comets were regulated by the same laws as those of the planetary bodies.    This result was one of great importance ; for as the comets enter our system in every possible direction, and at all angles with the ecliptic, and as a great part of their orbits extends far beyond the limits of the solar system, it demonstrated the existence of gravity in spaces beyond the planets, and proved that the law of the inverse ratio of the squares of the distance was true in every possible direction, and at very remote distances from the centre of our system.

Such is a brief view of the leading discoveries which the *Principia* first announced to the world.    The grandeur of the subjects of which it treats,—the beautiful simplicity of the system which it unfolds,—the clear and concise reasoning by which that system is explained,—and the irresistible evidence by which it is supported, might have insured it the warmest admiration of contemporary mathematicians, and the most welcome reception in all the schools of philosophy throughout Europe.    This, however, is not the way in which great truths are generally received.    Though the astronomical discoveries of Newton were not assailed by the class of ignorant pretenders who attacked his optical writings, yet they were everywhere resisted by the errors and prejudices which had taken a deep hold even of the strongest minds.    The philosophy of Descartes was predominant throughout Europe.    Appealing to the imagination more than to reason, it was quickly received into popular favour, and the same causes which facilitated its introduction, extended its influence, and completed its dominion over the human mind.    In explaining all the movements of the heavenly bodies by a system of vortices in a fluid medium diffused through the universe, Descartes had seized upon an analogy of the most alluring and deceitful kind.    Those who had seen heavy bodies revolving in the eddies of a whirlpool, or in the gyrations of a vessel of water thrown into a circular motion, had no difficulty in conceiving how the planets might revolve round the sun by analogous movements. The mind instantly grasped at an explanation of so palpable a character, and which required for its development neither the exercise of patient thought, nor the aid of mathematical skill. The talent and perspicuity with which the Cartesian system was expounded, and the show of experiments with which it was sustained, contributed powerfully to its adoption, while it derived a still higher sanction from the excellent character and the unaffected piety of its author.

Thus entrenched as the Cartesian system was, in the strongholds of the human mind, and fortified by its most obstinate prejudices, it was not to be wondered at that the pure and sublime doctrines of the Principia were distrustfully received and perseveringly resisted. The uninstructed mind could not readily admit the idea, that the great masses of the planets were suspended in empty space, and retained in their orbits by an invisible influence residing in the sun ; and even those philosophers who had been accustomed to the rigour of true scientific research, and who possessed sufficient mathematical skill for the examination of the Newtonian doctrines, viewed them at first as reviving the occult qualities of the ancient physics, and resisted their introduction with a pertinacity which it is not easy to explain. Prejudiced, no doubt, in favour of his own metaphysical views, Leibnitz himself misapprehended the principles of the Newtonian philosophy, and endeavoured to demonstrate the truths in the Principia by the application of different principles. Even two years after the publication of the Principia, he published a dissertation in which he explained the motions of the planets by an ethereal fluid. Huygens, who above all other men was qualified to appreciate the new philosophy, rejected the doctrine of gravitation as existing between the individual particles of matter, and received it only as an attribute of the planetary masses. John Bernouilli, also, one of the first mathematicians of the age, opposed the philosophy of Newton. Mairan, in the early part of his life, was a strenuous defender of the system of vortices. Cassini and Maraldi were quite ignorant of the Principia, and occupied themselves with the most absurd methods of calculating the orbits of the comets long after the Newtonian method had been established on the most impregnable basis ; and even Fontenelle, a man of liberal views and extensive information, continued throughout the whole of his life to maintain the doctrines of Descartes.

The Chevalier Louville, in his memoir " On the construction and Theory of Tables of the Sun," had applied the doctrine of central force to the motions of the planets, so early as 1720.[1] S'Gravesande had introduced it into the Dutch universities at a somewhat earlier period ; and Maupertuis, in consequence of a visit which he paid to England in 1728, zealously defended it in his Treatise on the Figures of the Celestial Bodies. But notwithstanding these and some other examples that might be quoted, we must admit the truth of the remark of Voltaire, that though Newton survived the publication of the Principia more than forty years, yet at the time of his death he had not above twenty followers in England.[2] With regard to the progress of the Newtonian philosophy in England, some difference of opinion has been entertained. Professor Playfair gives the following account of it :—" In the universities of England, though the Aristotelian physics had made an obstinate resistance, they had been supplanted by the Cartesian, which became firmly established about the time when their foundation began to be sapped by the general progress of science, and particularly by the discoveries of Newton. For more than thirty years after the publication of these discoveries, the system of vortices kept its ground, and a translation from French into Latin of the Physics of Rohault, a work entirely Cartesian, continued at Cambridge to be the text for philosophical instruction. About the year 1718, a new and more elegant translation of the same book was published by Dr. Samuel Clarke, with the addition of notes, in which that profound and ingenious writer explained the views of Newton on the principal subjects of discussion, so that the notes contained virtually a refutation of the text ; they did so, however, only virtually, all appearance of argument and controversy being carefully avoided.  Whether this escaped the notice of the learned Doctor or not is uncertain, but the new translation, from its better Latinity and the name of the editor, was readily admitted to all the academical honours which the old one had enjoyed.  Thus the stratagem of Dr. Clarke completely succeeded ; the tutor might prelect from the text, but the pupil would sometimes look into the notes ; and error is never so sure of being exposed, as when the truth is placed close to it, side by side, without anything to alarm prejudice, or awaken from its lethargy the dread of innovation.  Thus, therefore, the Newtonian philosophy first entered the University of Cambridge, under the protection of the Cartesian."  To this passage Professor Playfair adds the following as a note.

"The Universities of St. Andrews and Edinburgh were, I believe, the first in Britain where the Newtonian philosophy was made the subject of the academical prelections.  For this distinction they are indebted to James and David Gregory, the first in some respects the rival, but both the friends of Newton.  Whiston bewails, in the anguish of his heart, the difference in this respect between those universities and his own.  David Gregory taught in Edinburgh for several years prior to 1690, when he removed to Oxford ; and Whiston says[1] 'he had already caused several of his scholars to keep Acts, as we call them, upon several branches of the Newtonian philosophy, while we at Cambridge, poor wretches, were ignominiously studying the fictitious hypotheses of the Cartesians.'[2]  I do

[1] "Whiston's *Memoirs of his own Life,*" p. 36.
[2] It does not appear at what time the Newtonian Philosophy was received at Oxford. Judging from Addison's "Oration in Defence of the New Philosophy," spoken in the

not, however, mean to say that from this date the Cartesian philosophy was expelled from those universities ; the Physics of
Rohault were still in use as a text-book,—at least occasionally,
to a much later period than this, and a great deal, no doubt,
depended on the character of the individual.   Professor Keill
introduced the Newtonian philosophy in his lectures at Oxford
in 1697 ; but the instructions of the tutors, which constitute
the real and efficient system of the University, were not cast in
that mould till long afterwards."  Adopting the same view of
the subject, Mr. Dugald Stewart has stated, " that the philosophy of Newton was taught by David Gregory at Edinburgh,
and by his brother, James Gregory, at St. Andrews,[1] before it
was able to supplant the vortices of Descartes in that very
university of which Newton was a member.   It was in the

Theatre at Oxford, July 7, 1693, six years after the publication of the Principia, we have
no doubt that the Cartesian Philosophy, which is obviously the " New Philosophy,"
defended by Addison, was in full force at that date.  This oration, " done from the
Latin original," is appended to the English translation of Fontenelle on the Plurality of
Worlds ; and on the title-page to that work it is called " *Mr. Addison's Defence on the
Newtonian Philosophy.*"  Our readers will decide from the following extract whether
the New Philosophy means the Newtonian or the Cartesian Philosophy :—

" How long, gentlemen of the University, shall we slavishly tread in the steps of the
ancients, and be afraid of being wiser than our ancestors ?  How long shall we religiously
worship the triflings of antiquity as some do old wives' stories ?  It is indeed shameful,
when we survey the *great* ornament of the present age (NEWTON), to transfer our ap-
plauses to the ancients, and to take pains to search into ages past for persons fit for
panegyrick."  So far the New Philosophy may mean that of Newton, but the following
passage contradicts any such inference :—" The ancient philosophy has had more
allowed than it could reasonably pretend to ; how often has Sheldon's Theatre rung
with encomia on the Stagyrite, who, greater than his own Alexander, has long, un-
opposed, triumphed in our school desks, and had the whole world for his pupils ?  At
length rose CARTESIUS, a happier genius, who has bravely asserted the truth against the
united force of all opposers, and has brought on the stage a *new method of philosophizing.*  But shall we stigmatize with the name of *novelty, that philosophy* which, though
but lately revived, is more ancient than the peripatetic, and as old as the mother from
whence it is derived ?  A great man indeed he was, and the only one we envy France
(*Descartes*).  He solved the difficulties of the universe almost as well as if he had been its
architect."  The name of Newton or his philosophy is never again mentioned.—*Author.*

[1] Dr. Reid states, that James Gregory, Professor of Philosophy at St Andrews, printed
a Thesis at Edinburgh in 1690, containing twenty-five positions, of which twenty-two
were a compend of Newton's Principia.

Scottish universities that the philosophy of Locke, as well as that of Newton, was first adopted as a branch of academical education."

Anxious as we should have been to have awarded to Scotland the honour of having first adopted the Newtonian philosophy, yet a regard for historical truth compels us to take a different view of the subject. It is well known that Sir Isaac Newton delivered lectures on his own philosophy from the Lucasian chair before the publication of the Principia ; and in the very page of Whiston's life quoted by Professor Playfair, he informs us that he had heard him read such lectures in the public schools, though at that time he did not at all understand them. Newton continued to lecture till 1699, and occasionally, we presume, till 1703, when Whiston became his successor, having been appointed his deputy in 1699. In both of these capacities, Whiston delivered in the public schools a course of lectures on astronomy, and a course of physico-mathematical lectures, in which the mathematical philosophy of Newton was explained and demonstrated, and both these courses were published,—the one in 1707, and the other in 1710,—for the use of the young men in the University. In 1707, the celebrated blind mathematician, Nicholas Saunderson, took up his residence in Christ's College, without being admitted a member of that body. The society not only allotted to him apartments, but gave him the free use of their library. With the concurrence of Whiston, he delivered a course " On the Principia, Optics, and Universal Arithmetic of Newton," and the popularity of these lectures was so great, that Sir Isaac corresponded on the subject of them with their author ; and on the ejection of Whiston from the Lucasian chair in 1711, Saunderson was appointed his successor. In this important office he continued to teach the Newtonian philosophy till the time of his death, which took place in 1739.

But while the Newtonian philosophy was thus regularly taught in Cambridge, after the publication of the Principia, there were

not wanting other exertions for accelerating its progress. About
1694, the celebrated Dr. Samuel Clarke, while an under-gra-
duate, defended in the public schools, a question taken from the
Newtonian philosophy ; and his translation of Rohault's Physics,
which contains references in the notes to the Principia, and which
was published in 1697 (and not in 1718, as stated by Professor
Playfair), shows how early the Cartesian system was attacked
by the disciples of Newton.   The author of the life of Saunderson informs us, that public exercises or acts, founded on every
part of the Newtonian system, were very common about 1707,
and so general were such studies in the University, that the
Principia rose to four times its original price.[1]   One of the most
ardent votaries of the Newtonian philosophy was Dr. Laughton,
who had been tutor in Clare Hall from 1694, and it is probable that, during the whole, or at least a greater part of his
tutorship, he had inculcated the same doctrines.   In 1709-10,
when he was proctor in that college, instead of appointing a
moderator, he discharged the office himself, and devoted his
most active exertions to the promotion of mathematical knowledge.   Previous to this, he had even published a paper of
questions on the Newtonian philosophy, which appear to have
been used as theses for disputations ; and such was his ardour
and learning, that they powerfully contributed to the popularity of his college.[2]   About the same time the learned Dr.
Bentley, who first made known the philosophy of his friend to
general readers, filled the high office of Master of Trinity
College, and could not fail to have exerted his influence in pro-
pagating doctrines which he so greatly admired.   Had any
opposition been offered to the introduction of the true system

---

[1] Cotes states, in his preface to the second edition of the Principia, that copies of the
first edition were scarce, and could only be obtained at an immense price.  Sir William
Brown, when at college, gave more than two guineas for a copy, and owing to the difficulty of procuring one at a reasonable price, the father of Dr. John Moore of Glasgow
transcribed the whole work with his own hand.  See Nichol's *Literary Anecdotes*, vol.
iii p. 322, and *Encyc. Brit.* Art. MOORE.

[2] See the *Museum Criticum*, vol. ii. p. 514.

of the universe, the talents and influence of these individuals would have immediately suppressed it, but no such opposition seems to have been made ; and though there may have been individuals at Cambridge ignorant of mathematical science, who adhered to the system of Descartes, and patronized the study of the Physics of Rohault, yet it is probable that similar persons existed in the Universities of Edinburgh and St. Andrews ; and we cannot regard their adherence to error as disproving the general fact, that the philosophy of Newton was quickly introduced into all the universities of Great Britain.[1]

But while the mathematical principles of the Newtonian system were ably expounded in our seats of learning, its physi-

[1] The following passage in Whiston's Life of Dr. Clarke, is not in accordance with some of the preceding statements. " About the year 1697, while I was chaplain to Dr. John Moor, then Bishop of Norwich, I met at one of the coffee-houses in the market-place at Norwich, a young man, to me then wholly unknown ; his name was Clarke, pupil to that eminent and careful tutor, Mr. Ellis, of Gonvil and Caius College in Cambridge. Mr. Clarke knew me so far at the university, I being about eight years elder than himself, and so far knew the nature and success of my studies, as to enter into a conversation with me about that system of Cartesian philosophy his tutor had put him to translate,—I mean Rohault's Physics ; and to ask my opinion about the fitness of such a translation. I well remember the answer I made him, that, ' since the youth of the university must have, at present, some system of Natural Philosophy for their studies and exercises ; and since the true system of Sir Isaac Newton's was not yet made easy enough for the purpose ; it was not improper, for their sakes, yet to translate and use the system of Rohault (who was esteemed the best expositor of Descartes), but that as soon as Sir Isaac Newton's philosophy came to be better known, that only ought to be taught, and the other dropped.' Which last part of my advice, by the way, has not been followed, as it ought to have been, in that university. But, as Bishop Hoadley truly observes, Dr. Clarke's Rohault is still the principal book for the young students there. Though such an observation be no way to the honour of the tutors in that university, who, in reading Rohault, do only read a philosophical romance to their pupils, almost perpetually contradicted by the better notes thereto belonging. And certainly to use Cartesian fictitious hypotheses at this time of day, after the principal parts of Sir Isaac Newton's certain system have been made easy enough for the understanding of ordinary mathematicians, is like the continuing to eat old acorns after the discovery of new wheat, for the food of mankind. However, upon this occasion, Mr. Clarke and I fell into a discourse about the wonderful discoveries made in Sir Isaac Newton's philosophy ;—and the result of that discourse was, that I was greatly surprised that so young a man as Mr. Clarke then was, not much, I think, above twenty-two years of age, should know so much of those sublime discoveries which were then almost a secret to all, but to a few particular mathematicians."

cal truths had been studied by some of the most distinguished
scholars and philosophers of the times, and were subsequently
explained and communicated to the public by various lecturers
on experimental philosophy. The celebrated Locke, who was
incapable of understanding the Principia from his want of
geometrical knowledge, inquired of Huygens if all the mathematical propositions in that work were true. When he was
assured that he might depend upon their certainty, he took
them for granted, and carefully examined the reasonings and
corollaries deduced from them. In this manner he acquired a
knowledge of the physical truths in the Principia, and became
a firm believer in the discoveries which it contained. In the,
same manner he studied the treatise on Optics, and made himself master of every part of it which was not mathematical.[1]
From a manuscript of Sir Isaac Newton's, entitled, " A Demonstration that the Planets, by their gravity towards the Sun,
may move in Ellipses,[2] found among the papers of Mr. Locke,
and published by Lord King," it would appear that he himself
had been at considerable trouble in explaining to his friend
that interesting proposition. This manuscript is endorsed,
" Mr. Newton, March, 1689." It begins with three hypotheses (the two first being the two laws of motion, and the third
the parallelogram of motion), which introduce the proposition
of the proportionality of the areas to the times in motions
round an immovable centre of attraction.[3] Three lemmas, containing the properties of the ellipse, then prepare the reader for
the celebrated proposition, that when a body moves in an
ellipse,[4] the attraction is reciprocally as the square of the distance of the body from the focus to which it is attracted.
These propositions are demonstrated in a more popular manner
than in the Principia, but there can be no doubt that, even in

---

[1] Preface to Desaguliers' *Course of Experimental Philosophy*, vol. i. p. viii.   Dr. Desaguliers says that he was told this anecdote several times by Sir Isaac Newton himself.
[2] The *Life of John Locke*.   Edit. 1830, vol. i. pp. 389-400.
[3] *Principia*, lib. i. prop. i.                              [4] *Ibid*. lib. i. prop. xi.

their present modified form, they were beyond the capacity of Mr. Locke.

Among the learned men who were desirous of understanding the truths revealed in the Principia, Richard Bentley was one of the most distinguished. In 1691, when only thirty years of age, he applied to John Craige, a mathematician of some eminence, and a friend of Newton, for a list of works which would enable him to study the Principia. Alarmed at the list which Craige sent him, he was induced to apply to Newton himself, who drew up the directions which, along with those of Craige, we have given in the Appendix.[1]  When Bentley was appointed, in 1692, the first Lecturer on Robert Boyle's Foundation, he chose as the subject of his discourse, " A Confutation of Atheism." The insidious doctrines of Spinoza and Hobbes had at that time made considerable progress among the upper ranks of society, and as these authors denied a Divine Providence, and considered the existence of the universe as the result of necessity, Bentley proposed to conclude his course of lectures with the demonstration of a Divine Providence from the physical constitution of the universe, as demonstrated by Newton. Before printing his discourses, he consulted Newton on some points which required elucidation, and it was in reply to the Queries thus addressed to him, that Newton wrote the five remarkable letters already alluded to. By this means some of the great truths of the Newtonian philosophy were promulgated among a class of readers who would not otherwise have heard of them.[2]

[1] See APPENDIX, No. XIII. The original of these directions was given by Richard Cumberland, the relation of Bentley, to Trinity College, along with the originals of the four celebrated letters from Newton to Bentley, to which our attention will be afterwards directed.

[2] Lord Aston, "a great lover of the mathematics, who would gladly be satisfied in a difficulty or two on that science," requested Mr. Greves and Sir E. Southcote to submit these difficulties to Sir Isaac Newton. Mr. Greves accordingly went on Monday, the 30th November 1702, and gives the following account of the conversation. " He owns there are a great many faults in his book, and has crossed it and interleaved it, and writ in the margin of it, in a great many places. It is talked he designs to reprint it, though he would not own it  I asked him about his proof of a vacuum, and said that if there is

About the year 1718, Isaac Watts speaks of the exploded Physics of Descartes, and the noble inventions of Sir Isaac Newton, in his "hypotheses of the heavenly bodies and their motions ;" and he refers to previous writers who have explained Nature and its operations in a more sensible and geometrical manner than Aristotle, especially those who have followed the principles of that wonder of our age and nation, Sir Isaac Newton.[1]

Dr. John Keill was the first person who publicly taught natural philosophy " by experiments in a mathematical manner." Desaguliers informs us that this author " laid down very simple propositions, which he proved by experiments, and from these he deduced others more compound, which he still confirmed by experiments, till he had instructed his auditors in the laws of motion, the principles of hydrostatics and optics, and some of the chief propositions of Sir Isaac Newton, concerning light and colours. He began these courses in Oxford about the year 1704 or 1705, and in that way introduced the love of the Newtonian philosophy."[2] When Dr. Keill left the University, Desaguliers began to teach the new philosophy by experiments. He commenced his lectures at Harthall, in Oxford, in 1710, and delivered more than a hundred and twenty discourses ; and when he went to settle in London in 1713, he informs us that he found " the Newtonian philosophy generally received among persons of all ranks and professions, and even among the ladies by the help of experiments."[3]

---

such a matter as escapes through the pores of all sensible bodies, this could not be weighed. . . . I find he designs to alter that part, for he has writ on the margin, *Materia sensibilis ;* perceiving his reasons do not conclude in all matter whatsoever."—Edleston's *Correspondence,* Pref. p. xiv., and Tixall's *Letters,* II. 152, quoted there.

[1] *Improvement of the Mind,* Part I. chap. xx. Art. vi. and xvi., or his *Works,* vol. v. pp. 301, 306.

[2] These lectures were first published in Latin in 1718, and afterwards in English in 1721 and 1739, under the title of *An Introduction to the true Astronomy,* or *Astronomical Lectures read in the Astronomical School of the University of Oxford.* By John Keill, M.D. F.R.S.

[2] Desaguliers, *ut supra,* Preface, pp. viii. x.

Such were the steps by which the philosophy of Newton was established in Great Britain. From the time of the publication of the Principia, its mathematical doctrines formed a regular part of academical education, and before twenty years had elapsed, its physical truths were communicated to the public in popular lectures, illustrated by experiments, and accommodated to the capacities of those who were not versed in mathematical knowledge. The Cartesian system, though it may have lingered for a while in the recesses of our universities, was soon over-turned ; and long before his death, Newton enjoyed the high satisfaction of seeing his philosophy triumphant in his native land.

In closing our account of the Principia, and in justification of the high eulogium we have pronounced upon it, we may quote the opinions of two of the most distinguished men of the past or the present age. " It may be justly said," observes Halley, " that so many and so valuable philosophical truths, as are herein discovered, and put past dispute, were never yet owing to the capacity and industry of any one man." [1]  " The importance and generality of the discoveries," says Laplace, " and the immense number of original and profound views which has been the germ of the most brilliant theories of the philosophers of this century, and all presented with much elegance, will insure to the work, on the *Mathematical Principles of Natural Philosophy*, a pre-eminence above all the other productions of human genius." [2]

[1] *Phil. Trans.* vol. xvi. p. 296.
[2] *Système du Monde*, Edit. 2de, 1799, p. 336.

## CHAPTER XIII.

The Newtonian Philosophy stationary for half a Century, owing to the imperfect state of Mechanics, Optics, and Analysis—Developed and extended by the French Mathematicians—Influence of the Academy of Sciences—Improvements in the Infinitesimal Calculus—Christian Mayer of the Arithmetic of Sines—D'Alembert's Calculus of Partial Differences—Lagrange's Calculus of Variations—The Problem of Three Bodies—Importance of the Lunar Theory—Lunar Tables of Clairaut, D'Alembert, and Euler—The Superior Tables of Tobias Mayer gains the Prize offered by the English Board of Longitude—Euler receives part of the English Reward, and also a Reward from the French Board—Laplace discovers the cause of the Moon's Acceleration, and completes the Lunar Theory—Lagrange's Solution of the Problem of Three Bodies as applied to the Planets—Inequalities of Jupiter and Saturn explained by Laplace—Stability of the Solar System the proof of Design—Maclaurin, Laplace, and others, on the Figure of the Earth—Researches of Laplace on the Tides, and the stable Equilibrium of the Ocean—Theoretical Discovery of Neptune by Adams and Leverrier—New Satellites of Saturn and Neptune—Extension of Saturn's Ring and its partial fluidity—Twenty-seven Asteroids Discovered—Leverrier's Theory of them—Comets with Elliptic Orbits within our System—Law of Gravity applied to Double Stars—Spiral Nebulæ—Motion of the Solar System in Space.

WHEN Halley remarked that the author of the *Principia* "seemed to have exhausted his argument, and left little to be done by those who should succeed him," he committed a mistake which, though it had a tendency to check the progress of inquiry, was yet one into which philosophers are apt to fall when their science has made a great start by the discovery of some general and comprehensive law. Had Halley ventured to make this remark at the close of his life, rather than in 1687, he might have found some justification of it in the long interval which elapsed before any brilliant addition had been made to physical astronomy. During the half century which had passed away since the discovery of universal gravitation, no application of it of any importance had been made, and, as

Laplace has observed, "all this interval was required for this great truth to be generally comprehended, and for surmounting the opposition which it encountered from the system of vortices, and from the prejudices of contemporaneous mathematicians." The infinitesimal analysis, as it was left by Newton and Leibnitz, was incapable of conducting the physical astronomer to any higher results than those which were consigned in the Principia ; and it is a remarkable fact in the history of science, that the very men who spurned the new philosophy of gravitation, were strenuously engaged in improving that very calculus which was destined to establish and extend those great truths which they had so rashly denounced.

It has been remarked by Laplace, that " with the exception of his researches on the elliptical motion of the planets and comets, of the attraction of spherical bodies, and of the intensity of gravity at the surface of the sun, and of the planets that are accompanied by satellites, all the other discoveries which we have described were only blocked out by Newton. His theory of the figures of the planets was limited by the supposition of their homogeneity. His solution of the problem of the precession of the equinoxes, though very ingenious and accordant with observations, is in many respects defective. In the great number of perturbations in the celestial motions, he has considered only those of the lunar motions, the most important of which, namely, the evection, had escaped his researches. He has completely established the existence of the principle which he discovered, but the development of its consequences and of its advantages has been the work of the successors of this great geometer." [1]

In thus completing the great work of which Newton laid the foundation, it was necessary, as Laplace observes, " to bring to perfection at once the sciences of mechanics, optics, and analysis ; and though physical astronomy may still be improved and simplified, yet posterity will gratefully acknowledge that the

[1] *Système du Monde*, p. 336.

geometers of the eighteenth century have not transmitted to us a single astronomical phenomenon of which they have not determined the cause and the law. We owe to France the justice of observing, that if England had the advantage of giving birth to the discovery of universal gravitation, it is principally to the French geometers, and to the encouragement held out by the Academy of Sciences, that we owe the numerous developments of this discovery, and the revolution which it has produced in astronomy." [1]

In submitting to our readers a brief history of these developments, and of that revolution, we shall gather fresh laurels for the author of the Principia. It is from what he left undone, and what he enabled others to do, that we can rightly estimate the magnitude and appreciate the value of his achievement. The importance of a great discovery does not lie in its intrinsic novelty and beauty : It is the number of its applications, and the ubiquity of its range, that stamps its value ; and when we proclaim Newton the Father of the Philosophy of the Universe, we must regard the Eulers, the Clairauts, the D'Alemberts, the Lagranges, and the Laplaces of another age, as the intellectual progeny which he educated and reared. A distinguished philosopher has asked the question, why no British name is ever mentioned in the list of mathematicians who followed Newton in his brilliant career, and completed the magnificent edifice of which he laid the foundation ? [2] May we not make the question more special by asking why the University which he instructed and adorned, which possessed such noble endowments, and which claims the honour of having first adopted and taught his philosophy, did not rear a younger son, or even a sickly child, that .could be ranked in the great family we have named ? Scotland contributed

1 Laplace, *Système du Monde*, p. 340.

Professor Playfair adds, that this was " the more remarkable, as the interests of navigation were deeply involved in the question of the lunar theory, so that no motive which a regard to reputation or to interest could create was wanting to engage the mathematicians of England in the inquiry."—*Edinburgh Review*, vol. xi. p. 280. Jan. 1808.

her Maclaurin, but England no European name ; and a century and a half passed away till Airey and Adams adorned the birth-place of Newton's genius. In the same spirit in which we have asked these questions, M. Arago, equally jealous of the glory of his country, has freely confessed, " that no Frenchman can reflect, without an aching heart, on the small participation of his own country in the memorable achievement of the discovery of universal gravitation ;" and Mr. Grant, the latest historian of physical science,[1] in responding to this liberal sentiment, has added, in the language of just severity, that " *if an English-man could be supposed to be equally sensitive*, he has ample reason to regret the inglorious part his country played during the long period which marked the development of the Newto-nian theory."[2]

In the imperfect state in which the differential calculus was left by Newton and Leibnitz, its inventors, it was not fitted to

[1] *History of Physical Astronomy*, &c. p. 108.  London, 1852.  Mr. Grant also remarks, " that with the exception of Maclaurin and Thomas Simpson, hardly any individual of these islands deserves even to be mentioned in connexion with the history of physical astronomy during that period ;" and that, at the beginning of the present century, " there was hardly an individual in this country who possessed an intimate acquaintance with the methods of investigation which had conducted the foreign mathematicians to so many sublime results."

[2] Referring our readers to the statements at the end of Chapter IV., as showing the probable cause of the success of the French mathematicians, and of the inglorious failure of our own, we beg their attention to the following confirmation of our views by one of the wisest and most eminent of our Scottish mathematicians.  In a review of Laplace's *Système du Monde*, Professor Playfair makes the following observations.

" The literary institution which has most completely produced its effect of any in mo-dern times, and that has been most successful in promoting the interests of science, is that of the Royal Academy of Sciences of Paris, where *small pensions and great honours*, bestowed on a few men for devoting themselves exclusively to works of invention and discovery, have been the means of advancing the mathematical sciences in France to a state of unexampled prosperity.

" In England, *where such an institution as that just mentioned was wanting*, and where the public is perpetually prepared, with the question, *cui bono*, to repress what seems the luxury of science, the same progress has not been made ; and our mercantile prejudices have so far defeated our own purpose, that if the matter had been left to us, the theory of the moon's motion would still have been extremely imperfect, and the great nautical problem of finding the longitude could have received nothing like an accurate solution." —*Edinburgh Review*, vol. xv. p. 39.  Jan. 1810.

grapple with the higher problems in physical astronomy which still remained to be solved ; and it was fortunate for the future progress of the science, that distinguished mathematicians directed themselves to the improvement of the infinitesimal calculus, and to the discovery of new mechanical principles, or extended applications of those already known.

In 1727, the very year in which Newton died, Christian Mayer published in the Petersburg Commentaries, a valuable memoir on the application of algebra to geometry ; and the geometrical theorems which he demonstrated, formed the basis of the *Arithmetic of Sines*, for which Euler provided a notation and an algorithm, which has rendered it one of the most simple and valuable instruments of astronomical research. The invention of the calculus of *Partial Differences* by D'Alembert, which he first made known in 1747, was particularly applicable to the more difficult problems in physical astronomy, and when improved and extended by Euler, it became an invaluable instrument in every inquiry which demanded the aid of the pure or mixed mathematics.

But however valuable were these instruments of analysis, the *calculus of variations* discovered by Lagrange in 1760, was the greatest step in the improvement of the infinitesimal calculus which was made in the last century. It not only afforded the most complete solution of the problems that gave rise to it, but had an application of the most extensive kind, exceeding even the expectations of its inventor. Euler, who had made some progress in the same subject, at once acknowledged the superiority of his youthful rival, and with a nobility of mind not frequently displayed even by the greatest men, he renounced his own less perfect methods, and devoted himself to the study and extension of the new calculus.[1]

Nearly twenty years after the death of Newton, Euler, Clairaut, and D'Alembert were engaged in solving what has

---

[1] See the Article MATHEMATICS in the *Edinburgh Encyclopædia*, vol. xiii. p. 380, where Sir John Herschel pronounces a beautiful eulogy on the conduct of Euler.

been called the *problem of three bodies*,—that is, the determination of the motion of *one* body revolving round a *second* body, such as the *moon* round the *earth*, and disturbed by the attractions of a *third* body, such as the *sun*. The rigorous solution of this problem is beyond the reach of human genius, and the imperfect solution which has been obtained is only an approximate one depending for its accuracy on the more or less advanced state of the infinitesimal calculus. But even if the problem of three bodies had been susceptible of an accurate solution, it would not have diminished the difficulty of solving the more general problem of finding the motion of a planet, when simultaneously acted upon by all the other planets of the system. In this case the disturbances are very small, and when the separate action of each planet upon the disturbed body is determined, the sum of the perturbations, when applied to the place of the planet in its elliptic orbit, will give its true place in the heavens as seen from the centre of the sun.

When the three bodies are the sun, the moon, and the earth, the disturbance of the moon's motions by the action of the sun is very considerable, and hence the theory of the moon was the first subject to which the continental mathematicians directed their attention. The determination of the longitude at sea by observing the distance of the moon from the stars, had given a peculiar interest to the construction of accurate tables for computing the moon's place, and the Board of Longitude in England had offered a high reward. Mathematicians were urged to the inquiry by the united motives of wealth and fame. Newton had explained only five of the principal equations of the moon's orbit, and it was obvious that there were many other irregularities which observation alone was incapable of detecting. Clairaut seems to have been the first of the three mathematicians who undertook this inquiry ; but however this may be, the competitors arrived at the same goal with nearly equal success. Clairaut had at first endeavoured to compute the lunar inequalities by the method of Newton, but he was obliged to abandon it, and appeal to the higher powers of analysis. In 1746, Euler drew up a set of lunar tables, founded on the results of his researches, but they were not found to be very superior to those in common use. In 1754, Clairaut and D'Alembert published lunar tables, embodying the results of their theory. Those of Clairaut were far superior to any that had hitherto been published, while those of D'Alembert were very inferior in accuracy. Encouraged by the failure of his rivals, Euler resumed his investigations in 1755, and published a more complete set of lunar tables, along with his researches on the lunar theory ; but though more conformable with observation than his former set, they had not that degree of accuracy which was required for the determination of the longitude.

While the mathematicians, trusting too much to theory, were thus baffled in the useful application of their own results, a sagacious practical astronomer directed his attention to the improvement of the lunar tables, and carried off the prize. Tobias Mayer of Göttingen, comparing the results obtained by Euler with a number of accurate observations made by himself and others, produced a set of tables which, when compared with the observations of Bradley, gave the moon's place within *thirty seconds*. These tables were sent to the English Board of Longitude in 1755, in competition for the prize ; but they did not possess that degree of precision which was required. Mayer, however, continued till the day of his death to add to their accuracy, and he left behind him a complete set of solar and lunar tables, for which the Board of Longitude awarded his widow the sum of *three thousand pounds*, a portion of the reward which they had offered for the discovery of the longitude. These tables were first published in 1770, and their greatest error was found never to exceed *one minute and a quarter*. As these tables were founded on Euler's theorems, the Board presented this distinguished mathematician with the sum of *three hundred pounds*. Though advanced in years, Euler was full of intellectual life, and having continued to labour at the lunar theory, he constructed a new set of tables, which were published in 1771, and were rewarded by the Board of Longitude in France.

Notwithstanding the accuracy of Mayer's tables, an irregularity had been discovered by observation which was not indicated by the theory of gravity. Halley and other astronomers had placed it beyond a doubt that the moon performed her monthly revolution round the earth in a shorter time than formerly. This acceleration of the moon, as it was called, amounted to nearly *ten seconds* in a century, and various hypotheses were framed to account for it. The most plausible of these was, that all space was filled with an ethereal medium which opposed such a resistance to the motions of the planets, that the force which kept them in their orbit would gradually overpower their diminished velocity, and thus shorten their period round the central body. This hypothesis was supported by Euler, and by the abettors of the undulatory theory, who required the existence of a medium for the propagation of light, and it was adopted with equal eagerness by another class of theorists, who saw in the acceleration of the celestial motions the process by which the Almighty was to destroy the solar system, by precipitating the secondary planets upon their primaries, and the primary planets upon the sun. Laplace admitted the sufficiency of the hypothesis, but as he saw no reason for admitting the existence of a resisting medium, he did not consider himself warranted in adopting such an hypothesis till it was found that gravitation was incapable of accounting for the fact. Another theory of the moon's acceleration was founded on the supposition that the daily motion of the earth was retarded by the continued blowing of the easterly winds of the tropics against the mountain ranges which extend from the equator to the poles ; but Laplace satis-fied himself, from a rigorous examination of this supposition, that no retardation of the earth's motion could be thus produced. Another hypothesis still remained to which astronomers might appeal not only for the explanation of the moon's acceleration,

but also of some considerable inequalities in the motions of
Jupiter and Saturn, which appeared not to have a periodical
character, and therefore to be in the same category with the
moon's acceleration.  Newton and every other philosopher had
taken it for granted that the force of gravity was propagated
instantaneously from bodies, and not in time like the rays of
light ; but it occurred to Laplace that if time was required for
the transmission of gravity, it would affect the intensity of the
force.  He therefore computed the velocity of gravity that
would be required to produce the observed acceleration, and he
found it to be *eight millions* of times greater than the velocity
of light, that is 192,500 miles multiplied by 8,000,000, or
1,540,000,000,000 miles in a second—a velocity which no
language can express.  After arriving at this result, Laplace
found that if the acceleration is produced by another cause, then
the effect of the successive transmissions would be insensible,
and consequently the velocity of gravity, if it is not instanta-
neous, must at least be *fifty millions* of times greater than that
of light, that is, must be at least 9,625,000,000,000 miles in
a second.

In the course of these investigations it had been placed beyond a doubt that every inequality in the motion of the planets,
and in the form of their orbits produced by their mutual gravitation, must be periodical, that is, that the inequality, after
reaching its maximum, will diminish according to the same law
by which it increased, and hence it became doubly interesting
to discover the cause of phenomena which had this character.
Although foiled in so many attempts to refer the moon's acceleration to the action of gravity, Laplace returned to the
inquiry with fresh zeal, and about the end of 1787, his labours
were crowned with success.  It was well known to Lagrange
and to himself, that the eccentricities of the planetary orbits
underwent extremely slow changes, which had a very long
period.  To such a change the eccentricity of the earth's orbit
is subject from the action of the planets.  The mean action

of the sun must therefore vary with the earth's eccentricity, and the earth, thus exerting a greater or a less force over the moon, will accelerate or retard her, and thus produce the secular inequality which has been observed in her mean motion. When the eccentricity is diminishing, which it has been doing since the date of the earliest astronomical observations, the moon's mean motion will be accelerated ; but when the diminution ceases, and the orbit returns to its former ellipticity, the sun's action will increase, and the moon's mean motion will be retarded.[1]  Laplace found the acceleration to be *ten seconds* during a century,—a rate which, notwithstanding its variable character, may be considered as uniform for two thousand years.

Although Halley suspected the existence of this inequality so early as 1693, yet it is to Mr. Dunthorne that we owe the first accurate determination of its magnitude.  By means of lunar eclipses observed at Babylon in 721 B.C., and at Alexandria in 201 B.C.,—a solar eclipse observed by Theon, A.D. 364, and other two by Ibyn Jounis at Cairo, about the end of the tenth century, he found the acceleration to be *ten* seconds in a hundred years.[2]  The consequence of this inequality is, that the moon is about *two hours* later in coming to the meridian than she would have been had she performed her monthly revolution in the same time that she did when the earliest Chaldean observations were made.  " It is indeed a wonderful fact in the history of science," as Mr. Grant remarks, " that these rude notes of the priests of Babylon should escape the ruins of successive empires, and finally, after the lapse of three thousand years, should become subservient in establishing a phenomenon of so refined and complicated a character as the inequality we

---

[1] M. Leverrier has recently shown that the earth's eccentricity will diminish during the period of *twenty-four thousand years!*

[2] Mr. Airy has more recently found by discussing three ancient total eclipses (Aug. 15, B.C. 309 ; May 19, B.C. 556 ; May 28, B.C. 584), that the secular acceleration is at least 12′ 12″, as adopted by Hansen in his Lunar Tables.  See *Memoirs of the Astronomical Society*, vol. xxvi.

have just been considering."[1]  And in referring to the long
period of the same inequality, Professor Playfair remarks, that
"two thousand years are little more than an infinitesimal in
this reckoning ; and as an astronomer thinks that he commits
no error when he considers the rate of the sun's motion as
uniform for twenty-four hours, so he commits none when he
regards the rate of this equation as continuing the same for
twenty centuries.  That man, whose life, nay, the history of
whose species occupies such a mere point in the duration of the
world, should come to the knowledge of laws that embrace
myriads of ages in their revolution, is perhaps the most astonish-
ing fact that the history of science exhibits."[2]

By this great discovery, which had eluded the grasp of Euler
and Lagrange,[3] Laplace may be regarded as having completed
the lunar theory exactly one hundred years after it had been
sketched out in the first edition of the Principia.

The curious subject of the moon's acceleration has recently
excited much interest in consequence of Professor Adams[4] having
proposed an important correction upon the theory of Laplace,
by which the secular acceleration was reduced to $6''\cdot11$.
M. Delaunay, by a different process, has since found it to be
$6''\cdot11$, exactly the same as that obtained by Mr. Adams.[5]
M. Plana, the distinguished Sardinian mathematician, and M.
Pontecoulant,[6] still adhere to the theory of Laplace, on grounds
which are not yet published.   M. Delaunay is of opinion that

---

[1] *History of Physical Astronomy*, pp. 63, 64.

[2] *Edinburgh Review*, vol. xi. p. 261.

[3] The Academy of Sciences proposed the moon's acceleration as the subject of their
prize for 1770.  Euler gained it, but came to the conclusion that it was not produced by
the force of gravity.  The same subject was again proposed in 1772, and the prize was
divided between Euler and Lagrange.  Euler ascribed the acceleration to a resisting
medium, and Lagrange evaded the difficulty.  The prize was again offered in 1774, and
was gained by Lagrange, and he now doubted the existence of the inequality.  It was
under these circumstances that Laplace took up the subject, and obtained the results
which we have mentioned.

[4] *Phil. Trans.* 1853, p. 398.

[5] *Comptes Rendus*, tom. xlviii. pp. 137, 249, 817, 1031 ; tom. xlix. p. 309.

[6] *Id.* tom. xlviii. p. 1023.

this difference has arisen from M. Plana having regarded the equal description of areas as constant, whereas it is variable. The difference between the results of MM. Adams and Delaunay, if correct, and those obtained from ancient eclipses, is very remarkable, and indicates the operation of some cause which remains to be discovered.

The theory of the lunar motions being thus completed, Euler, Lagrange, and Laplace directed all the powers of their mind, and all the refinements of analysis, to the determination of the mutual action of the primary planets. In this case the three bodies were the sun, the disturbed and the disturbing planet. In 1748, the Academy of Sciences proposed the Inequalities of Jupiter and Saturn as the subject of their prize. In his Memoir, which gained the prize, Euler proved that both Jupiter and Saturn were subject to considerable inequalities, arising from their mutual action, but all of them periodical, and returning nearly in the same order after short intervals of not much more than twenty or thirty years. But though these results accorded with observation, they afforded no explanation of the great secular inequalities which in twenty centuries had produced in Jupiter an acceleration of $3° 33'$, and in Saturn a retardation of $5° 13'$. The Academy, therefore, again offered their prize of 1752 for the best Memoir on the same subject. Euler a second time carried off the prize ; but though he found two inequalities of long periods depending on the angle formed by the line of the apsides of each planet, yet he made them equal and additive, contrary to observation. Lagrange failed in the same inquiry ; and Laplace, after carrying his approximation farther than either of his rivals, came to the conclusion that no change in the mean motion of Jupiter and Saturn could be produced by their mutual action. Under this grave embarrassment, apparently threatening the truth or accuracy of the law of gravity, but really heralding a great discovery, Lagrange appeared with a new solution of the problem of three bodies. At the age of twenty-seven he published this solution in the Turin Memoirs

for 1763, and, in applying it to the motions of Jupiter and
Saturn, he obtained for the former an additive secular equation
of nearly *three* seconds, and for the latter a subtractive one of
*fourteen* seconds ; but though this result was in its general
character superior to that of Euler, it yet afforded no explanation of the great inequalities we have mentioned.   Having
observed that the calculus had never given any inequalities but
periodical ones, Lagrange now set himself to inquire, whether
in the planetary system, continually increasing or continually
diminishing inequalities, affecting the mean motions, could be
produced by the mutual action of the two planets.   Independently of any approximation, and by a method peculiarly his
own, he found that all inequalities produced by gravity must
be periodical, and that amid all the changes arising from the
mutual action of the planets, two elements are unchangeable—
the length of the major axis of the planet's elliptical orbit, and
the time in which that orbit is described.   The inclination of
the orbit to the ecliptic changes, the ellipse and its eccentricity
change, but its greater axis and the time of the planet's revolution are unalterable.   This grand discovery, excluding every
source of disorder, and securing the stability of the system, is
doubtless one of the noblest in physical astronomy, and more
than any other displays the wisdom of the Creator.

    But though Lagrange had made this great step in celestial
physics, he failed in discovering the cause of the inequalities of
Jupiter and Saturn, and left to Laplace the honour of solving
this perplexing problem.   By a more rigorous inquiry into the
effects of their mutual action, Laplace found that the mean
motion of Jupiter would be accelerated, while that of Saturn
would be retarded, and that the relative derangement of the
two planets would be as *five* to *ten*, the ratio of their mean
motion, or as 3° 58' to 5° 16', the result for Jupiter differing
only *nine* minutes from that given by Halley.   In continuing
the inquiry, he found that each planet was subject to an
inequality whose period was 969 years ;—that of Saturn, when

a maximum, being 48' 44", and that of Jupiter 20' 49", with an opposite sign. These inequalities were a maximum in 1560, and from that epoch the apparent mean motions of the two planets have been approaching to their true mean motions, and became the same in 1790. By a comparison of these results with forty-three observed oppositions of Saturn, Laplace found them generally correct, and the error never exceeding *two minutes* of a degree. This difference he afterwards reduced in the case of both planets to *twelve seconds*, although the best tables of Saturn often erred *twenty minutes*. By these brilliant researches theory and observation were reconciled,—the last difficulty which beset the Newtonian theory was removed,—every inequality in the Solar System was explained,—and the law of gravitation established as a law of the universe.

In concluding this brief notice of the progress of physical astronomy since the time of Newton in a few of its leading features, we are naturally led to ponder on the great truth of the stability and permanence of the solar system as demonstrated by the discoveries of Lagrange and Laplace. In the present day, when worlds and systems of worlds, when life physical and life intellectual are supposed to be the result of general law, it is interesting to study those conditions of the planetary system which are necessary to its stability, and to consider whether they appear to be the result of necessity or design. It follows, from the discoveries of Laplace, that there are three conditions essential to the stability and permanence of the solar system, namely, the motion of all the planets in the same direction,—their motion in orbits slightly elliptical, or nearly circular,—and the commensurability of their periods of revolution. That these conditions are not necessary is very obvious. Any one of them may be supposed different from what it is, while the rest remained the same. The planets, like the comets, might have been launched in different directions, and moved in planes of various and great inclinations to the ecliptic. They might have been propelled with such varie-

ties of tangential force as to have moved in orbits of great
ellipticity ; and no reason, even of the most hypothetical nature,
can be assigned why their annual periods might not have been
incommensurable.  The arrangements, therefore, upon which
the stability of the system depends, must have been the result
of design, the contrivance of that omniscience which foresaw all
that was future, and of that infinite skill which knew how to
provide for the permanence of His work.  How far the comets,
whose motions are not regulated by such laws, and which move
in so many directions, may in the future interfere with the
order of our system, can only be conjectured.  They have not
interfered with it in the past, owing no doubt to the smallness
of their density ; and we cannot doubt that the same wisdom
which has established so great a harmony in the movements of
the planetary system, that the inequalities which necessarily
arise from their mutual action arrive at a maximum, and then
disappear, will also have made provision for the future stability
of the system.

Although it is only a general view that we can take of the
important discoveries in physical astronomy which have sprung
from those of Newton, yet we should scarcely be justified in
omitting those which relate to the figure of our earth and the
tides of its ocean.  Newton inferred that the figure of the earth
was an oblate spheroid, whose equatorial diameter was to its
polar axis in the ratio of 231 to 230, but it was reserved for
Maclaurin to demonstrate, *a priori*, that the earth, if homogeneous, might assume such a form.  The method which he
employed, though synthetical, was remarkable for its accuracy
and elegance.  In 1743, Clairaut published his Treatise on the
Figure of the Earth, in which he investigated the form it would
assume on the supposition of its density being heterogeneous.
He found that the earth would have the form of an elliptic
spheroid, if its mass was arranged in homogeneous concentric
strata of the same form ; and he investigated the beautiful
theorem which bears his name, by which we can determine the

ellipticity of the earth from measures of the force of gravity, taken in two different latitudes by the aid of the pendulum. D'Alembert, Lagrange, Legendre, Laplace, Ivory, Plana, Gauss, Poisson, and Airy, have directed their attention to the subject of the earth's figure, but without adding much to the results obtained by Clairaut. In his *Mécanique Céleste*, Laplace has applied the deductions of his calculus to the determination of the figure of the earth, from the measurement of degrees on its surface, and the observations made in different latitudes on the length of a pendulum vibrating seconds, and he finds that the result cannot be reconciled with the hypothesis of an elliptic spheroid, unless a greater error than is probable be admitted in some of the measurements.[1] Upon discussing, however, all the more recent measurements of a degree, and all the observations with the pendulum, the ellipticity of the earth in the former case has been found to be $\frac{1}{299}$, and, in the latter, $\frac{1}{289}$, the ellipticity indicated by the lunar perturbation being $\frac{1}{305}$, an agreement which is very remarkable, when we consider the local causes which necessarily affect the observations with the pendulum, as first noticed by General Sabine, and the measurement of an arc of the meridian.

The theory of the tides of our ocean, though treated by a master mind in the Principia, was nevertheless susceptible of extension and improvement. The Academy of Sciences proposed it as the subject of their prize for 1740. Four dissertations competed for the prize, three of them of great merit, by Euler, Daniel Bernouilli, and Maclaurin, and a fourth by Father Cavalleri, a Jesuit, who founded his investigation on the system of Vortices. The prize was divided among all the four competitors,—a proof, doubtless, that the Cartesian doctrines were not entirely exploded. These dissertations, and others on the same subject, are founded on what is called the equilibrium theory, which supposes that the sun and moon draw the waters of the ocean into the form of an aqueous spheroid, in which

---

[1] *Mécanique Céleste*, tom. ii. liv. iii. chap. v.; and *Système du Monde*, liv. iv. chap. vii.

the molecules of water are maintained at rest by the action of
these forces.    In consequence, however, of the daily motion of
the earth, such a spheroid never can be formed,—there can
only be a tendency to it ; and hence the tides are the consequence of the perpetual oscillation of the waters of the ocean,—
a result which the state of mechanical and mathematical science
will not allow us to determine.    Laplace, however, undertook
the task, and communicated to the Academy of Sciences in
1755, 1779, and 1790, a series of valuable memoirs on the
subject.    The theory to which he was led by these researches
rests upon two suppositions not strictly true, namely, that the
earth is covered with water, and that the depth of the ocean is
uniform under the same parallel of latitude.    Regarding every
particle of water as under the influence of three forces, namely,
the attraction of the earth, the attraction of the sun and moon,
and that which arises from the earth's rotation, he found that
three kinds of oscillation are produced ; the first depending on
the sun and moon, and varying periodically, so as not to return
till after a long interval ; the second depending on the earth's
rotation, and returning in the same order after the interval of
about a day ; and the third depending on double the angular
rotation of the earth, and returning after an interval of about
half a day.    As the oscillations of the second class are affected
by the depth of the sea as well as the earth's rotation, and as
the differences between the two tides in the same day depend
chiefly upon them, Laplace has from this been able to determine
that the mean depth of the sea -is about four leagues.    The
general correctness of this theory• has been placed beyond a
doubt by a comparison of its results, with observations on the
tides made at Brest during a long succession of years. [1]

As the ocean is often agitated by several irregular causes,
such as storms and earthquakes, which raise it to great heights,
and sometimes make it overstep its limits, Laplace has endea-

_Mecanique Céleste_, part i. liv. iv. chap. i. tom. ii. p. 171 ; and _Système du Monde_,
liv. iv. chap. x. p. 248.

voured to ascertain the " stability of the equilibrium of our seas." Although we find that the sea falls into its hollow bed after the ordinary commotions to which it is subject, yet we may reasonably fear that some extraordinary cause may communicate to it such a disturbance, that, though inconsiderable in its origin, may go on increasing till it raises it above the highest mountains. As such a result would afford an explanation of several phenomena of natural history, it becomes interesting to determine the conditions necessary to the absolute stability of the equilibrium of our seas, and to see if these conditions exist in nature. In submitting this question to analysis, Laplace has found that *the equilibrium of the ocean is stable if its density is less than the mean density of the earth*, and that its equilibrium cannot be subverted unless these two densities are equal, or that of the earth less than that of its waters. The experiments on the attraction of Schehallion and Mount Cenis, and those made by Mr. Cavendish, Reich, and Bailey, with balls of lead, demonstrate that the mean density of the earth is at least *five* times that of water, and hence the stability of the ocean is placed beyond a doubt. As the seas, therefore, have at one time covered continents which are now raised above their level, we must seek for some other cause of it than any want of stability in the equilibrium of the ocean.[1]

We have already seen how Newton deduced the precession of the equinoxes from the action of the sun and moon upon the excess of matter accumulated at the equator of the terrestrial spheroid. This investigation, however, was founded on principles not rigorously correct, and therefore the complete solution of the problem was left to his successors. The discovery, too, of the nutation and of its cause, by Bradley, gave a new character to the investigation, which now required the aid of the calculus of partial differences. It fell to the lot of D'Alembert to give a complete solution of the problem, whatever were the figure

[1] See *Mécanique Céleste*, part i. liv. iv. chap. ii. tom. ii. p. 204 ; and *Système du Monde*, liv. iv. chap. xi. p. 265.

and the density of the strata of the terrestrial spheroid. The results which he obtained agreed accurately with observations on the precession, and he obtained also the true measure of the nutation, or the dimensions of the small ellipse described by the pole of the equator, which the observations of Bradley had left in some uncertainty.

In viewing the subject under a more general aspect than D'Alembert, Laplace was led to some very interesting results. From his researches on the oscillations of the ocean, he was led to the remarkable theorem, " that whatever be the law of the depth of the sea, and the form of the spheroid which it covers, the phenomena of the precession and the nutation are the same as if the sea formed a solid mass with this spheroid." Laplace has also shown that the rotation of the earth upon its axis, or the length of the day, cannot be affected either by currents on the ocean, rivers, trade-winds, or even earthquakes, or in general any force which can shake the earth either in its interior or upon its surface. It might have been expected that the trade-winds blowing between the tropics would, by their action upon the sea, and upon the continents and mountains which they meet, insensibly diminish the rotatory motion of the earth ; but upon the same principle the other motions of the atmosphere, which take place beyond the tropics, would accelerate that motion by the same quantity. In order to produce any sensible change in the length of the day, a very considerable displacement in the parts of the earth would be required. A great mass of matter, for example, transported from the poles to the equator, would increase the length of the day, and it would be diminished if dense bodies approached either pole, or the axis of the earth. But as there appears to be no cause which is capable of displacing masses sufficiently large to produce such effects, we may regard the length of the day as one of the most unchangeable elements in the system of the world. " The same thing is true," as Laplace observes, " with respect to the points where the earth's axis meets its surface. If this planet turned

successively round different diameters inclined to one another
at considerable angles, the equator and the poles would change
their place upon the earth ; and the seas on rushing to the new
equator, would cover and uncover alternately the highest mountains ; but all the researches which I have made on the displacement of the poles of rotation at the surface of the earth,
have proved to me that it is insensible."[1]   After discussing the
consequences respecting the constitution of the earth, which
are accordant with his theory of the precession and nutation,
Laplace states, that though it does not enable us to determine
the ellipticity of the earth, it fixes its limit between $\frac{1}{304}$ and
$\frac{1}{578}$ part of the radius of the equator.   The same theory indicates as the most probable constitution of the earth, that the
density of its strata increases from its surface to its centre.[2]

Such is a brief and general view of the important discoveries
in physical astronomy which have illustrated the century that
followed the publication of the Principia.   Brilliant as they are,
and evincing as they do the highest genius, yet the century in
which we live has been rendered remarkable by a discovery
which, whether we view it in its theoretical relations, or in its
practical results, is the most remarkable in the history of physical
astronomy.   In the motions of the planet Uranus, discovered
since the time of Newton, astronomers had been for a long time
perplexed with certain irregularities, which could not be deduced
from the action of the other planets.   M. Bouvard, who constructed tables of this planet, seeing the impossibility of reconciling
the ancient with the modern observations, threw out the idea
that the irregularities from which this discrepancy arose might
be owing to the action of an unknown planet.   Our countryman,
the Rev. Mr. Hussey, conceived " the possibility of some disturbing body beyond Uranus ;" and Hansen, with whom Bouvard
corresponded on the subject, was of opinion that there must be

---

[1] *Système du Monde,* liv. iv. chap. xiii. pp. 276, 277.   See also *Mécanique Céleste,*
part i. liv. v. chap. i. tom. ii. p. 347.        [2] *Méc. Céleste,* tom. ii. pp. 354, 355.

*two new planets beyond Uranus* to account for the irregularities. In 1834, Mr. Hussey was anxious that the Astronomer-Royal should assist him in detecting the invisible planet, and other astronomers expressed the same desire, to have so important a question examined and settled. On his return to Berlin from the meeting of the British Association in 1846, the celebrated astronomer, M. Bessel, commenced the task of determining the actual position of the planet ; but in consequence of the death of M. Flemming, the young German astronomer to whom he had intrusted some of the preliminary calculations, and of his own death not long afterwards, the inquiry was stopped.

While the leading astronomers in Europe were thus thinking and talking about the possible existence of a new planet beyond the orbit of Uranus, two young astronomers, Mr. Adams of St. John's College, Cambridge, and M. Leverrier of Paris, were diligently engaged in attempting to deduce from the irregularities which it produced in the motions of Uranus, the elements of the planet's orbit, and its actual position in the heavens. In October 1845, Mr. Adams had solved this intricate problem— the *inverse problem of perturbations,* as it has been called, placing beyond a doubt the theoretical existence of the planet, and assigning to it a place in the heavens, which was afterwards found to be little more than a single degree from its exact place ! Anxious for the discovery of the planet in the heavens, Mr. Adams communicated his results to the Astronomer-Royal and Professor Challis ; but more than *nine* months were allowed to pass away before a single telescope was directed in search of it to the heavens. On the 29th July, Professor Challis began his observations, and on the 4th and 12th of August, when he directed his telescope to the theoretical place of the planet as given him by Mr. Adams, *he saw the planet, and obtained two positions of it.*

While Mr. Adams was engaged in this important inquiry, M. Leverrier, who had distinguished himself by a series of valuable memoirs on the great inequality of Pallas,—on the perturbations of Mercury,—and on the rectification of the orbits of comets, was busily occupied with the same problem. In the summer of 1845, M. Arago represented to Leverrier the importance of studying the perturbations of Uranus. Abandoning his researches on comets, he devoted himself to the task suggested by his friend, and on the 10th November 1845, he communicated to the Academy of Sciences his *First Memoir on the Theory of Uranus.* In the following June he submitted to the Academy his Second Memoir, entitled, *Researches on the Motions of Uranus,* in which, after examining the different hypotheses that had been adduced to explain the irregularities of that planet, he is driven to the conclusion that *they are due to the action of a planet situated in the ecliptic at a mean distance double that of Uranus.* He then proceeds to determine where this planet is actually situated, what is its mass, and what are the elements of the orbit which it describes : After giving a rigorous solution of this problem, and showing that there are not two quarters of the heavens in which we can place the planet at a given epoch, he computes its heliocentric place on the 1st January 1847, which he finds to be in the 325th degree of longitude, and he boldly asserts that in assigning to it this place, he does not commit an error of more than 10°. The position thus given to it is within a degree of that found by Mr. Adams. Anxious, like Mr. Adams, for the actual discovery of the planet, M. Leverrier naturally expected that practical astronomers would exert themselves in searching for it. The place which he assigned to it was published on the 1st of June, and yet no attempt seems to have been made to find it for nearly five months. The *exact position* of the planet was published on the 31st August, and on the 18th September was communicated to M. Galle, of the Royal Observatory of Berlin, who discovered it as a star of the eighth magnitude the very evening on which he received the request to look for it. Professor Challis had *secured* the discovery of this remarkable body six weeks before, but the honour of having actually found it belongs to the Prussian astronomer.

With the universal concurrence of the astronomical world, the new planet received the name of NEPTUNE.   It revolves round the sun in about 172 years, at a mean distance of thirty, that of Uranus being nineteen, and that of the Earth one ; and by its discovery the Solar System has been extended *one thousand millions of miles* beyond its former limits.

The honour of having made this discovery belongs equally to Adams and Leverrier.   It is the greatest intellectual achievement in the annals of astronomy, and the noblest triumph of the Newtonian Philosophy.   To detect a planet by the eye, or to track it to its place by the mind, are acts as incommensurable as those of muscular and intellectual power.   Recumbent on his easy chair, the practical astronomer has but to look through the cleft in his revolving cupola, in order to trace the pilgrim star in its course ; or by the application of magnifying power, to expand its tiny disc, and thus transfer it from among its sidereal companions to the planetary domains.   The physical astronomer, on the contrary, has no such auxiliaries : he calculates at noon, when the stars disappear under a meridian sun : he computes at midnight, when clouds and darkness shroud the heavens ; and from within that cerebral dome, which has no opening heavenward, and no instrument but the Eye of Reason, he sees in the disturbing agencies of an unseen planet, upon a planet by him equally unseen, the existence of the disturbing agent, and from the nature and amount of its action, he computes its magnitude and indicates its place.   If man has ever been permitted to see otherwise than by the eye, it is when the clairvoyance of reason, piercing through screens of epidermis and walls of bone, grasps, amid the abstractions of number and of quantity, those sublime realities which have eluded the keenest touch, and evaded the sharpest eye.

Although the philosophy of Newton has since his day enjoyed such signal triumphs, it has yet other strongholds to storm, and other conquests to achieve.   In his survey of the sidereal and planetary domains, the practical astronomer has in the present century laid open new fields of research ripe for the intellectual sickle, and fitted to yield to the accomplished analyst the richest harvest of discovery.

Within our own system the detection of a satellite to Neptune, by Mr. Lassels,—of an eighth satellite to Saturn, by Mr. Lassels and Mr. Bond, between the orbits of the 4th and 5th of these bodies,—and of a new fluid ring gradually advancing to the body of the planet, will furnish interesting materials to the physical astronomer. This new and remarkable feature in the system of Saturn has been recently studied by Mr. Bond of the United States, and M. Otto Struve, at the observatory of Pulkova, with the great Munich telescope. With that fine instrument they saw distinctly the dark interval which separates this new ring from the two old ones, and the boundaries of this interval were so well marked, that they succeeded in measuring its dimensions. They perceived, also, at the inner margin of the new ring, an edge or border feebly illuminated, which they conceived might be the commencement of another similar appendage, though the line of separation had not yet become visible. The following are the principal results which these two able astronomers have obtained :—" 1. The new ring is not subject to very rapid changes. 2. It is not of very recent formation ; for it is quite certain that it has been seen, if not recognised, according to its true character, ever since the improvements upon astronomical telescopes have enabled astronomers to see the belts upon the surface of the planet, or at least since the beginning of the last century. 3. *That the inner border of the annular system of Saturn has, since the time of Huygens, been gradually approaching to the body of the planet,* and therefore it follows, that there has been a successive enlargement of this system. 4. That it is at least very probable that the approach of the rings towards the planet is caused particularly by the successive extension of the inner or middle ring. Hence it follows, that Saturn's system of rings does not exist, as has been generally supposed, in a state of stable equilibrium, and that *we may expect sooner or later, perhaps in some dozen of years, to see the rings united with the body of the planet.*" [1]

Of all the celestial phenomena which have been discovered since the time of Newton, the most remarkable are the *fifty-six* small planets which have been discovered between the orbits of Mars and Jupiter. Dr. Olbèrs of Bremen, who discovered two of them, hazarded the idea that a large planet which had once occupied the same place, had been burst in pieces by some internal force. This opinion, which has been long considered as a very probable one, has only recently been called in question. M. Leverrier, the first mathematician who has directed his attention to the theory of this remarkable group of bodies, considers the opinion of Olbers as contradicted by the great inclination of the orbit of Pallas ; and in place of explaining the existence of these planets by an alteration of the primitive system of the universe, he believes " that they have been regularly formed like all the other planets, and in virtue of the same laws." In a very interesting communication on this subject, lately made to the Academy of Sciences,[2] M. Leverrier has endeavoured to ascertain the limit of the sum of the magnitudes of the whole group, known and unknown, by the disturbing action which they exercise on the motion of the perihelion of Mars and the Earth. If the perihelions of these small planets were distributed uniformly in all the regions of the zodiac, the action of these masses of matter, situated in one half or semi-circumference of the heavens, would be destroyed by the action of the equal masses situated in the opposite half

---

[1] Laplace has shown that the stability of the equilibrium of the rings requires that they be irregular solids, unequally wide in different parts of their circumference, so that their centres of gravity do not coincide with their centres of figure.—See *Mécanique Céleste*, part i. liv. iii. chap. vi. tom. ii. p. 155 ; *Système du Monde*, liv. chap. viii. p. 242.

[2] *Considérations sur l'ensemble du Système des petites Planètes situées entre Mars et Jupiter*, par M. U. J. LEVERRIER. Lu 28 Nov. 1853. *Comptes Rendus*, &c., tom. xxxvii. pp. 793-798.

or semi-circumference. But M. Leverrier finds that *twenty* out of *twenty-six* of the planets have the longitudes of their peri-helion between 4° and 184°, a semi-circumference of the heavens, and hence their action as one mass on Mars and the Earth is not destroyed by the action of the other six planets. It is possible that the small planets, which may yet be disco-vered, may have more of their perihelions in the latter of their semi-circumferences than in the former; but the possibility is that there will be more of them conjoined with the larger than the smaller group, or, at least, that they will be equally diffused over the zodiac in reference to their perihelion points.

Having shown that the perihelion of Mars is placed much more advantageously than that of the Earth, in relation to the mean direction of the perihelions of the small planets, and that the greater eccentricity of the orbit of Mars is more favourable for determining the amount of their action, he finds that if the total mass of the small planets were equal to the mass of the Earth, it would produce in the heliocentric longitude of the perihelion of Mars, an inequality which in a century would amount to *eleven seconds*, a quantity which could not have escaped the notice of astronomers. Considering, therefore, that this inequality would become particularly sensible at the oppo-sitions of Mars, M. Leverrier is led to believe, that though the orbit of Mars has not received its final improvements, yet it will not admit of an error in longitude greater than *one-fourth* of the above quantity, and hence he concludes, *that the sum total of the matter constituting the small planets situated between the mean distances* 2·20 *and* 3·16, *cannot exceed about the fourth part of the mass of the Earth.*

In examining the place of the nodes of twenty-six of the small planets, M. Leverrier finds that *twenty-two* of the ascending nodes of their orbits have their longitudes between 36° and 216°, that is, within a semi-circumference of the heavens,[1] a result almost

[1] M. Leverrier takes occasion to remark, "that we might perhaps find some systematic difference between the mean direction of the ascending nodes of the planets near the

the same as that which takes place in their perihelions. From this fact he observes, that in considering the motion of the plane of the ecliptic, we may arrive at conclusions of the same kind respecting the magnitude of the mass of the small planets, though the limit would be less strict than in that which is derived from the grouping of their perihelions.

In his theory of the motion of comets, Sir Isaac Newton did not anticipate that bodies of this kind would be discovered moving in elliptical orbits, contained within the limits of our own system, and thus affording a new application of the law of gravity, and remarkable examples of the action of the planets upon this new class of wandering stars. It had long been the universal belief among astronomers, that every comet strayed far beyond the limits of our system, the shortest period being about seventy years. In 1818, however, M. Pons announced the discovery of a very faint comet, without a tail, the motions of which could not be reconciled with a parabolic orbit. After its fourth appearance, Professor M. Encke of Berlin, whose name is now attached to the comet, found that it moved in an elliptic orbit with a period of about 1211 days, or three years and a third, and that its orbit was included within our system, extending inward as far as Mercury, and outward only a little beyond the orbit of Pallas. He computed the perturbations produced by the action of Venus, the Earth, Mars, Jupiter, and Saturn, and he found that its periods had been diminishing between 1786 and 1838, at the rate of about $2\frac{1}{2}$ hours in each revolution—an effect which he ascribed to the resistance of an ethereal medium.

A still more remarkable comet, supposed to be the same as that of 1772, 1805, 1839, &c., was discovered in 1826 by M. Biela. Its period was found to be about 2410 days, or $6\frac{3}{4}$ years, and its orbit did not reach so far as that of Saturn.

Sun, and that of the ascending nodes of the more distant planets, and that we may thus conjecture that these planets belong in reality to three distinct groups."—*Comptes Rendus,* &c., tom. xxxvii. p. 795.

M. Damoiseau found that its arrival at its perihelion would be retarded nine days and sixteen hours by the action of Saturn, Jupiter, and the Earth ; and that on the 29th October 1832, about a month before its perihelion passage, it would cross the plane of the ecliptic, within 18,000 miles of a point in the Earth's orbit.   The announcement of this fact excited such an alarm in Paris, that M. Arago was summoned to allay the fears of the community.   According to prediction, the comet returned in 1839 and 1846 ; but, strange to say, it was on this last occasion *separated into two distinct comets*, the one a little fainter than the other.   Their tails were parallel, and their distance, which was the same till the comet became single by the gradual disappearance of the smaller one, was found by M. Plantamour to be equal to about two-thirds of the radius of the moon's orbit, that is, about 160,000 miles !¹

Another comet belonging to our system was discovered by M. Faye in November 1843.   Dr. Goldsmicht found that its period was about 2718 days, or $7\frac{1}{2}$ years, and M. Leverrier computed that its arrival would be delayed 7 days and 16 hours by the action of the planets.   Its orbit is more circular than that of any other comet, and is included between the orbits of Mars and Saturn.   It had been suggested by M. Valz, that this comet might be Lexell's comet of 1770,² which had been rendered visible by the action of Jupiter in 1767, and which was afterwards thrown into a larger orbit and rendered invisible in 1779 by the action of the same planet.   M. Leverrier, however, has shown that the two bodies cannot be identical.

Before another year had expired, a fourth comet belonging to our system was discovered by M. De Vico of Rome.   He first

¹ Sir John Herschel has ventured to say, " that the orbit of Biela's comet so nearly intersects that of the Earth, that an actual collision is not impossible, and indeed (supposing neither orbit variable) must, *in all likelihood*, happen in the lapse of some millions of years."—*Outlines of Astronomy*, § 585.

² This comet ought to have appeared *thirteen* times since 1770, and, as it has not been since seen, it must be lost.   Burckhardt supposed that it might have become a satellite to Jupiter, from its aphelion being near that planet !

saw it on the 29th August 1844, and M. Faye found that it revolved in an elliptic orbit with a period of about 2000 days, or $5\frac{1}{2}$ years. It was supposed by some astronomers that this comet was the same as that of 1585, observed by Tycho ; but M. Leverrier has shown that they are not identical, and that the comet of De Vico is not the same as that of Lexell. He discovered, however, such a striking similarity between it and the comet observed by De la Hire in 1678, that he considers them clearly identical. It is strange, however, that this comet should only have been seen once previous to 1844, although it has frequently come very near the Earth.

Another comet of the Solar system was discovered by M. Brorsen on the 26th February 1846. Its period is 2042 days, or about $5\frac{4}{7}$ years. It is very faint, and is almost identical in its elements with the comet of 1532.

A seventh comet, discovered by M. Peters on the 26th June 1846, has been placed by the calculations of M. Arrest among those having elliptic elements and a short period, and therefore belonging to our system. Its period is 5804 days, or about 16 years.

Such are some of the important celestial phenomena within the limits of our own Solar system, to which the Newtonian theory is applicable, and to which it has been to some extent successfully applied. The sidereal phenomena which have been discovered beyond our system, in which movements of long periods, round visible and invisible centres, have been traced and measured, possess a higher interest, and to some of them also the Newtonian law of gravitation has been actually extended.

The most important of this class of phenomena are those of binary and multiple systems of stars. Among the many stars of this kind which have been discovered by Sir William Herschel and succeeding observers, there must be a large number in which the two, three, or four stars constituting a group have no other connexion than that of being placed nearly in the same line. There are others, however, in which, as Sir W.

Herschel long ago announced, one of two stars revolves round the other in regular orbits, and with periods which have been determined—that of Castor, being 334 years, $\gamma$ Virginis 708 years, and $\gamma$ Leonis 1200 years. Although the list of double stars has been greatly extended, yet those whose orbits and periods have been determined with any accuracy, amount only to twenty-one. Nine of these have been computed by Mr. Madler of Dorpat, five by Sir John Herschel, four by Mr. Hind, and one by M. Savary.[1] The first calculation of the orbit of a double star was made in 1830 by M. Savary (in the case of $\xi$ of the Great Bear), who showed that the changes of place in one of the stars could be explained by an elliptic orbit, and a period of $58\frac{1}{4}$ years. The periods of the other twenty double stars vary from $31\frac{1}{2}$ to 737 years, eleven having their periods below 100 years, three below two hundred, two below 300, and three between 600 and 700 years. These orbits are calculated on the supposition that the force exerted by the stars varies inversely as the square of the distance, and the accuracy with which the observations are represented allows us to conclude that the Newtonian law of gravity extends to the distant region of the double stars.[2]

Another sidereal phenomenon, in which we have the appearance of motion round a centre, is displayed in the spiral nebulæ discovered by Lord Rosse ; that the stars which compose these spirals have been placed there in virtue of some movement related to the central mass, cannot be doubted, although it is vain for man to attempt the solution of such a problem. To suppose these spirals to be nothing more than vaporous matter, like the tail of a comet, whirled round into spiral branches, because we cannot find any explanation compatible with the almost universally admitted fact, that every nebula is composed

[1] A table of the elements of their orbits is given by Sir John Herschel in his *Outlines of Astronomy*, § 843.

[2] M. Madler has adduced an instance (p Ophiuchi), where he regards the deviations from an elliptic orbit too considerable to be accounted for by an error of observation ; but we cannot view a single fact of this kind as affecting the generality of the law of gravity.

of stars, is to renounce all faith in the great truths of astronomy, and seek for some resting-place to the mind, when reason stands aghast amid the infinite and the incomprehensible.

Beside the motions of one of the bodies which compose a binary system, a proper motion of a very peculiar kind has been observed in the stars. In one region of the heavens the distance between the stars is increasing, and in the opposite region diminishing, while in intermediate localities little or no change of place is observed. It is obvious that such changes indicate a motion of our earth, and consequently of the whole Solar system, to a point in the heavens where the increasing distance of the stars is a maximum. Before the proper motion of the fixed stars had been measured, various speculators, among whom Hooke was the earliest, hazarded the supposition that the whole Solar system was in continual motion. Tobias Mayer, in 1771, attempted in vain to deduce such a movement of the system from the proper motions of eighty stars; but a few years afterwards, in 1783, when better observations were accessible, Sir W. Herschel and M. Prévost came to the conclusion that the Solar system was advancing to a point in the heavens whose right ascension was 257°,[1] and north declination 25°. Although both Biot and Bessel came to the same conclusion as Tobias Mayer, that no such motion existed, yet the existence of a proper motion has been more recently placed beyond a doubt by the observations made at the observatories of Dorpat, Abo, and Pulkova : And it has been shown by the united studies of Argelander, Otto Struve, and Peters, that the point to which the Solar system is advancing at the epoch of 1840, is situated in,—

Right ascension, 259° 35', with a probable error of 2° 57'
North declination, 34° 33', with a probable error of 3° 24'

Not content with determining the direction of the solar motion, Otto Struve has computed the angular value of this motion, as seen at a right angle to the Sun's path, and at the

[1] M. Prévost, who used Mayer's proper motions, made the right ascension only 230°.

mean distance of the stars of the first magnitude.   His results are as follows :—

From the right ascension of the stars, $0''\cdot 32122$, with a probable error of $0''\cdot 03684$
From their declination,    .    .    $0\ \cdot 35719$, with a probable error of $0\ \cdot 03562$

Or, taking the mean of these results,   $0''\cdot 33920$                    $0''\cdot 03623$

But as the parallax of stars of the first magnitude is $0''\cdot 209$, we can change the angular motion of the Sun into a linear motion in space ; and hence taking the radius of the Earth's orbit as unity, M. Struve finds that the annual motion of the Sun in space is $\frac{0°\cdot 3392}{0\cdot 209} = 1\cdot 623$ radii of the Earth's orbit, with a probable error of $0\cdot 229$.

In his interesting work on Stellar Astronomy,[1] he has expressed these results in the following manner :—" *The motion of the solar system in space is directed to a point of the celestial vault situated on the right line which joins the two stars π and μ Herculis at a quarter of the apparent distance of these stars, reckoning from π Herculis.   The velocity of this motion is such, that the Sun, with all the bodies which depend upon it, advances annually in the above direction* $1\cdot 623$ *times the radius of the Earth's orbit, or* $33,550,000$ *geographical miles. The possible error of this last number amounts to* $1,733,000$ *geographical miles, or to a seventh part of the whole.   We may then wager* $400,000$ *to* $1$ *that the Sun has a proper progressive motion, and* $1$ *to* $1$ *that it is comprised between the limits of thirty-eight and twenty-nine millions of geographical miles.*

If we take $95$ millions of English miles as the mean radius of the Earth's orbit, we have $95 \times 1\cdot 623 = 154\cdot 185$ millions of miles, and, consequently,

The velocity of the Solar system is 154,185,000 miles in the year.
,,                    ,,              422,424 miles in a day.
,,                    ,,              17,601 miles in an hour.
,,                    ,,              293 miles in a minute.
,,                    ,,              4·9 miles in a second.

As none of the celestial motions are rectilineal, the advance

[1] *Etudes d' Astronomie Stellaire*, of which we have given a copious abstract in the *North British Review*, vol. viii. pp. 523-534.

of the system in space must be round some distant centre, which M. Madler, without much reason, supposes to be *Alcyone*, the brightest star in the Pleiades. In the course of time, however, the point to which the system is advancing must change its place, and from the nature and magnitude of that change, its curvilineal motion, and perhaps the form of its orbit, may be established. But even if so grand a result were obtained, we may never be able to ascertain whether our Sun and planets revolve like a multiple star round a single centre, or, as in our planetary system, they form only one of a number of systems revolving round the same centre. On such a subject speculation is vain. We must rest satisfied with the simple truth, that since the earliest observation of the stars, our system has described so small a portion of its curvilineal orbit, that it cannot be distinguished from a straight line. If the buried relics of primeval life have taught us how brief has been our tenure of this terrestrial paradise, compared with its occupancy by the brutes that perish, the great sidereal truth which we have been expounding, impresses upon us the no less humbling lesson, that from the birth of man to the extinction of his race, the system to which he belongs will have described but an infinitesimal arc of that immeasurable circle in which it is destined to revolve.

Such are the great sidereal movements to some of which the law of gravitation has been already applied, and nobody has ventured to doubt that all of them will, in due time, come under its rule. Every new satellite, every new asteroid, every new comet, every new planet, every new star circulating round its fellow, proclaims the universality of Newton's philosophy, and adds fresh lustre to his name. It is otherwise, however, in the general history of science. The reputation achieved by a great invention is often transferred to another which supersedes it, and a discovery which is the glory of one age is eclipsed by the extension of it in another. The fame of having invented the steam-engine has disappeared beside the reputation of the philosophers who have improved it ; and the laurels which the discoverer of Ceres has worn for half a century, have been almost withered by the discovery of fifty-six similar bodies. It is the peculiar glory of Newton, however, that every discovery in the heavens attests the universality of his laws, and adds a greener leaf to the laurel chaplet which he wears.

## CHAPTER XIV.

History of the Infinitesimal Calculus—Archimedes—Pappus—Napier—Edward Wright —Kepler's Treatise on Stereometry—Cavalieri's Geometria Indivisibilium—Roberval —Toricelli—Fermat—Wallis's Arithmetica Infinitorum—Hudde—Gregory—Slusius— Newton's discovery of Fluxions in 1655—General Account of the Method, and of its Applications—His Analysis per Equationes, etc.—His Discoveries communicated to English and Foreign Mathematicians—The Method of Fluxions and Quadratures— Account of his other Mathematical Writings—He solves the Problems proposed by Bernouilli and Leibuitz—Leibnitz visits London, and corresponds with the English Mathematicians, and with Newton through Oldenburg—He discovers the Differential Calculus, and communicates it to Newton—Notice of Oldenburg—Celebrated Scholium respecting Fluxions in the Principia—Account of the Changes upon it—Leibnitz's Manuscripts in Hanover.

In the history of Newton's optical and astronomical discoveries, which we have given in the preceding chapters, we
have seen him involved in disputes with his own countrymen as
well as with foreigners, in reference to the value and the priority
of his labours. Such extreme sensitiveness as that with which
he felt the criticisms and discussed the claims of his opponents,
has been seldom exhibited in the annals of science ; and so
great was his dread of controversy, and so feeble his love of
wealth and of fame, that, but for the importunities of his
friends, his most important researches would have been withheld from the world. If he had been warned of the dangers of
a scientific career by the troubled lives of Galileo and of Kepler,
he must have learned from their history that great truths have
never been received with implicit submission, and that in every
age and every state of society the newest and the highest must
undergo more than one ordeal—the ordeal of the ignorant,

whose capacity they transcend—the ordeal of philosophy, by which they are to be tested and confirmed—and the ordeal of personal jealousy and rival schools, by which they are to be misrepresented and condemned. The discoveries of Newton were tried by all these tests : they emerged purer and greater from the opposition of the Dutch savans : they were placed on a firmer basis by the skilful analysis of Hooke and of Huygens ; and they were more warmly received and more widely extended after they had triumphed over the rival speculations of the followers of Aristotle and Descartes.

In the history of Newton's mathematical discoveries, which the same dread of controversy had induced him to withhold from the world, we shall find him involved in more exciting discussions,—in what may even be called quarrels, in which both the temper and the character of the disputants were severely tried. In the controversy respecting the discovery of fluxions, or of the differential calculus, Newton took up arms in his own cause, and though he never placed himself in the front rank of danger, he yet combated with all the ardour of his comrades. Hitherto it had been his lot to contend with individuals unknown to science, or with the philosophers of his own country who were occupied with the same studies ; but interests of a larger kind, and feelings of a higher class, sprung up around him. National sympathies mingled themselves with the abstractions of number and of quantity. The greatest mathematicians of the age took the field, and statesmen and princes contributed an auxiliary force to the settlement of questions upon which, after the lapse of nearly 200 years, a verdict has not yet been pronounced.

Painful as the sight must always be when superior minds are brought into collision, society gains from the contest more than the parties lose. We are too apt to regard great men, of the order of Newton and Leibnitz, as exempt from the common infirmities of our nature, and to worship them as demigods more than to admire them as sages. In the history upon which we are about to enter we shall see distinguished philosophers upon the stage, superior, doubtless, to their fellows, but partaking in all the frailties of temper, and exposed to all the suspicions of injustice, which embitter the controversies of ordinary life.

Although the honour of having invented the calculus of fluxions, or the differential calculus, has been conferred upon Newton and Leibnitz, yet, as in every other great invention, they were but the individuals who combined the scattered lights of their predecessors, and gave a method, a notation, and a name, to the doctrine of quantities infinitely small.

By an ingenious attempt to determine the area of curves the ancients made the first step in this interesting inquiry. Their principles were sound, but their want of an organized method of operation prevented them from even forming a calculus. The method of exhaustions which they employed for this purpose consisted in making the curve a limiting area, to which the inscribed and circumscribed polygonal figures continually approached by increasing the number of their sides. The area thus obtained was obviously the area of the curve. In the case of the parabola, Archimedes showed that its area is two-thirds of its circumscribing rectangle, or of the product of the ordinate and the abscissa ; and he proved that the superficies of the sphere was equal to the convex superficies of the circumscribing cylinder, or to four times one of its great circles, and that the solidity of the sphere was two-thirds of that of the cylinder. His writings abound in trains of thought, which are strictly conducted on the principles of the modern calculus, but in place of this calculus we have only an imperfect arithmetic.

Pappus of Alexandria, who flourished about the close of the fourth century, followed Archimedes in the same inquiries, and his celebrated theorems on the centre of gravity[1] is the only

---

[1] Guldinus gave this theorem in 1635, and seeing that he was acquainted with Pappus, Montucla and others were disposed to regard him as a plagiarist. Had they studied Pappus in Condamine's Latin, in place of that of Halley, they never would have known the theorem but from Guldinus.

fruit which sprung from the seed sown by the Greek geometer till we reach the commencement of the seventeenth century. We search in vain the writings of Cardan, Tartaglia, Vieta, and Stevinus, for any proof of their power to employ the infinitesimal principle.

Our countryman, John Napier of Merchiston, and his contemporary, Edward Wright, were not only the first to revive the use of the infinitesimal principle, but the first who applied it in an arithmetical form. They distinctly apprehended the idea of a sufficient approach to the calculation of gradual change by the substitution of small and discontinuous changes. In this way Napier arrived at the representation of the results of arithmetical and geometrical progression taking place continuously in two different magnitudes, and associated the logarithm of any quantity with its primitive. In this manner, too, Wright exhibited what we now call an integration by quadrature, in his celebrated construction of the meridional parts. Both of these geometers fully conceived the idea, as it was embodied in their several problems ; and though we cannot ascribe to either a distinct conception of it, we cannot withhold from them the honour of being the first of modern writers who assisted their successors in its conception.

In his treatise on Stereometry, published in 1615, Kepler made some advances in the doctrine of infinitesimals. In consequence of a dispute with a wine-merchant he studied the mensuration of round solids, or those which are formed by the revolution of the conic sections round any line whatever within or without the section. He considered the circle as consisting of an infinite number of triangles, having their vertices in the centre, and their infinitely small bases in the circumference. In like manner, he considered the cone as composed of an infinite number of pyramids, and the cylinder of an infinite number of prisms, and by thus rendering familiar the idea of quantities infinitely great and infinitely small, he gave an impulse to this branch of mathematics.

The failure of Kepler in solving some of the more difficult problems which he himself proposed, drew the attention of geometers to the subject of infinitely small quantities, and seems particularly to have attracted the attention of Cavalieri. This celebrated mathematician, who was the friend as well as the disciple of Galileo, was born at Milan in 1598, and was professor of geometry at Bologna. Although he had invented his method of indivisibles so early as 1629, his work entitled *Geometria Indivisibilium* did not appear till 1635, nor his *Exercitationes*, containing his most remarkable results, till 1647. He considers a line as composed of an infinite number of points, a surface of an infinite number of lines, and a solid of an infinite number of surfaces, and he assumes as an axiom, that the infinite sums of such lines and surfaces have the same ratio, existing in equal numbers in different surfaces or solids, as the surfaces or solids to be determined. As it is not true that an infinite number of infinitely small points can make a line, nor an infinite number of infinitely small lines a surface, Pascal proposed to return to the idea of Kepler by considering a line as composed of an infinite number of infinitely short lines,—a surface as composed of an infinite number of infinitely narrow parallelograms, and a solid of an infinite number of infinitely thin solids. If Cavalieri had been more advanced in algebra he might, perhaps, have gone farther ; but he was undoubtedly the first who applied the algebraical process to the quadrature of parabolas of an integer order ; and his chief instrument, as it was afterwards that of Wallis, was the theorem, that $1^n + 2^n + \ldots x^n$, divided by $\left( x^n + x^n \ldots x'' \right)$ is $1 : (n + 1)$ when $x$ is infinite.

Previous to the publication of Cavalieri's work, Roberval had adopted the same principle, and proved that the area of the cycloid was equal to three times that of its generating circle. He determined also the centre of gravity of its area, and the solids formed by its revolution about its axis or its base. We owe to the same mathematician a general method of drawing tangents to certain curves, mechanical and geometrical, which was in some respects similar to that of fluxions. Regarding every curve as described by a point, Roberval[1] considered the point as influenced by two motions, by the composition of which it moves in the direction of a tangent ; and had he possessed the method of fluxions he could have determined in every case the relative velocities of these motions, which depend on the nature of the curve, and, consequently, the direction of the tangent, which he assumed to be the diagonal of a parallelogram whose sides were as the velocities.

Without knowing what had been done by Roberval, Toricelli, a pupil of Galileo, published, in 1644, a solution of the cycloidal problems ; but though the demonstrations were so different as to prove that he had not seen those of Roberval, and though his character and talents might have protected him from so ungenerous a charge, the French mathematician did not scruple to accuse him of plagiarism. Toricelli made much use of the infinitesimal methods, and was one of those who most clearly foresaw the approach of a new calculus.

The methods of Peter Fermat, counsellor of the Parliament of Toulouse, for obtaining maxima and minima, and for drawing tangents to curves, had such a striking resemblance to those of the differential calculus, that Laplace, and, in a more qualified manner, Lagrange, have pronounced Fermat[2] to be the inventor. We need not say that this is an exaggeration : Fermat and others came so close to the calculus as actually to invent cases of it ; but none before Newton and Leibnitz ever imagined, far less organized, a general method which should combine the scattered cases of their predecessors into a uniform and extensible system.

---

[1] Roberval's concealment of his discovery, and his forgery of a work of Aristarchus, greatly lower his credit, when he bears testimony in his own favour.

[2] These methods were published in the sixth or supplemental volume of the second edition of Herigon's *Cursus*, Paris, 1644, 8vo : and an example was given by Schooten in the second edition of his Commentary on the second Book of Descartes's Geometry, in 1659.

As the time for the real invention approached, the anticipa-
tory cases were multiplied. The *Arithmetica Infinitorum* of
Wallis (1655), not to speak of any other of his writings,
applied and extended the ideas of Cavalieri, and produced an
ample field of results. It appears, in modern language, like a
treatise on $\int x^n dx$ for all values of $n$ except $-1$, and on
$\int (a^2-x^2)^n dx$ for all integer values of $n$. It gives the first
description of the method of rectifying a curve. In the work
before cited, Schooten publishes a letter from Henry Van
Heuraet, written in 1659, giving the algebraic rectification of
every parabola of the form $y^n = ax^{n+1}$, except in the case of $n=1$,
which case is shown to depend on the quadrature of the hyperbola. This had been completed a year or two before, about the
same time at which William Neile communicated to Wallis his
rectification of the semicubical parabola. Fermat also did the
same as Neile, under the forms of the old geometry. Descartes,
in 1648, showed that he had made progress in a method of
finding areas, centres of gravity, and tangents ; and he afterwards determined the character of a curve by what we should
now call a transformation of a differential equation.

In his Commentary on Descartes, Schooten published two
letters of John Hudde, the second of which is dated January
27, 1658. It shows how to make a rational function integral
or fractional, a maximum or minimum, and even treats the case
in which the function and its variable are connected by an un-
solved rational equation. The rules are, for the first time,
extricated from algebraical process, and presented in calcular
form. These very remarkable results were well known to both
Newton and Leibnitz, and are freely cited by both.

James Gregory, in 1668, gave two of what we should now
call integrations of trigonometrical functions. He demonstrated
the connexion which had been observed between Wright's meridional parts and the logarithms of cotangents.

The methods of drawing tangents, invented by Barrow and
by Slusius, were published in 1670 and in 1673. Such

methods were then common ; and Barrow, in announcing his, says he scarcely perceives the use of publishing it, because several similar methods were well known.   But both these methods obtained an undue importance in the great controversy, and this probably arose from their being both published in England.

Such are the methods which Newton and Leibnitz received from their predecessors, and, were we obliged to describe them in modern terms, we should call them isolated instances of differentiation and integration, of calcular rules of differentiation, of quadrature, rectification, and determination of centres of gravity, of determination of maxima and minima, both of explicit and implicit functions, &c.   But we can hardly permit ourselves to invite the reader to look back under general terms, because he can hardly use the general terms without having the idea of a general system.   Some will almost be inclined to ask what was left for Newton and Leibnitz to do ?   The best answer is, that it was left for them to put the querist in a position to ask the question.   Had it not been for Newton and Leibnitz, that is, supposing their place had never been supplied, the close approach of the investigators to each other, and to a common method, would never have been visible.

We have already seen[1] that the attention of Newton had been directed to these subjects so early as 1663 and 1664. Upon reading Dr. Wallis's work in the winter of 1664-5, he obtained an expression in series for the area of circular sectors ; and from the consideration that the arch has the same proportion to its sector that an arch of 90° has to the whole quadrant, he found an expression for the length of the arch.   At the same time he determined the area of the rectangular hyperbola intercepted between the curve, its asymptote, and two ordinates parallel to the other asymptote ; and it was by this series that he computed the area of the hyperbola to fifty-two figures, when the plague had, in the summer of 1669, driven him from

[1] See pp. 20-22.

Cambridge to Boothby. At the same time he was led, by the happy thought of substituting indefinite indices of powers for definite ones, to give a more general form to the 59th proposition of Dr. Wallis's Arithmetic of Infinites. In the beginning of 1665, he likewise discovered a method of tangents similar to those of Hudde, Gregory, and Slusius, and a method of finding the curvature of curve lines at any given point ; and, continuing to pursue the method of interpolation, he found the quadrature of all curves whose ordinates are the powers of binomials affected with indices whole, fractional, or surd, affirmative or negative ; together with a rule for reducing any power of a binomial into an approximating or converging series. In the spring of the same year he discovered a method of doing the same thing by the continual division and extraction of roots ; and he soon after extended the method to the extraction of the roots of adfected equations in species.

Having met with an example of the method of Fermat, in Schooten's Commentary on the Second Book of Descartes, Newton succeeded in applying it to adfected equations, and determining the proportion of the increments of indeterminate quantities. These increments he called *moments*, and to the velocities with which the quantities increase he gave the names of *motions, velocities* of *increase*, and *fluxions*. He considered quantities not as composed of indivisibles, but as generated by motion ; and as the ancients considered rectangles as generated by drawing one side into the other, that is, by moving one side upon the other to describe the area of the rectangle, so Newton regarded the areas of curves as generated by drawing the ordinate into the abscissa, and all indeterminate quantities as generated by continual increase. Hence, from the flowing of time and the moments thereof, he gave the name of *flowing quantities* to all quantities which increase in time, that of *fluxions* to the velocities of their increase, and that of *moments* to their parts generated in moments of time. He considered time as flowing uniformly, and represented it by any other quantity,

which is regarded as flowing uniformly, and its fluxion by a
unit. These moments of time, or of its exponent, he considers
as equal to one another, and represents by the letter $o$, or by
any other mark multiplied by unity. The other flowing quantities are represented by any letters or marks, but most commonly by the letters at the end of the alphabet ; while their
fluxions are represented by any other letters or marks, or by
the same letters in a different form or size, and their moments
by their fluxions multiplied by a moment of time.

In a manuscript, dated 13th November 1665, the direct
method of fluxions is described with examples, and the following problem is resolved :—" An equation being given expressing
the relation of two or more lines, $x$, $y$, $z$, &c., described in the
same time by two or more moving bodies, A, B, C, &c., to
find the relation of their velocities, $p$, $q$, $r$, &c., with which
these lines are described." In the same manuscript we find
an application of this method to the drawing of tangents, by
determining the motion of any point which describes the curve,
and also to the determination of the radius of curvature of any
curve line, by making the perpendicular to the curve move
upon it at right angles, and finding that point of the perpendicular which is in least motion, for that point will be the
centre of curvature of the curve at that point upon which the
perpendicular stands. On another leaf of the same book,
dated May 20, 1665, the same method is given, but in different words, and fluxions are represented with dots superfixed.
In another leaf, dated May 16, 1666, there is given a general
method, consisting of seven propositions, of solving problems
by motion, the seventh proposition being the same, though
differently expressed, from that in the paper of November 13,
1665.

In a small tract, written in October 1666, we find the same
method in the same number of propositions ; but the seventh
is improved by showing how to proceed in equations involving
fractions and surds, and such quantities as were afterwards

called transcendental. To this tract there is added an eighth proposition, containing the inverse method of fluxions, in so far as he had then attained it, namely, by the method of quadratures, and by most of the theorems in the Scholium to the tenth proposition of his Book of Quadratures, which with many more are contained in this tract. Newton then proceeds to show the application of the propositions to the solution of the twelve following problems, many of which were at that time entirely new :—

" 1. To draw tangents to curve lines.

" 2. To find the quantity of the crookedness of lines.

" 3. To find the points distinguishing between the concave and convex portions of curved lines.

" 4. To find the point at which lines are most or least curved.

" 5. To find the nature of the curve line whose area is expressed by any given equation.

" 6. The nature of any curve line being given, to find other lines whose areas may be compared to the area of that given line.

" 7. The nature of any curve line being given, to find its area when it may be done ; or two curved lines being given, to find the relation of their areas when it may be.

" 8. To find such curved lines whose lengths may be found, and also to find their lengths.

" 9. Any curve line being given, to find other lines whose lengths may be compared to its length, or to its area, and to compare them.

" 10. To find curve lines whose areas shall be equal, or have any given relations to the length of any given curve line drawn into a given right line.

" 11. To find the length of any curve line when it may be.

" 12. To find the nature of a curve line whose length is expressed by any given equation when it may be done."

Such were the improvements in the higher geometry which

Newton had made before the end of 1666. His analysis, consisting of the method of series and fluxions combined, was so universal as to apply to almost all kinds of problems. He had not only invented the method of fluxions in 1665, in which the motions or velocities of flowing quantities increase or decrease, but he had considered the increase or decrease of these motions or velocities themselves, to which he afterwards gave the name of *second fluxions*,—using sometimes letters with one or two dots, to represent first and second fluxions.

It does not appear that Newton imparted any of these methods to his mathematical friends ; but in order to communicate some of his results, he composed his treatise entitled *Analysis per Equationes Numero Terminorum Infinitas*, in which the method of fluxions and its applications are supposed by some to be explained ; while others are of opinion, that it treats only of moments or infinitely small increments, and exhibits the algebraical processes involved in their use. In June 1669, he communicated his work to Dr. Barrow, who, in letters to Collins of the 20th June, the 31st July, and the 20th August, mentions it, as we have already seen,[1] as the production of Newton, a young man of great genius. Having taken a copy of this treatise, Collins returned the original to Dr. Barrow, from whom it again passed into the hands of Newton. At the death of Collins, Mr. William Jones found the copy among his papers ; and having compared it with the original given him by Newton, it was published, along with some other analytical tracts of the same author, in 1711, nearly fifty years after it was composed.

Although the discoveries contained in this treatise were not at first given to the world, yet they were generally known to mathematicians by the correspondence of Collins, who communicated them to James Gregory in Scotland ; to M. Bertet, and an English gentleman, Francis Vernon, secretary to the English ambassador in Paris ; to Slusius in Holland ; to Bo-

[1] See p. 32, and note 3, p. 24.

relli in Italy ; and to Thomas Strode, Oldenburg, Dary, and others in England, in letters dated between 1669 and 1672.

In the years 1669 and 1670, Newton had prepared for the press a new and enlarged edition of Kinckhuysen's Introduction to Algebra.[1] He at first proposed to add to it, as an introduction, a treatise entitled, a *Method of Fluxions and Quadratures ;* but the fear of being involved in disputes as annoying as those into which his optical discoveries had led him, and which were not yet concluded, prevented him from giving this treatise to the world. At a later period of our author's life, Dr. Pemberton had prevailed upon him to publish it, and for this purpose had examined all the calculations and prepared the diagrams. The latter part of the treatise, however, in which he intended to show the manner of resolving problems which cannot be reduced to quadratures, was never finished ; and when Newton was about to supply this defect, his death put a stop to the plan.[2] It was therefore not till the year 1736 that a translation of the work appeared, with a commentary by Mr. John Colson, Professor of Mathematics in Cambridge.[3]

Between the years 1671 and 1676, Newton did not pursue his mathematical studies. His optical researches, and the disputes in which they involved him, occupied all his time ; and there is reason to believe, that as soon as these disputes were over, he directed the whole energy of his mind to those researches which constitute the *Principia.*

Hitherto the method of fluxions was known only to the

---

[1] This task seems to have been pressed upon him by some friends in London. In sending to Collins the notes upon the book, in July 1670, he wishes his name to be suppressed, and suggests that in the title-page, after the words *Nunc e Belgico Latine versa,* the words *et ab alio authore locupletata* should be added. In a letter to Collins, dated September 5, 1676, he thus speaks of the work :—" I have nothing in the press, only Kinckhuysen's Algebra, I would have got printed here, to satisfy the expectation of some friends in London, but our press cannot do it. This, I suppose, is the book Dr. Lloyd means. It is now in the hands of a bookseller here to get it printed ; but if it do come out, I shall add nothing to it.—Macclesfield *Correspondence,* vol. ii. p. 398.

[2] Pemberton's *Account of Sir Isaac Newton's Discoveries,* Pref. p. 6.

[3] It is entitled *Method of Fluxions and Infinite Series.* Lond. 1736, 1737. 4to.

friends of Newton and their correspondents ; but in the first
edition of the *Principia*, which appeared in 1687, he published
for the first time one of the most important rules of the fluxionary calculus, which forms the Second Lemma of the Second
Book, and points out the method of finding the moment of the
products of any power whatsoever.

In writing the *Principia*, Newton made great use of both
the direct and the inverse method of fluxions ; but though all
the difficult propositions in that work were invented by the
aid of the calculus, yet the calculations were not put down,
and the propositions were demonstrated by the method of the
ancients, shortened by the substitution of the doctrine of limits
for that of exhaustions.   No information, however, is given in
the *Principia* respecting the algorithm or notation of the calculus ; and it was not till 1693 that it was communicated to
the mathematical world, in the Second Volume of Dr. Wallis's
Works, which was published in that year.   The friends of
Newton in Holland had informed Dr. Wallis that Newton's
" Method of Fluxions " had passed there with great applause
by the name of Leibnitz's *Calculus Differentialis*.   The Doctor,
who was at that time printing the Preface to his First Volume,
inserted in it a brief notice of Newton's claim to the discovery
of fluxions, and published in his second volume some extracts
from the *Quadratura Curvarum*, with which Newton had
furnished him.[1]

To the first edition of Newton's Optics, which appeared in
1704, there were added two mathematical treatises, entitled,
*Tractatus duo de speciebus et magnitudine figurarum curviline-
arum*, the one bearing the title of *Tractatus de Quadratura
Curvarum*,[2] and the other *Enumeratio linearum tertii ordinis*.[3]
The first contains an explanation of the doctrine of fluxions, and

---

[1] Wallisii *Opera*, tom. i. Præf. pp. 2, 3 ; and tom. iii. cap. xciv. xcv.  See also Letter of
Wallis to Newton, April 10, 1695, in Edleston's *Correspondence*, &c., p. 309, and part of
it in Raphson's *Hist. of Fluxions*, pp. 120, 121.

[2] Newtoni *Opera*, tom. i. pp. 333-386.          [3] Ibid. tom. i. pp. 531-560.

of its application to the quadrature of curves ; and the second a
classification of seventy-two curves of the third order, with an
account of their properties.  The reason for publishing these
two tracts in his Optics (in the subsequent editions of which
they are omitted) is thus stated in the advertisement :—
" In a letter written to M. Leibnitz in the year 1679, and
published by Dr. Wallis, I mentioned a method by which I
had found some general theorems about squaring curvilinear
figures on comparing them with the conic sections, or other the
simplest figures with which they might be compared.  And
some years ago I lent out a manuscript containing such theorems ;
and having since met with some things copied out of it, I have
on this occasion made it public, prefixing to it an introduction,
and joining a scholium concerning that method.  And I have
joined with it another small tract concerning the curvilinear
figures of the second kind, which was also written many years
ago, and made known to some friends, who have solicited the
making it public."

In the year 1707, Mr. Whiston published the algebraical
lectures which Newton had delivered at Cambridge, under the
title of *Arithmetica Universalis, sive de Compositione et Reso-
lutione Arithmetica Liber.*[1]  This work, which is still in the
University Library, was soon afterwards translated into English
by Mr. Raphson ; and a second edition of it, with improvements
by the author, was published at London in 1712, by Dr.
Machin, secretary to the Royal Society.  With the view of
stimulating mathematicians to write annotations on this admirable work, the celebrated S'Gravesande published a tract, entitled, *Specimen Commentarii in Arithmeticam Universalem ;*
and Maclaurin's Algebra seems to have been drawn up in consequence of this appeal.

Among the mathematical works of Newton we must not
omit to enumerate a small tract entitled, *Methodus Differentialis,* which was published with his consent in 1711.  It

[1] Newtoni *Opera,* tom. i. pp. 1-251.

consists of six propositions, which contain a method of drawing
a parabolic curve through any given number of points, and which
are useful for constructing tables by the interpolation of series,
and for solving problems depending on the quadrature of curves.

Another mathematical treatise of Newton was published for
the first time in 1799, in Dr. Horsley's edition of his works.
It is entitled, *Artis Analyticæ Specimina, vel Geometria Analytica.*[1] In editing this work, which occupies about 130 quarto
pages, Dr. Horsley used three manuscripts, one of which was
in the handwriting of the author ; another, written in an unknown hand, was given by Mr. William Jones to the Honourable Charles Cavendish ; and a third, copied from this by Mr.
James Wilson, the editor of Robins's works, was given to Dr.
Horsley by Mr. John Nourse, bookseller to the king. Dr.
Horsley has divided it into twelve chapters, which treat of
infinite series, of the reduction of affected equations, of the
specious resolution of equations, of the doctrine of fluxions, of
maxima and minima, of drawing tangents to curves, of the
radius of curvature, of the quadrature of curves, of the area of
curves which are comparable with the conic sections ; of the
construction of mechanical problems, and on finding the length
of curves.

In enumerating the mathematical works of our author, we
must not overlook his solutions of the celebrated problems
proposed by John Bernoulli and Leibnitz. In June 1696,
John Bernoulli addressed a letter to the most distinguished
mathematicians in Europe,[2] challenging them to solve the two
following problems :—

1. To determine the curve line connecting two given points
which are at different distances from the horizon, and not in the
same vertical line, along which a body passing by its own gravity,
and beginning to move at the upper point, shall descend to the
lower point in the shortest time possible.

[1] Newtoni *Opera,* tom. i. pp. 388-519.
[2] " Acutissimis qui toto orbe florent Mathematicis."

2. To find a curve line of this property that the two segments of a right line drawn from a given point through the curve, being raised to any given power, and taken together, may make everywhere the same sum.[1] This challenge was first made in the Leipsic Acts, for June 1696.[2] Six months were allowed by Bernoulli for the solution of the problem, and in the event of none being sent to him he promised to publish his own. The six months, however, elapsed without any solution being produced ; but he received a letter from Leibnitz, stating that he had " cut the knot of the most beautiful of these problems," and requesting that the period for their solution should be extended to Christmas next, that the French and Italian mathematicians might have no reason to complain of the shortness of the period. Bernoulli adopted the suggestion, and publicly announced the prorogation for the information of those who might not see the Leipsic Acts.

On the 29th January 1696-7, Newton received from France two copies of the printed paper containing the problems, and on the following day he transmitted a solution of them to Charles Montague, Chancellor of the Exchequer, and then President of the Royal Society.[3] He announced that the curve required in the first problem must be a cycloid, and he gave a method of determining it. He solved also the second problem, and he showed that by the same method other curves might be found which shall cut off three or more segments having the like properties. Solutions were also obtained from Leibnitz and the Marquis de l'Hôpital ; and although that of Newton was anonymous, yet Bernoulli recognised in it his powerful mind ; " *tan-*

---

[1] John Bernoulli had already published, in the Leipsic Acts for June, p. 266, a solution of the most simple case in which the exponent of the power was unity.

[2] *Acta Lipsiensia*, in June, p. 269.

[3] The original manuscript of this letter with the solution of the problem is preserved at the Royal Society ; and one of the two papers, a folio printed half-sheet, still exists in their archives. At the bottom, in Newton's hand, are the words, " Chartam hanc ex Gallia missam accepi, Jan 29, 1696-7."—Edleston's *Correspondence*, &c. &c., p. lxviii. For a copy of the document, see Newtoni *Opera*, tom. iv. pp. 411-418.

*quam,*" says he, " *ex ungue leonem,*" as the lion is known by his claw.

One of the *last* mathematical efforts of our author was made, with his usual success, in solving a problem which Leibnitz proposed in 1716, in a letter to the Abbé Conti, " for the purpose, as he expressed it, of feeling the pulse of the English analysts." The object of this problem was to determine the curve which should cut at right angles an infinity of curves of a given nature, but expressible by the same equation. Newton received this problem about five o'clock in the afternoon, as he was returning from the Mint ; and though the problem was difficult, and he himself fatigued with business, he reduced it to a fluxional equation before he went to bed.

In his reply to Leibnitz,[1] Conti does not even mention the solution of Newton ; but as if such a problem had been beneath the notice of the English geometers, he says :—" Your problem was very easily resolved, and in a short time. Several geometers, both in London and Oxford, have given the solution. It is general, and extends to all sorts of curves, whether geometrical or mechanical. The problem is proposed somewhat equivocally ; but I believe that M. De Moivre is not wrong when he says that we must fix the idea of a series of curves, and suppose, for example, that they have the same subtangent for the same abscissa, which would correspond not only with the conic sections, but with an infinity of other curves, both geometrical and mechanical."

Such is a brief account of the mathematical writings of Sir Isaac Newton, not one of which was voluntarily communicated to the world by himself. The publication of his Universal Arithmetic is said to have been made by Whiston against his will ; and, however this may be, it was an unfinished work, never designed for the public. The publication of his *Quadrature of Curves,* and of his *Enumeration of Curve Lines,* was in Newton's opinion rendered necessary, in consequence of plagiar-

[1] Dated London, March 1716.

isms from the manuscripts of them which he had lent to his friends, and the rest of his analytical writings did not appear till after his death. It is not easy to penetrate into the motives by which this great man was actuated. If his object was to keep possession of his discoveries till he had brought them to a higher degree of perfection, we may approve of the propriety, though we cannot admire the prudence, of such a step. If he wished to retain to himself his own methods, in order that he alone might have the advantage of them, in prosecuting his physical inquiries, we cannot reconcile so selfish a measure with that openness and generosity of character which marked the whole of his life, nor with the communications which he so freely made to Barrow, Collins, and others. If he withheld his labours from the world in order to avoid the disputes and contentions to which they might give rise, he adopted the very worst method of securing his tranquillity. That this was the leading motive under which he acted, there is little reason to doubt. The early delay in the publication of his *Method of Fluxions*, after the breaking out of the plague at Cambridge, was probably owing to his not having completed the whole of his design ; but no apology can be made for the imprudence of withholding it any longer from the public,—an imprudence which is the more inexplicable, as he was repeatedly urged by Wallis, Halley, and his other friends, to present it to the world.[1] Had he published this noble discovery previous to 1673, when his great rival had made but little progress in those studies which led him to the same method, he would have secured to himself the undivided honour of the invention, and Leibnitz could have aspired to no other fame but that of an improver of the doctrine of fluxions. But he unfortunately acted otherwise. He announced to his friends that he possessed a method, of great generality and power : He communicated to them a general account of its principles and applications ; and the information which was thus conveyed, might have directed the attention of

[1] Wallis to Newton, April 10, 1695. See Edleston's *Correspondence*. pp. 301. 302

mathematicians to subjects to which they would not have otherwise applied their powers.    The discoveries which he had
previously made were made subsequently by others ; and
Leibnitz, instead of appearing on the theatre of science as the
disciple and the follower of Newton, stood forth with all the
dignity of a second inventor ; and, by the early publication of
his discoveries, had nearly placed himself on the throne which
Newton was destined to ascend.

It would be inconsistent with the nature of this work to
enter into a detailed history of the dispute between Newton
and Leibnitz respecting the invention of fluxions.    A brief and
general account of it, however, is indispensable.

In the beginning of 1673, when Leibnitz came to London in
the suite of the Duke of Hanover, he became acquainted with
the great men who then adorned the capital of England.
Among these was Henry Oldenburg, a countryman of his own,
who was at that time Secretary to the Royal Society,    Leibnitz
had not then, as he himself assures us,[1] entered upon the study
of the higher geometry, but he eagerly embraced the opportunity which was now offered to him of learning the discoveries of
the English mathematician.    With this view he kept up a correspondence with Oldenburg, communicating to him freely certain
arithmetical and analytical methods of his own, and receiving
in return an account of the discoveries in series made by James
Gregory and Newton.    In the two letters[2] written in London
to Oldenburg, and in the first four which he addressed to him
from Paris,[3] he refers only to certain properties of numbers
which he had discovered ; but in those of a subsequent date,
he mentions a theorem of his own for expressing the area of a
circle, or of any given sector of it, by an infinite series or

[1] Two years before this, in 1671, Leibnitz presented to the Academy of Sciences a
paper containing the germ of the differential method, so that he must have been able to
appreciate the information he received in England.—See page 71.

[2] Dated February 3d and 20th, 1673.

[3] March 30, April 26, May 26, and June 8, 1673.

rational numbers ;[1] and of deducing, by the same method, the arc of a circle from its sine.[2]    In reply to these letters, Oldenburg acquainted him with the previous discoveries of Newton, and transmitted to him a communication from Collins, describing several series which had been sent to him by Gregory on the 15th February 1671.    Leibnitz stated in reply,[3] that he was so much distracted with business, that he had not time to compare these series with his own ; and he promises to communicate his opinion to Oldenburg as soon as he has made the comparison.    In continuing his correspondence with Oldenburg, Leibnitz requested farther information respecting the analytical discoveries recently made in England ; and it was in compliance with this request that Newton, at the pressing solicitation of Oldenburg and Collins, wrote a long letter, dated 13th June 1676, to be communicated to Leibnitz.

This letter, which was sent to Leibnitz in Paris, along with extracts from Gregory's letters, on the 26th June, contained Newton's method of series, and, after describing it,' he added, " that analysis, by the assistance of infinite equations of this kind, extends to almost all problems except some numerical ones like those of Diophantus, but does not become altogether universal without some farther methods of reducing problems to infinite equations, and infinite equations to finite ones, when it might be done."

Leibnitz answered this letter on the 27th August, and, in return for Newton's method of series, he sent to Oldenburg a theorem for transmuting figures into one another ; and thus demonstrated the series of Gregory for finding the arch from its tangent.    In consequence of Leibnitz having requested still farther information, Newton addressed to Oldenburg his celebrated letter of the 24th October 1676.    In this letter he gave an account of his discovery of the method of series before the plague in the summer of 1665.    He stated, that on the publication of Mercator's *Logarithmotechnia*, he had communicated

---

[1] July 15, 1673.    [2] October 26, 1673.    [3] May 20, 1675.

a compendium of this method through Dr. Barrow to Mr. Collins, and, that five years after, he had, at the suggestion of the latter, written a large tract on the same subject, joining with it a method from which the determination of maxima and minima, and the method of tangents of Slusius and some others flowed. "This method," he continued, "was not limited to surds, but was founded upon the following proposition, which he communicated enigmatically in a series of transposed letters, *Data equatione quotcunque fluentes quantitates involvente, fluxiones invenire, et vice versa.* This proposition," he added, "facilitated the quadrature of curves, and afforded him infinite series, which broke off and became finite when the curve was capable of being squared by a finite equation." In the conclusion of this letter, Newton stated that his method extended to inverse problems of tangents, and others more difficult, and that in solving these he used two methods, one more general than the other, which he expressed enigmatically in transposed letters, which formed the following sentence :—"Una methodus consistit in extractione fluentis quantitatis ex equatione simul involvente fluxionem ejus : altera tantum in assumptione seriei pro quantitate quâlibet incognita, ex quâ cetera commodè derivari possunt, et in collatione terminorum homologorum æquationis resultantis, ad eruendos terminos assumptæ seriei."

This letter, though dated 24th October, had not been forwarded to Leibnitz on the 5th March 1677. At the time Newton was writing it, Leibnitz spent a week in London, on his return from Paris to Germany ; but it must have reached him in the spring of that year, as he sent an answer to it dated June 21, 1677.

In this remarkable letter he frankly describes his differential calculus and its algorithm. He says that he agrees with Newton in the opinion that Slusius's methods of tangents is not absolute, and that he himself had long ago (*a multo tempore*) treated the subject of tangents much more generally by the differences of ordinates. He gives an example of drawing tangents, and shows how to proceed, as Newton expresses it, " without sticking at surds." He then expresses the opinion, that the method of drawing tangents, which Newton wished to conceal, does not differ from his ; and he regards this opinion as confirmed by the statement of Newton, that his method facilitated the quadrature of curves.

No answer seems to have been returned to this communication either by Oldenburg or Newton, and, with the exception of a short letter from Leibnitz to the former, dated 12th July 1677, no farther correspondence between them seems to have taken place. This no doubt arose from the death of Oldenburg in the month of September 1677 ;[1] and the two rival geometers, having through him become acquainted with each other's labours, were left to pursue them with all the ardour which the importance of the subject could not fail to inspire.

In the hands of Leibnitz, the differential calculus made rapid progress. In the *Acta Eruditorum*, which appeared at Leipsic in October 1684, he describes its algorithm in the same manner as he had done in his letter to Oldenburg. He points out its

[1] Henry Oldenburg, whose name is so intimately associated with the history of Newton's discoveries, was born at Bremen, and was consul from that town to London during the usurpation of Cromwell. Having lost his office, and been compelled to seek the means of subsistence, he became tutor to an English nobleman, whom he accompanied to Oxford in 1656. During his residence in that city he was introduced to the philosophers who established the Royal Society, and, upon the death of William Crown, the first secretary, he was appointed, in 1663, joint secretary along with Mr. Wilkins. He kept up an extensive correspondence with more than *seventy* philosophers and literary men in all parts of the world,—a privilege especially given to the Society in their charter. The suspicions of the Government, however, were, somehow or other, excited against him, and he was committed to the Tower on the 20th June 1667, "for dangerous designs and practices." Although no evidence was produced to justify so harsh a proceeding, he was kept a close prisoner till the 26th August 1667, when he was discharged. " This remarkable event," as Mr. Weld remarks, "had so much influence on the Society as to cause a suspension of the meetings from the 30th May to the 3d October." It is remarkable that there is no notice of this fact in the council or journal-books of the Society.

Oldenburg was the author of several papers in the Philosophical Transactions, and of some works which have not acquired much celebrity. He died at Charlton, near Greenwich, in August 1678. See Weld's *History of the Royal Society*, vol. i. pp. 200-204.

application to the drawing of tangents, and the determination of maxima and minima ;[1] and he adds, that these are only the beginnings of a much more sublime geometry, applicable to the most difficult and beautiful problems even of mixed mathematics, which, without his differential calculus, or one SIMILAR to it, could not be treated with equal facility. The suppression of Newton's name in this reference to a *similar* calculus, which was obviously that of Newton, indicated in the letters of 1676, was the first false step in the fluxionary controversy, and may be regarded as its commencement.

While Leibnitz was thus making known the principles of his Calculus, Newton was occupied in preparing his Principia for the press.   In the autumn of 1684, he had sent the principal propositions of his work to the Royal Society ; but it would appear from his letter to Halley of the 20th June 1686, that the second book of the Principia had not then been sent to him.   He must therefore have been acquainted with the paper of Leibnitz in the *Acta Eruditorum,* before he sent the manuscript of the second book to press ; and it was doubtless from this cause that he was led to compose the second lemma of that book, in which he, for the first time, explains the fundamental principle of the fluxionary calculus. This lemma, which occupies only three pages, was terminated with the following scholium, which has been the subject of such angry discussion.

" The correspondence which took place about ten years ago, between that very skilful geometer G. G. Leibnitz and myself, when I had announced to him that I possessed a method of determining maxima and minima, of drawing tangents, and of performing similar operations, which was equally applicable to surds and to rational quantities, and concealed the same in transposed letters, involving this sentence (*Data Æquatione quotcunque Fluentes quantitates involvente, Fluxiones invenire,*

---

[1] This article was entitled, " Nova methodus pro maximis et minimis, itemque tangentibus quæ nec fractas nec irrationales moratur, et singulare pro illis calculi genus, per G. G. L."—*Acta Erudit.* 1684, pp. 472, 473.

*et vice versa*), this illustrious man replied that he also had fallen on a method of the same kind, and he communicated his method, which scarcely differed from my own,[1] except in the forms of words and notation (and in the idea of the generation of quantities[2]). The fundamental principle of both is contained in this lemma."

This celebrated scholium has been viewed in different lights by Leibnitz and his followers. Leibnitz asserts,[3] that Newton " has accorded to him in this scholium the invention of the differential calculus independently of his own ;" and M. Biot considers the scholium as " eternalizing the rights of Leibnitz by recognising them in the Principia." But the scholium has no such meaning, and it was not the intention of the author that it should be thus understood. It is a statement of the simple fact, that Leibnitz communicated to him a method which was nearly the same as his own,—a sentiment which he might have expressed whether he believed that Leibnitz was an independent inventor of his calculus, or had derived it from his communication and correspondence with his friend.[4]

The manuscripts of Newton furnish us with some curious information on this subject, and place it beyond a doubt that he regarded the silence of Leibnitz, in his communication of 1684, as an aggressive movement, which he was bound to repel. " After seven years," says Newton,[5] " viz., in October

---

[1] " *A mea vix abludentem*"—the same expression which Leibnitz used in his letter to Oldenburg of June 21, 1677, " *ab his non abludere.*" The similarity of the Method of Fluxions and the Differential Calculus, may be considered as admitted both by Newton and Leibnitz.

[2] These words were inserted in the 2d edition of the Principia.

[3] Letter to the Abbé Conti, April 9, 1716, and to Madame de Kilmansegg, April 18, 1716.

[4] We have, fortunately, Newton's own opinions on the subject. " And as for the *scholium* upon the second *lemma* of the second book of the *Principia Philosophiæ Mathematicæ*, which is *so much wrested against me*, it was written not to give away that *lemma* to *Mr. Leibnitz*, but, on the contrary, to assert it to myself. Whether *Mr. Leibnitz* invented it after me, or had it from me, is a question of no consequence ; for second inventors have no right."—Raphson's *History of Fluxions*, 1715, p. 122, see also p. 115 ; and Newtoni *Opera*, tom. iv. p. 616.

[5] In a manuscript of seven closely written pages, entitled, " A Supplement to the

1684, he published the elements of this method (the method mentioned to Leibnitz in his letter of October 24, 1676), as his own, without referring to the correspondence which he formerly had with the English about these matters. He mentioned, indeed, a *methodus similis, but whose that method was,* and *what he knew of it,* he did not say, as he should have done. And thus *his silence put me upon a necessity* of writing the scholium upon the second lemma of the second Book of Principles, *lest it should be thought that I borrowed* that lemma from Mr. Leibnitz. In my letter of 24th October 1676, when I had been speaking of the Method of Fluxions, I added, Fundamentum harum operationum, satis obvium quidem, quoniam non possum explicationem ejus prosequi, sic potius celavi 6*œccdœ* 13*eff* 7*i* 3*l* 9*n* 4*o* 4*qrr* 4*s* 9*t* 12*vx.* And in the said scholium I opened this enigma, saying, that it contained the sentence, *Data œquatione quotcunque fluentes quantitates involvente, fluxiones invenire, et vice versa ;* and was written in the year 1676, for I looked upon this *as a sufficient security, without entering into a wrangle;* but Mr. Leibnitz was of another opinion."

In 1724, when the third edition of the Principia was preparing for the press, Newton had resolved to substantiate his claims to the first, if not the sole invention, of the new calculus, and we have found several rough draughts of the changes which he intended to have made upon the scholium. In one of these[1] he gives an account of the fundamental principle of the fluxionary calculus, and distinctly states that it " might have been *easily collected* even from the letter which he wrote to Collins on the 10th December 1672,[2] a copy of which was sent to Leibnitz in 1676."[3]

---

Remarks;" that is, to some observations upon Leibnitz's letter to Conti, dated 9th April 1716, published in Raphson's *Fluxions,* p. 111.

[1] The title of this addition, which occupies more than a folio page, is, " In the end of the Scholium in Princip. Philos., p. 227, after the words, *Utriusque fundamentum continetur in hoc Lemmate,* add, *Sunto quantitates datæ, a, b, c ; fluentes x, y, z.*" &c.

[2] A copy of this letter was sent to Tschirnhausen in May 1675, thirteen months before it was sent to Leibnitz.

[3] "Doubts have been expressed," Mr. Edleston remarks, " whether these papers were

In another folio sheet, we have the scholium in three different forms, including the substance of the one previously published.[1] In all of them it is distinctly stated that Newton's letter to Collins, of the 10th December 1672, containing the

actually sent to Leibnitz." That papers were sent and received by Leibnitz, his own testimony and that of others prove ; but there is some reason to believe, as first indicated by Mr. Edleston, and made much more probable by Professor De Morgan, that Newton's letter of the 10th December was sent, without the example of drawing a tangent to a curve, which it actually contained, and which was relied upon as giving Leibnitz a knowledge of the new calculus. In support of this opinion, we find that what are called the originals, said to have been received by Leibnitz, and Collins' draught of the papers preserved in the Royal Society, contain merely an allusion to that method. These originals have been printed in Leibnitz's *Mathematical Works*, published at Berlin in 1849, but fac-similes have not been given to enable us to judge of their genuineness. It is difficult to reconcile with these statements that of Newton himself, who declares that the *originals* of the letters in question were sent to Leibnitz in Paris to be *returned*, and that these originals were in the archives of the Royal Society. Leibnitz may have retained imperfect copies of these *originals*, which must have contained the method of tangents. If it be true that the original letters of Newton were sent to Leibnitz, we have nothing to do with the copies either at Hanover or the Royal Society.

With regard to the *seven* "study exercises by Leibnitz, on the use of both the differential and integral calculus," as Professor De Morgan calls them, dated November 11, 21, 22, 1675, June 26, July, November 1676, which were published by Gerhardt in 1848, we cannot, without seeing the originals or proper fac-similes of the hand-writing, receive them as evidence. Gerhardt admits that some person had been *turning the 5 of 1675 into a 3* (from an obvious motive) ; and when we recollect how Leibnitz altered grave documents to give him a priority to Bernoulli, as we shall presently see, we are entitled to pause before we decide on any writings that have passed through his hands. But even if we admit these documents to be genuine, the allegation of Newton's friends that copies of his papers were in circulation before 1675, requires to be considered in the controversy. We recommend to the reader the careful study of Mr. Edleston's statement in the *Correspondence of Sir Isaac Newton*, p. xlvii., and of the very interesting paper by Professor De Morgan, on the *Companion to the Almanac for* 1852, p. 8.

To these observations we may add, that Keill published in the *Journal Littéraire* for May and June 1713, vol. i. p. 215, the extract from the letter of December 10, 1672, as the chief document upon which the report of the committee of the Royal Society was founded, and at the same time distinctly stated *that this letter was sent to Leibnitz.* Now Leibnitz, as we know, read this letter, and never contradicted the allegation of Keill. If the paper actually sent to him had been merely an abridgment of that letter, from which the example was omitted, he would undoubtedly have come forward, and proved by the production of what he did receive, and what we know he possessed, that the principal argument used against him had no foundation.

Three years afterwards, in 1716, when Newton had challenged him to the discussion, he had another opportunity which he did not use, of disowning the reception of the letter.

[1] See APPENDIX, No. XIII.

method of drawing tangents, with an example, had been sent to
Leibnitz in June 1676, and that on his return from France
through England to Germany, he had consulted Newton's letters in the hands of Collins, and had not long after this fallen
upon a similar method. We have not succeeded in finding a
copy of the scholium, as it was published in the first edition of
the Principia,[1] or any traces of the grounds upon which he
omitted the historical details in the original draughts of it.

It would be interesting to know why these contemplated
additions to the scholium were not adopted, and a single paragraph from the letter of December 10, 1672, substituted for
the original scholium. In the letters of Pemberton to Newton,
in 1724 and 1725, I have found no reference to this change
upon the scholium.

It appears, therefore, that Newton had resolved to overlook
the aggressive movement of Leibnitz in 1684 ; and on another
occasion, when he believed his rights to be invaded, he exercised the same forbearance.[2]   Circumstances, however, now
occurred which induced his friends to come forward in his

[1] On a separate folio sheet I have found the following form of the scholium. The
words in italics are not in the printed scholium, in which there is the word *eandem* here
omitted.   " In literis quæ mihi cum geometra peritissimo G. G. Leibnitio annis abhinc
decem intercedebant, cum significarem me compotem esse methodi determinandi maximas et minimas, ducendi tangentes, *quadrandi figuras curvilineas*, et similia peragendi
quæ in terminis surdis æque ac in rationalibus procederet, *methodumque exemplis illustrarem, sed fundamentum ejus* literis transpositis hanc sententiam involventibus [Data
æquatione quotcunque fluentes quantitates involvente, fluxiones invenire, et vice versa]
celarem : rescripsit vir clarissimus, *anno proximo*, se quoque in ejusmodi methodum in-
cidisse, et methodum suam communicavit a mea vix abludentem, præterquam in verborum et notarum formulis.   Utriusque fundamentum continetur in hoc Lemmate."
This copy does not contain the few words added in the second edition of the Principia.

[2] In the *Acta Eruditorum* for January and February 1689, Leibnitz published two
papers, one " On the Motion of Projectiles in a resisting Medium," and the other,
" On the Causes of the Celestial Motions."   Newton regarded the propositions in these
papers, and in a third, *De Lineis Opticis,* as plagiarisms from the Principia, Leibnitz, as
he said, " pretending that he had found them all before that book came abroad," and
" to make the principal proposition his own, adapting to it an erroneous demonstration,
and thereby discovering that he did not yet understand how to work in second differences."—See Raphson's *Fluxions,* p. 117 ; and *Recensio Commercii Epistolici;* Newtoni
*Opera,* tom. iv p. 481, No. lxxii.

cause. Having learned, as we have seen, that Newton's "notions of Fluxions passed there by the name of Leibnitz's Differential Calculus," Dr. Wallis stopped the printing of the Preface to the first volume of his Works, in order to claim for Newton the invention of Fluxions, as contained in the letters of June and October 1676, which had been sent to Leibnitz. In intimating to Newton what he had done, he said, "You are not so kind to your reputation (and that of the nation) as you might be, when you let things of worth lie by you so long, till others carry away the reputation which is due to you."[1]

Early in the year 1691, the celebrated James Bernoulli "spoke contemptuously" of the Differential Calculus, maintaining that it differed from that of Barrow only in notation, and in an abridgment of the operation ;[2] but it nevertheless "grew into reputation," and made great progress after the Marquis de l'Hospital had published, in 1696, his excellent work on the Analysis of Infinitesimals. The claims of the two rival geometers increased in value with the stake for which they contended, and an event soon occurred which placed them in open combat. Hitherto neither Newton nor Leibnitz had claimed to

---

[1] See APPENDIX, No. XIV. " At the request of Dr. Wallis," says Newton, " I sent to him in two letters, dated 27th August and 17th September 1692, the first proposition of the Book of Quadratures, copied almost verbatim from the book, and also the method of extracting fluents out of equations involving fluxions, mentioned in my letter of 24th October 1676, and copied from an older paper, and an explication of the method of fluxions direct and inverse, comprehended in the sentence, *Data equatione,* &c. &c , and the Doctor printed them all the same year (viz. anno 1692), in the second volume of his works, pp. 391-396. This volume being then in the press, and coming abroad the next year, two years before the first volume was printed off, and this is the first time that the use of letters with pricks, and a rule for finding second, third, and fourth fluxions were published, though they were long before in manuscript. When I considered only first fluxions, I seldom used letters with a prick ; but when I considered also second, third, and fourth fluxions, &c., I distinguished them by letters with one, two, or more pricks ; and for fluents I put the fluxions either included within a square (as in the aforesaid analysis), or with a square prefixed as in some other papers, or with an oblique line upon it. And these notations by pricks and oblique lines, are the most compendious yet used, but were not known to the Marquis de l'Hospital when he recommended the differential notation, nor are necessary to the method."—*A Supplement to the Remarks,* p. 4.

[2] *Acta Eruditorum,* Jan. 1691, p. 14.

himself the merit of being the sole inventor of the new calculus. Newton was acknowledged even by his rival as the first inventor, and in his scholium he was supposed to have allowed Leibnitz in return the merit of a second inventor.    Newton, however, had always believed, without publicly avowing it, that Leibnitz had derived his calculus from the communications made to him by Oldenburg ;  and Leibnitz, though he had repeatedly declared that he and Newton had borrowed nothing from each other, was yet inclined to consider his rival as a plagiarist.

This celebrated controversy, rendered interesting by the transcendent talents of its promoters, and instructive by the moral frailties with which it was stained, will form the subject of the following chapter.

# APPENDIX.

## No. I.

*(Referred to in page 30.)*

LETTER FROM MR. NEWTON TO FRANCIS ASTON, ESQ., A YOUNG FRIEND WHO
WAS ON THE EVE OF SETTING OUT UPON HIS TRAVELS.

MR. ASTON was elected a Fellow of the Royal Society in 1678. He was
an active member, and was frequently in the Council. He was chosen one
of the Secretaries on the 30th November 1681, and held that office till the
9th December 1685. He had been re-elected on the 30th of November, but,
at a meeting of the Council on the 9th December, "he threw up," says Mr.
Weld,[1] "the Secretaryship in so sudden and violent a manner, that the
Council resolved not to run the risk of being similarly treated on any
future occasion, and determined on having an officer more immediately
under their command." Halley's letter (dated March 27, 1686, and giving
an account of this affair to Mr. William Molyneux) will better explain the
circumstances of the case :—

"The history of our affairs," says Halley, "is briefly this. On St. An-
drew's day last, being our anniversary day of election, Mr. Pepys was
continued President, Mr. Aston, Secretary, and Tancred Robinson chosen
in the room of Mr. Musgrave. Every body seemed satisfied, and no dis-
content appeared anywhere, when, on a sudden, Mr. Aston, as I suppose,
willing to gain better terms of reward from the Society than formerly, on
December 9th, in Council, declared that he would not serve them as Secretary ; and therefore desired them to provide some other to supply that
office ; and that after such a passionate manner, that I fear he has lost
several of his friends by it. The Council, resolved not to be so served for
the future, thought it expedient to have only honorary secretaries, and a
clerk or amanuensis, upon whom the whole burthen of the business should
lie, and to give him a fixed salary, so as to make it worth his while, and
he to be accountable to the secretaries for the performance of his office ;
and, on January 27th last, they chose me for their under officer, with a
promise of a salary of fifty pounds per annum at least."[2]
Mr. Aston does not seem to have taken offence at these proceedings of the

---

[1] *History of the Royal Society*, vol. i. pp. 302, 303.

[2] Notwithstanding Mr. Aston's conduct, the Council ordered that he be presented
with a gratuity of £60.

Council.  He communicated to the Society some observations on certain
unknown ancient characters, which were published in the Philosophical
Transactions for 1692 ; and, previous to his death, which seems to have
taken place in 1715, he bequeathed to the Royal Society a small estate,
still in their possession, at Mablesthorpe, in Lincolnshire, consisting of 55
acres, 2 roods, and 2 perches.  He likewise left to the Society a considerable number of books and some personal property, which, after paying off
certain debts, amounted to £445.[1]

On the 27th February 1684-5, Newton addressed to Mr. Aston a letter,
in which he states, that the attempt made by himself and Mr. Charles
Montague to establish a Philosophical Society at Cambridge, had failed.

The following letter was written when Newton was only twenty-six years
of age.  We have not been able to find any account of the information
which Mr. Aston communicated to his friend, either during his travels or
after his return :—

" TRINITY COLLEGE, CAMBRIDGE, May 18, 1669.

SIR,—Since in your letter you give mee so much liberty of spending my
judgment about what may be to your advantage in travelling, I shall do
it more freely than perhaps otherwise would have been decent.  First,
then, I will lay down some general rules, most of which, I believe, you
have considered already ; but if any of them be new to you, they may excuse the rest ; if none at all, yet is my punishment more in writing than
your's in reading.

" When you come into any fresh company, 1. Observe their humours.
2. Suit your own carriage thereto, by which insinuation you will make
their converse more free and open.    3. Let your discourse be more in
querys and doubtings than peremptory assertions or disputings, it being
the designe of travellers to learne, not to teach.  Besides, it will persuade
your acquaintance that you have the greater esteem of them, and soe make
them more ready to communicate what they know to you ; whereas nothing sooner occasions disrespect and quarrels than peremptorinesse.  You
will find little or no advantage in seeming wiser, or much more ignorant
than your company.    4. Seldom discommend any thing though never so
bad, or doe it but moderately, lest you bee unexpectedly forced to an un-
hansom retraction.  It is safer to commend any thing more than it deserves,
than to discommend a thing soe much as it deserves ; for commendations
meet not soe often with oppositions, or, at least, are not usually soe ill
resented by men that think otherwise, as discommendations ; and you will
insinuate into men's favour by nothing sooner than seeming to approve
and commend what they like ; but beware of doing it by a comparison.
5. If you bee affronted, it is better, in a forraine country, to pass it by in
silence, and with a jest, though with some dishonour, than to endeavour
revenge ; for, in the first case, your credit's ne'er the worse when you return into England, or come into other company that have not heard of the
quarrell.  But, in the second case, you may beare the marks of the quarrell
while you live, if you outlive it at all.  But, if you find yourself unavoid-
ably engaged, 'tis best, I think, if you can command your passion and
language, to keep them pretty eavenly at some certain moderate pitch, not
much hightning them to exasperate your adversary, or provoke his friends,

<hr>

[1] Weld's History of the Royal Society, vol. i. p. 428.

nor letting them grow over much dejected to make him insult. In a word, if you can keep reason above passion, that and watchfullnesse will be your best defendants. To which purpose you may consider, that, though such excuses as this,—He provok't mee so much I could not forbear,—may pass among friends, yet amongst strangers they are insignificant, and only argue a traveller's weaknesse.

"To these I may add some general heads for inquirys or observations, such as at present I can think on. As, 1. To observe the policys, wealth, and state affairs of nations, so far as a solitary traveller may conveniently doe. 2. Their impositions upon all sorts of people, trades, or commoditys, that are remarkable. 3. Their laws and customs, how far they differ from ours. 4. Their trades and arts, wherein they excell or come short of us in England. 5. Such fortifications as you shall meet with, their fashion, strength, and advantages for defence, and other such military affairs as are considerable. 6. The power and respect belonging to their degrees of nobility or magistracy. 7. It will not be time mispent to make a catalogue of the names and excellencys of those men that are most wise, learned, or esteemed in any nation. 8. Observe the mechanisme and manner of guiding ships. 9. Observe the products of nature in several places, especially in mines, with the circumstances of mining and of extracting metals or minerals out of their oare, and of refining them ; and if you meet with any transmutations out of their own species into another (as out of iron into copper, out of any metall into quicksilver, out of one salt into another, or into an insipid body, &c.), those, above all, will be worth your noting, being the most luciferous, and many times lucriferous experiments too in philosophy. 10. The prices of diet and other things. 11. And the staple commoditys of places.

"These generals (such as at present I could think of), if they will serve for nothing else, yet they may assist you in drawing up a modell to regulate your travels by.

"As for particulars, these that follow are all that I can now think of, viz., Whether at Schemnitium, in Hungary (where there are mines of gold, copper, iron, vitriol, antimony, &c.), they change iron into copper by dissolving it in a vitriolate water, which they find in cavitys of rocks in the mines, and then melting the slimy solution in a strong fire, which in the cooling proves copper. The like is said to be done in other places, which I cannot now remember ; perhaps, too, it may done in Italy. For about twenty or thirty years agone there was a certain vitrioll came from thence (called Roman vitrioll), but of a nobler virtue than that which is now called by that name ; which vitrioll is not now to be gotten, because, perhaps, they make a greater gain by some such trick as turning iron into copper with it, than by selling it. 2. Whether, in Hungary, Sclavonia, Bohemia, near the town Eila, or at the mountains of Bohemia near Silesia, there be rivers whose waters are impregnated with gold ; perhaps, the gold being dissolved by some corrosive waters like *aqua regis*, and the solution carried along with the streame, that runs through the mines. And whether the practise of laying mercury in the rivers, till it be tinged with gold, and then straining the mercury through leather, that the gold may stay behind, be a secret yet, or openly practised. 3. There is newly contrived, in Holland, a mill to grind glasses plane withall, and I think polishing them too ; perhaps it will be worth the while to see it. 4. There is in Holland one —— Borry, who some years since was imprisoned by the Pope, to have extorted from him secrets (as I am told) of great worth, both as to medicine and profit, but he escaped into Holland, where they have granted him a guard.  I think he usually goes cloathed in green.  Pray inquire what you can of him, and whether his ingenuity be any profit to the Dutch.  You may inform yourself whether the Dutch have any tricks to keep their ships from being all worm-eaten in their voyages to the Indies.  Whether pendulum clocks do any service in finding out the longitude, &c.

"I am very weary, and shall not stay to part with a long compliment, only I wish you a good journey, and God be with you.

"Is. NEWTON.

"Pray let us hear from you in your travels.  I have given your two books to Dr. Arrowsmith."

---

## No. II.

*(Referred to in page 118.)*

As Newton's Hypothesis "touching his Theory of Light and Colours," which he communicated to the Royal Society on the 9th December 1675, and which he afterwards illustrated and extended in his celebrated letter to Robert Boyle in 1679, is very little known, and must ever be referred to in the History of Optical Discovery, we have reprinted these two interesting documents :—

AN HYPOTHESIS[1] EXPLAINING THE PROPERTIES OF LIGHT DISCOURSED OF IN MY SEVERAL PAPERS.

"SIR,—In my answer to Mr. Hook, you may remember I had occasion to say something of hypotheses, where I gave a reason why all allowable hypotheses in their genuine constitution should be conformable to my theories, and said of Mr. Hook's hypothesis, that I took the most free and natural application of it to phænomena to be this :—'That the agitated parts of bodies, according to their several sizes, figure, and motions, do excite vibrations in the æther of various depths or bignesses, which being promiscuously propagated through that medium to our eyes, effect in us a sensation of light of a white colour ; but if by any means those of unequal bignesses be separated from one another, the largest beget a sensation of a red colour, the least or shortest of a deep violet, and the intermediate ones of intermediate colours, much after the manner that bodies, according to their several sizes, shapes, and motions excite vibrations in the air of various bignesses, which, according to those bignesses, make several tones in sound, &c.  I was glad to understand, as I apprehended from Mr. Hook's discourse at my last being at one of your assemblies, that he had changed his former notion of all colours being compounded of only two

1 In a letter to Oldenburg, dated January 25, 1675-76.

original ones, made by the two sides of an oblique pulse, and accommodated his hypothesis to this my suggestion of colours, like sounds, being various, according to the various bigness of the pulses. For this I take to be a more plausible hypothesis than any other described by former authors ; because I see not how the colours of thin transparent plates, or skins, can be handsomely explained without having recourse to ætherial pulses. But yet I like another hypothesis better, which I had occasion to hint something of in the same letter in these words :—' The hypothesis of light's being a body, had I propounded it, has a much greater affinity with the objector's own hypothesis than he seems to be aware of, the vibrations of the æther being as useful and necessary in this as in his. For assuming the rays of light to be small bodies emitted every way from shining substances, those, when they impinge on any refracting or reflecting superficies, must as necessarily excite vibrations in the æther as stones do in water when thrown into it. And supposing these vibrations to be of several depths or thicknesses, accordingly as they are excited by the said corpuscular rays of various sizes and velocities, of what use they will be for explicating the manner of reflexion and refraction, the production of heat by the sunbeams, the emission of light from burning, putrifying, or other substances whose parts are vehemently agitated, the phænomena of thin transparent plates and bubbles, and of all natural bodies, the manner of vision, and the difference of colours, as also their harmony and discord, I shall leave to their consideration who may think it worth their endeavour to apply this hypothesis to the solution of phænomena.' Were I to assume an hypothesis, it should be this, if propounded more generally so as not to determine what light is, further than that it is something or other capable of exciting vibrations in the æther ; for thus it will become so general and comprehensive of other hypotheses as to leave little room for new ones to be invented ; and therefore because I have observed the heads of some great virtuosos to run much upon hypotheses, as if my discourses wanted an hypothesis to explain them by, and found that some, when I could not make them take my meaning when I spake of the nature of light and colours abstractedly, have readily apprehended it when I illustrated my discourse by an hypothesis ; for this reason I have here thought fit to send you a description of the circumstances of this hypothesis, as much tending to the illustration of the papers I herewith send you ; and though I shall not assume either this or any other hypothesis, not thinking it necessary to concern myself whether the properties of light discovered by me be explained by this, or Mr. Hook's, or any other hypothesis capable of explaining them ; yet while I am describing this, I shall sometimes, to avoid circumlocution and to represent it more conveniently, speak of it as if I assumed it and propounded it to be believed. This I thought fit to express, that no man may confound this with my other discourses, or measure the certainty of one by the other, or think me obliged to answer objections against this script ; for I desire to decline being involved in such troublesome, insignificant disputes.

"But to proceed to the hypothesis :—1. It is to be supposed therein, that there is an ætherial medium, much of the same constitution with air, but far rarer, subtiler, and more strongly elastic. Of the existence of this medium, the motion of a pendulum in a glass exhausted of air almost as quickly as in the open air is no inconsiderable argument. But it is not to be supposed that this medium is one uniform matter, but composed partly of the main phlegmatic body of æther, partly of other various ætherial spirits, much after the manner that air is compounded of the phlegmatic body of air intermixed with various vapours and exhalations. For the electric and magnetic effluvia, and the gravitating principle, seem to argue such variety. Perhaps the whole frame of nature may be nothing but various contextures of some certain ætherial spirits or vapours, condensed as it were by precipitation, much after the manner that vapours are condensed into water, or exhalations into grosser substances, though not so easily condensable ; and after condensation wrought into various forms, at first by the immediate hand of the Creator, and ever since by the power of nature, which, by virtue of the command, increase and multiply, became a complete imitator of the copy set her by the Protoplast. Thus perhaps may all things be originated from æther.

" At least the electric effluvia seem to instruct us that there is something of an ætherial nature condensed in bodies. I have sometimes laid upon a table a round piece of glass about two inches broad, set in a brass ring, so that the glass might be about one-eighth or one-sixth of an inch from the table, and the air between them inclosed on all sides by the ring, after the manner as if I had whelmed a little sieve upon the table. And then rubbing a pretty while the glass briskly with some rough and raking stuff, till some very little fragments of very thin paper laid on the table under the glass began to be attracted and move nimbly too and fro ; after I had done rubbing the glass, the papers would continue a pretty while in various motions, sometimes leaping up to the glass and resting there a while, then leaping down and resting there, then leaping up, and perhaps down and up again, and this sometimes in lines seeming perpendicular to the table, sometimes in oblique ones ; sometimes also they would leap up in one arch and down in another divers times together, without sensible resting between ; sometimes skip in a bow from one part of the glass to another without touching the table, and sometimes hang by a corner and turn often about very nimbly, as if they had been carried about in the midst of a whirlwind, and be otherwise variously moved,—every paper with a divers motion. And upon sliding my finger on the upper side of the glass, though neither the glass nor the enclosed air below were moved thereby, yet would the papers as they hang under the glass receive some new motion, inclining this way or that way, accordingly as I moved my finger. Now whence all these irregular motions should spring I cannot imagine, unless from some kind of subtile matter lying condensed in the glass, and rarefied by rubbing, as water is rarefied into vapour by heat, and in that rarefaction diffused through the space round the glass to a great distance, and made to move and circulate variously, and accordingly to actuate the papers, till it returns into the glass again, and be recondensed there. And as this condensed matter by rarefaction into an ætherial wind (for by its easy penetrating and circulating through glass I esteem it ætherial) may cause these odd motions, and by condensing again may cause electrical attraction with its returning to the glass to succeed in the place of what is there continually recondensed ; so may the gravitating attraction of the earth be caused by the continual condensation of some other such like ætherial spirit, not of the main body of phlegmatic æther, but of something very thinly and subtilely diffused through it, perhaps of an unctuous, or gummy

tenacious and springy nature ; and bearing much the same relation to
æther which the vital aërial spirit requisite for the conservation of flame
and vital motions does to air. For if such an ætherial spirit may be condensed in fermenting or burning bodies, or otherwise coagulated in the
pores of the earth and water into some kind of humid active matter for the
continual uses of nature (adhering to the sides of those pores after 'the
manner that vapours condense on the sides of a vessel), the vast body of
the earth, which may be everywhere to the very centre in perpetual working, may continually condense so much of this spirit as to cause it from
above to descend with greater celerity for a supply : in which descent it
may bear down with it the bodies it pervades with force proportional to
the superficies of all their parts it acts upon, nature making a circulation
by the slow ascent of as much matter out of the bowels of the earth in an
aërial form, which for a time constitutes the atmosphere, but being continually buoyed up by the new air, exhalations, and vapours rising under-
neath, at length (some part of the vapours which return in rain excepted)
vanishes again into the ætherial spaces, and there perhaps in time relents
and is attenuated into its first principle. For nature is a perpetual circula-
tory worker, generating fluids out of solids, and solids out of fluids, fixed
things out of volatile, and volatile out of fixed, subtile out of gross, and
gross out of subtile, some things to ascend and make the upper terrestrial
juices, rivers, and the atmosphere, and by consequence others to descend
for a requital to the former. And as the earth, so perhaps may the sun
imbibe this spirit copiously, to conserve his shining, and keep the planets
from receding further from him ; and they that will may also suppose that
this spirit affords or carries with it thither the solary fuel and material
principle of light, and that the vast ætherial spaces between us and the
stars are for a sufficient repository for this food of the sun and planets.
But this of the constitution of ætherial natures by the bye.

" In the second place, it is to be supposed that the æther is a vibrating
medium like air, only the vibrations far more swift and minute ; those of
air made by a man's ordinary voice, succeeding one another at more than
half a foot or a foot distance, but those of æther at a less distance than the
hundred-thousandth part of an inch. And as in air the vibrations are
some larger than others, but yet all equally swift (for in a ring of bells the
sound of every tone is heard at two or three miles' distance in the same
order that the bells are struck), so I suppose the ætherial vibrations differ
in bigness, but not in swiftness. Now these vibrations, besides their use in
reflection and refraction, may be supposed the chief means by which the
parts of fermenting or putrifying substances, fluid liquors, or melted, burning, or other hot bodies, continue in motion, are shaken asunder like a
ship by waves, and dissipated into vapours, exhalations, or smoke, and
light loosed or excited in those bodies, and consequently by which a body
becomes a burning coal, and smoke flame ; and I suppose flame is nothing
but the particles of smoke turned by the access of light and heat to burning coals, little and innumerable.

" Thirdly, the air can pervade the bores of small glass pipes, but yet not
so easily as if they were wider, and therefore stands at a greater degree of
rarity than in the free aërial spaces, and at so much greater a degree of
rarity as the pipe is smaller, as is known by the rising of water in such
pipes to a much greater height than the surface of the stagnating water

into which they are dipped. So I suppose æther, though it pervades the pores of crystal, glass, water, and other natural bodies, yet it stands at a greater degree of rarity in those pores than in the free ætherial spaces, and at so much a greater degree of rarity as the pores of the body are smaller. Whence it may be that spirit of wine, for instance, though a lighter body, yet having subtler parts, and consequently smaller pores than water, is the more strongly refracting liquor. This also may be the principal cause of the cohesion of the parts of solids and fluids, of the springiness of glass and other bodies whose parts slide not one upon another in bending, and of the standing of the mercury in the Torricellian experiment, sometimes to the top of the glass, though a much greater height than twenty-nine inches. For the denser æther which surrounds these bodies must crowd and press their parts together, much after the manner that air surrounding two marbles presses them together if there be little or no air between them. Yea, and that puzzling problem, *by what means the muscles are contracted and dilated to cause animal motion, may receive greater light from hence than from any other means men have hitherto been thinking on.* For if there be any power in man to condense and dilate at will the æther that pervades the muscle, that condensation or dilatation must vary the compression of the muscle made by the ambient æther, and cause it to swell or shrink, accordingly ; for though common water will scarce shrink by compression and swell by relaxation, yet (so far as my observation reaches) spirit of wine and oil will ; and Mr. Boyle's experiment of a tadpole shrinking very much by hard compressing the water in which it swam, is an argument that animal juices do the same : and as for their various pression by the ambient æther, it is plain that that must be more or less, accordingly as there is more or less æther within to sustain and counterpoise the pressure of that without. If both æthers were equally dense, the muscle would be at liberty as if pressed by neither : if there were no æther within, the ambient would compress it with the whole force of its spring. If the æther within were twice as much dilated as that without, so as to have but half as much springiness, the ambient would have half the force of its springiness counterpoised thereby, and exercise but the other half upon the muscle ; and so in all other cases the ambient compresses the muscle by the excess of the force of its springiness above that of the springiness of the included. To vary the compression of the muscle therefore, and so to swell and shrink it, there needs nothing but to change the consistence of the included æther ; and a very little change may suffice, if the spring of æther be supposed very strong, as I take it to be many degrees stronger than that of air.

"Now for the changing the consistence of the æther, some may be ready to grant that the soul may have an immediate power over the whole æther in any part of the body, to swell or shrink it at will ; but then how depends the muscular motion on the nerves ? Others therefore may be more apt to think it done by some certain ætherial spirits included within the *dura mater*, which the soul may have power to contract or dilate at will in any muscle, and so cause it to flow thither through the nerves ; but still there is a difficulty why this force of the soul upon it does not take off the power of springiness, whereby it should sustain more or less the force of the outward æther. A third supposition may be, that the soul has a power to inspire any muscle with this spirit, by impelling it thither through the nerves; but this too has its difficulties; for it requires a for-cible intruding the spring of the æther in the muscles by pressure exerted from the parts of the brain; and it is hard to conceive how so great force can be exercised amidst so tender matter as the brain is; and besides, why does not this ætherial spirit, being subtile enough, and urged with so great force, go away through the *dura mater* and skins of the muscle, or at least so much of the other æther go out to make way for this which is crowded in? To take away these difficulties is a digression, but seeing the subject is a deserving one, I shall not stick to tell you how I think it may be done.

"First, then, I suppose there *is* such a spirit; that is, that the animal spirits are neither like the liquor, vapour, or gas, of spirits of wine; but of an ætherial nature, subtile enough to pervade the animal juices as freely as the electric, or perhaps magnetic, effluvia do glass. And to know how the coats of the brain, nerves, and muscles, may become a convenient vessel to hold so subtile a spirit, you may consider how liquors and spirits are disposed to pervade, or not pervade, things on other accounts than their subtilty; water and oil pervade wood and stone, which quicksilver does not; and quicksilver, metals, which water and oil do not; water and acid spirits pervade salts, which oil and spirit of wine do not; and oil and spirit of wine pervade sulphur, which water and acid spirits do not; so some fluids (as oil and water), though their parts are in freedom enough to mix with one another, yet by some secret principle of *unsociableness* they keep asunder; and some that are *sociable* may become *unsociable* by adding a third thing to one of them, as water to spirit of wine by dissolv-ing salt of tartar in it. The like *unsociableness* may be in ætherial natures, as perhaps between the æthers in the vortices of the sun and planets; and the reason why air stands rarer in the bores of small glass pipes, and æther in the pores of bodies, may be, not want of subtilty, but *sociable-ness;* and on this ground, if the ætherial vital spirit in a man be very *sociable* to the marrow and juices, and *unsociable* to the coats of the brain, nerves, and muscles, or to anything lodged in the pores of those coats, it may be contained thereby, notwithstanding its subtilty; especially if we suppose no great violence done to it to squeeze it out, and that it may not be altogether so subtile as the main body of æther, though subtile enough to pervade readily the animal juices, and that as any of it is spent, it is continually supplied by new spirit from the heart.

"In the next place, for knowing how this spirit may be used for animal motion, you may consider how some things unsociable are made sociable by the mediation of a third. Water, which will not dissolve copper, will do it if the copper be melted with sulphur. Aquafortis, which will not pervade gold, will do it by addition of a little sal-ammoniac or spirit of salt. Lead will not mix in melting with copper; but if a little tin, or antimony, be added, they mix readily, and part again of their own accord, if the antimony be wasted by throwing saltpetre, or otherwise. And so lead melted with silver quickly pervades and liquifies the silver in a much less heat than is required to melt the silver alone; but if they be kept in the test till that little substance that reconciled them be wasted or altered, they part again of their own accord. And in like manner the ætherial animal spirit in a man may be a mediator between the common æther, and the muscular juices, to make them mix more freely; and so by sending a little of this spirit into any muscle, though so little as to cause no sensible tension of the muscle by its own force, yet by rendering the juices more sociable to the common external æther, it may cause that æther to pervade the muscle of its own accord in a moment more freely and more copiously than it would otherwise do, and to recede again as freely, so soon as this mediator of sociableness is retracted ; whence, according to what I said above, will proceed the swelling or shrinking of the muscle, and consequently the animal motion depending thereon.

"Thus may therefore the soul, by determining this ætherial animal spirit or wind into this or that nerve, perhaps with as much ease as air is moved in open spaces, cause all the motions we see in animals ; for the making which motions strong, it is not necessary that we should suppose the æther within the muscle very much condensed, or rarefied, by this means, but only that its spring is so very great that a little alteration of its density shall cause a great alteration in the pressure. And what is said of muscular motion may be applied to the motion of the heart, only with this difference ; that the spirit is not sent thither as into other muscles, but continually generated there by the fermentation of the juices with which its flesh is replenished, and as it is generated, let out by starts into the brain, through some convenient *ductus*, to perform those motions in other muscles by inspiration, which it did in the heart by its generation. For I see not why the ferment in the heart may not raise as subtile a spirit out of its juices, to cause those motions, as rubbing does out of a glass to cause electric attraction, or burning out of fuel to penetrate glass, as Mr. Boyle has shown, and calcine by corrosion metals melted therein.[1]

"Hitherto I have been contemplating the nature of æther and ætherial substances by their effects and uses, and now I come to join therewith the consideration of light.

"In the fourth place, therefore, I suppose light is neither æther, nor its vibrating motion, but something of a different kind propagated from lucid bodies. They that will may suppose it an aggregate of various peripatetic qualities. Others may suppose it multitudes of unimaginable small and swift corpuscles of various sizes springing from shining bodies at great distances one after another, but yet without any sensible interval of time, and continually urged forward by a principle of motion, which in the beginning accelerates them, till the resistance of the ætherial medium equal the force of that principle, much after the manner that bodies let fall in water are accelerated till the resistance of the water equals the force of gravity. God, who gave animals motion beyond our understanding, is, without doubt, able to implant other principles of motions in bodies which we may understand as little. Some would readily grant this may be a spiritual one ; yet a mechanical one might be shown, did not I think it better to pass it by. But they that like not this, may suppose light any other corporeal emanation, or an impulse or motion of any other medium or ætherial spirit diffused through the main body of æther, or what else they imagine proper for this purpose. To avoid dispute, and make this hypothesis general, let every man here take his fancy ; only whatever light be, I would suppose it consists of successive rays differing from one another in contingent circumstances, as bigness, force, or vigour, like as the sands on the shore, the

---

[1] Boyle's Essays of the strange subtilty, &c., of effluviums, &c., together with a discovery of the perviousness of glass to ponderable parts of flame.

waves of the sea, the faces of men, and all other natural things of the same kind differ, it being almost impossible for any sort of things to be found without some contingent variety. And further, I would suppose it diverse from the vibrations of the æther, because (besides that were it those vibrations, it ought always to verge copiously in crooked lines into the dark or quiescent medium, destroying all shadows, and to comply readily with any crooked pores or passages as sounds do) I see not how any superficies (as the side of a glass prism on which the rays within are incident at an angle of about forty degrees) can be totally opake. For the vibrations beating against the refracting confine of the rarer and denser æther must needs make that pliant superficies undulate, and those undulations will stir up and propagate vibrations on the other side. And further, how light, incident on very thin skins or plates of any transparent body, should for many successive thicknesses of the plate in arithmetical progression, be alternately reflected and transmitted, as I find it is, puzzles me as much. For though the arithmetical progression of those thicknesses, which reflect and transmit the rays alternately, argues that it depends upon the number of vibrations between the two superficies of the plate, whether the ray shall be reflected or transmitted, yet I cannot see how the number should vary the case, be it greater or less, whole or broken, unless light be supposed something else than these vibrations. Something indeed I could fancy towards helping the two last difficulties, but nothing which I see not insufficient.

"Fifthly, it is to be supposed that light and æther mutually act upon one another, æther in refracting light, and light in warming æther, and that the densest æther acts most strongly. When a ray therefore moves through æther of uneven density, I suppose it most pressed, urged, or acted upon by the medium on that side towards the denser æther, and receives a continual impulse or ply from that side to recede towards the rarer, and so is accelerated if it move that way, or retarded if the contrary. On this ground, if a ray move obliquely through such an unevenly dense medium (that is, obliquely to those imaginary superficies which run through the equally dense parts of the medium, and may be called the refracting superficies), it must be incurved, as it is found to be by observation in water,[1] whose lower parts were made gradually more salt, and so more dense than the upper. And this may be the ground of all refraction and reflexion. For as the rarer air within a small glass pipe, and the denser without, are not distinguished by a mere mathematical superficies, but have air between them at the orifice of the pipe running through all intermediate degrees of density, so I suppose the refracting superficies of æther between unequally dense mediums to be not a mathematical one, but of some breadth, the æther therein at the orifices of the pores of the solid body being of all intermediate degrees of density between the rarer and the denser ætherial mediums; and the refraction I conceive to proceed from the continual incurvation of the ray all the while it is passing the physical superficies. Now if the motion of the ray be supposed in this passage to be increased or diminished in a certain proportion, according to the difference of the densities of the ætherial mediums, and the addition or detraction of the motion be reckoned in the perpendicular from the refracting superficies, as

---

[1] Mr. Hook's Micrographia where he speaks of the inflexion of rays.

it ought to be, the sines of incidence and refraction will be proportional according to what Descartes has demonstrated.

"The ray, therefore, in passing out of the rarer medium into the denser, inclines continually more and more towards parallelism with the refracting superficies; and if the different densities of the mediums be not so great, nor the incidence of the ray so oblique as to make it parallel to that superficies before it gets through, then it goes through and is refracted; but if through the aforesaid causes the ray becomes parallel to that superficies before it can get through, then it must turn back and be reflected. Thus, for instance, it may be observed in a triangular glass prism O E F, that the

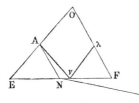

rays A N that tend out of the glass into air, do, by inclining them more to the refracting superficies, emerge more and more obliquely till they be infinitely oblique, that is, in a manner parallel to the superficies, which happens when the angle of incidence is about 40°; and then if they be a little more inclined, are all reflected, as at A ν λ, becoming, I suppose, parallel to the superficies before they can get through it.

"Let A B C D represent the rarer medium, E F H G the denser, C D F E the space between them or refracting physical superficies, in which the æther

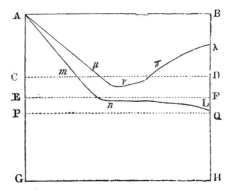

is of all intermediate degrees of density, from the rarest æther at C D to the densest at E F; A m n L a ray, A m its incident part, m n its incurvation by the refracting superficies, and n L its emergent part. Now, if the ray A m be so much incurved as to become at its emergence n, as nearly as may be, parallel to C D, it is plain that if that ray had been incident a little more obliquely, it must have become parallel to C D before it had arrived at E F, the further side of the refracting superficies, and so could have got no nearer to E F, but must have turned back by further incurvation, and been reflected as it is represented at A μ ν λ : and the like would have happened if the density of the æther had further increased from E F to P Q, so that P Q H G might be a denser medium than E F G H was supposed ; for then the ray in passing from m to n, being so much incurved as at n to become parallel to C D or P Q, it's impossible it should ever get nearer to P Q, but must at n begin by further incurvation to turn back, and so be reflected. And because if a refracted ray (as n L) be made incident, the incident (A m) shall become the refracted ; and therefore if the ray A μ ν, after it is arrived at ν, where I suppose it parallel to the refracting superficies, should be reflected perpendicularly back, it would return back in the line of incidence ν μ A ; therefore going forward, it must go forward in such another line ν π λ, both cases being alike, and so be reflected at an angle equal to that of incidence.

" This may be the cause and manner of reflexion, when light tends from the rarer towards the denser æther ; but to know how it should be reflected when it tends from the denser towards the rarer, you are farther to consider, how fluids near their superficies are less pliant and yielding than in their more inward parts, and if formed into thin plates or shells, they become much more stiff and tenacious than otherwise. Thus things which readily fall in water, if let fall upon a bubble of water, they do not easily break through it, but are apt to slide down by the sides of it, if they be not too big and heavy. So if two well-polished convex glasses, ground on very large spheres, be laid one upon the other, the air between them easily recedes till they almost touch, but then begins to resist so much that the weight of the upper glass is too little to bring them together, so as to make the black (mentioned in the papers I sent you) appear in the midst of the rings of colours. And if the glasses be plain, though no broader than a twopence, a man with his whole strength is not able to press all the air out from between them, so as to make them fully touch. You may observe also that insects will walk upon water without wetting their feet, and the water bearing them up ; also motes falling upon water will often lie long upon it without being wetted. And so I suppose æther in the confine of two mediums is less pliant and yielding than in other places, and so much the less pliant by how much the mediums differ more in density ; so that in passing out of denser æther into rarer, when there remains but a very little of the denser æther to be passed through, a ray finds more than ordinary difficulty to get through, and so great difficulty where the mediums are of a very differing density as to be reflected by incurvation after the manner described above, the parts of æther on the side where they are less pliant and yielding, acting upon the ray much after the manner that they would do were they denser there than on the other side ; for the resistance of the medium ought to have the same effect on the ray from whatsoever cause it arises. And this I suppose may be the cause of the reflexion of quicksilver and other metalline bodies. It must also concur to increase the reflective virtue of the superficies when rays tend out of the rarer medium into the denser ; and in that case therefore the reflexion having a double cause ought to be stronger than in the æther, as it is apparently. But in refraction this rigid tenacity or unpliableness of the superficies need not be considered, because so much as the ray is thereby bent in passing to the most tenacious and rigid part of the superficies, so much is it thereby unbent again in passing on from thence through the next parts gradually less tenacious.

"Thus may rays be refracted by some superficies, and reflected by others, be the medium they tend into denser or rarer. But it remains further to be explained, how rays alike incident on the same superficies (suppose of crystal, glass, or water) may be, at the same time, some refracted, others reflected ; and for explaining this, I suppose that the rays when they impinge on the rigid resisting ætherial superficies, as they are acted upon by it, so they react upon it, and cause vibrations in it, as stones thrown into water do in its surface ; and that these vibrations are propagated every way into both the rarer and denser mediums, as the vibrations of air which cause sound are from a stroke, but yet continue strongest where they began, and alternately contract and dilate the æther in that physical superficies. For it's plain by the heat which light produces in bodies that it is able to put their parts in motion, and much more to heat and put in motion the more tender æther ; and it's more probable that it communicates motion to the gross parts of bodies by the mediation of æther than immediately ; as, for instance, in the inward parts of quicksilver, tin, silver, and other very opake bodies, by generating vibrations that run through them, than by striking the outward parts only without entering the body. The shock of every single ray may generate many thousand vibrations, and by sending them all over the body, move all the parts, and that perhaps with more motion than it could move one single part by an immediate stroke ; for the vibrations, by shaking each particle backward and forward, may every time increase its motion, as a ringer does a bell by often pulling it, and so at length move the particles to a very great degree of agitation, which neither the simple shock of a ray, nor any other motion in the æther, besides a vibrating one, could do. Thus in air shut up in a vessel, the motion of its parts caused by heat, how violent soever, is unable to move the bodies hung in it with either a trembling or progressive motion ; but if air be put into a vibrating motion by beating a drum or two, it shakes glass windows, the whole body of a man, and other massy things, especially those of a congruous tone ; yea, I have observed it manifestly shake under my feet a cellared free-stone floor of a large hall ; so as I believe the immediate stroke of five hundred drum-sticks could not have done, unless perhaps quickly succeeding one another at equal intervals of time. Ætherial vibrations are therefore the best means by which such a subtile agent as light can shake the gross particles of solid bodies to heat them. And so supposing that light impinging on a refracting or reflecting ætherial superficies puts it into a vibrating motion, that physical superficies being by the perpetual appulse of rays always kept in a vibrating motion, and the æther therein continually expanded and compressed by turns ; if a ray of light impinge upon it while it is much compressed, I suppose it is then too dense and stiff to let the ray pass through, and so reflects it ; but the rays that impinge on it at other times, when it is either expanded by the interval of two vibrations, or not too much compressed and condensed, go through, and are refracted.

"These may be the causes of refractions and reflexions in all cases, but

for understanding how they come to be so regular, it's further to be considered, that, as in a heap of sand, although the surface be rugged, yet if
water be poured on it to fill its pores, the water, so soon as its pores are
filled, will evenly overspread the surface, and so much the more evenly as
the sand is finer ; so, although the surface of all bodies, even the most
polished, be rugged, as I conceive, yet when that ruggedness is not too
gross and coarse, the refracting ætherial superficies may evenly overspread
it. In polishing glass or metal, it is not to be imagined that sand, putty,
or other fretting powders should wear the surface so regularly as to make
the front of every particle exactly plane, and all those planes look the
same way, as they ought to do in well-polished bodies, were reflexion performed by their parts ; but, that those fretting powders should wear the
bodies first to a coarse ruggedness, such as is sensible, and then to a finer
and finer ruggedness, till it be so fine that the ætherial superficies evenly
overspreads it, and so makes the body put on the appearance of a polish,
is a very natural and intelligible supposition. So in fluids it is not well to
be conceived that the surfaces of their parts should be all plain, and the planes
of the superficial parts always kept looking all the same way, notwithstanding that they are in perpetual motion, and yet without these two
suppositions, the superficies of fluids could not be so regularly reflexive as
they are, were the reflexion done by the parts themselves, and not by an
ætherial superficies evenly overspreading the fluid.

" Further, considering the regular motion of light, it might be suspected
whether the various vibrations of the fluid through which it passes may
not much disturb it ; but that suspicion I suppose will vanish by considering, that if at any time the foremost part of an oblique wave begin to turn
it awry, the hindermost part by a contrary action must soon set it straight
again.

" Lastly, because without doubt there are in every transparent body
pores of various sizes, and I said that æther stands at the greatest rarity
in the smallest pores, hence the æther in every pore should be of a differing
rarity, and so light be refracted in its passage out of every pore into the
next, which would cause a great confusion, and spoil the body's transparency ; but, considering that the æther in all dense bodies is agitated by
continual vibrations, and these vibrations cannot be performed without
forcing the parts of æther forward and backward from one pore to another
by a kind of tremor, so that the æther which one moment is in a great pore
is the next moment forced into a less ; and, on the contrary, this must
evenly spread the æther into all the pores not exceeding some certain bigness, suppose the breadth of a vibration, and so make it of an even density
throughout the transparent body, agreeable to the middle sort of pores.
But where the pores exceed a certain bigness, I suppose the æther suits its
density to the bigness of the pore or to the medium within it, and so, being
of a divers density from the æther that surrounds it, refracts, or reflects
light in its superficies, and so makes the body where many such interstices
are, appear opake.

" Thus much of refraction, reflexion, transparency, and opacity ;—and
now to explain colours. I suppose that as bodies of various sizes, densities, or tensions, do by percussion or other action, excite sounds of various
tones, and consequently vibrations in the air of various bignesses ; so, when

the rays of light, by impinging on the stiff refracting superficies, excite vibrations in the æther, those rays, whatever they be, as they happen to differ in magnitude, strength, or vigour, excite vibrations of various bignesses ; the biggest, strongest, or most potent rays, the largest vibrations, and others shorter, according to their bigness, strength, or power ; and therefore the ends of the capillamenta of the optic nerve, which front or face the retina, being such refracting superficies, when the rays impinge upon them, they must there excite these vibrations ; which vibrations (like those of sound in a trumpet) will run along the aqueous pores or crystalline pith of the capillamenta, through the optic nerves into the sensorium (which light itself cannot do), and there, I suppose, affect the sense with various colours, according to their bigness and mixture : the biggest with the strongest colours, reds and yellows ; the least with the weakest, blues and violets ; the middle with green, and a confusion of all, with white ; much after the manner that in the sense of hearing nature makes use of aërial vibrations of several bignesses, to generate sounds of divers tones ; for the analogy of nature is to be observed.   And further, as the harmony and discord of sounds proceed from the proportions of the aërial vibrations, so may the harmony of some colours, as of a golden and blue, and the discord of other, as of red and blue, proceed from the proportions of the ætherial.   And possibly colour may be distinguished into its principal degrees : red, orange, yellow, green, blue, indigo, and deep violet,—on the same ground that sound within an eighth is graduated into tones.   For, some years past, the prismatic colours, being in a well-darkened room, cast perpendicularly upon a paper about two-and-twenty foot distant from the prism, I desired a friend to draw with a pencil lines across the image or pillar of·colours, where every one of the seven aforenamed colours was most full and brisk, and also where he judged the truest confines of them to be, whilst I held the paper so that the said image might fall within a certain compass marked on it.   And this I did, partly because my own eyes are not very critical in distinguishing colours, partly because another to whom I had not communicated my thoughts about this matter could have nothing but his eyes to determine his fancy in making those marks. This observation we repeated divers times, both in the same and divers days, to see how the marks on several papers would agree ; and comparing the observations, though the just confines of the colours are hard to be assigned, because they passed into one another by insensible gradation, yet the differences of the observations were but little, especially towards the red end ; and taking means between those differences that were, the length of the image (reckoned not by the distance of the verges of the semicircular ends, but by the distance of the centres of those semicircles, or length of the straight sides, as it ought to be) was divided in about the same proportion that a string is between the end and the middle to sound the tones in an eighth.  ꟼ You will understand me best by viewing the annexed figure, in which A B and C D represent the straight sides about ten inches long, A P C and B T D the semicircular ends, x and y the centres of those semicircles, x z the length of a musical string double to x y, and divided between x and y so as to sound the tones expressed at the side (that is, x H the half, x G and G I the third part, y K the fifth part, y M the eighth part, and G E the ninth part of x y) ; and the intervals between these divisions express the spaces which the colours written there took up, every colour being most briskly specific in the middle of those spaces.  Now for the cause of

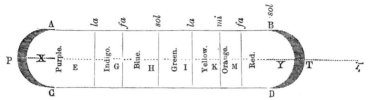

these and such like colours made by refraction, the biggest or strongest rays must penetrate the refracting superficies more freely and easier than the weaker, and so be less turned awry by it, that is less refracted ; which is as much as to say, the rays which make red are least refrangible, those which which make blue, or violet, most refrangible, and others otherwise refrangible according to their colour.  Whence if the rays which come promiscuously from the sun be refracted by a prism, as in the aforesaid experiment, those of several sorts being variously refracted, must go to several places on an opposite paper or wall, and so parted, exhibit every one their own colours, which they could not do while blended together.  And because refraction only severs them, and changes not the bigness or strength of the ray, thence it is, that after they are once well-severed, refraction cannot make any further changes in their colour.  On this ground may all the phænomena of refractions be understood."

### LETTER FROM NEWTON TO ROBERT BOYLE.

"HONOURED SIR,—I have so long deferred to send you my thoughts about the physical qualities we speak of, that did I not esteem myself obliged by promise, I think I should be ashamed to send them at all.  The truth is, my notions about things of this kind are so indigested, that I am not well satisfied myself in them ; and what I am not satisfied in, I can scarce esteem fit to be communicated to others ; especially in natural philosophy, where there is no end of fancying.  But because I am indebted to you, and yesterday met with a friend, Mr. Maulyverer, who told me he was going to London, and intended to give you the trouble of a visit, I could not forbear to take the opportunity of conveying this to you by him.

" It being only an explication of qualities which you desire of me, I shall set down my apprehensions in the form of suppositions as follows.  And first, I suppose that there is diffused through all places an ætherial substance, capable of contraction and dilatation, strongly elastic, and, in a word, much like air in all respects, but far more subtile.

" 2.  I suppose this æther pervades all gross bodies, but yet so as to stand rarer in their pores than in free spaces, and so much the rarer, as their pores are less ; and this I suppose (with others) to be the cause why light incident on those bodies is refracted towards the perpendicular ; why two well-polished metals cohere in a receiver exhausted of air ; why ☿ stands sometimes up to the top of a glass pipe, though much higher than thirty inches ; and one of the main causes why the parts of all bodies cohere ; also the cause of filtration, and of the rising of water in small glass pipes above the surface of the stagnating water they are dipped into ; for I suspect the æther may stand rarer, not only in the insensible pores of bodies, but even in the very sensible cavities of those pipes ; and the same principle may cause menstruums to pervade with violence the pores of the bodies they dissolve, the surrounding æther, as well as the atmosphere, pressing them together.

    " 3. I suppose the rarer æther within bodies, and the denser without them, not to be terminated in a mathematical superficies, but to grow gradually into one another ; the external æther beginning to grow rarer, and the internal to grow denser, at some little distance from the superficies of the body, and running through all intermediate degrees of density in the intermediate spaces ; and this may be the cause why light, in Grimaldo's experiment, passing by the edge of a knife, or other opake body, is turned aside, and as it were refracted, and by that refraction makes several colours. Let A B C D be a dense body, whether opake or transparent, E F G H the outside of the uniform æther, which is within it, I K L M the inside of the uniform æther, which is without it ; and conceive the æther, which is between E F G H and I K L M, to run through all intermediate degrees of density

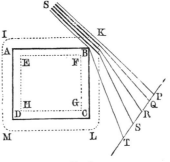

Fɪɢ. 1.

between that of the two uniform æthers on either side. This being supposed, the rays of the sun s B, s K, which pass by the edge of this body between B and K, ought in their passage through the unequally dense æther there, to receive a ply from the denser æther, which is on that side towards K, and that the more by how much they pass nearer to the body, and thereby to be scattered through the space P Q R S T, as by experience they are found to be. Now the space between the limits E F G H and I K L M, I shall call the space of the æther's graduated rarity.

    " 4. When two bodies moving towards one another come near together, I suppose the æther between them to grow rarer than before, and the spaces of its graduated rarity to extend further from the superficies of the bodies towards one another ; and this, by reason that the æther cannot move and play up and down so freely in the straight passage between the bodies, as it could before they came so near together : thus, if the space of the æther's graduated rarity reach from the body A B C D F E only to the distance G H L M R S, when no other body is near it, yet may it reach further, as to I K, when another body N O P Q approaches ; and as the other body approaches more and more, I suppose the æther between them will grow rarer and rarer. These suppositions I have so described, as if I thought the spaces of graduated æther had precise limits, as is expressed at I K L M

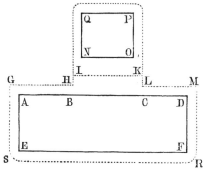

FIG. 2.

in the first figure, and G M R S in the second ; for thus I thought I could better express myself. But really I do not think they have such precise limits, but rather decay insensibly, and, in so decaying, extend to a much greater distance than can easily be believed or need be supposed.

"5. Now, from the fourth supposition it follows, that when two bodies approaching one another come so near together as to make the æther between them begin to rarefy, they will begin to have a reluctance from being brought nearer together, and an endeavour to recede from one another ; which reluctance and endeavour will increase as they come nearer together, because thereby they cause the interjacent æther to rarefy more and more. But at length, when they come so near together that the excess of pressure of the external æther which surrounds the bodies, above that of the rarefied æther, which is between them, is so great as to overcome the reluctance which the bodies have from being brought together ; then will that excess of pressure drive them with violence together, and make them adhere strongly to one another, as was said in the second supposition. For instance, in the second figure, when the bodies E D and N P are so near together that the spaces of the æther's graduated rarity begin to reach to one another, and meet in the line I K, the æther between them will have suffered much rarefaction, which rarefaction requires much force, that is, much pressing of the bodies together ; and the endeavour which the æther between them has to return to its former natural state of condensation, will cause the bodies to have an endeavour of receding from one another. But, on the other hand, to counterpoise this endeavour, there will not yet be any excess of density of the æther which surrounds the bodies, above that of the æther which is between them at the line I K. But if the bodies come nearer together, so as to make the æther in the mid-way line I K grow rarer than the surrounding æther, there will arise from the excess of density of the surrounding æther a compressure of the bodies towards one another, which, when by the nearer approach of the bodies it become so great as to overcome the aforesaid endeavour the bodies have to recede from one another, they will then go towards one another and adhere together. And, on the contrary, if any power force them asunder to that distance, where the endeavour to recede begins to over-come the endeavour to accede, they will again leap from one another. Now hence I conceive it is chiefly that a fly walks on water without wet-ting her feet, and consequently without touching the water; that two polished pieces of glass are not without pressure brought to contact, no, not though the one be plain, the other a little convex; that the particles of dust cannot by pressing be made to cohere, as they would do, if they did but fully touch; that the particles of tinging substances and salts dissolved in water do not of their own account concrete and fall to the bottom, but diffuse themselves all over the liquor, and expand still more if you add more liquor to them. Also, that the particles of vapours, ex-halations, and air do stand at a distance from one another, and endeavour to recede as far from one another as the pressure of the incumbent atmos-phere will let them; for I conceive the confused mass of vapours, air, and exhalations which we call the atmosphere, to be nothing else but the particles of all sorts of bodies, of which the earth consists, separated from one another, and kept at a distance, by the said principle.

"From these principles the action of menstruums upon bodies may be thus explained: suppose any tinging body, as cochineal or logwood be put into water; so soon as the water sinks into its pores and wets on all sides any particle which adheres to the body only by the principle in the second supposition, it takes off, or at least much diminishes, the efficacy of that principle to hold the particle to the body, because it makes the æther on all sides the particle to be of a more uniform density than before. And then the particle being shaken off by any little motion, floats in the water, and with many such others makes a tincture; which tincture will be of some lively colour, if the particles be all of the same size and density; otherwise of a dirty one. For the colours of all natural bodies whatever seem to depend on nothing but the various sizes and densities of their particles, as I think you have seen described by me more at large in another paper. If the particles be very small (as are those of salts, vitriols, and gums), they are transparent; and as they are supposed bigger and bigger, they put on these colours in order, black, white, yellow, red; violet, blue, pale green, yellow, orange, red; purple, blue, green, yellow, orange, red, &c., as it is discerned by the colours, which appear at the several thicknesses of very thin plates of transparent bodies. Whence, to know the causes of the changes of colours, which are often made by the mixtures of several liquors, it is to be considered how the particles of any tincture may have their size or density altered by the infusion of another liquor. When any metal is put into common water the water cannot enter into its pores, to act on it and dissolve it. Not that water consists of too gross parts for this purpose, but because it is unsociable to metal. For there is a certain secret principle in nature, by which liquors are sociable to some things and unsociable to others ; thus water will not mix with oil, but readily with spirit of wine, or with salts ; it sinks also into wood, which quicksilver will not ; but quicksilver sinks into metals, which, as I said, water will not. So aquafortis dissolves ☽, not ☉ ; aqua regis ☉, not ☽, &c. But a liquor, which is of itself unsociable to a body, may, by the mixture of a convenient mediator, be made sociable ; so molten lead, which alone will not mix with copper, or with regulus of Mars, by the addition of tin is made to mix with either. And water, by the mediation of saline spirits, will mix with metal. Now when any metal is put in water impregnated with such spirits, as into aquafortis, aqua regis, spirit of vitriol, or the like, the particles of the spirits, as they, in floating in the water, strike on the metal, will by their sociableness enter into its' pores and gather round its outside particles, and by advantage of the continual tremor the particles of the metals are in, hitch themselves in by degrees between those particles and the body, and loosen them from it ; and the water entering into the pores together with the saline spirits, the particles of the metal will be thereby still more loosed, so as by that motion the solution puts them into, to be easily shaken off, and made to float in the water : the saline particles still encompassing the metallic ones as a coat or shell does a kernel, after the manner expressed in the annexed figure, in which figure I have made the particles round, though they may be cubical, or of any other shape.

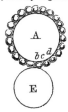

Fig. 3.

"If into a solution of metal thus made be poured a liquor abounding with particles, to which the former saline particles are more sociable than to the particles of the metal (suppose with particles of salt of tartar), then so soon as they strike on one another in the liquor, the saline particles will adhere to those more firmly than to the metalline ones, and by degrees be wrought off from those to enclose these. Suppose A a metalline particle, inclosed with saline ones of spirit of nitre, E a particle of salt of tartar, contiguous to two of the particles of spirit of nitre, b and c ; and suppose the particle E is impelled by any motion towards d, so as to roll about the particle c till it touch the particle d, the particle b adhering more firmly to E than to A, will be forced off from A ; and by the same means the particle E, as it rolls about A, will tear off the rest of the saline particles from A one after another, till it has got them all, or almost all, about itself. And when the metallic particles are thus divested of the nitrous ones, which, as a mediator between them and the water, held them floating

Fig. 4.

in it, the alcalizate ones, crowding for the room the metallic ones took up before, will press these towards one another, and make them come more easily together : so that by the motion they continually have in the water, they shall be made to strike on one another ; and then, by means of the principle in the second supposition, they will cohere and grow into clus-

ters, and fall down by their weight to the bottom, which is called precipitation. In the solution of metals, when a particle is loosing from the
body, so soon as it gets to that distance from it, where the principle of
receding described in the fourth and fifth supposition begins to overcome
the principle of acceding, described in the second supposition, the receding
of the particle will be thereby accelerated ; so that the particle shall, as it
were, with violence leap from the body, and putting the liquor into a brisk
agitation, beget and promote that heat we often find to be caused in solutions of metals. And if any particle happen to leap off thus from the
body, before it is surrounded with water, or to leap off with that smart-
ness as to get loose from the water, the water, by the principle in the
fourth and fifth suppositions, will be kept off from the particle, and stand
round about it, like a spherically hollow arch, not being able to come to
a full contact with it any more ; and several of these particles afterwards
gathering into a cluster, so as by the same principle to stand at a distance
from one another, without any water between them, will compose a bubble. Whence I suppose it is, that in brisk solutions there usually happens
an ebullition. This is one way of transmuting gross compact substance
into aërial ones. Another way is by heat ; for as fast as the motion of
heat can shake off the particles of water from the surface of it, those particles, by the said principle, will float up and down in the air, at a distance
both from one another, and from the particles of air, and make that substance we call vapour. Thus I suppose it is, when the particles of a body
are very small (as I suppose those of water are), so that the action of heat
alone may be sufficient to shake them asunder. But if the particles be
much larger, they then require the greater force of dissolving menstruums
to separate them, unless by any means the particles can be first broken
into smaller ones. For the most fixed bodies, even gold itself, some have
said, will become volatile, only by breaking their parts smaller. Thus
may the volatility and fixedness of bodies depend on the different sizes of
their parts. And on the same difference of size may depend the more or
less permanency of aërial substances, in their state of rarefaction. To

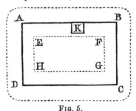

understand this, let us suppose A B C D to
be a large piece of any metal, E F G H the
limit of the interior uniform æther, and K
a part of the metal at the superficies A B.
If this part or particle K be so little that it
reaches not to the limit E F, it is plain that
the æther at its centre must be less rare
than if the particle were greater ; for
were it greater, its centre would be further
from the superficies A B, that is, in a place
where the æther (by supposition) is rarer ;

the less the particle K therefore, the denser
the æther at its centre ; because its centre comes nearer to the edge A B,
where the æther is denser than within the limit E F G H. And if the particle were divided from the body, and removed to a distance from it, where
the æther is still denser, the æther within it must proportionally grow
denser. If you consider this, you may apprehend how, by diminishing the
particle, the rarity of the æther within it will be diminished, till between
the density of the æther without, and the density of the æther within it,

there be little difference ; that is, till the cause be almost taken away, which should keep this and other such particles at a distance from one another.   For that cause explained in the fourth and fifth suppositions, was the excess of density of the external æther above that of the internal. This may be the reason then why the small particles of vapours easily come together, and are reduced back into water, unless the heat, which keeps them in agitation, be so great as to dissipate them as fast as they come together ; but the grosser particles of exhalations raised by fermentation keep their aërial form more obstinately, because the æther within them is rarer.

"Nor does the size only, but the density of the particles also, conduce to the permanency of aërial substances ; for the excess of density of the æther without such particles above that of the æther within them is still greater ; which has made me sometimes think that the true permanent air may be of a metallic original ; the particles of no substances being more dense than those of metals.   This, I think, is also favoured by experience, for I remember I once read in the Philosophical Transactions, how M. Huygens at Paris, found that the air made by dissolving salt of tartar would in two or three days' time condense and fall down again, but the air made by dissolving a metal continued without condensing or relenting in the least.   If you consider then, how by the continual fermentations made in the bowels of the earth there are aërial substances raised out of all kinds of bodies, all which together make the atmosphere, and that of all these the metallic are the most permanent, you will not perhaps think it absurd, that the most permanent part of the atmosphere, which is the true air, should be constituted of these, especially since they are the heaviest of all other, and so must subside to the lower parts of the atmosphere and float upon the surface of the earth, and buoy up the lighter exhalations and vapours to float in greatest plenty above them.   Thus, I say, it ought to be with the metallic exhalations raised in the bowels of the earth by the action of acid menstruums, and thus it is with the true permanent air ; for this, as in reason it ought to be esteemed the most ponderous part of the atmosphere, because the lowest, so it betrays its ponderosity by making vapours ascend readily in it, by sustaining mists and clouds of snow, and by buoying up gross and ponderous smoke.   The air also is the most gross unactive part of the atmosphere, affording living things no nourishment, if deprived of the more tender exhalations and spirits that float in it ; and what more unactive and remote from nourishment than metallic bodies ?

"I shall set down one conjecture more, which came into my mind now as I was writing this letter ; it is about the cause of gravity.   For this end I will suppose æther to consist of parts differing from one another in *subtilty* by indefinite degrees ; that in the pores of bodies there is less of the grosser æther, in proportion to the finer, than in open spaces ; and consequently, that in the great body of the earth there is much less of the grosser æther, in proportion to the finer, than in the regions of the air ; and that yet the grosser æther in the air affects the upper regions of the earth ; and the finer æther in the earth the lower regions of the air, in such a manner, that from the top of the air to the surface of the earth, and again from the surface of the earth to the centre thereof, the æther is insensibly finer and finer.   Imagine now any body suspended in the air, or lying on the earth, and the æther being by the hypothesis grosser in the pores, which are in the upper parts of the body, than in those which are in its lower parts, and that grosser æther being less apt to be lodged in those pores than the finer æther below, it will endeavour to get out and give way to the finer æther below, which cannot be, without the bodies descending to make room above for it to go out into.

" From this supposed gradual subtilty of the parts of æther some things above might be further illustrated and made more intelligible ; but by what has been said, you will easily discern whether in these conjectures there be any degree of probability, which is all I am at.   For my own part, I have so little fancy to things of this nature, that had not your encouragement moved me to it, I should never, I think, have thus far set pen to paper about them.   What is amiss, therefore, I hope you will the more easily pardon in

" Your most humble servant and honourer,
" ISAAC NEWTON.

" CAMBRIDGE, *Feb.* 28, 1678-9."

---

# No. III.

### (*Referred to in page* 190.)

THE following is an accurate copy of the large drawing of a sheep's eye, as mentioned in the text, and of the manuscript which accompanied it.

"1. Ellipsis A X T Y talis est ut parallel. (ad medium inter vitrum et aquam medium refractos projiciat in Z).

2. S Z est fere ⅓ A S.

3. Retinæ superficies plano      duplo      magis      quam superficies utravis crystallini.

4. Crystallini superficies anterior posteriore plenius est.

5. Convexitatis corneæ et araneæ fere commune centrum est  .  .  .  .

6. Centrum anterioris araneæ istis aliquanto inferior habetur.   2 R Z est ¼ A R.

A T : X Y : : 25 : 18 (: : 7 : 5 proxime.)

E R : $\pi \xi$ : : 83 : 101 (: : 23 : 28 : : 9 : 11 pr.)

F R : $\zeta \theta$ : : 9 : 8.

A R : $\xi \pi$ : : 13 : 12.[1]

A T : E B.

A E : E B.

A B : A R.

R S : A R.

I commune centrum curvaturæ tunicarum ad A, B, et R.

I A : I R : : 13 : 21.

I B : I R : : 19 : 36 (: : 1 : 2 fere.)

F P : $\zeta \theta$.

---

[1] This is obviously a mistake.

F P : O C.
F O : V W.
F O : O H.
F H : H O.

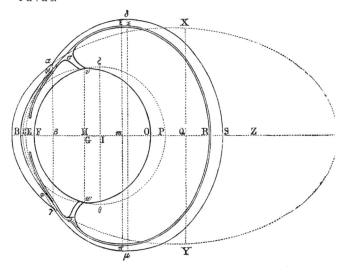

The dimensions of this figure, taken from a sheep's eye, are as followeth :—

*By Experiment.*

A S =   975.
$\mu\,\delta$ = 1025.
A B =    52.
R S =    60.
$\epsilon\,\delta$ =    16.
$a\,\gamma$ =   686.
A $\beta$ =   196.
F O =   429.
$v\,w$ =   530.
H O =   248.
The angle F $v$ O about 160 degrees.
$v$ O $w$ is a circle whose radius is G O = 265; and I A = 350, I B = 298,
    I R = 565, and I F = 307, are the radii of spheres so much concave or convex as the surfaces of the horny tunic $a$ A $\gamma$, $\omega$ B $\phi$, of the retina $\xi$ R $\pi$,

and of the exterior aranea $v$ F $w$, at their vertices A, B, R, F.   Lastly,
A $a\,\sigma$ = 968 = arcui A $\gamma\,\tau$.

### *By Deduction.*

A T = 1350 = 2 A Q, and X Y = 972.
E R =   816 = 2 $m$ R, and $\mu\,\delta$ = 993.
E P =   481 = 2 F K, and $\zeta\,\theta$ = 542.
And A Z = 1143.   The said lines A T, X Y, E R, &c., being the right and transverse axes of the ellipses A $a$ X $\tau$ Y $\gamma$, E $\xi$ R $\pi$, and F $\zeta$ P $\omega$, and Z the exterior focus of A $a\,\tau\,\gamma$.

I was prevented by an accident from taking the distance of the crystalline humour from the horny tunic, which I would gladly have done to have had the conformity of all the parts one to another in one and the same eye ; but by all circumstances 'tis near the truth' to make A H = 340, or A F = 159.   I have made the same centre I to both the horny and network tunic, they happening to be very near together.   But I am apt to suspect that it is somewhat too remote from the cornea by reason of the difficulty of measuring the least convexity of the cornea, or the greatest convexity of the retina.   Perhaps it may not be amiss to make I A = 344, I R = 571, and the point H (since it is so near it) coincident with I."

---

## No. IV.

### *(Referred to in page 192.)*

#### LETTER FROM NEWTON TO DR. WILLIAM BRIGGS.[1]

"For his Hon$^d$ ffriend D$^r$ W$^m$ BRIGGS.

"S$^r$

"Though I am of all men grown y$^e$ most shy of setting pen to paper about any thing that may lead into disputes yet yo$^r$ friendship overcomes me so far as y$^t$ I shall set down my suspicions about yo$^r$ Theory, yet on this condition, that if I can write but plain enough to make you understand me, I may leave all to yo$^r$ use w$^{th}$out pressing it further on.   For I designe not to confute or convince you but only to present & submit my thoughts to yo$^r$ consideration & judgment.

"First then it seems not necessary that the bending of y$^e$ nerves in y$^e$ Thalamus opticus should cause a differing tension of y$^e$ ffibres.   ffor those w$^{ch}$ have y$^e$ further way about, will be apt by nature to grow the longer. If y$^e$ arm of a tree be grown bent it follows not that the fibres on y$^e$ elbow are more stretcht then those on the concave side, but that they are longer. And if a straight arm of a tree be bent by force for some time, the fibres on y$^e$ elbow w$^{ch}$ were at first on y$^e$ stretch will by degrees grow longer &

¹ Edleston's *Correspondence*, &c., p. 265.

longer till at length the arm stand of it's self in y$^e$ bended figure it was at first by force put into, that is till y$^e$ fibres on y$^e$ elbow be grown as much longer then y$^e$ rest as they go further about, & so have but the same degree of tension w$^{th}$ them.  The observation is ordinary in twisted Codling hedges, fruit trees nailed up against a wall &c.  And y$^e$ younger & more tender a tree is the sooner will it stand bent.  How much more therefore ought it to be so in that most tender substance of y$^e$ Optick nerves w$^{ch}$ grew bent from y$^e$ very beginning?  And whether if those nerves were carefully cut out of y$^e$ brain & outward coat & put into brine made as neare as could be of the same specific gravity w$^{th}$ y$^e$ nerves, they would unbend or exactly keep the same bent they had in y$^e$ brain may be worth considering.  ffor though y$^e$ strength of a single fibre upon the stretch be inconsiderably little, yet all together ought to have as much strength to unbend y$^e$ nerve, as would suffice by outward application of y$^e$ hand to bend a straight nerve of y$^e$ same thickness, the dura Mater being taken off.

"M$^r$ Sheldrake further suggests wittily that an object whether the axis opticus be directed above it, under it, or directly towards it, appears in all cases alike as to figure & colour excepting that in y$^e$ 3$^d$ case tis distincter, w$^{ch}$ proceeds not from y$^e$ frame of y$^e$ nerves but from y$^e$ distinctness of y$^e$ picture made in y$^e$ Retina in that case.  But in y$^e$ first case where y$^e$ vision is made by y$^e$ fibres above & second where tis made by those below, the object appearing alike : he thinks it argues that the fibres above & below are of y$^e$ same constitution & tension, or at least if they be of a differing tension, that that tension has no effect on y$^e$ mode of vision, but I understand you are already made acquainted w$^{th}$ his thoughts.

"It may be further considered that the cause of an objects appearing one to both eyes is not its appearing of y$^e$ same colour form & bigness to both, but in y$^e$ same situation or place.  Distort one eye & you will see y$^e$ coincident images of y$^e$ object divide from one another & one of them remove from y$^e$ other upwards downwards or sideways to a greater or less distance according as y$^e$ distortion is ; & when the eyes are let return to their natural posture the two images advance towards one another till they become coincident & by that coincidence appear but one.  If we would then know why they appear but one, we must e[n]quire why they appear in one & y$^e$ same place & if we would know y$^e$ cause of that we must enquire why in other cases they appear in divers places variously situate & distant one from another.  ffor that w$^{ch}$ can make their distance greater or less can make it none at all.  Consider whats the cause of their being in y$^e$ same altitude when one is directly to y$^e$ right hand y$^e$ other to y$^e$ left & what of their being in y$^e$ same coast or point of y$^e$ compas, when one is directly over y$^e$ other : these two causes joyned will make them in y$^e$ same altitude & coast at once that is in y$^e$ same place.  The cause of situations is therefore to be enquired into.  Now for finding out this y$^e$ analogy will stand between y$^e$ situations of sounds & the situations of visible things, if we will compare these two senses.  But the situations of sounds depend not on their tones.  I can judge from whence an echo or other sound comes tho I see not y$^e$ sounding body, & this judgment depends not at all on y$^e$ tone.  I judge it not from east because acute, from west because grave : but be y$^e$ tone what it will I judge it from hence or thence by some other principle.  And by that principle I am apt to think a blind man may distinguish unisons one from another when y$^e$ one is on his right hand y$^e$

other on his left.   And were our ears as good & accurate at distinguishing y$^e$ coasts of audibles as our eyes are at distinguishing y$^e$ coasts of visibles I conceive we should judge no two sounds the same for being unisons unless they came so exactly from y$^e$ same coast as not to vary from one another a sensible point in situation to any side.   Suppose then you had to do with one of so accurate an ear in distinguishing y$^e$ situation of sounds.  how would you deale with him?   Would you tell him that you heard all unisons as but one sound?   He would tell you he had a better ear than so.   He accounted no sounds y$^e$ same w$^{ch}$ differed in situation : & if your eyes were no better at y$^e$ situation of things then your ears, you would perhaps think all objects y$^e$ same, w$^{ch}$ were of y$^e$ same colour.   But for his part he found y$^t$ y$^e$ like tension of strings & other sounding bodies did not make sounds one, but only of y$^e$ same tone : & therefore not allowing the supposition that it does make them one, the inference from thence that y$^e$ like tension of y$^e$ optick fibres made y$^e$ object to y$^e$ two eyes appeare one, he did not think himself obliged to admit.   As he found y$^t$ tones depended on those tensions so perhaps might colours, but the situation of audibles depended not on those tensions, & therefore if the two senses hold analogy with one another, that of visibles does not, & consequently the union of visibles as well as audibles which depends on the agreement of situation as well as of colour or tone must have some other cause.

"But to leave this imaginary disputant, let us now consider what may be y$^e$ cause of y$^e$ various situations of things to y$^e$ eyes.   If when we look w$^{th}$ one eye it may be asked why objects appear thus & thus situated one to another the answer would be because they are really so situated among themselves & make their coloured pictures in y$^e$ Retina so situated one to another as they are & those pictures transmit motional pictures into y$^e$ sensorium in y$^e$ same situation & by the situation of those motional pictures one to another the soul judges of y$^e$ situation of things without.   In like manner when we look with two eyes distorted so as to see y$^e$ same object double if it be asked why those objects appeare in this or that situation & distance one from another, the answer should be because through y$^e$ two eyes are transmitted into y$^e$ sensorium two motional pictures by whose situation & distance then from one another the soule judges she sees two things so situate & distant.   And if this be true then the reason why when the distortion ceases & y$^e$ eyes return to their natural posture the doubled object grows a single one is that the two motional pictures in y$^e$ sensorium come together & become coincident.

"But you will say, how is this coincidence made?   I answer, what if I know not?   Perhaps in y$^e$ sensorium, after some such way as y$^e$ Cartesians would have beleived or by some other way.   Perhaps by y$^e$ mixing of y$^e$ marrow of y$^e$ nerves in their juncture before they enter the brain, the fibres on y$^e$ right side of each eye going to y$^e$ right side of y$^e$ head those on y$^e$ left side to y$^e$ left.   If you mention y$^e$ experim$^t$ of y$^e$ nerve shrunck all y$^e$ way on one side y$^e$ head, that might be either by some unkind juyce abounding more on one side y$^e$ head y$^n$ on y$^e$ other, or by y$^e$ shrinking of y$^e$ coate of y$^e$ nerve whose fibres & vessels for nourishment perhaps do not cross in y$^e$ juncture as y$^e$ fibres of y$^e$ marrow may do.   And its more probable y$^t$ y$^e$ stubborn coate being vitiated or wanting due nourishment shrank and made y$^e$ tender marrow yeild to its capacity, than that y$^e$ tender marrow by shrinking should make yᵉ coate yeild. I know not whether you would have yᵉ succus nutricius run along yᵉ marrow. If you would, 'tis an opinion not yet proved & so not fit to ground an argument on. If you say yᵗ in yᵉ Camælion & ffishes yᵉ nerves only touch one another without mixture & sometimes do not so much as touch; 'Tis true, but makes altogether against you. ffishes looke one way with one eye yᵉ other way with yᵉ other: the Chamælion looks up wᵗʰ one eye, down wᵗʰ t'other, to yᵉ right hand wᵗʰ this, to yᵉ left wᵗʰ yᵗ, twisting his eyes severally this way or that way as he pleases. And in these Animals which do not look yᵉ same way wᵗʰ both eyes what wonder if yᵉ nerves do not joyn? To make them joyn would have been to no purpose & nature does nothing in vain. But then whilst in these animals where tis not necessary they are not joyned, in all others wᶜʰ look yᵉ same way wᵗʰ both eyes, so far as I can yet learn, they are joyned. Consider therefore for what reason they are joyned in yᵉ one & not in the other. ffor God in yᵉ frame of animals has done nothing wᵗʰout reason.

" There is one thing more comes into my mind to object. Let yᵉ circle D J represent the Retina, or if you will the end of yᵉ optick nerve cut cross. A the end of a fibre above of most tension, C yᵉ end of one below of least tension. D & G yᵉ ends of fibres above on either hand almost of as much tension as A, F & J the ends of others below almost of as little tension as C. E yᵉ end of a fibre of less tension then A or G & of more then C or. J. And between A & C, G & J there will [be] fibres of equal tension wᵗʰ E because between them there are in a continual series fibres of all degrees of tension between yᵉ most tended at A & G & least tended at C & J. And by the same argument that 3 fibres E, B & H of like tension are noted let the whole line of fibres of the same Degree of tension running from E to H be noted. Do you now say yᵗ yᵉ reason why an object seen wᵗʰ two eyes appears but one is that yᵉ fibres in yᵉ two eyes by wᶜʰ 'tis seen are unisons? then all objects seen by unison fibres must for yᵉ same reason appear in one & yᵉ same place that is all yᵉ objects seen by the line of fibres E B H running from one side of the eye to yᵉ other. ffor instance two stars one to yᵉ right hand seen by yᵉ fibres about H, the other to yᵉ left seen by yᵉ fibres about E ought to appear but one starr, & so of other objects. ffor if consonance unite objects seen wᵗʰ the fibres of two eyes much more will it unite those seen wᵗʰ those of yᵉ same eye. And yet we find it much otherwise. What soever it is that causes the two images of an object seen with both eyes to appear in yᵉ same place so as to seem but one can make them upon distorting yᵉ eyes separate one from yᵉ other & go as readily & as far asunder to yᵉ right hand & to yᵉ left as upwards & downwards.

" You have now yᵉ summ of what I can think of worth objecting set down in a tumultuary way as I could get time from my Sturbridge ffair friends. If I have any where exprest myself in a more peremptory way

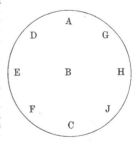

then becomes yᵉ weaknes of yᵉ argument pray look on that as done not in earnestness but for yᵉ mode of discoursing.   Whether any thing be so material as yᵗ it may prove any way useful to you I cannot tell.   But pray accept of it as written for that end.   ffor having laid Philosophical speculations aside nothing but yᵉ gratification of a friend would easily invite me to so large a scribble about things of this nature.

" Sʳ I am
" Yoʳ humble Servant

" Trin. Coll. Cambr. Sept. 12ᵗʰ. 1682.                          Is. Newton."[1]

---

## No. V.

### (*Referred to in page* 195.)

[This letter is prefixed to the Latin version of Briggs' *Theory of Vision*, Lond. 1685, which was made at Newton's request, and must have been intended as a recommendation of that work as well as of his *Ophthalmographia.*]

" Isaacus Newtonus Doctori Gulielmo Briggio.

" Vir Clarissime,
" Hisce tuis Tractatibus[2] duas magni nominis scientias uno opere promoves, *Anatomiam* dico & *Opticam.*   Organi enim (in quo utraque versatur) artificio summo constructi diligenter perscrutaris mysteria.   In hujus dissectione peritiam & dexteritatem tuam non exiguo olim mihi oblectamento fuisse recordor.   Musculis motoriis secundùm situm suum naturalem elegantèr à te expansis, cæterisque partibus coràm expositis, sic ut singularum usus & ministeria non tàm intelligere liceret quàm cernere, effeceret dudùm ut ex cultro tuo nihil non accuratum sperarem.   Nec spem fallebat eximius ille Tractatus Anatomicus, quem postmodùm edidisti.   Jam praxeos hujus ἀκρίβειαν pergis ingeniosissimâ Theoriâ instruere & exornare.   Et quis Theoriis condendis aptior extiterit, quàm qui phænomenis accuratè observandis navârit operam ?   Nervos opticos *ex capillamentis variè tensis* constare supponis, eaque magis esse tensa quæ per iter longius porriguntur ; ex diversâ autem tensione fieri ut objectorum partes singulæ non coincidant & confundantur inter se, sed pro situ suo naturali diversis in locis appareant ; & *capillamentis* amborum oculorum æquali tensione factis *concordibus*, geminas objectorum species uniri.   Sic ex tensione chordarum, quâ soni· vel variantur vel concordant in Musicâ, colligere videris quid fieri debet in Opticâ.   Simplex etenim est *Natura*, & eodem operandi tenore in immensâ

---

¹ From the original in the British Museum, Add. MSS. 4237, fol. 34.
² i.e., *Ophthalmographia*, Cantab. 1676 (2d edit. Lond. 1687), and his *Theory of Vision.*

effectuum varietate sibi ipsa constare solet.  Quantò verò magìs in sensuum cognatorum causis ?  Et quamvis aliam etiam horum sensuum analogiam suspicari possim, ingeniosam tamen esse quam tute excogitasti, certè nemo non lubentèr fatebitur.  Nec inutilem censeo Dissertationem ultimam quâ diluis objectiones.  Inde Lector attentus & pleniùs intelliget Hypothesin totam, & in quæstiones incidet vel tuis Meditationibus illustratas, vel novis experimentis & disquisitionibus posthàc dirimendas.  Id quod in usum cedet juventuti Academicæ, & provectiores ad ulteriores in Philosophiâ progressus manuducet.  Pergas itaque, vir ornatissime, scientias hascę præclaris inventis, uti facis, excolere ;  doceasque difficultates causarum naturaliam tàm facilè solertiâ vinci posse, quàm solent conatibus vulgaribus difficultèr cedere.

" Vale."

" *Dabam Cantabrigiæ* 7 *Kal. Maii.*
1685."

---

# No. VI.

*(Referred to in page* 197.)

### NEWTON'S *Fifteenth* QUERY.[1]

ARE not the species of objects seen with both eyes united where the optic nerves meet before they come into the brain, the fibres on the right side of both nerves uniting there, and, after union, going thence into the brain in the nerve which is on the right side of the heart ; and the fibres on the left side of both nerves uniting in the same place, and, after union, going into the brain in the nerve which is on the left side of the head, and these two nerves meeting in the brain, in such a manner that their fibres make but one entire species or picture, half of which on the right side of the sensorium, comes from the right side of both eyes through the right side of both optic nerves, to the place where the nerves meet, and from thence on the right side of the head into the brain ; and the other half on the left side of the sensorium comes in like manner from the left side of both eyes.  For the optic nerves of such animals as look the same way with both eyes (as of men, dogs, sheep, oxen, &c.), meet before they come into the brain, but the optic nerves of such animals as do not look the same way with both eyes (as of fishes and of the chameleon) do not meet, if I am rightly informed.

---

# No. VII.

*(Referred to in page* 197.)

ALTHOUGH we have extracted a part of this document in the text, for the sake of illustration, we shall give the whole of it as published by Mr. Harris.

[1] *Optics*, 3d edit. 1721, pp. 320, 321.

DESCRIPTION OF THE OPTIC NERVES AND THEIR JUNCTURE IN THE
BRAIN, BY SIR ISAAC NEWTON.[1]

"The *tunic retina* grows not from the sides of the optic nerve (as the
other two which rise one from the *dura,* the other from the *pia mater*), but
it grows from the middle of the nerve, sticking to it all over the extremity
of its marrow. Which marrow, if the nerve be any where cut cross-wise
betwixt the eye and the union of the nerves, appears full of small spots or
pimples, which are a little prominent, especially if the nerve be pressed, or
warmed at a candle ; and these shoot into the very eye, and may be seen
within side, where the retina grows to the nerve ; and they also continue
to the very juncture E F G H. But at the juncture they end on a sudden
into a more tender white pap, like the anterior part of the brain ; and so
the nerve continues after the juncture into the brain filled with a white
tender pap, in which can be seen no distinction of parts as betwixt the
said juncture and the eye.

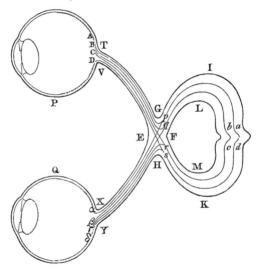

" Now I conceive that every point in the retina of one eye, hath its correspondent point in the other ; from which two very slender pipes filled
with a most limpid liquor do, without either interruption or any other unevenness or irregularity in their process, go along the optic nerves to the

1 The original of this drawing and description I found at Hurtzbourne Park in a
manuscript book without one of its boards, p. 17.

juncture E F G H, where they meet either betwixt G F or F H, and there unite into one pipe as big as both of them ; and so continue in one, passing either betwixt I L or M K, into the brain, where they are terminated perhaps at the next meeting of the nerves betwixt the *cerebrum* and *cerebellum*, in the same order that their extremities were situated in the retina's. And so there are a vast multitude of these slender pipes which flow from the brain, the one half through the right side nerve I L, till they come at the juncture G F, where they are each divided into two branches, the one passing by G and T to the right side of the right eye A B, the other half shooting through the space E F, and so passing by X to the right side of the left eye α β. And in like manner the other half shooting through the left side nerve M K, divide themselves at F H, and their branches passing by E V to the right eye, and by H Y to the left, compose that half of the retina in both eyes, which is towards the left side C D and γ δ.

"Hence it appears, 1. Why the two images of both eyes make but one image *a b c d* in the brain.

"2. Why, when one eye is distorted, objects appear double ; for if the image of any object be made upon A in the one eye, and β in the other, that object shall have two images in the brain at *a* and *b*. Therefore the pictures of any object ought to be made upon the corresponding points of the two retinas ; if upon A in the right eye, then upon *a* in the left ; if upon B, then also upon β. And so shall the motions concur after they have passed the juncture G H, and make one image at *a* or *b* more vivid than one eye alone could do.

"3. Why, though one thing may appear in two places by distorting the eyes, yet two things cannot appear in one place. If the picture of one thing fall upon A, and of another upon *a*, they may both proceed to *p*, but no farther ; they cannot both be carried on the same pipes *p a* into the brain ; that which is strongest or most helped by phantasy will there prevail, and blot out the other.

"4. Why, if one of the branches of the nerve beyond the juncture, as at G F or F H, should be cut, that half of both eyes towards the wounded nerve would be blind, the other half remaining perfect.

"5. Why the juncture is almost as broad again betwixt G and H, as between E and F ; because all the tubuli of both eyes pass between G and H, and but half of them betwixt E and F.

"6. Why the nerve G I L F buts not directly upon the nerve X E H Y, but deviates a little towards T V ; because its tubuli are to pass only into that side of the nerve E H X Y towards E X. The like of F M K H.

"7. Why the marrow of the nerve T V E G grows soft on a sudden, when it comes at the juncture E F, and more suddenly on that side towards G than towards E. And the like of the nerve E X Y H : For it being necessary that the nerve T V E G should be stretched and bended several ways by the motion of the eye ; therefore the tubuli are involved or wrought up within the substances of several tough skins, which, being folded up together, compose the marrow of the nerve pretty solid and flexible, lest the tubuli should be prejudiced by the several motions of the nerve. And those small pimples or prominencies which appear in the nerve cut crosswise, I conceive to be made by the foldings of those crasser skins. But the nerve at the juncture E G F H, being well guarded from all violence and motion by the bones into which it is closely adapted ; 'tis not necessary the said membraneous substance should be continued any farther than E G ; therefore the tubuli there on a sudden unsheath themselves, that those on the inner side of the nerves towards V E and X E may severally cross 'twixt E F, and be united with their correspondents on the other sides Y H and T G. Now, because the inner tubuli must first cross, before they can concur with the outmost tubuli of the opposite nerve ; hence it is, that the nerves grow soft sooner on the inner side at E, than on the outer side at G and H.

" 8. Why the two nerves meet a second time in the brain : because the two half images carried along I L and M K may be united in one compleat image, in the sensory.   *Note,* that the nerves at their meeting, are round about disjoined from the rest of the brain ; nor are they so thick there, as a little before their meeting.   But by their external figure, they seem as if the *capillamenta* concentered like the radii of a hemisphere to a point in the lower part of the juncture.   And 'tis probable that the visive faculty is there : for else why do the nerves swell there to so great a bulk, as it were preparing for their last office ?   Why do they run directly cross from either side the brain to meet there, if the design was to have the motions conveyed by the shortest cut from the eye to the sensorium, before they grew too weak.   If they were to proceed farther, they might have gone a shorter cut, and in a less channel.   There is indeed a marrow shoots from under them towards the *cerebellum,* to which they are united ; but the greatest part of their substance, if not all of it, lies above this marrow, and also shoots cross beyond it to the centre of the brain, where they meet. Lastly, the substance here is most pure, the situation in the midst of the brain, constituting the upper part of that small passage 'twixt all the ventricles, where all superfluous humours have the greatest advantage to slide away, that they may not incumber that precious organ.

" Light seldom strikes upon the parts of gross bodies (as may be seen in its passing through them) ; its reflection and refraction is made by the diversity of æthers ; and therefore its effect upon the retina can only be to make this vibrate : which motion then must be either carried in the optic nerves to the sensorium, or produce other motions that are carried thither. Not the latter, for water is too gross for such subtile impressions ; and as for animal spirits, tho' I tied a piece of the optic nerve at one end, and warmed it in the middle, to see if any airy substance by that means would disclose itself in bubbles at the other end, I could not spy the least bubble ; a little moisture only, and the marrow itself squeezed out.   And indeed they that know how difficultly air enters small pores of bodies, have reason to suspect that an airy body, tho' much finer than air, can pervade and without violence (as it ought to do) the small pores of the brain and nerves, I should say of water ; because those pores are filled with water : and if it could, it would be too subtile to be imprisoned by the *dura mater* and skull, and might pass for *æther.*   However, what need of such spirits ? Much motion is ever lost by communication, especially betwixt bodies of different constitutions.   And therefore it can no way be conveyed to the sensorium so entirely, as by the æther itself.   Nay, granting me, but that there are pipes filled with a pure transparent liquor passing from the eye to the sensorium, and the vibrating motion of the æther will of necessity run along thither.   For nothing interrupts that motion but reflecting surfaces ; and therefore also that motion cannot stray through the reflecting surfaces of the pipe, but must run along (like a sound in a trunk) entire to the sensorium.   And that vision thus made, is very conformable to the sense of hearing, which is made by like vibrations."

# No. VIII.

(*Referred to in page* 269, *as* No. IX.)

THE interesting correspondence between Halley and Newton, consisting of fifteen letters, which, with the exception of one given in Chap. XVI., Vol. II., we give in this Appendix, forms an essential part of the History of the Principia, and throws much light on the personal character of Newton. The *eight* letters, Nos. 1, 3, 4, 5, 6, 8, 10, and 11, having been preserved in the archives of the Royal Society, were published in their entire state by my late amiable and learned friend, Professor Rigaud of Oxford, in the *Appendix* to his interesting volume, entitled *Historical Essay on the First Publication of the Principia.*[1] The greater number of them had been printed in a garbled and imperfect state by the authors of the articles HALLEY, HOOKE, and NEWTON, in the *General Dictionary* and in the *Biographia Britannica,* and therefore Mr. Rigaud had them carefully copied from the guard-book of the Royal Society. At the end of each letter he has mentioned the parts that have been omitted, and the changes that have been made upon it in the different works where it has been used. We have adopted these important notes of Mr. Rigaud.

The other *six* letters, Nos. 2, 7, 9, 12, 13, and 14, which, with the one already referred to, complete the correspondence, were. found among the Newtonian papers in the possession of the Earl of Portsmouth, and are now printed for the first time.

## 1.—HALLEY TO NEWTON.

" *May* 22, 1686.

" SIR,

" Your incomparable treatise, entitled Philosophiæ Naturalis Principia Mathematica, was by Dr. Vincent presented to the Royal Society on the 28th past ; and they were so very sensible of the great honour you do them by your dedication, that they immediately ordered you their most hearty thanks, and that a council should be summoned to consider about the printing thereof ; but by reason of the president's attendance upon the King, and the absence of our vice-presidents, whom the good weather has drawn out of town, there has not since been any authentic council to resolve what to do in the matter : so that on Wednesday last the Society, in their meeting, judging that so excellent a work ought not to have its publication any longer delayed, resolved to print it at their own charge in a large quarto of a fair letter ; and that this their resolution should be signified to you, and your opinion therein be desired, that so it might be gone about with all speed. I am intrusted to look after the printing it, and will take care that it shall be performed as well as possible ; only I would first have your directions in what you shall think necessary for the embellishing thereof, and particularly whether you think it not better that the schemes

[1] Oxford, 1838.

should be enlarged, which is the opinion of some here : but what you signify as your desire shall be punctually observed.

"There is one thing more that I ought to inform you of, viz., that Mr. Hooke has some pretensions upon the invention of the rule of the decrease of gravity being reciprocally as the squares of the distances from the centre. He says you had the notion from him, though he owns the demonstration of the curves generated thereby to be wholly your own. How much of this is so, you know best, as likewise what you have to do in this matter, only Mr. Hooke seems to expect you should make some mention of him in the preface, which 'tis possible you may see reason to prefix. I must beg your pardon, that 'tis I that send you this ungrateful account; but I thought it my duty to let you know it, that so you might act accordingly, being in myself fully satisfied, that nothing but the greatest candour imaginable is to be expected from a person, who has of all men the least need to borrow reputation."

The following paragraph and conclusion of the letter, taken from the original, did not exist in any of the previously printed copies of it.

"When I shall have received your directions, the printing shall be pushed on with all expedition, which, therefore, I entreat you to send me as soon as may be. You may please to direct to me, to be left with Mr. Hunt at Gresham College, and your line will come to the hands of,

"Sir,
"Your most affectionate humble servant,
"EDM. HALLEY."

"This letter was printed from the copy in the Letter Book of the Royal Society (Supplement, vol. iv. p. 340), by Birch, in his History of the Royal Society (vol. iv. p. 484). It is also printed in the Biographia Britannica (vol. v. p. 3225)."


2.—HALLEY TO NEWTON.

"LONDON, *June* 7, 1686.

"SIR,
"I here send you a proof of the first sheet of your book, which we think to print on this paper, and in this character; if you have any objection, it shall be attended to: and if you approve it, we will proceed; and care shall be taken that it shall not be published before the end of Michaelmas term, since you desire it. I hope you will please to bestow the second part, or what remains of this, upon us as soon as you shall have finished it, for the application of this mathematical part to the system of the world, is what will render it acceptable to all naturalists, as well as mathematicians; and must advance the sale of the book. Pray, please to revise this proof, and send it me up with your answer. I have already corrected it, but cannot say I have spied all the faults. When it has passed your eye, I doubt not but it will be clear from errata. The printer begs your excuse of the diphthongs, which are of a character a little bigger, but he has some a casting of the just size. This sheet being a proof, is not so clear as it ought to be; but the letter is new, and I have seen a book of a very fair character,

which was the last thing printed from this set of letter ; so that I hope the Edition may in that particular be to your satisfaction.—I am, Sir,
                    " Your most affectionate humble servant,
                                        " E. HALLEY.

" Please to send by the coach, directed to me, to be left with Mr. Hunt, at Gresham College.

" *To his honoured Friend,*
      MR. ISAAC NEWTON,
            *at his Chamber in* TRINITY COLLEGE,
                        CAMBRIDGE."


### 3.—NEWTON TO HALLEY.

" SIR,
" In order to let you know the case between Mr. Hooke and me, I gave you an account of what passed between us in our letters, so far as I could remember ; for, 'tis long since they were writ, and I do not know that I have seen them since.  I am almost confident by circumstances, that Sir Chr. Wren knew the duplicate proportion when I gave him a visit ; and then Mr. Hooke (by his book Cometa written afterwards) will prove the last of us three that knew it.  I intended in this letter to let you understand the case fully ; but it being a frivolous business, I shall content myself to give you the heads of it in short, viz., that I never extended the duplicate proportion lower than to the superficies of the earth, and before a certain demonstration I found the last year, have suspected it did not reach accurately enough down so low ; and therefore in the doctrine of projectiles never used it nor considered the motions of the heavens ; and consequently Mr. Hooke could not from my letters, which were about projectiles and the regions descending hence to the centre, conclude me ignorant of the theory of the heavens.  That what he told me of the duplicate proportion was erroneous, namely, that it reached down from hence to .the centre of the earth.  That it is not candid to require me now to confess myself, in print, then ignorant of the duplicate proportion in the heavens ; for no other reason, but because he had told it me in the case of projectiles, and so upon mistaken grounds accused me of that ignorance. That in my answer to his first letter I refused his correspondence, told him I had laid philosophy aside, sent him only the experiment of projectiles (rather shortly hinted than carefully described), in compliment to sweeten my answer, expected to hear no further from him ; could scarce persuade myself to answer his second letter ; did not answer his third, was upon other things ; thought no further of philosophical matters than his letters put me upon it, and therefore may be allowed not to have had my thoughts of that kind about me so well at that time.  That by the same reason he concludes me then ignorant of the rest of the duplicate proportion, he may as well conclude me ignorant of the rest of that theory I had read before in his book.  That in one of my papers writ (I cannot say in what year, but I am sure some time before I had any correspondence with Mr. Oldenburg, and that's) above fifteen years ago, the proportion of the forces of

the planets from the sun, reciprocally duplicate of their distances from him, is expressed, and the proportion of our gravity to the moon's conatus recedendi a centro terræ is calculated, though not accurately enough. That when Hugenius put out his Horol. Oscil., a copy being presented to me, in my letter of thanks to him, I gave those rules in the end thereof a particular commendation for their usefulness in Philosophy, and added out of my aforesaid paper an instance of their usefulness, in comparing the forces of the moon from the earth, and earth from the sun; in determining a problem about the moon's phase, and putting a limit to the sun's parallax, which shows that I had then my eye upon comparing the forces of the planets arising from their circular motion, and understood it; so that a while after, when Mr. Hooke propounded the problem solemnly, in the end of his Attempt to prove the Motion of the Earth, if I had not known the duplicate proportion before, I could not but have found it now. Between ten and eleven years ago, there was an hypothesis of mine registered in your books, wherein I hinted a cause of gravity towards the earth, sun, and planets, with the dependence of the celestial motions thereon; in which the proportion of the decrease of gravity from the superficies of the planet (though for brevity's sake not there expressed) can be no other than reciprocally duplicate of the distance from the centre. And I hope I shall not be urged to declare, in print, that I understood not the obvious mathematical conditions of my own hypothesis. But grant I received it afterwards from Mr. Hooke, yet have I as great a right to it as to the ellipsis. For as Kepler knew the orb to be not circular but oval, and guessed it to be elliptical, so Mr. Hooke, without knowing what I have found out since his letters to me, can know no more, but that the proportion was duplicate quam proximè at great distances from the centre, and only guessed it to be so accurately, and guessed amiss in extending that proportion down to the very centre, whereas Kepler guessed right at the ellipsis. And so Mr. Hooke found less of the proportion than Kepler of the ellipsis. There is so strong an objection against the accurateness of this proportion, that without my demonstrations, to which Mr. Hooke is yet a stranger, it cannot be believed by a judicious philosopher to be any where accurate. And so, in stating this business, I do pretend to have done as much for the proportion as for the ellipsis, and to have as much right to the one from Mr. Hooke and all men, as to the other from Kepler; and therefore on this account also he must at least moderate his pretences.

" The proof you sent me I like very well. I designed the whole to consist of three books; the second was finished last summer being short, and only wants transcribing, and drawing the cuts fairly. Some new propositions I have since thought on, which I can as well let alone. The third wants the theory of comets. In autumn last I spent two months in calculations to no purpose for want of a good method, which made me afterwards return to the first book, and enlarge it with divers propositions, some relating to comets, others to other things, found out last winter. The third I now design to suppress. Philosophy is such an impertinently litigious Lady, that a man had as good be engaged in lawsuits, as have to do with her. I found it so formerly, and now I am no sooner come near her again, but she gives me warning. The two first books, without the third, will not so well bear the title of Philosophiæ Naturalis Principia Mathematica; and therefore I had altered it to this, De Motu Corporum libri duo. But, upon second thoughts, I retain the former title. 'Twill help the sale of the book, which I ought not to diminish now 'tis yours. The articles are, with the largest, to be called by that name ; if you please you may change the word to *sections*, though it be not material ; which is all at present from

" your affectionate friend,
" and humble servant,
Is. NEWTON.

" CAMBRIDGE, *June* 20, 1686.

" Since my writing this letter, I am told by one, who had it from another lately present at one of your meetings, how that Mr. Hooke should there make a great stir, pretending that I had all from him, and desiring they would see that he had justice done him. This carriage towards me is very strange and undeserved ; so that I cannot forbear, in stating the point of justice, to tell you further, that he has published Borell's hypothesis in his own name ; and the asserting of this to himself, and completing it as his own, seems to me the ground of all the stir he makes. Borell did something in it, and wrote modestly. He has done nothing, and yet written in such a way, as if he knew and had sufficiently hinted all but what remained to be determined by the drudgery of calculations and observations, excusing himself from that labour by reason of his other business, whereas he should rather have excused himself by reason of his inability. For 'tis plain, by his words, he knew not how to go about it. Now is not this very fine ? Mathematicians, that find out, settle, and do all the business, must content themselves with being nothing but dry calculators and drudges ; and another, that does nothing but pretend and grasp at all things, must carry away all the invention, as well of those that were to follow him, as of those that went before. Much after the same manner were his letters writ to me, telling me that gravity, in descent from hence to the centre of the earth, was reciprocally in a duplicate ratio of the altitude, that the figure described by projectiles in this region would be an ellipsis, and that all the motions of the heavens were thus to be accounted for ; and this he did in such a way, as if he had found out all, and knew it most certainly. And, upon this information, I must now acknowledge, in print, I had all from him, and so did nothing myself but drudge in calculating, demonstrating, and writing, upon the inventions of this great man. And yet, after all, the first of those three things he told of me is false, and very unphilosophical ; the second is as false ; and the third was more than he knew, or could affirm me ignorant of by any thing that past between us in our letters. Nor do I understand by what right he claims it as his own ; for as Borell wrote, long before him, that by a tendency of the planets towards the sun, like that of gravity or magnetism, the planets would move in ellipses, so Bullialdus wrote that all force, respecting the sun as its centre, and depending on matter, must be reciprocally in a duplicate ratio of the distance from the centre, and used that very argument for it, by which you, sir, in the last Transactions, have proved this ratio in gravity. Now if Mr. Hooke, from this general proposition in Bullialdus, might learn the proportion in gravity, why must this proportion here go for his invention? My letter to Hugenius, which I mentioned above, was directed to Mr. Oldenburg, who used to keep the originals. His papers came into

Mr. Hooke's possession. Mr. Hooke, knowing my hand, might have the curiosity to look into that letter, and thence take the notion of comparing the forces of the planets arising from their circular motion; and so what he wrote to me afterwards, about the rate of gravity, might be nothing but the fruit of my own garden. And it's more than I can affirm, that the duplicate proportion was not expressed in that letter. However, he knew it not (as I gather from his books) till five years after any mathematician could have told it him. For when Hugenius had told how to find the force in all cases of circular motion, he had told 'em how to do it in this as well as in all others. And so the honour of doing it in this is due to Hugenius. For another, five years after, to claim it as his own invention is as if some mechanic, who had learned the art of surveying from a master, should afterwards claim the surveying of this or that piece of ground for his own invention, and keep a heavy quarter to be in print for't. But what, if this surveyor be a bungler, and give an erroneous survey? Mr. Hooke has erred in the invention he pretends to, and his error is the cause of all the stir he makes. For his extending the duplicate proportion down to the centre (which I do not) made him correct me, and tell me the rest of his theory as a new thing to me, and now stand upon it, that I had all from that his letter, notwithstanding that he had told it to all the world before, and I had seen it in his printed books, all but the proportion. And why should I record a man for an invention, who founds his claim upon an error therein, and on that score gives me trouble? He imagines he obliged me by telling me his theory, but I thought myself disobliged by being, upon his own mistake, corrected magisterially, and taught a theory, which every body knew, and I had a truer notion of than himself. Should a man who thinks himself knowing, and loves to show it in correcting and instructing others, come to you, when you are busy, and notwithstanding your excuse press discourses upon you, and through his own mistakes correct you, and multiply discourses; and then make this use of it, to boast that he taught you all he spake, and oblige you to acknowledge it, and cry out injury and injustice if you do not; I believe you would think him a man of strange unsociable temper. Mr. Hooke's letters in several respects abounded too much with that humour, which Hevelius and others complain of; and therefore he may do well in time to consider, whether, after this new provocation, I be much more bound (in doing him that justice he claims) to make an honourable mention of him in print, especially since this is the third time that he has given me trouble in this kind. For your further satisfaction in this business, I beg the favour you would consult your books for a paper of mine entitled, An Hypothesis explaining properties of Light. It was dated Dec. 7, 1675, and registered in your book about January or February following. Not far from the beginning there is a paragraph ending with these words: ' And as the earth, so perhaps may the sun imbibe this spirit copiously to conserve his shining, and keep the planets from receding further from him; and they that will may also suppose that this spirit affords or carries thither the solary fuel and material principle of light. And that the vast ethereal spaces between us and the stars are for a sufficient repository for this food of the sun and planets. But this of the constitution of ethereal natures by the by.'

"In these and the foregoing words you have the common cause of gravity towards the earth, sun, and all the planets, and that by this cause

the planets are kept in their orbs about the sun. And this is all the philosophy Mr. Hooke pretends I had from his letters some years after, the
duplicate proportion only excepted. The preceding words contain the
cause of the phænomena of gravity, as we find it on the surface of the
earth, without any regard to the various distances from the centre. For at
first I designed to write of nothing more. Afterwards, as my manuscript
shews, I interlined the words above cited relating to the heavens; and in
so short and transitory an interlined hint of things, the expression of the
proportion may well be excused. But if you consider the nature of the
hypothesis, you'll find that gravity decreases upwards, and can be no other
from the superficies of the planet than reciprocally duplicate of the distance from the centre, but downwards that proportion does not hold. This
was but an hypothesis, and so to be looked upon only as one of my
guesses, which I did not rely on ; but it sufficiently explains to you, why
in considering the descent of a body down to the centre, I used not the
duplicate proportion. In the small ascent and descent of projectiles above
the earth, the variation of gravity is so inconsiderable, that Mathematicians
neglect it. Hence the vulgar hypothesis with them is uniform gravity.
And why might not I, as a Mathematician, use it frequently, without
thinking on the philosophy of the heavens, or believing it to be philosophically true ?

"This letter, with the postscript belonging to it, was printed in the
General Dictionary by Bernard, Birch, and Lockman (vol. vii. p. 797).
The writers in the Biographia Britannica likewise adopted it; but have
separated the different parts, and printed one portion twice. They have
given the beginning (p. 401 to p. 402, line 37) in the life of Hooke (vol. iv.
p. 2659); the next part (p. 402) in the life of Newton (vol. v. p. 3225), and
the end (p. 403) is repeated in the life of Halley (vol. iv. p. 2504). The
postscript (p. 403 to p. 405) was added to the part annexed to the life of
Hooke (vol. iv. p. 2660)."

## 4.—HALLEY TO NEWTON.

"SIR,                                          "LONDON, 29 *June*, 1686.

"I am heartily sorry, that in this matter, wherein all mankind ought
to acknowledge their obligations to you, you should meet with any thing
that should give you disquiet; or that any disgust should make you think
of desisting in your pretensions to a Lady, whose favours you have so
much reason to boast of. 'Tis not she, but your rivals, envying your
happiness, that endeavour to disturb your quiet enjoyment ; which when
you consider, I hope you will see cause to alter your resolution of supress-
ing your third book, there being nothing which you can have compiled
therein, which the learned world will not be concerned to have concealed.
Those gentlemen of the Society, to whom I have communicated it, are
very much troubled at it, and that this unlucky business should have
happened to give trouble, having a just sentiment of the author thereof.
According to your desire in your former, I waited upon Sir Christopher
Wren, to inquire of him, if he had the first notion of the reciprocal duplicate proportion from Mr. Hooke. His answer was, that he himself very

many years since had had his thoughts upon the making out the planets' motions by a composition of a descent towards the sun, and an impressed motion; but that at length he gave it over, not finding the means of doing it. Since which time Mr. Hooke had frequently told him, that he had done it, and attempted to make it out to him; but that he never was satisfied that his demonstrations were cogent. And this I know to be true, that in January 168⅘, I having, from the considerations of the sesqui-alter proportion of Kepler, concluded that the centripetal force decreased in the proportion of the squares of the distances reciprocally, came on Wednesday to town, where I met with Sir Christopher Wren and Mr. Hooke, and falling in discourse about it, Mr. Hooke affirmed, that upon that principle all the laws of the celestial motions were to be demonstrated, and that he himself had done it. I declared the ill success of my own attempts; and Sir Christopher, to encourage the inquiry, said, that he would give Mr. Hooke, or me, two months' time, to bring him a convincing demonstration thereof; and besides the honour, he of us, that did it, should have from him a present of a book of 40 shillings. Mr. Hooke then said, that he would conceal it for some time, that others trying and failing might know how to value it, when he should make it public. However 'I remember, that Sir Christopher was little satisfied that he could do it; and though Mr. Hooke then promised to shew it him, I do not find, that in that particular he has been so good as his word. The August following, when I did myself the honour to visit you, I then learned the good news, that you had brought this demonstration to perfection: and you were pleased to promise me a copy thereof, which the November following I received with a great deal of satisfaction from Mr. Paget; and thereupon took another journey to Cambridge, on purpose to confer with you about it, since which time it has been entered upon the Register Books of the Society. As all this passed, Mr. Hooke was acquainted with it, and according to the philosophically ambitious temper he is of, he would, had he been master of a like demonstration, no longer have concealed it, the reason, he told Sir Christopher and me, now ceasing. But now he says, this is but one small part of an excellent system of nature, which he has conceived, but has not yet completely made out, so that he thinks not fit to publish one part without the other. But I have plainly told him, that unless he produce another differing demonstration, and let the world judge of it, neither I nor any one else can believe it. As to the manner of Mr. Hooke's claiming the discovery, I fear it has been represented in worse colours than it ought; for he neither made public application to the Society for justice, nor pretended you had all from him. The truth is this: Sir John Hoskyns, his particular friend, being in the chair, when Dr. Vincent presented your book, the Doctor gave it its just encomium both as to the novelty and dignity of the subject. It was replied by another gentleman, that you had carried the thing so far, that there was no more to be added. To which the Vice-president replied, that it was so much the more to be prized, for that it was both invented and perfected at the same time. This gave Mr. Hooke offence, that Sir John did not, at that time, make mention of what he had, as he said, discovered to him; upon which they two, who till then were the most inseparable cronies, have since scarce seen one another, and are utterly fallen out. After the breaking up of that meeting, being adjourned to the coffee-house, Mr. Hooke did there endeavour to gain belief, that he had some such thing by him, and that he gave you the first hint of this invention. But I found, that they were all of opinion, that nothing thereof appearing in print, nor on the books of the Society, you ought to be considered as the inventor. And if in truth he knew it before you, he ought not to blame any but himself, for having taken no more care to secure a discovery, which he puts so much value on. What application he has made in private, I know not; but I am sure that the Society have a very great satisfaction, in the honour you do them, by the dedication of so worthy a treatise. Sir, I must now again beg you, not to let your resentments run so high, as to deprive us of your third book, wherein the application of your mathematical doctrine to the theory of comets and several curious experiments, which, as I guess by what you write, ought to compose it, will undoubtedly render it acceptable to those, who will call themselves Philosophers without Mathematics, which are much the greater number. Now you approve of the character and paper, I will push on the edition vigorously. I have sometimes had thoughts of having the cuts neatly done in wood, so as to stand in the page with the demonstrations. It will be more convenient, and not much more charge. If it please you to have it so, I will try how well it can be done; otherwise I will have them in somewhat a larger size than those you have sent up. I am, Sir,

"Your most affectionate humble servant,

"E. HALLEY.

"This letter was printed in the Gen. Dic. (vol. vii. p. 799.) In the Biographia Britannica the parts are separated, and some, as was done for No. 3, are repeated. The beginning (p. 405 to p. 406) is annexed to the life of Newton (vol. v. p. 3226), and the first part of it appears also (to p. 406) in the life of Halley (vol. iv. p. 2504). The middle (p. 406) will be found in the life of Hooke (vol. iv. p. 2661); the end (p. 407) printed in the life of Newton (vol. v. p. 3226), and the latter part also in the life of Halley (vol. iv. p. 2504). The words (p. 406), 'As all this passed, Mr. Hooke was acquainted with it, and'—are wholly omitted."

### 5.—NEWTON TO HALLEY.

"July 14, 1686.

"SIR,

"I have considered your proposal about wooden cuts, and believe it will be much convenienter for the reader, and may be sufficiently handsome, but I leave it to your determination. If you go this way, then I desire you would divide the first figure into these two:[1] I crowded them into one to save the trouble of altering the numbers in the schemes you have. I am very sensible of the great kindness of the gentlemen of your Society to me, far beyond what I could ever expect or deserve, and know how to distinguish between their favour and another's humour. Now I understand he was in some respects misrepresented to me, I wish I had spared the postscript to my last. This is true, that his letters occasioned my finding the method of determining figures, which when I had tried in the ellipsis, I threw the calculations by, being upon other studies; and so it rested for

[1] The figures here are unnecessary.

about five years, till upon your request I sought for that paper ; and not finding it, did it again, and reduced it into the propositions shewed you by Mr. Paget : but for the duplicate proportion I can affirm that I gathered it from Kepler's theorem about twenty years ago. And so Sir Christopher Wren's examining the ellipsis over against the focus shews, that he knew it many years ago, before he left off his enquiry after the figure by an impressed motion and a descent compounded together. There was another thing in Mr. Hooke's letters, which he will think I had from him. He told me, that my proposed experiment about the descent of falling bodies was not the only way to prove the motion of the earth ; and so added the experiment of your pendulum clock at St. Helena as an argument of gravity's being lessened at the equator by the diurnal motion. The experiment was new to me, but not the notion ; for in that very paper, which I told you was writ some time above fifteen years ago, and to the best of my memory was writ eighteen or nineteen years ago, I calculated the force of ascent at the equator, arising from the earth's diurnal motion, in order to know what would be the diminution of gravity thereby. But yet to do this business right, is a thing of far greater difficulty than I was aware of. A third thing there was in his letters, which was new to me, and I shall acknowledge it, if I make use of it. 'Twas the deflexion of falling bodies to the south-east in our latitude. And now having sincerely told you the case between Mr. Hooke and me, I hope I shall be free for the future from the prejudice of his letters. I have considered how best to compose the present dispute, and I think it may be done by the inclosed scholium to the fourth proposition. In turning over some old papers I met with another demonstration of that proposition, which I have added at the end of this scholium. Which is all at present from

" your affectionate friend,<br>
" and humble servant,<br>
" Is. NEWTON.

" This letter was printed in the Gen. Dic. (vol. vii. p. 800) ; but the first fourteen lines and the diagrams belonging to them are omitted. It was reprinted in the Biographia Britannica (life of Hooke, vol. iv. p. 2661), where the last sentence (' In turning over,' &c. p. 41) is omitted, as well as the beginning, which was left out in the General Dictionary."

6.—NEWTON TO HALLEY.

" SIR,

" Yesterday I unexpectedly struck upon a copy of the letter, I tola you of, to Hugenius. 'Tis in the hand of one Mr. John Wickins, who was then my chamber-fellow, and is now parson of Stoke Edith near Monmouth [Hereford], and so is authentic. It begins thus, being directed to Mr. Oldenburg.

" ' SIR,

" ' I receiv'd your letters, with M. Hugens's kind present, which I have viewed with great satisfaction, finding it full of very subtile and useful

speculations very worthy of the author.  I am glad, that we are to expect
another discourse of the Vis Centrifuga, which speculation may prove of
good use in Natural Philosophy and Astronomy, as well as Mechanics.
Thus, for instance, if the reason, why the same side of the moon is ever
towards the earth, be the greater conatus of the other side to recede from
it, it will follow (upon supposition of the earth's motion about the sun),
that the greatest distance of the sun from the earth is to the greatest distance of the moon from the earth, not greater than 10000 to 56 ; and
therefore the parallax of the sun not less than $\frac{56}{10000}$ of the parallax
of the moon ; because were the sun's distance less in proportion to that of
the moon, she would have a greater conatus from the sun than from the
earth.  I thought also some time that the moon's libration might depend
upon her conatus from the sun and earth compared together, till I apprehended a better cause.'

"Thus far this letter concerning the Vis Centrifuga.  The rest of it, for
the most part concerning colours, is printed in the Phil. Trans. of July 21,
1673, No. 96.  Now from these words it's evident, that I was at that time
versed in the theory of the force arising from circular motion, and had an
eye upon the forces of the planets, knowing how to compare them by the
proportions of their periodical revolutions and distances from the centre
they move about : an instance of which you have here in the comparison
of the forces of the moon arising from her menstrual motion about the
earth, and annual about the sun.  So then in this theory I am plainly before Mr. Hooke.  For he about a year after, in his Attempt to prove the
Motion of the Earth, declared expressly, that the degrees, by which gravity
decreased, he had not then experimentally verified ; that is, he knew not
how to gather it from phenomena ; and therefore he there recommends
it to the prosecution of others.

"Now, though I do not find the duplicate proportion expressed in this
letter (as I hoped it might), yet if you compare this passage of it here
transcribed, with that hypothesis of mine, registered by Mr. Oldenburg in
your book, you will see that I then understood it.  For I there suppose
that the descending spirit acts upon bodies here on the superficies of the
earth with force proportional to the superficies of their parts ; which cannot be, unless the diminution of its velocity in acting upon the first parts
of any body it meets with, be recompensed by the increase of its density
arising from that retardation.  Whether this be true is not material.  It
suffices, that 'twas the hypothesis.  Now if this spirit descend from above
with uniform velocity, its density, and consequently its force, will be reciprocally proportional to the square of its distance from the centre.  But
if it descend with accelerated motion, its density will everywhere diminish
as much as its velocity increases ; and so its force (according to the hypothesis) will be the same as before, that is, still reciprocally as the square of
its distance from the centre.

"In short, as these things compared together shew, that I was before Mr.
Hooke in what he pretends to have been my master, so I learned nothing
by his letters but this, that bodies fall not only to the east, but also in our
latitude to the south.  In the rest his correcting and informing me was to
be complain'd of.  And tho' his correcting my spiral occasioned my finding
the theorem, by which I afterwards examined the ellipsis ; yet am I not
beholden to him for any light into the business, but only for the diversion

he gave me from my other studies to think on these things, and for his dog-maticalness in writing, as if he had found the motion in the ellipsis, which inclined me to try it, after I saw by what method it was to be done.  Sir, I am,

" your affectionate friend,
" and humble servant,
" Is. Newton.

"*July* 27, 1686.

" This letter was printed in the Gen. Dict. (vol. vii. p. 800), and reprinted in the Biographia Britannica (life of Hooke, vol. iv. p. 2661).  The original letter to Oldenburg, from which an extract is given here by Newton, is in the guard-book (No. 1), and the date of it is there preserved, ' June 23, 73.' It likewise contains a passage, in addition to what Newton has quoted, and which is omitted in the copy that is printed in the Phil. Transactions (vol. viii. p. 6087).  It does not indeed bear upon the present subject, but still the completion of the letter may be some apology for inserting it in this place.  It is as follows :

" In the demonstration of the 8th proposition de descensu gravium, there seems to be an illegitimate supposition, namely, that the flextures at B and c do not hinder the motion of the descending body.  For in reality they will hinder it, so that a body which descends from A shall not acquire so great velocity, when arrived at D, as one which descends from E.  If this supposition be made because a body descending by a curve line meets with no such opposition, and this proposition is laid down in order to the con-templation of motion in curve lines, then it should have been shewn that though rectilinear flextures do hinder, yet the infinitely little flextures which are in curves, though infinite in number, do not at all hinder the motion.

" The rectifying curve lines by that way which Mr. Hugens calls evolu-tion, I have been sometimes considering also, and here met with a way of resolving it, which seems more ready and free from the trouble of calcula-tion than that of M. Hugens.  If he please, I will send it him.  The pro-blem also is capable of being improved by being propounded thus more generally.

" ' Curvas invenire quotascunque, quarum longitudines cum propositæ alicujus curvæ longitudine, vel cum area ejus ad datam lineam applicata, comparari possunt.' "

7.—Halley to Newton.

" London, *October* 14, 1686.

" Sir,
" By reason you are desirous that your book should not be public before Hilary Term, the impression has not been expedited as it might have been ; but I hope that it is the more correct for proceeding so slow.  I have sent you by the coach which goes from hence to-morrow morning, all the sheets that are done, desiring you would be pleased to mark all the errata you shall find, that so if there be any material one, the reader may be adver-

tised thereof, but this at your leisure. At present I more immediately want to be informed concerning your geometrical effection of the problem XXIII, as much as relates to the 63d figure, for upon trial (there being no demonstration annexed) there seems to be some mistake committed: wherefore I intreat you would please to send me, revised by yourself, those few lines that relate thereto, and, if it be not too much trouble, be prevailed upon to subjoin something of the Demonstration. In your transmutation of figures according to the 22d lemma, which you use in the two following problems, to me it seems that the manner of transmuting a trapezium into a parallelogram needs some further explanation ; I have printed it as you sent it, but I pray you please a little farther to describe by an example the manner of doing it, for I am not perfectly master of it ; a short hint will suffice. Pray, defer the answer hereto as little as may stand with your convenience, for we are now within a sheet of the 23d problem, and shall want your amendments, if there be occasion for them. If there be any service I can do you here in town, pray command, Sir,

" Your most affectionate humble servant,

" EDM. HALLEY.

> " *To his honoured Friend,*
>     MR. ISAAC NEWTON,
>        *at* TRINITY COLLEDG, CAMBRIDG,
>           These."

8.—NEWTON TO HALLEY.

" SIR,
    " In the scholium you write of, the words ' vel hyperbolæ' in the 3d line are to be struck out, and in the 5th and 6th lines the words ' quæ sit ad G K' should be ' quæ sit ad ½ G K.' I send you inclosed the beginning of this scholium with the 63d figure as I would have them printed. I thank you heartily for giving me notice that it was amiss. The ground of the transmutation of a trapezium into a parallelogram I lay down, pag. 87, in these words : ' Nam rectæ quævis convergentes transmutantur in parallelas, adhibendo pro radio ordinato primo A O lineam quamvis rectam, quæ per concursum convergentium transit : id adeo quia concursus ille hoc pacto abit in infinitum, lineæ autem parallelæ sunt quæ ad punctum infinite distans tendunt.' In the figure, pag. 86, conceive the curve H G I to be produced both ways till it meet and intersect itself any where in the radius ordinatus primus A O : and when the point G moving up and down in the curve H I arrives at that intersection point, I say the point g moving in like manner up and down in the curve h i will become infinitely distant. For the point G falling upon the line O A, the point D will fall upon the point A, and the line O D upon the line O A ; and so becoming parallel to a B their intersection point d will become infinitely distant, and consequently the line d g will become infinitely distant, and so will its point g. Q. E. D. So then if any two lines of the primary figure H G I D intersect in the radius ordinatus primus A O, their intersection in the new figure h g i d shall become infinitely distant ; and, therefore, if the two intersecting lines be right ones, they shall become parallel. For right lines, which lead to a point infinitely dis-

tant, do not intersect one another and diverge, but are parallel. Therefore, if in the primary figure there be any trapezium, whose opposite sides converge to points in the radius ordinatus primus O A, those sides in the new figure shall become parallel, and so the trapezium be converted into a parallelogram.

"The printed sheets I intend to look over. Mr. Paget, in his stay here, has noted these errata, of which the 3d is a fault in the copy.

"P. 6, l. 27, velocitate ; p. 8, l. 19, tur Sunt. ; p. 14, l. 30, reciproce ut D O ; p. 18, l. 1, recta. I wish the printer be careful to mend all you note. Sir, I am very sensible of the great trouble you are at in this business, and the great care you take about it. Pray take your own time. And if you meet with any thing else, which you think need either correcting or further explaining, be pleased to signify it to

"your humble and obliged servant,
"Is. NEWTON.

"TRIN. COLL.
*Octob.* 18, 1686.

" My thanks for your note of De la Hire."


### 9.—HALLEY to NEWTON.

" LONDON. *Feb.* 24 [1686-7].

"HONOURED SIR,
" I return you most hearty thanks for the copy you sent me of the sheet which was lost by the printer's negligence ; I will now do nothing else till the whole be finished, which I hope may be soon after Easter ; and to redeem the time I have lost, I will employ another press to go on with the second part, which I am glad to understand you have perfected, and if you please to send it up to me, as soon as I have it I will set the printer to work on it, and will not be wanting to do my part to let it appear to the world to your satisfaction. I am sorry the Society should be represented to you so unsteady as to fall so frequently into variance,[1] but there is no such thing ; and I am bold to say, that I serve them to their satisfaction, though six out of thirty-eight last general election did their endeavour to have put me by.[2] Dr. Wallis his papers I will send you ; the result is much the same with yours, and he had from an account I gave him of what you had demonstrated, I will send it you with some more sheets this next week ; it is as yours founded on the hypothesis of the opposition being proportionate to the celerity which you say you find reason to dispute. Your demonstration of the parallax of the sun from the inequalities of the moon's motions, is what the Society has commanded me to request of you, it being the best means of determining the dimensions of the planetary system, which all other ways are deficient in ; and they entreat you not to desist when you are come so near the solution of so noble a problem. This done, there remains nothing more to be enquired in this matter, and

---

[1] Mr. Weld, in his History of the Royal Society, does not mention any " variances" as taking place at this time.
[2] Halley was at this time Clerk and Assistant Secretary, and continued so till 1698.

you will do yourself the honour of perfecting scientifically what all past ages have but blindly groped after.  I have your two propositions you sent me some time since, and shall insert them in their proper place.

"I am, Sir, to the utmost of my power,
          "Your most affectionate humble servant,
                                        "EDM. HALLEY.
"*To his Honoured Friend,*
      *Mr.* ISAAC NEWTON,
          *in* TRINTY COLLEDG, CAMBRIDG,
                    These."

### 10.—NEWTON TO HALLEY.

"SIR,

"I have sent you the sheet you want.  The second book I made ready for you in autumn, having wrote to you in summer that it should come out with the first, and be ready against the time you might need it, and guessing by the rate of the press in summer you might need it about November or December.  But not hearing from you, and being told (though not truly) that, upon some differences in the Royal Society, you had left your secretary's place, I desired my intimate friend Mr. C. Montague[1] to enquire of Mr. Paget how things were, and send me word.  He writes, that Dr. Wallis has sent up some things about projectiles pretty like those of mine in the papers Mr. Paget first shewed you, and that 'twas ordered I should be consulted whether I intend to print mine.  I have inserted them into the beginning of the second book with divers others of that kind : which therefore, if you desire to see, you may command the book when you please, though otherwise I should choose to let it lie by me till you are ready for it.  I think I have the solution of your problem about the sun's parallax, but through other occasions shall scarce have time to think further on these things : and besides, I want something of observation, for if my notion be right, the sun draws the moon in the quadratures, so that there needs an equation of about 4 or $4\frac{1}{2}$ minutes to be subducted from her motion in the first quarter and added in the last.  I hope you received a letter with two corollaries I sent you in autumn.  I have eleven sheets already, that is, to M.  When you have seven more printed off I desire you would send them.  I thank you for putting forward the press again, being very sensible of the great trouble I give you amidst so much business of your own and the Royal Society's.  In this, as well as in divers other things, you will much oblige

                    "your affectionate friend,
                         "and humble servant,
                              "IS. NEWTON.

"TRIN. COLL. CAMBRIDGE,
   *Feb.* 28, 1686.  [1686-7.]"

[1] Afterwards the Earl of Halifax.

## 11.—NEWTON TO HALLEY.

" SIR,

" You'll receive the 2nd book on Thursday night or Friday by the coach. I have directed it to be left with Mr. Hunt at Gresham Coll. Pray let me beg the favour of a line or two to know of the receipt. I am obliged to you for pushing on the edition, because of people's expectation, tho' otherwise I could be as well satisfied to let it rest a year or two longer. 'Tis a double favour, that you are pleased to double your pains about it. Dr. Wallis's papers may be long, and I would not give you the trouble of transcribing them all. The heads may suffice. The resistance, in swift motions, is in a duplicate proportion to the celerity. The deduction of the sun's parallax from the moon's variation, I cannot promise now to consider. When astronomers have examined whether there be such an inequality of her motion in the quadratures, as I mentioned in my last, and determined the quantity thereof, I may take some occasion perhaps to tell them the reason. No more at present from

" your most affectionate humble servant,

" Is. NEWTON.

" CAMBRIDGE,
*March* 1, 86-7."

## 12.—HALLEY TO NEWTON.

" LONDON, *March* 7, 1686-7.

" HONOURED SIR,

"I received yours, and according to it your Second Book, which this week I will put to the press, having agreed with one that promises me to get it done in seven weeks, it making much about twenty sheets. The First Book will be about thirty, which will be finished much about the same time. This week you shall have the eighteenth sheet according to your directions. You mention in this Second your Third Book *De Systemate Mundi*, which from such firm principles, as in the preceding you have laid down, cannot choose but give universal satisfaction, if this be likewise ready, and not too long to get printed at the same time, and you think fit to send it ; I will endeavour by a third hand, to get it all done together, being resolved to engage in no other business till such time as all is done, desiring hereby to clear myself from all imputations of negligence in a business wherein I am much rejoiced to be any ways concerned in handing to the world that that all future ages will admire, and as being,

" Sir, your most obedient servant,

" EDM. HALLEY.

" *To* Mr. ISAAC NEWTON,
*at* TRINITY COLLEDG CAMBRIDG."

No answer to this letter, or any of the subsequent letters, has been preserved.

### 13.—HALLEY TO NEWTON.

"SIR,

"I have now sent you the eighteenth sheet of your book, but could not be as good as my word, by reason of the extraordinary trouble of the last sheet, which was the reason it could not be finished time enough to send it you the last week. I have not been wanting to endeavour the clearing it of errata, but am sensible that, notwithstanding all my care, some have crept in; but I hope none of consequence. Pray, please to examine it yourself, and note what mistakes are committed, that so they may be noted at the end; and if they be very material, the sheet shall be done over again, as I was forced to do the sheet P must be done, for the figure is turned upside down by the negligence of the printer, in p. 112. I hope, in a fortnight more, to send you as many more sheets, and very suddenly to have the first part finished—being,

"Sir, your most humble servant,

EDM. HALLEY.

"*To* MR. ISAAC NEWTON,
        *at* TRINITY COLL.,
                CAMBRIDGE.

"*Post-p*ᵈ.
                These present—
With a small parcel."

### 14.—HALLEY TO NEWTON.

"HONOURED SIR,

"I received not the last part of your divine treatise till yesterday, though it came to town that day se'ennight, having had occasion to be out of town the last week. The first part will be finished within the three weeks, and, considering the shortness of the third over the second, the same press that did the first will get it done so soon as the second can be finished by another press; but I find some difficulty to match the letter justly. Your method of determining the orb of a comet deserves to be practised upon more of them, as far as may ascertain whether any of those that have passed in former times may have returned again; for their nodes and perihelia being fixed, will prove it sufficiently, and, by their periods, the transverse diameters will be given, which possibly may render the problem more easy. If you can remove the fault in the comet's latitudes, 'twill be better; but as it is, the numbers you have laid down do make out the verity of the hypothesis past dispute. I do not find that you have touched that notable appearance of comets' tails, and their opposition to the sun, which seems rather to argue an efflux from the sun than a gravitation towards him. I doubt not but this may follow from your principles with the like ease as all the other phenomena; but a proposition or two concerning these will add much to the beauty and perfection of your theory of comets. I find I shall not get the whole completed before Trinity Term, when I hope to have it published, when the world will not be more instructed by the demonstrative doctrine thereof, than it will pride itself to have a subject capable of penetrating so far into the abstrusest secrets of nature, and exalting human reason to so sublime a pitch by this utmost effort of the mind.  But least my affection should make me transgress, I remain,

" Your most obedient servant,
EDM. HALLEY.

" *To* MR. ISAAC NEWTON,
*to be left with Mr. Parish Rector oj*
*Coulsterworth, in Lincolnshire.*
*These—*"

---

## No. IX.

*(Referred to in page 272, as No. XI.)*

THE following is a copy of the verses written by Halley, and prefixed to the First Edition of the Principia.  In imitation of Professor Rigaud, the original verses are printed in the larger type.  The alterations made by Bentley, in the second edition of 1713, are in a smaller type, and the parts between brackets are the alterations adopted in the third edition, published by Pemberton in 1726.

#### HALLEY'S VERSES PREFIXED TO THE PRINCIPIA.

In
viri præstantissimi
D. ISAACI NEWTONI
opus hocce
mathematico-physicum
sæculi gentisque nostræ decus egregium.

En tibi norma Poli, et divæ libramina Molis,
        [en]        [et]
Computus atque Jovis ; quas, dum primordia rerum
Conderet, omnipotens sibi        ipse
Pangeret, omniparens Leges violare Creator
Dixerit, [atque operum quæ fundamenta locarit.]
Noluit, æternique operis fundamina fixit.
Intima panduntur victi penetralia cœli,
                circumrotet,
Nec latet extremos quæ Vis circumrotat Orbes.
Sol solio residens ad se jubet omnia prono
Tendere descensu, nec recto tramite currus
Sidereos patitur vastum per inane moveri ;
Sed rapit immotis, se centro, singula Gyris.

Hinc          qua
Jam patet horrificis quæ sit via flexa Cometis ;
Jam non miramur barbati Phænomena Astri.[1]
Discimus hinc tandem qua causa argentea Phœbe
         eat, et
Passibus haud æquis graditur ; cur subdita nulli
Hactenus Astronomo numerorum fræna recuset :
  remeent        progrediantur
Cur remeant Nodi, curque Auges progrediuntur.
Discimus et quantis refluum vaga Cynthia Pontum
      impellat ; [fessis dum]
Viribus impellit, dum fractis fluctibus Ulvam
Deserit, ac Nautis suspectas nudat arenas ;
Alternisve ruens spumantia     pulsat.
Alternis vicibus suprema ad littora pulsans.
Quæ toties animos veterum torsere Sophorum,
     hodie
Quæque Scholas frustra rauco certamine vexant
Obvia conspicimus nubem pellente Mathesi.
Jam dubios nulla caligine prægravat error,[2]
  Quæ superas
Queis Superum penetrare domos atque ardua Cœli
Newtoni auspiciis, jam dat contingere Templa.
Scandere sublimis Genii concessit acumen.
  Surgite Mortales, terrenas mittite curas ;
           cognoscite
Atque hinc cœligenæ vires dignoscite Mentis,
A pecudum vita longe lateque remotæ.
    primus
Qui scriptis jussit Tabulis compescere Cædes,
Furta et Adulteria, et perjuræ crimina Fraudis ;
Quive vagis populis circumdare mœnibus Urbes
Autor erat ; Cererisve beavit munere gentes ;
Vel qui curarum lenimen pressit ab Uva ;
Vel qui Niliaca monstravit arundine pictos
Consociare sonos, oculisque exponere Voces ;
Humanam sortem minus extulit ; utpote pauca
In commune ferens miseræ solatia
        [tantum solamina]
Respiciens miseræ solummodo commoda vitæ.
Jam vero Superis convivæ admittimur, alti
          diæ
Jura poli tractare licet, jamque abdita cœcæ
     Naturæ, et
Claustra patent Terræ, rerumque[3] immobilis ordo,
      præteritis latuere incognita sæclis.
Et quæ præteriti latuerunt sæcula mundi.
     justis
Talia monstrantem mecum celebrate Camœnis,

[1] This line was entirely omitted in 1713, and restored in 1726.
[2] This line also was omitted in 1713, and restored in 1726.
[3] que—omitted in 1713, restored in 1726.   The parts in italics are alterations, made in the third, though not in the second edition.

[*o cœlicolum gaudentes*]
Vos qui cœlesti gaudetis nectare vesci,
Newtonum clausi reserantem scrinia Veri
carum
Newtonum Musis charum, cui pectore puro
Phœbus adest, totoque incessit Numine mentem :
Nec fas est propius Mortali attingere Divos.
EDM. HALLEY.

It does not appear on what authority those changes were introduced into the third edition, which did not exist in the two first. It is quite certain that they were made without the authority either of Halley or Newton. It is probable, from the following anecdote, which we found in Conduitt's manuscripts, that Pemberton was the author of them.

"Bentley," says Conduitt, "altered Halley's verses when he printed the Principia. Halley told me that Sir Isaac Newton made him hope that in Pemberton's edition his verses would be printed from his own copy, but complained they were not, for he made it—

Æternique operis fundamenta fixit.

And it is printed,

Operumque fundamenta locavit.

And when I said that perhaps Sir Isaac Newton did not care for having anything appear before his book, that seemed to favour the idea that the world was eternal ;—'Yes,' said he, 'that is what Pemberton would fix upon me, but *æternum* is only *æviternum*, and I meant no more.'"—Conduitt's MSS.

No. X.

(*Referred to in page* 278, *as* No. XII.)

IT is either a great privilege or a great misfortune to be the associate of distinguished individuals. The light of the halo which surrounds them falls brightest on their companions, but though it generally illustrates and adorns, it sometimes displays failings and imperfections of character, and transmits them to posterity. We have already seen how unfortunate for the memory of Mr. Paget was his connexion with Newton and Flamsteed. We shall now see the reverse in the case of Cotes, who, though justly distinguished by his own talents and acquirements, has yet derived a considerable portion of his reputation from being the friend of Newton, and an editor of the Principia. It is probable, indeed, from the fact that Bentley was the proprietor of the second edition of the Principia, and a worshipper of Mammon, that Fame was the only reward which fell to the lot of Cotes.

Roger Cotes was born at Burbage, in Leicestershire, on the 10th July 1682. His father, who was rector of the parish, placed him at Leicester school, where, at the age of twelve, he displayed a great taste for mathematics. At the house of his uncle, the Rev. John Smith, and with his assistance, he made great progress in mathematics, and at St. Paul's School in London, he made equal progress in classical learning.

From St. Paul's School he went to Trinity College, Cambridge, where he was entered pensioner on the 6th April 1699. He was elected scholar in May 1701, took his degree of B.A. in 1703, and was sworn minor Fellow of the College, on the 3d of October 1705. On the 6th October 1707, he was appointed the first Plumian Professor of Astronomy and Experimental Philosophy. In 1713 he took orders, and in the same year undertook to superintend the second edition of the Principia.

In 1714 he published in the Philosophical Transactions a paper, entitled *Logometria*, the first part of the treatise on the same subject, which forms the principal part of his posthumous work, entitled *Harmonia Mensurarum*, edited in 1722 by his cousin, Dr. Robert Smith. In 1716, he communicated to the Society an account of the great fiery meteor seen on the 6th March of that year, but it is obvious from his description of it that it was only an Aurora Borealis.

In a few weeks after he wrote this communication to the Society, he was seized with fever, and, after a relapse, accompanied with violent diarrhœa and constant delirium, he died on the 5th June 1716, amid the deep regrets of the University and the scientific world. When Newton received the sad intelligence of the loss of his friend, he made the memorable observation, " If Mr. Cotes had lived we might have known something."

A short time before his death, when he was only in his thirty-second year, he demonstrated the beautiful optical theorem, that " the magnitude of the image of an object seen through any number of lenses is to that of the object itself, as the distance of the image from the eye is to the apparent distance of the object." [1]

In 1722, there appeared the *Epistola ad Amicum de Cotesii Inventis*, addressed to Mr. James Wilson, by Henry Pemberton, and an Appendix, bearing the date of May 1722. Beside some tracts in Latin, which have not been published, he left behind him a course of lectures on Hydrostatics and Pneumatics, which was published by Dr. Smith in 1738. In Mr. Edleston's Correspondence, he has published twenty-four letters from Cotes to his friends, from one of which it appears that he had anticipated S'Gravesende in the invention of the Heliostate. [2]

Cotes was interred in the chapel of Trinity College, and the following and much admired inscription on his monument, was written by Dr. Bentley.

H. S. E.
ROGERUS ROBERTI FILIUS COTES,
Hujus Collegii S. Trinitatis Socius,
Et Astronomiæ et Experimentalis
Philosophiæ Professor Plumianus ;

[1] See Smith's *Optics*, vol. i. p. 191, cor. 19 ; and vol. ii., *Remarks*, p. 76.

[2] Mr. Edleston refers to the Register of the Royal Society for evidence, that Hooke and Halley had previously invented the Heliostate. The first publication, however, of the invention, is due to the Dutch philosopher.—See S'Gravesende's *Physices Elem. Math.* vol. ii. p. 715, § 2660, Tab. 84, 85. Edit. 1742.

Qui immatura morte præreptus,
Pauca quidem ingenii sui
Pignora reliquit,
Sed egregia, sed admiranda,
Ex intimis Matheseos penetralibus
Felici solertia tum primum eruta ;
Post magnum illum Newtonum,
Societatis hujus spes altera,
Et decus gemellum ;
Cui ad summam doctrinæ laudem
Omnes morum virtutumque dotes
In cumulum accesserunt ;
Eo magis spectabilis amabilisque,
Quod in formoso corpore
Gratiores venirent.
Natus Burbagii
In agro Leicestriensi
Jul. x. MDCLXXXII.
Obiit Jun. v. MDCCXVI.

## No. XI.

*(Referred to in page 297, as No. XIII.)*

THE great interest excited by the Principia even among persons who
were not qualified by their mathematical knowledge to comprehend it, led
some individuals of active and powerful minds to acquire as much geometrical and analytical knowledge as would enable them to understand
and appreciate the leading truths which Newton had discovered.   Dr.
Bentley, as we have already seen, was anxious to expound the discoveries
of Newton[1] in a popular form, and to adduce them as proofs of the wisdom
and benevolence of the Deity ; and having resolved to study the work
which contained them, he applied, through his friend, Mr. William Wotton,[2] to John Craige, an able Scotch mathematician, for a list of works

---

[1] Dr. Monk is of opinion that Bentley had previously attended Newton's lectures.
" The true system of the universe," he says, " and the proper methods of philosophical
investigation, had not become public by the writings of Newton, but the light of the
Newtonian discoveries was partially revealed to Cambridge before the rest of the world
by the lectures of the philosopher himself, delivered in the character of the Lucasian
Professor.  These Bentley had an opportunity of attending; and that he did not neglect
it, I am induced to believe, by his selection of the Newtonian discoveries as a prominent
subject of his Boyle's Lectures, and his familiarity with the train of reasoning by which
they are established."—Monk's *Life of Bentley*, pp. 6, 7.
[2] William Wotton, the friend of Bentley and of Craige, was a very remarkable person ;
and Dr. Monk informs us that he was the only one of Bentley's contemporaries with

which should be read in order to understand the Principia. Alarmed with the long list of authors sent him by Craige on the 24th June 1691, Bentley seems to have applied to Newton himself, from whom he received the following directions. Mr. Edleston thinks that the date of it is probably about July 1691:—

*Directions given by Newton to Bentley respecting the books necessary to be read before studying the Principia.*[1]

"Next after Euclid's Elements the Elements of y$^e$ Conic sections are to be understood. And for this end you may read either the first part of y$^e$ Elementa Curvarum of John De Witt, or De la Hire's late treatise of y$^e$ conick sections, or D$^r$ Barrow's Epitome of Apollonius.

"For Algebra read first Barth[ol]in's introduction, & then peruse such Problems as you will find scattered up & down in y$^e$ Commentaries on Cartes's Geometry & other Algebraical [*sic*] writings of Francis Schooten. I do not mean y$^t$ you should read over all those Commentaries, but only y$^e$ solutions of such Problems as you will here & there meet with. You may meet with De Witt's Elementa Curvarum & Bartholin's Introduction bound up together w$^{th}$ Carte's Geometry & Schooten's Commentaries.

"For Astronomy read first y$^e$ short account of y$^e$ Copernican System in the end of Gassendus's Astronomy & then so much of Mercator's Astronomy as concerns y$^e$ same system & the new discoveries made in the heavens by Telescopes in the Appendix.

"These are sufficient for understanding my book : but if you can procure Hugenius's Horologium Oscillatorium, the perusal of that will make you much more ready.

"At y$^e$ first perusal of my Book it's enough if you understand y$^e$ Propositions w$^{th}$ some of y$^e$ Demonstrations w$^{ch}$ are easier than the rest. For when you understand y$^e$ easier they will afterwards give you light into y$^e$ harder. When you have read y$^e$ first 60 pages, pass on to y$^e$ 3$^d$ Book & when you see the design of it you may turn back to such Propositions

whom he maintained a friendship in after life. "He was," adds Dr. Monk, "the able antagonist of Sir W. Temple on the controversy 'On Ancient and Modern Learning.' As their combined efforts on that occasion have associated together the names of Wotton and Bentley, it is right to take some notice of the former, who, when he entered the University, was a child, and presents the best authenticated instance of a juvenile prodigy that I have ever found upon record. It is certified by the testimony, not of one, but many persons of sense and learning, that at *six* years of age he was able to read and translate Latin, Greek, and Hebrew ; to which at *seven* he added some knowledge of the Arabic and Syriac. On his admission at Catherine Hall, in his *tenth* year, the master, Dr. Eachard, the antagonist of Hobbes, recorded '*Gulielmus Wotton, infra decem annos, nec Hammondo nec Grotio secundus.*' This surprising proficiency during his academical career is testified by some of the best scholars of that day . . . When he proceeded Bachelor of Arts, he was acquainted with twelve languages, and, as there was no precedent of granting that degree to a boy of thirteen, Dr. H. Gower, one of the Caput, thought fit to put upon record a notice of his proficiency in every species of literature, as a justification of the University."—Monk's *Life of Bentley*, pp. 7, 8; see also Nichol's *Literary Anecdotes*, vol. iv. pp. 253-259.

[1] We have given this paper exactly as it is printed in Mr. Edleston's *Correspondence*, &c., pp. 273, 274. It is copied from the original, presented, along with the original MSS. of Newton's four celebrated letters to Bentley, by his grandson, Richard Cumberland, to Trinity College.—Cumberland's *Memoirs*, vol. i. p. 94.

as you shall have a desire to know,.or peruse the whole in order if you think fit."

The following memorandum is written upon the MS. by Bentley:—

"Directions from Mr Newton by his own Hand."

### Directions given by John Craige for understanding the Principia.

The course of reading proposed by John Craige for understanding the Principia is much more extensive than that of Newton. It is published in Bentley's Correspondence,[1] in a very interesting letter addressed to William Wotton, which, we have no doubt, will be gratifying to some of our readers :—

"WINDSOR, 24 *June*, 1691.

"SIR,

"I would have sent you this line before this, if I had thought you had returned from Cambridge. You may tell your Friend that 'nothing less than a thorough knowledge of all that is yet known in the most curious parts of Mathematicks can make him capable to read Mr. Newton's book with that advantage which I believe he proposes to himself. Upon this account, then, it may justly seem a very undecent piece of vanity to undertake to give a method for reading a book that involves so much in it, and so far above my strength ; however, in compliance with your desire, I shall give you that which appears to me to be the shortest and most proper method for such an end.

"Next to Euclid's Elements, let him apply himself to the Conick Sections, for which he need only read *De Witt's First Book De Elementis Linearum Curvarum ;* but let him not meddle with the second, which treats of the *Loca Geometrica*. After he has made himself Master of the Conick Sections, he must read some good System of Algebra : I know none better than *Jo. Prestet's Elémens des Mathématiques*, especially if he can get the new edition : here it is absolutely necessary to be constantly exercising himself in the resolving of Problems ; but let him forbear meddling with any geometrical Problem, until he be entirely Master of all the precepts of common Algebra ; afterwards he may look over *Wallis, De Beaun, Fermott, Hudden,* and pick out several things which he will scarcely meet with in Prestet, or any one System. When this is done, the great difficulty of the work is over: this is the foundation of all ; and, therefore, he must not grudge to bestow more time and application upon it, than, perhaps, he would willingly allow, if he knew how much of both are requisite. I must not forget to desire him to have a care not to begin with Kersey's Algebra, which is apt (by its pompous bulk and title) to deceive new beginners, as sad experience has taught myself. I can assure him there was never a duller book writ; and, as far as I can judge, there was never a man who pretended to write of Algebra that understood the design of it less than Mr. Kersey did : but, to do him justice, he treats the Arithmetical part of Algebra (both as to rational and Surd Quantities) in a very plain, full, and clear method. The prodigious loss of time which this unlucky book made me sustain (when I had no guide to direct me in my studies of this kind), drew this severe character of Mr. Kersey from me ; and I doubt

[1] See vol. ii. pp. 736-740 ; and vol. i. p. xxxii.

not but this advertisement will be of some use to your friend. When he is thus well instructed with the Elements both of Geometry and Algebra, he must study the use of both, which consists in these two things, viz., the inventing of Theorems and resolving of Geometrical Problems; for which end he must begin with *Cartes his Geometry,* reading only the first and third book; but let him forbear the second till such time as he perfectly understands the first and last, which is Cartes his own advice in one of his Letters, and, indeed, the nature of the thing shows it should be so. This will give him a vaster idea of Geometry and of the great use of Algebra than is possible for me to express, or for one that has not read it to imagine. In the next place, let him peruse diligently *De Witt's* second book, which treats of the *Loca Geometrica;* and immediately after that read Cartes his second book, which treats of the same subject: and because the method of Tangents is the chief part of this 2nd book, and, indeed, of all his whole Geometry (as he himself confesses), let him read *Slusius his Method,* which he'll find in the *Philosophical Transactions; Dr. Barrow's Method,* which he'll find (if I remember right) at the end of his 10*th Geometrical Lecture;* and *Mr. Leibnitz his Method,* which he'll find in the *Acta Eruditorum,* which is the best of all; for by these four (not to mention several others of less note) various methods he will become master of this famous Problem, which, of all others, is of the greatest use in the solution of the hardest Problems in Geometry. Here it will be again necessary to exercise his pen much in the solving of Geometrical, as before in the solving of Arithmetical Problems; which he may furnish himself with out of any books that are by him, particularly out of *Vieta, Reinaldini, Henderson, Schooten, Kersey,* &c.; but he must keep close to Cartes his General Method, and make no other use (as yet) of those books, but only to provide himself with good store of Problems.

" Another great Invention, which has extremely promoted Geometry in our Age, is the Method of Indivisibles. Wherefore, in the next place, let him read the famous *Cavalerius* on that subject, who is, if not the Inventor, yet, at least, the great Restorer of that Method. After him must be read *Dr. Barrow's Geometrical Lectures,* who has carried that Method further than any, and who will inform him with more excellent and universal Theorems than any book that has been written in this Age. When your friend has gone so far, he needs not be much solicitous in what order he read any book of pure Geometry or Algebra, but may take them promiscuously as they come to his hand; for scarce any thing will occur which he will not be able to overcome: but the books that I think will be most worthy of his application are, *Archimedes and Apollonius,* his works of Dr. Barrow's edition; *Slusius his Mesolabium; Vieta; Gregorius a Sancto Vincentio; Mr. James Gregory's Works; Hugenius his Horologium Oscillatorium; La Hire his Conick Sections;* and *Tschirnhaus his Medicina Mentis:* but in this last, as also in Archimed and Hugenius, he must pass over all that is not pure Geometry or Algebra.

" Then he must advance to those parts that are of a more compounded nature, and which have a more immediate Relation to Mr. Newton's book. First, then, he must read with a great deal of care *Galileus his Works De Motu;* in reading of which he will find vast help from *Dr. Barrow's five first Lectures.* Then he must read *Torricelli's book De Motu,* who carries on Galileus his design. He will find also much to the same purpose in *Gas-*

*sendus, Hugenius, and Mersennus ;* after them he must read *Mariot, who treats of 'the Laws of Motion;* then let him read what *Sir Christopher Wren* and *Dr. Wallis* hath printed in the *Philosophical Transactions* concerning the said Laws ; after this it will not be amiss to read *Dr. Wallis his Mechanicks,* but he may pass over all that part *De Calculo Centri gravitatis.* There are several things in *Mr. Hobbes De Motu* which will be of some use to him : and indeed, without a good understanding of what these Authors have already written concerning Motion, it is simply impossible to understand this unparalleled book of Mr. Newton's, which treats of nothing else but Motion, but in such a manner as tends to the perfecting of Philosophy, and particularly that part of it which relates to the motion of the Stars and Planets. Therefore, in the next place, your friend must make himself perfect in Astronomy, in studying of which let him begin with *Tacquet ;* for though he follows a false Hypothesis, yet none has treated this matter in so clear and full a method. But here I suppose your friend to be skilled in Trigonometry (both plane and spherical, for which *Norwood* first, and *Ward* afterwards, are to be read), and the use of the Sphere. When he has done with Tacquet, let him get *Kepler, Bulliald, Seth Ward, Mercator and Gassendus, and Copernicus,* who ought to have been first mentioned : by the help of these he will have a perfect understanding of the state of Astronomy as it was before Mr. Newton published his book ; which he might safely now begin with, were it not for some collateral things which he brings in from the Opticks, Hydrostaticks, &c. For the Opticks he must read *Cartes, Ja. Gregory, Dr. Barrow, Honoratus Fabri, and Tacquet ;* and till he hath read these, he must pass over what Cartes speaks of his Ovals in the 2d book of his Geometry. For Hydrostaticks, he must read *Archimed and Borelli,* and something which he'll find in *Dr. Wallis his Mechanicks.* And because much of Master Newton's book refers to the Quadratures of Figures, he must read what has been written on this subject by *Dr. Wallis and Mr. David Gregory.*

" Here, you see, is a vast deal to be done, even enough to discourage a man whose inclinations have not a great bias this way ; but he that seriously considers the real pleasure and advantage that arises from this, and (if I be not mistaken) only from this kind of study, will not be disheartened either by the tediousness or difficulty that attends it ; but my business was not to persuade, but, as far as I am able, to instruct your friend in what Order he ought to proceed in this matter : which I have done with all the care and exactness that was possible. And if this shall chance to be of no use to him, yet I shall not fail entirely in the end for which I writ it, which was to show my readiness, at least, to serve you, for whose sake there is nothing that I will refuse to do that lies within the compass of my power, though it were even to the discovery of my own weakness and ignorance, which, perhaps, I have sufficiently done already ; and, therefore, shall add no more, but that I am and ever shall be,

" Your most real friend and humble servant,

" JO. CRAIGE.

" *For Mr.* WILLIAM WOTTON,
*Chaplain to The* EARLE OF NOTTINGHAME,
*at* CLEVELAND-HOUSE,
LONDON."

The following note in Bentley's handwriting is written on the fourth page or cover of Mr. Craige's letter :—

" Ex Newtono
　　Cartesii geometria in De la Hire Lectiones Conicæ
　　Barthii Introductio in Algebra
　　Mercatoris Astronomia
　　Hugenii Horologium Oscillatorium."

THE most complete and successful attempt to make the *Principia* accessible to those who are "little skilled in mathematical science," has been made by Lord Brougham, in his admirable analysis of that work, which forms the greater part of the second volume of his edition of Paley's *Natural Theology.*[1]

"The reader of the *Principia*," says Lord Brougham, "if he be a tolerably good mathematician, can follow the whole chain of demonstration by which the universality of gravitation is deduced from the fact, that it is a power acting inversely, as the square of the distance to the centre of attraction. Satisfying himself of the laws which regulate the motion of bodies in trajectories around given centres, he can convince himself of the sublime truths unfolded in that immortal work, and must yield his assent to this position, that the moon is deflected from the tangent of her orbit round the earth, by the same force by which the satellites of Jupiter are deflected from the tangent of theirs, the very same force which makes a stone unsupported fall to the ground. The reader of the *Mécanique Céleste*, if he be a still more learned mathematician, and versed in the modern improvements of the calculus which Newton discovered, can follow the chain of demonstration by which the wonderful provision made for the stability of the universe, is deduced from the fact, that the direction of all the planetary motions is the same—the eccentricity of their orbits small, and the angle formed by the plane of their orbits with the ecliptic acute. Satisfying himself of the laws which regulate the mutual actions of these bodies, he can convince himself of a truth yet more sublime than Newton's discovery, though flowing from it, and must yield his assent to the marvellous position, that all the irregularities occasioned in the system of the universe, by the mutual attraction of its members, are periodical, and subject to an eternal law which prevents them from ever exceeding a stated amount, and secures through all time the balanced structure of a universe composed of bodies whose mighty bulk and prodigious swiftness of motion, mock the utmost efforts of the human imagination. All these truths are to the skilful mathematician as thoroughly known, and their evidence is as clear, as the simplest proposition of arithmetic is to common understandings. But how few are those who thus know and comprehend them ! Of all the millions that thoroughly believe these truths, certainly not a thousand individuals are capable of following even any considerable portion of the demonstrations upon which they rest ; and probably not a hundred now living have ever gone through the whole steps of these demonstrations."[2]

---

[1] *Dissertations on Subjects of Science connected with Natural Theology.* By Henry Lord Brougham, F.R.S., and Member of the National Institute of France.　Vol. ii. pp. 243-480.　Lond. 1839.

[2] Ibid. vol. ii. pp. 172, 173.

This *analytical view* of the *Principia* has since been published in a separate form (1855) by Lord Brougham and Mr. Routh of St. Peter's College, Cambridge.    Mr. Routh has extended it to the second and third book. The only addition made by Lord Brougham to the publication of 1839, is an elaborate Appendix, chiefly upon central forces directed to more than one centre, which it is greatly to be lamented that Sir Isaac Newton did not treat of.

---

I have mentioned in page 271, on the authority of Conduitt's MSS., the time when different parts of the *Principia* were written.    I have found, in Sir Isaac's own handwriting, the following memorandum, which contains some additional information of considerable interest :—

"In the tenth proposition of the second book, there was a mistake in the first edition, by drawing the tangent of the arch G H from the wrong end of the arch, which caused an error in the conclusion ; but in the second edition I rectified the mistake.    And there may have been some other mistakes occasioned by the shortness of the time in which the book was written, and by its being copied by an amanuensis who understood not what he copied ; besides the press faults, for I wrote it in seventeen or eighteen months, beginning in the end of December 1684, and sending it to the Royal Society in May 1686, excepting that about ten or twelve of the propositions were composed before, viz., the 1st and 11th in December 1679, the 6th, 7th, 8th, 9th, 10th, 12th, 13th, and 17th, Lib. I., and the 1st, 2d, 3d, and 4th, Lib. II., in June and July 1684."

---

# No. XII.

(*Referred to in page* 360, *as* No. XIII.)

AFTER the publication of the second edition of the *Principia*, when an erroneous interpretation had been given of the Scholium, Newton was very anxious that the motive under which he wrote it, and the precise meaning which he attached to it, should be understood.    I have, therefore, given in page 359 an explanation of his views, which is more full than that quoted in the note from Raphson ; but I have found another MS. in which an additional motive is stated.    "And because," he says, "Mr. Leibnitz had published those elements (meaning those in the Lemma) a year and some months before, without making any mention of the correspondence which I had with him by means of Mr. Oldenburg ten years before that time, I added a Scholium, not to give away the Lemma, but to put him in mind of that correspondence, *in order to his making a public acknowledgment thereof before he proceeded to claim that Lemma from me.*" [1]

[1] The words in Italics are an interlineation.

DRAUGHT COPIES OF THE SCHOLIUM TO THE LEMMA.

SCHOLIUM.

*In literis quæ mihi cum Geometra peritissimo G. G. Leibnitio, anno 1676, intercedebant, cum significarem me compotem esse methodi* analyticæ *determinandi Maximas et Minimas, ducendi Tangentes,* quadrandi figuras curvilineas, conferendi easdem inter se, *et similia peragendi quæ in terminis surdis æque ac in rationalibus procederent, et* Tractatus quos de hujusmodi rebus scripsisse, alterum quem Barrovius, anno 1669, ad Collinium misit, et alterum anno 1671 in quo hanc methodum prius exposueram; cumque fundamentum hujus methodi *literis transpositis hanc sententiam involventibus (Data Equatione quotcunque fluentes quantitates involvente Fluxiones invenire et vice versa), celarem,* specimen vero ejusdem in curvis quadrandis subjungerem et exemplis illustrarem; et cum Collinius Epistolam, 10 Decem. 1672 datam, a me accepisset in qua methodum hanc descripseram et exemplo Tangentium more Slusiano ducendarum illustraveram, et hujus Epistolæ exemplar mense Junio anno 1676 in Galliam ad D. Leibnitium misisset, *et vir clarissimus* sub finem mensis Octobris, in reditu suo e Gallia per Angliam in Germaniam, epistolas meas in manu Collinii insuper consuluisset : incidit is tandem *in methodum* similem sub diversis verborum et notarum formulis, et mense Junio sequente specimen ejusdem in Tangentibus more Slusiano ducendis ad me misit, et subjunxit se credere *methodum meam a sua non abludere* presertim cum quadraturæ curvarum per utramque methodum faciliores redderentur. Methodi vero *utriusque fundamentum continetur in hoc* Lemmate.

Almost the whole of the Scholium printed in the *first* and *second* editions of the *Principia* is put in Italics, in order to show the change upon it which Sir Isaac had proposed for the *third* edition.

In the other two forms of the Scholium, written on the same sheet with'the preceding, the first and second half of it are partly transposed ; and at the end of one of them after *in hoc Lemmate,* are the words *et hæc methodus plenius exponitur in Tractatu.*

It is singular that both Newton and Cotes should have permitted the words *annis abhinc decem* to remain in the second edition, seeing that in 1713, *thirty-seven years* had elapsed. In the draughts, however, of the Scholium under consideration, the more correct words *anno 1676* are substituted.

I have found another draught of the Scholium, distinctly written, without any important correction, which differs only from the printed one in the first edition of the *Principia* in the following points :—

1. After *ducendi tangentes* the words *quadrandi figuras curvilineas* are added.

2. After *procederet,* the words *methodumque exemplis illustrarem* are added ; and

3. Before *celarem,* the word *eandem* is inserted.

## No. XIII.

(*Referred to in page* 362, *as* No. XIV.)

John Wallis, D.D., the author of the following letter, was one of the most distinguished mathematicians of the seventeenth century. He was born at Ashford in Kent on the 23d November 1616. He studied at Emanuel College, Cambridge, and was a Fellow of Queens'. In 1644 he was chosen one of the Secretaries to the Westminster Assembly of Divines, and in 1649 Savilian Professor of Geometry at Oxford. Between the years 1654 and 1662 he carried on a keen controversy with Hobbes. His principal work is his *Arithmetica Infinitorum,* published in 1655.[1] His works, both theological and mathematical, were published by the curators of the University of Oxford in 1699, in 3 vols. folio. He died at Oxford on the 28th October 1703, and was in the 82d year of his age when he wrote the two following letters :—

### 1.—LETTER FROM WALLIS TO NEWTON.

"OXFORD, *April* 30, 1695.

"SIR,
"I thank you for your letter of April 21st by Mr. Conon. But I can by no means admit your excuse for not publishing your Treatise of Light and Colours. You say you dare not *yet* publish it. And why *not yet?* Or if not now, when then? You add, lest it create you some trouble. What trouble *now* more than at another time. Pray consider how many years this hath layn upon your hands already, and while it lyes upon your hands it will still be some trouble ; (for I know your thoughts must still be running upon it.) But when published that trouble will be over. You think, perhaps, it may occasion some letters (of exceptions) to you, which you shall be obliged to answer. What if so ? 'Twill be at your choice whether to answer them or not. The treatise will answer for itself. But are you troubled with no letters for not publishing it ? I suppose your other friends call upon you for it as well as I, and are as little satisfied with the delay. Meanwhile you lose the reputation of it, and we the benefit, so that you are neither just to yourself nor kind to the public. And perhaps some other may get scraps of the notion and publish it as his own ; and then 'twill be his, not yours, though he may perhaps never attain to the tenth part of what you be already master of. Consider that 'tis now about thirty years since you were master of these notions about *Fluxions* and *Infinite Series* ; but you have never published aught of it to this day (which is worse than *nonumque prematur in annum*). 'Tis true I have endeavoured to do you right in that point. But if I had published the same or like notions without naming you, and the world possessed of another *calculus differentialis* instead of your *fluxions:* how should this or the next age know of your share therein ? And even what I have said is but playing an after game for you to recover (precariously *ex postliminio*) what you had let slip in its due time. And even yet I see you make no great haste to

[1] See this Volume, page 340.

publish these letters[1] which are to be my vouchers for what I say of it. And even these letters at first were rather extorted from you than voluntary. You may say, perhaps, the last piece of this concerning colour is not quite finished. It may be so (and perhaps never will), but pray let us have what is ; and while that is printing, you may (if ever) perfect the rest. But if, during the delay, you chance to die, or those papers chance to take fire (as some others have done), 'tis all lost both as to you and as to the public. It hath been an old complaint that an Englishman never knows when a thing is well (but will still be overdoing), and thereby loseth, or spoils many times what was well before. I own that modesty is a virtue, but too much diffidence (especially as the world now goes) is a fault. And if men will never publish aught till it be so perfect that nothing more can be added to it, themselves and the public will both be losers. I hope, Sir, you will forgive me this freedom (while I speak the sense of others as well as my own), or else I know not how we shall forgive these delays. I could say a great deal more, but if you think I have said too much already, pray forgive this kindness of

" Your real friend and humble servant,

" JOHN WALLIS.

" Dr. Gregory gives you his service."

## 2.—LETTER FROM WALLIS TO NEWTON.

The following letter, written more than two years afterwards, is partly on the same subject, but is interesting from the message which it contains from Leibnitz in the postscript of a letter to Wallis, dated May 28, 1697 :—[2]

" OXONIÆ, *Julii* 1, 1697.

" CLARISSIME VIR,

" Accepi nuper a D. Leibnitio literas Hanoveræ datas Mai 28, 1697. In quibus cum nonnulla sint quæ te quadamtenus spectant, liberem tibi suis verbis exponere, viz., ' *Si qua esset occasio, D. Newtono, summi ingenii viro (forte per amicum) salutem officiosissimam a me nunciandi, eumque meo nomine precandi ne se ab edendis præclaris meditationibus diverti pateretur, beneficio hoc a te petere auderem. Item methodum Fluxionum profundissimi Newtoni cognitam esse methodo mea differentiali non tamen animadverti, postquam opus ejus ad lucem prodiit, sed etiam professus sum in Actis Eruditorum ; et alios quoque monui. .Id enim candori meo convenire judicavi non minus quam ipsius merito. Itaque communi nomine designare soleo Analyseos Infinitesimalis (quæ latius quam Methodus Tetragonista patet) interim ; quemadmodum et Vietiana et Cartesiana methodus, Analyseos Speciosa nomine venit ; discrimina tamen nonnulla supersunt. Ita fortasse Newtoniana et mea differunt in nonnullis.*' Hæc ea verbatim transcripsi ex nobilissimi Leibnitii literis ut videas id ab exteris etiam desiderari, quod ego non tantum petii sed obtestatus sum aliquoties, aliique mecum, nec tamen hactenus obtinuimus ut quæ apud te primis desideratissima

[1] The letters on Fluxions in Wallis's *Works*, vol. ii. pp. 391-396.
[2] The letter of Leibnitz is dated 28*th March*, though in the title prefixed to it by Wallis, and in the following letter, the date is made 28th May.

ederentur. Quippe cum hoc aut negas aut differs; non tantum tuæ famæ sed et bono publico deesse videris. Duas illas Epistolas (longiusculas et refertissimas) anno 1676 scriptas (unde ego Excerpta quædam antehac edidi) curabo ego (nisi me id vetes) subjungi volumini cuidam meo (jam aliquandiu sub prælo) quamprimum per præli moras licebit. Tuam de Lumine et Coloribus Hypothesin novam (cujus aliquot specimina jam ante multis annis dederis) quam per annos (si recte conjicio) triginta apud te supprimere dictum est, spero ut propediem edendam cures; ut quam ego insignem Naturali Philosophiæ accessionem jamdudum existimavi et publice deberi: Quam et Prælo fuisse diu paratam audio.) Idem dixerim de pluribus quæ apud te latent, quorum ego non sum conscius. Hæc interim raptim monenda duxi.

"Tuus ad officia,
"JOHANNES WALLIS.

"I put it into this form, that if you think it proper you may desire Dr. Sloan to insert it in the Transactions."[1]

The letter is addressed on the back,
"To MR. ISAAC NEWTON, Controller
of the Mint at The Tower,
LONDON."

The first paragraph of this message to Newton, in the preceding letter, is given in Leibnitz's letter to Wallis, as printed in the third volume of his works, and the following reason is assigned for withholding the rest of the message :—[Sequebantur pauca quæ rem Mathematicam non spectant.]—Wallisii Opera, tom. iii. p. 680.

In Wallis's reply to Leibnitz, dated July 30, 1697, he says,—"Quæ Newtonum spectant, ad eum scripsi tuis verbis, simulque obtestatus sum meo nomine ut imprimi curet quæ sua supprimit scripta. Quod et sæpe ante feceram, sed hactenus in cassum."—Ibid. p. 685.

---

[1] This memorandum is placed at the very foot of the page, apparently for the purpose of its being cut off.

END OF VOLUME FIRST.

EDINBURGH : T. CONSTABLE,
PRINTER TO THE QUEEN, AND TO THE UNIVERSITY.

Printed in Great Britain
by Amazon

61177343R00274